ADVANCES IN COGNITIVE-BEHAVIORAL THERAPY

BANFF INTERNATIONAL BEHAVIORAL SCIENCE Series

SERIES EDITORS

Kenneth D. Craig, *University of British Columbia*
Keith S. Dobson, *University of Calgary*
Robert J. McMahon, *University of Washington*
Ray DeV. Peters, *Queen's University*

Volumes in the **Banff International Behavioral Science Series** take the behavioral science perspective on important basic and applied challenges that confront practitioners working in the fields of the social, psychological, and health services. The editors invite leading investigators and practitioners to contribute because of their expertise on emergent issues and topics. Contributions to the volumes integrate information on themes and key issues relating to current research and professional practice. The chapters reflect the authors' personal, critical analysis of the topics, the current scientific and professional literature, and discussions and deliberations with other experts and practitioners. It is our intention to have this continuing series of publications provide an "expressive" early indicator of the developing nature and composition of the behavioral sciences and scientific applications to human problems and issues. The volumes should appeal to practitioners, scientists, and students interested in the interface between professional practice and research advances.

Volumes in This Series:

- *Anxiety and Depression in Adults and Children*   Edited by Kenneth D. Craig and Keith S. Dobson
- *Advances in Cognitive-Behavioral Therapy*   Edited by Keith S. Dobson and Kenneth D. Craig
- *Preventing Childhood Disorders, Substance Abuse, and Delinquency*   Edited by Ray DeV. Peters and Robert J. McMahon

ADVANCES IN COGNITIVE- BEHAVIORAL THERAPY

Keith S. Dobson
Kenneth D. Craig
editors

Banff International Behavioral Science Series

 SAGE Publications
International Educational and Professional Publisher
Thousand Oaks   London   New Delhi

For information address:

 SAGE Publications, Inc.
2455 Teller Road
Thousand Oaks, California 91320
E-mail: order@sagepub.com

SAGE Publications Ltd.
6 Bonhill Street
London EC2A 4PU
United Kingdom

SAGE Publications India Pvt. Ltd.
M-32 Market
Greater Kailash I
New Delhi 110048 India

Printed in the United States of America

Library of Congress Cataloging-in-Publication Data

Advances in cognitive-behavioral therapy / editors, Keith S. Dobson
  Kenneth D. Craig.
    p. cm. — (Banff international behavioral science series; v. 2)
  Chiefly papers presented at the 24th Banff International
Conference on Behavioural Science.
  Includes bibliographical references (p.) and index.
  ISBN 0-8039-7006-4 (cloth: alk. paper)
  ISBN 0-7619-0643-6 (pbk.: alk. paper)
    1. Cognitive therapy—Congresses. I. Dobson, Keith S.
II. Craig, Kenneth D., 1937- . III. Banff International
Conference on Behavioural Science (24th: 1992: Banff, Alta.)
IV. Series.
RC489.C63A384 1996
616.89'143—dc20   95-50226

96 97 98 99 10 9 8 7 6 5 4 3 2

Sage Production Editor: Vicki Baker

Contents

Preface

There is little doubt that cognitive-behavioral models are among the most influential in modern psychotherapy. This influence is not coincidental but has rather arisen for a number of important reasons, many of which have been cited previously (Dobson & Block, 1988; Mahoney, 1993; Meichenbaum, 1993). Critical among these reasons are the following:

1. These models are in agreement with the general "cognitive revolution" within psychology, including the development of information-processing and other cognitive models of mind and personality (Carver & Scheier, 1981; Neisser, 1967).

2. It is widely accepted that these models enjoy a closer correspondence with human experience than their more limited and focused behavioral forebears (Ellis, 1993; Mahoney, 1974; Meichenbaum, 1977, 1993). The explicit discussion of cognitive, behavioral, and emotional aspects of functioning in cognitive-behavioral therapies has no doubt been one aspect of their wide acceptability among psychotherapy practitioners (Hunsley & Lefebvre, 1990; Norcross, Prochaska, & Gallagher, 1989).

3. These therapies are built on a sound empirical basis, often with measurable behavioral outcomes as part of the assessment process. The continued focus on methodological behaviorism (Mahoney, 1974) has ensured that these interventions are empirically validated (Chambless et al., 1995)—a phenomenon that in turn has increased their acceptability to third-party payers for psychological services and the public.

4. The flexibility inherent in the cognitive-behavioral therapies has helped to ensure their wide applicability. As there is not a single cognitive-behavioral therapy but rather a number of complex and adaptable therapies (see Dobson, 1988; Mahoney, 1993), these interventions have commended themselves to a large number of practitioners working in diverse clinical areas. This very text is a testament to the diversity of ages and clinical problems that can be addressed by these therapeutic models.

OVERVIEW OF THIS BOOK

Given the interest and growth in the cognitive-behavioral tradition, the 24th Banff International Congress on Behavioural Science devoted itself to an assessment of the theoretical and practical developments in this field. Experts in different areas came together to present and discuss their work and to provide an update of recent developments in the cognitive-behavioral therapy movement. This volume not only represents the ideas shared at the conference but also includes discussion about broader issues related to these therapies. Although not exhaustive in its survey of all applications of cognitive-behavioral therapies, it is a comprehensive view of the field. It is our hope that readers of this book will gain (or increase) an appreciation of the cognitive-behavioral field and will realize further innovations beyond those already presented.

In organizing the conference and this ensuing volume, a decision was made not to focus extensively on the theoretical underpinnings of cognitive-behaviorism but rather to focus on developments in their applications. Readers of this book will notice that only one chapter, that of Kanfer, is addressed to theoretical issues, without a specific application or problem area. Kanfer's work on self-regulation, which has influenced the field for decades (Kanfer, 1971, 1975; Kanfer & Schefft, 1988), offers a conceptual model of the processes involved in the commitment to making change and then actually implementing that commitment. His chapter in this text offers an excellent summary of his vision of and the data related to these processes and is a framework within which more specific applications can be considered.

The remaining chapters in this text present applications of the cognitive-behavioral therapies to specific problem areas. Deffenbacher's chapter (Chapter 2) discusses the nature of anger and the cognitive and behavioral-emotional processes involved. Having laid this groundwork, Deffenbacher proceeds to delineate a range of interventions, including stimulus control, response disruption, relaxation, and more explicitly cognitive methods that have an empirical basis in either reducing anger reactions or managing those reactions once they are present.

The third chapter of this volume examines the commonalities among the various cognitive-behavioral treatments for depression. Drawing on both historical and current formulations, Dobson and Jackman-Cram posit that behavior change is critical to the successful treatment of depression and may be the common pathway of the cognitive-behavioral interventions. They leave open the best methods to evoke that behavioral change but certainly imply that cognitive-behavioral therapies can be effective in those processes. In many respects, their chapter is an invitation to cognitive-behavioral theorists and therapists to validate their causal models of cognition in depression.

Turk (Chapter 4) offers an excellent review of the primary features of chronic pain and the various cognitive, behavioral, physiological, and emotional regulation processes that are disrupted or influenced by pain. He points out that limitations of previous models of pain necessitated the inclusion of cognitive factors (Flor, Birbaumer, & Turk, 1990) and that the success of cognitive interventions has provided fodder for even more elaborated and more successful treatment. He notes the particular role of self-efficacy (Bandura, 1977), cognitive errors, and coping self-statements as significant components of successful pain treatment regimens. He concludes with a strong argument for the reciprocal influence of various aspects of pain and the need to include cognition as an integral aspect of these influences.

In Chapter 5, Chambless and Gillis examine the effectiveness of cognitive-behavioral therapies in the treatment of panic disorders, social phobia, and generalized anxiety disorder (GAD), and the following chapter by Craske focuses on the cognitive-behavioral therapies (notably those of Barlow and associates; see Barlow, Craske, Cerny, & Klosko, 1989) in the treatment of panic and agoraphobia. Both chapters show that the cognitive-behavioral models have well-developed and internally consistent ideas about the mechanisms involved in the anxiety disorders and that the therapies based on these models have demonstrated effectiveness not only for the reduction of anxiety symptoms but also for correlated symptomatology such as depression. Both chapters highlight that although we can safely conclude that these therapies are effective, we still need further research examining individual differences that may enhance or impede overall treatment effectiveness, as well as studies that more clearly attempt to (in)validate causal models of anxiety. Both chapters also discuss the role of evolving conceptions of anxiety itself (e.g., the changing conceptualization of agoraphobia as primarily defined by panic and anxious mood, as in the third edition of the *Diagnostic and Statistical Manual of Mental Disorders [DSM-III]*, or as defined primarily by avoidant behavior, as in the revised third edition of that manual [*DSM-III-R*]; American Psychiatric Association, 1980, 1987) in the efficacy of the interventions used for these disorders.

Chapter 7, by Alexander and colleagues, is the first of three chapters in this volume that focus on the application of cognitive-behavioral models in interpersonal contexts. Their chapter addresses the rhetorical question of whether cognitive change is necessary to modify dysfunctional family behavior and concludes that behavior change strategies must explicitly include cognitive, emotional, *and* behavioral aspects (see Alexander & Parsons, 1982). Like other contributors to this volume, these authors note that the various human systems depend on each other and that a complete analysis of function and dysfunction requires an attention to all of these processes.

In Chapter 8, Johnston examines the influence of parents' cognitions on dysfunctional child behavior and demonstrates how attention to these cognitions can be used in a positive way in family interventions for childhood behavioral problems. Such phenomena as parental expectations of and attributions for negative child behavior have been shown to be good predictors of the outcome of family therapy, and paying attention to these patterns is viewed by Johnston as critical to treatment process (Cunningham, 1990; Patterson & Forgatch, 1985).

In Chapter 9, Baucom and his associates present a cognitive-behavioral model of marital distress and show how cognitive-behavioral interventions can be applied to this population. Beginning with an analysis of some of the shortcomings of the traditional behavioral marital therapy approach, they show that there are a number of significant cognitive patterns in marital distress and that these patterns can be meaningfully addressed in cognitive-behavioral marital therapy (Baucom & Epstein, 1990). Their chapter hints at the sizable database that supports the efficacy of the cognitive-behavioral approach to marital distress. It also offers some ideas for further research and for integration of basic cognitive and marital research.

The final chapter of the volume, by Howes and Vallis, addresses the application of cognitive-behavioral therapies to the "nontraditional populations" of persons with post-traumatic stress disorder (PTSD) and personality disorders. The authors note that cognitive-behavioral models of these dysfunctions are just beginning to emerge, and they reveal how these applications are being developed. Although they are not able to cite any large set of empirical studies that confirms the value of cognitive-behavioral therapies for these populations, their chapter does provide an elegant discussion of the cognitive and behavioral features of these areas that argues for the development of these models. The authors then use this basic information to suggest how existing cognitive-behavioral therapies can be modified for the treatment of PTSD and personality disorders. Of the various chapters in this text, this one best exemplifies how the boundaries of the cognitive-behavioral therapies can be pushed back. Indeed, it is such clinical issues as the personality disorders that will maximally stretch and challenge the flexibility of these models (see also Freeman & Leaf, 1989).

Several chapters could have appeared in this book but were not a part of the Banff conference on which this text is based. Recent developments of the cognitive-behavioral therapies include interventions for impulsivity in children, sexual dysfunctions, and even delusional thinking. A truly complete clinical handbook of the cognitive-behavioral therapies would be advantageous. But this volume does represent well the diversity of clinical problems that are being tackled by the field and serves as a good documentation of these issues for theorists, researchers, and practitioners alike.

FUTURE ISSUES FOR THE COGNITIVE-BEHAVIORAL THERAPIES

Any publication is defined by the time and context in which it is produced; this volume is no different. Between the generation of the chapters and the publication of the book, there will already be developments that one could argue "should" have been included in this text. For such "omissions," we as coeditors assume responsibility. We are also acutely aware that the cognitive-behavioral therapies are themselves in a state of dynamic development and that any effort to capture their range and scope is at best a "snapshot" of a moving target. The expanding scope of these interventions, the need for more basic psychopathology and treatment validational research, and simply the raw excitement captured by these approaches guarantee that even in a few short years the field will have evolved.

The evolution and direction of future development of the cognitive-behavioral therapies cannot be predicted with certainty. But we predict that several phenomena will exert an influence on these processes, and we conclude this preface with a brief discussion of them.

The *DSM-IV* and Changing Conceptions of Psychopathology

In the years intervening between the Banff conference on which this volume is predicated and this publication, the fourth edition of the *Diagnostic and Statistical Manual of Mental Disorders* (*DSM-IV;* American Psychiatric Association, 1994) was released. As much as the *DSM-IV* was influenced by cognitive psychopathology research (Dobson & Kendall, 1993), it will also no doubt stimulate even further research on cognitive correlates of psychopathology and cognitive-behavioral treatments. More generally, the conceptions of psychopathology and treatment will undoubtedly continue to influence each other in a dynamic process. The prominence of cognitive symptomatology in many disorders and the effectiveness of the cognitive-behavioral therapies in modifying these symptoms will provide inspiration for both to develop.

The Empirical Validation Movement

As psychotherapy practitioners everywhere know, parties that pay for psychological services are increasingly strident in their demands for proven treatments. The scientist-practitioner ideal professed by psychology also implies that the interventions and services offered should have a validational basis. In recent years, these two "conspiratorial" factors have led to a re-examination of therapies in terms of their empirical justification. Perhaps most clearly seen in the American Psychological Association's Division 12 Task Force on Promotion and Dissemination of Psychological Procedures (Chambless et al., 1995), there has been a specific response to the calls for empirical validation and an emerging list of validated treatments.

It is not a coincidence that the list of validated treatments includes a number of those that are cited in this volume, for the cognitive-behavioral therapy movement has from its beginnings made a conscious effort to document outcome and process issues with quantitative measures. Thus, although other therapy approaches may be able to be validated, to some extent the cognitive-behavioral movement has generally been given the benefit of first validation by the empirical validation efforts. This benefit will include further research attention, which in turn is likely to prompt even further innovations and justifications. Indeed, the 1996 Banff conference itself has been given the theme of "developing and promoting empirically validated treatments"!

Managed Care and Third-Party Payment

Although the trend is considered insidious by some, it is undeniable that psychotherapies are increasingly sought by the public but paid for by third parties. In the United States, the recent and rapid development of managed-care programs and practice guidelines (Clinton, McCormick, & Besterman, 1994), often with demands for brief therapies of maximal benefit and minimal cost, may further accelerate the use and perceived advantage of cognitive-behavioral therapies. Even in countries with socialized medicine (e.g., Finland) or mixed models of private and public funding for such services (e.g., Canada), the availability of lists of empirically validated cognitive-behavioral treatments will undoubtedly be used by third-party payers to justify their decisions about which treatments will (or will not) be provided to the ultimate consumers of these services.

As certain therapies become favored for insurance or public coverage, it is almost certain that these models will grow in stature and presence. It can be expected that training programs for these therapies will be sought out and that graduate programs preparing the next generation of therapists will emphasize these therapies over, or possibly even to the exclusion of, other therapy models. In the short term, the above processes are likely to benefit the cognitive-behavioral therapies and their practitioners. How these processes will unfold over the long term is difficult to predict.

CONCLUSION

We have tried to use this preface to provide a sense of the excitement and innovation that is currently encompassed by the cognitive-behavioral therapy movement. From its beginnings in the late 1970s, cognitive-behavioral therapy has expanded in complexity and scope. Most clinical phenomena have now been analyzed from a cognitive-behavioral perspective, and intervention packages have been developed for a large number of problems commonly seen in clinical practice. There is clearly a zeitgeist phenomenon around the cognitive-behavioral therapies, and many are currently in development or undergoing empirical assessment. The next 10 years or so will be a time of continued growth, although summative evaluations, such as those now beginning to appear for anxiety and depression, will doubtless emerge in a number of specific new areas.

We were pleased to have co-chaired the Banff conference on which this volume is predicated and to have co-edited this volume. We watch with interest these developments in the field and commend this book to those who share this interest.

KEITH S. DOBSON
KENNETH D. CRAIG

REFERENCES

Alexander, J. F., & Parsons, B. V. (1982). *Functional family therapy: Principles and procedures.* Carmel, CA: Brooks/Cole.

American Psychiatric Association. (1980). *Diagnostic and statistical manual of mental disorders* (3rd ed.). Washington, DC: Author.

American Psychiatric Association. (1987). *Diagnostic and statistical manual of mental disorders* (3rd ed., Rev.). Washington, DC: Author.

American Psychiatric Association. (1994). *Diagnostic and statistical manual of mental disorders* (4th ed.). Washington, DC: Author.

Bandura, A. (1977). Self-efficacy: Toward a unifying theory of behavior change. *Psychological Review, 84,* 191-215.

Barlow, D. H., Craske, M. G., Cerny, J. A., & Klosko, J. S. (1989). Behavioral treatment of panic disorder. *Behavior Therapy, 20,* 261-282.

Baucom, D. H., & Epstein, N. (1990). *Cognitive behavioral marital therapy.* New York: Brunner/Mazel.

Carver, C. S., & Scheier, M. F. (1981). *Attention and self-regulation: A control theory approach to human behavior.* New York: Springer-Verlag.

Chambless, D. L., Babich, K., Crits-Christoph, P., Frank, E., Gilson, M., Montgomery, R., Rich, R., Steinberg, J., & Weinberger, J. (1995). Training in and dissemination of empirically-validated psychological treatments: Report and recommendations. *Clinical Psychologist, 48,* 3-24.

Clinton, J. J., McCormick, K., & Besterman, J. (1994). Enhancing clinical practice: The role of practice guidelines. *American Psychologist, 49,* 30-33.

Cunningham, C. E. (1990). A family systems approach to parent training. In R. A. Barkley (Ed.), *Attention deficit hyperactivity disorder* (pp. 432-461). New York: Guilford.

Dobson, K. S. (Ed.). (1988). *Handbook of the cognitive-behavioral therapies.* New York: Guilford.

Dobson, K. S., & Block, L. (1988). Historical and philosophical bases of the cognitive-behavioral therapies. In K. S. Dobson (Ed.), *Handbook of the cognitive-behavioral therapies* (pp. 5-37). New York: Guilford.

Dobson, K. S., & Kendall, P. (1993). *Psychopathology and cognition.* New York: Academic Press.

Ellis, A. (1993). Reflections on rational-emotive therapy. *Journal of Consulting and Clinical Psychology, 61,* 199-201.

Flor, H., Birbaumer, N., & Turk, D. C. (1990). The psychobiology of chronic pain. *Advances in Behaviour Research and Therapy, 12,* 47-84.

Freeman, A., & Leaf, R. C. (1989). Cognitive therapy applied to personality disorders. In
    A. Freeman, K. Simon, L. Butler, & H. Arkowitz (Eds.), *Comprehensive handbook of
    cognitive therapy* (pp. 403-434). New York: Plenum.
Hunsley, J., & Lefebvre, M. (1990). A survey of the practices and activities of Canadian
    clinical psychologists. *Canadian Psychology, 31,* 350-358.
Kanfer, F. H. (1971). The maintenance of behavior by self-generated stimuli and reinforce-
    ment. In A. Jacobs & L. B. Sachs (Eds.), *The psychology of private events* (pp. 39-57).
    New York: Academic Press.
Kanfer, F. H. (1975). Self-management methods. In F. H. Kanfer & A. P. Goldstein (Eds.),
    Helping people change: A textbook of methods (pp. 309-356). New York: Pergamon.
Kanfer, F. H., & Schefft, B. K. (1988). *Guiding the process of therapeutic change.* Cham-
    paign, IL: Research Press.
Mahoney, M. J. (1974). *Cognition and behavior modification.* Cambridge, MA: Ballinger.
Mahoney, M. J. (ed.) (April 1993). *Journal of Consulting and Clinical Psychology,* Recent
    developments in cognitive and constructivist psychotherapies. Special issue.
Mahoney, M. J. (1993). *Human change processes.* New York: Basic Books.
Meichenbaum, D. (1977). *Cognitive-behavior modification.* New York: Plenum.
Meichenbaum, D. (1993). Changing conceptions of cognitive-behavior modification: Retro-
    spect and prospect. *Journal of Consulting and Clinical Psychology, 61,* 202-204.
Neisser, U. (1967). *Cognitive psychology.* New York: Appleton-Century-Crofts.
Norcross, J., Prochaska, J., & Gallagher, K. (1989). Clinical psychologists in the 1980s: II.
    Theory, research and practice. *Clinical Psychologist, 42,* 45-53.
Patterson, G. R., & Forgatch, M. S. (1985). Therapist behavior as a determinant for patient
    noncompliance: A paradox for the behavior modifier. *Journal of Consulting and
    Clinical Psychology, 53,* 846-851.

The Banff Conferences
on Behavioural Science

This volume is one of a continuing series of publications sponsored by the Banff International Conferences on Behavioural Science. We are pleased to join Sage Publications in bringing this series to an audience of practitioners, investigators, and students. The publications arise from conferences held each spring since 1969 in Banff, Alberta, Canada, with papers representing the product of deliberations on themes and key issues. The conferences serve the purpose of bringing together outstanding behavioral scientists and professionals in a forum where they can present and discuss data related to emergent issues and topics. As a continuing event, the Banff International Conferences have served as an expressive "early indicator" of the developing nature and composition of the behavioral sciences and scientific applications to human problems and issues.

Because distance, schedules, and restricted audience preclude wide attendance at the conferences, the resulting publications have equal status with the conferences proper. Presenters at each Banff Conference are required to write a chapter specifically for the forthcoming book, separate from their presentation and discussion at the conference itself. Consequently, this volume is not a set of conference proceedings. Rather, it is an integrated volume of chapters contributed by leading researchers and practitioners who have had the unique opportunity of spending several days together presenting and discussing ideas prior to preparing their chapters.

Our "conference of colleagues" format provides for formal and informal interactions among all participants through invited addresses, workshops, poster presentations, and conversation hours. When combined with sight-seeing expeditions, cross-country and downhill skiing, and other recreations in the spectacular Canadian Rockies, the conferences have generated great enthusiasm and satisfaction among participants. The Banff Centre, our venue for the conferences for many years, has contributed immeasurably to the success of these meetings through its very comfortable accommodation, dining, and conference facilities. The following documents conference themes over the past 28 years.

1969 I
Ideal Mental Health Services

1970 II
Services and Programs for Exceptional Children and Youth

1971 III
Implementing Behavioural Programs for Schools and Clinics

1972 IV
Behaviour Change: Methodology, Concepts, and Practice

1973 V
Evaluation of Behavioural Programs in Community, Residential, and School Settings

1974 VI
Behaviour Modification and Families and Behavioural Approaches to Parenting

1975 VII
The Behavioural Management of Anxiety, Depression, and Pain

1976 VIII
Behavioural Self-Management Strategies, Techniques, and Outcomes

1977 IX
Behavioural Systems for the Developmentally Disabled
    A. School and Family Environments
    B. Institutional, Clinical, and Community Environments

1978 X
Behavioural Medicine: Changing Health Lifestyles

1979 XI
Violent Behaviour: Social Learning Approaches to Prediction,
Management, and Treatment

1980 XII
Adherence, Compliance, and Generalization in Behavioural Medicine

1981 XIII
Essentials of Behavioural Treatments for Families

1982 XIV
Advances in Clinical Behaviour Therapy

1983 XV
Childhood Disorders: Behavioural-Developmental Approaches

1984 XVI
Education in "1984"

1985 XVII
Social Learning and Systems Approaches to Marriage and the Family

1986 XVIII
Health Enhancement, Disease Prevention, and Early Intervention:
Biobehavioural Perspectives

1987 XIX
Early Intervention in the Coming Decade

1988 XX
Behaviour Disorders of Adolescence: Research, Intervention,
and Policy in Clinical and School Settings

1989 XXI
Psychology, Sport, and Health Promotion

1990 XXII
Aggression and Violence Throughout the Lifespan

1991 XXIII
Addictive Behaviours Across the Lifespan: Prevention, Treatment,
and Policy Issues

1992 XXIV
State of the Art in Cognitive-Behaviour Therapy

1

Motivation and Emotion in Behavior Therapy

FREDERICK H. KANFER

During the last 40 years, the focus of American psychology has moved from a strong emphasis on observable learned behaviors to the study of cognitive processes and more recently to biological processes as determinants of human behavior. Behavior therapy has reflected these shifts. The conceptual base of behavior therapy has gradually moved from a simple conditioning model for a specific response toward a complex-systems-oriented model that can account for the full range of human activities.

The first extension occurred in the context of the cognitive revolution and was founded on a philosophy of neobehaviorism. In this context, models of self-regulation have been developed to supplement the doctrine of environmental behavior control with self-generated goals and processes. In the 1976 Banff Conference on Behavioural Self-Management (Kanfer, 1977), I described the implications of self-regulation research and theories for clinical practice. Work in this area has resulted in the development of self-management and self-control strategies (Kanfer, 1970, 1975) that have now been well integrated into what has come to be known as "cognitive-behavioral therapy." The next step requires analysis of motivation.

1

There is general agreement among therapists of different schools that "the patient must have an adequate degree of motivation in order to continue and eventually profit from psychotherapy" (Garfield, 1986, p. 137). However, there have been few attempts to improve on traditional strategies of motivation derived from theories of neurosis and personality. Early philosophers have considered conation, the willful goal-oriented nature of human actions, a critical "component of the mind." In American psychology at the beginning of the century, controversies revolved around the role of instincts, cognition, or will as determinants of action. Hunter (1924) and Hudgins (1933), cited in Gardner Murphy (1949), were the first to describe the motivational construct of *will* or *voluntary action* from a learning theory perspective. Later, classical learning theorists dealt with motivation in terms of incentives and reinforcement histories. Deprivation operation and subsequent anticipation of the consequences via discriminative stimuli were the backbone of this approach. Such a model works fairly well with laboratory animals, in which biological drives and incentives are easily manipulated. A motivational analysis of human behavior, however, defies a simple recourse to conditioning of secondary or tertiary drives based on the child's biological nature. Today there is still no adequate comprehensive model of the motivational and affective mechanisms that provide continuity, goal orientation, and persistence in human activities.

Most early views on motivation in therapy assigned the locus of motivation to internal processes in the patient. My model rests on a functional analysis of the therapy process, not of the client in isolation. It views change as the common goal of therapy and the individual's capacity for generating incentives, goal states, and motives by means of anticipatory self-regulation (Cofer & Appley, 1964; Kanfer, 1987) as the primary processes to be enlisted for behavior changes. Motivation in therapy cannot be regarded as a personal characteristic, a stable trait, something a person does or does not have, or a driving force channeled by biology and experience. Instead, a conceptual analysis of the therapeutic process must take into account the capacity of the human organism for self-direction and continuing adjustment to the fluctuating environmental and biological conditions at any moment and also over the course of therapy (Ford, 1987; Kanfer & Schefft, 1988; Miller, 1985; Powers, 1973). Further, a person's behavior may be under control of conflicting motives, changing expectations of attaining specific goals, or changes in the appraised value of a goal state. As a consequence, we must ask specific questions about all current incentives and their salience: for example, what moves the client to return to sessions and what incentives are needed for doing an assigned task or for tolerating the anxiety or pain associated with some therapy procedures. Reallocation of motivational resources is required so that the client's concern for attaining therapeutic goals is higher and the goals are more valued than other current concerns or the continuation of dysfunctional behaviors, despite their inherent benefits or "secondary gains."

We assume that the development of "good motivation" for therapy requires consideration of five critical questions: (a) how to help a client set realistic goals, (b) how to relate these goals to the client's current needs and behaviors and to his or her higher-order goals and values, (c) how to assist the client to allocate resources and to give the pursuit of the goal a high priority, (d) how to offer the client specific techniques to facilitate goal attainment, and (e) how to maintain the new pattern despite setbacks.

It is assumed that all clients go through some common stages from the initiation of a motivating state to its termination. A tentative model for these stages is suggested by action theorists (Heckhausen & Kuhl, 1985; Klinger, 1975; Semmer & Frese, 1985) and others who have described the sequences in the course of seeking and terminating therapy (Prochaska & DiClemente, 1982). These models, like the present one, focus on self-generated motivators for actions and invoke controlled processes that include both cognitive and metacognitive subroutines governed by self-regulatory actions.

As we have previously noted (Kanfer & Schefft, 1988), an essential feature of therapy lies in the breaking of automatic processes associated with maladaptive behaviors, including "automatic thoughts" (Beck, 1976), well-established avoidance responses, pessimistic perspectives, misattributions, and other faulty but well-learned automatic behavior sequences. These behaviors, and the processes associated with them, minimize clients' responsibility for planning actions (Greenberg & Safran, 1990). They make fewer demands on clients' resources and run off with little effort. Clients therefore find them hard to change. To instigate a shift to controlled processing requires powerful incentives. To enlist effective self-regulation and problem solving requires use of factors that make therapeutic steps as simple, attractive, and rewarding as possible. To achieve this, the complexity or novelty of the specific tasks must also be considered. High attentional demands of a task may compete with self-regulation (Kanfer, 1991; Kanfer & Ackerman, 1989; Kanfer & Stevenson, 1985), whereas on well-practiced tasks self-regulation enhances performance by strengthening goal commitment and increasing effort.

THE MOTIVATIONAL STAGES IN THERAPY

Current cognitive-behavioral therapy metamodels are anchored in general systems theory. In general, it is assumed that a goal-directed behavior originates when an ongoing sequence is interrupted, a previous goal has been reached, or a more highly valued goal preempts current goal-directed pursuits and that it continues until the newly set goal is reached (e.g., Carver & Scheier, 1981; Ford, 1987; Kanfer, 1970, 1987; Klinger, 1975). In clients who come to therapy, the interruptions are often created by environmental demands (extrinsic motivation) such as the loss of a job or referral by a physician. It is the first task of the therapist to develop self-generated goals (intrinsic motivation) for which therapy represents the instrumental pathways. Frequently, these personal goals are more distant, more abstract, and of lower value than the desire for immediate removal of a current distress.

The present model conceptualizes therapeutic tasks as instances of problem solving (Kanfer & Busemeyer, 1982; Nezu & Nezu, 1989). Early in therapy, the focus is on helping clients to *realize the benefits* of change. Later segments center on *reducing the cost* of the change. Targeting motivation in therapy involves self-regulatory processes at three different time points. During early sessions, anticipatory self-regulation (self-monitoring, self-evaluation, and self-consequation) focuses on possible future goal states and actions that would alleviate the current distress and attain a more desirable state. Cognitive simulations (Taylor & Schneider, 1989) and "thought experiments" use the age-old technique of creatively rearranging past experiences and new information, with logic and imagination, to represent cognitively and interact with different scenarios. Different goal states, the necessary instrumental behaviors to attain them, and the client's affective reactions to them can then be compared and appraised from the client's point of view with regard to their desirability.

Only after preliminary and transitory goal-state scenarios are played out does therapy shift to the behavioral stage in the motivational sequence: the enactment of the plan and the maintenance of a new behavior pattern. This road from wish to action has been described by Heckhausen and Kuhl (1985) as passing through several way stations. The relevance of the wish to the present situation, desirability of expected outcome, and perceived competence to execute the necessary behaviors are among the most significant factors that determine whether a commitment is formed and persists until the goal is attained. The person's actual skills, the presence of obstacles or facilitators at the time, and the prevalence of social and personal norms for this situation are other variables that influence the formation and behavioral enactment of an intention. Factors that influence the likelihood of making a commitment, however, may be quite different from those that affect later execution of the intention (Kanfer, 1973). Heckhausen and Kuhl (1985) called the earlier phase that is primarily cognitive and imaginal the *motivation* phase and differentiated it from the actual enactment of the intention, which they described as the *volitional* phase. A critical transition is made at this point, a crossing of the Rubicon (Heckhausen, Gollwitzer, & Weinert, 1987), in which resources are devoted to action. As an individual begins to carry out goal-directed actions, the therapist's support shifts to the fine tuning of the behavior for maximum effectiveness. The more careful the preparation in previous stages, the less likely it is that unexpected obstacles, skill deficits, or weak behavior-outcome links will result in termination of the action sequence prior to attainment of the goal.

Attainment of the goal usually leads to disengagement and termination of the overall sequence. However, the ultimate purpose of change programs is not only the achievement of a new behavioral pattern but also its maintenance. A feedforward stage lays the groundwork for executing the behavior in the future. The last stage, the maintenance of motivation, protects the strength of the incentive from newly arising competing incentives and from a decay in strength of the goal-directed behavior. The conceptual model is iterative and recursive, with overlap of the stages and simultaneous pursuit of several subgoals. Progress toward each goal may be at a different stage, requiring activation of separate components of the model concurrently.

The conceptual model is intended to guide clinical judgment on what steps need to be worked through to maximize the client's investment in the therapeutic process. Throughout therapy, two separate levels of goals must be considered: (a) the client's motivation to form and continue a therapeutic relationship and (b) the client's motivation to change toward a more satisfying and effective life. The model is most applicable for clients whose dysfunctions do not prevent them from establishing some relationship with a therapist or seriously limit their cognitive capacities. For example, clients in acute psychotic episodes or neurologically impaired clients are not easily amenable to an approach using intrinsic motivators. Nevertheless, the general model can be applied by use of extrinsic reinforcers, as employed in token economies or other conditioning-based procedures.

THE THREE-STAGE SELF-REGULATION MODEL

Onset

Self-regulation is activated when two conditions are met: (a) The person is goal-oriented—that is, there is some representation of an instrumental action and intended outcome—and (b) there is no established behavior pattern available to achieve the goal. Behavior under such conditions is often described as voluntary and conscious. It is observed when a person is learning a new task, when a smooth behavioral sequence is disrupted, or when other strong behavioral tendencies or emotional dispositions compete with or inhibit a well-learned sequence. Essentially, self-regulatory processes are characterized by predominantly controlled processing of information (Bargh, 1989; Logan, 1989; Schneider & Shiffrin, 1977). They tend to be invoked in any situation in which new components, perspectives, or obstacles make it impossible to use a well-established behavior sequence. However, components of self-regulation can themselves be learned to the point at which they become routinized or automatically processed.

Attribution

Once the self-regulatory process is initiated, the goal-directed behavior and outcome are subject to attributional evaluation. If the person believes that the requisite action or the desired outcome is not attainable because of limitations in skills, knowledge, or ability, the person exits from the sequence and either changes goals or executes some other automatic response triggered by the situation. If the required action is judged to be under the person's control, it is evaluated next with regard to its relevance to the actor's current concern (Klinger, 1975, 1987). If the goal is irrelevant or of low concern, the person exits from the self-regulation cycle (Kanfer & Hagerman, 1987).

Stage 1: Self-Monitoring

If the goal is judged to be attainable and is currently relevant, the individual shifts attention to the ongoing behavior, with reference to the desired performance. Self-monitoring is affected by many different variables (see Figure 1.1). Among them are the person's current mood, selective attention to different dimensions of the ongoing behavior, and focus on

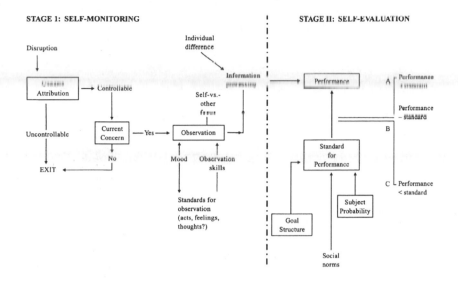

Figure 1.1. Self-Monitoring and Self-Evaluation Stages
SOURCE: Adapted from Kanfer (1987).

feelings or acts of self or others. These factors determine the accuracy and contents of the observation. Competing action tendencies, such as those generated by emotional states, may interfere with the observation and set up a conflict between goal states. Self-control techniques may be required to overcome such conflicts and to maintain focus on the original goal-oriented behavior.

Stage 2: Self-Evaluation

The second stage, the self-evaluation stage, consists of a comparison between the information obtained from self-monitoring and the goal toward which the person's behavior has been directed (see Figure 1.1). It is a comparison between what one is doing and what one believes one ought to be doing. Distortion in self-monitoring can interfere with effective self-regulatory behavior because it further distorts self-evaluation. The person's information-processing skills, momentary mood, emotional state, or attention may also alter the self-observation product (Duval & Wicklund, 1972; Kanfer, 1991; Smith, 1987). Self-evaluation is further affected by the goal structure

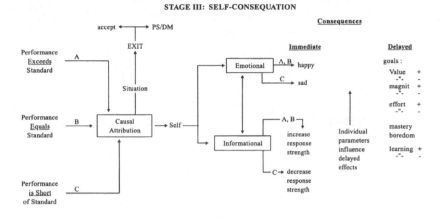

Figure 1.2.   Self-Consequation Stage
SOURCE: Adapted from Kanfer (1987).

and the many factors that influence the development of performance criteria in individuals (Cervone & Peake, 1986; Dweck, 1986; Locke, 1968; Locke, Shaw, Saari, & Latham, 1981). Other factors that contribute toward goal development are social norms, subjective probability estimates of success or failure, effectance motivation (White, 1959), and self-efficacy beliefs (Bandura, 1977). The initial step in self-evaluation is to ascertain the degree of overlap or discrepancy between performance and goal. The second step is the attachment of a utility value to the observed action. The outcome of the performance-versus-criterion comparison is also assessed by considering the causal attribution for the action. If the behavior is attributed to external factors, the individual exits the self-regulation cycle, either to accept the behavior without further evaluation or to engage in problem solving and decision making in an iteration of the cycle. Explanatory style of the individual (e.g., Peterson & Seligman, 1987) and other factors influence causal attribution at this stage.

Stage 3: Self-Consequation

If behavioral control is attributed to the self, the person enters the self-consequation stage (see Figure 1.2). In this stage, the immediate and long-term emotional and cognitive consequences of the preceding comparison are assessed. Positive self-evaluation can result in enhancement of mood and increased response strength of the preceding behavior, thus motivating further progression toward the goal. It can also have long-term effects on various self-reactions in relation to the behavior. In addition, these consequences may change the individual's future goals with regard to value, magnitude, or effort to be invested.

Regulation Based on Anticipated, Concurrent, or Past Events

Essentially the same mechanism is involved whether a person is contemplating an action, assessing an ongoing action, or reviewing a past episode. However, in the first case, *anticipatory* (or *prospective*) *self-regulation* (Kanfer, 1987, 1988), the only source of input during the cogitation is the actor. Imagining that one is acting assertively and anticipating the reactions of others are heavily influenced by the actor's biases about his or her skills and biased expectations about the behavior of others.

Transactional self-regulation occurs at a time when the behavior is part of the actual transactional fabric between a person and an environment. The direct contact with the environment provides physiological and external feedback that continuously changes as the sequence is run off. It yields information that is less affected by the actor's memory and idiosyncratic biases than in prospective self-regulation. The steering function of self-regulation is more realistically achieved when feedback is derived from a mixture of direct affective and sensorimotor consequences and information from the environment than when it is derived from imagining an event. Confronting an attacker with a gun, hearing the applause of an audience after a good performance, or engaging in lovemaking provides richer feedback than playing out these scenarios cognitively, though the latter can be useful for preparing for the actual episode.

Retrospective self-regulation also occurs in absence of real-world feedback. It is similar to prospective self-regulation in that all processes are intraindividual, but the memory of some external feedback is usually available. It differs from prospective self-regulation in its temporal focus on a previous experience. It aims at developing standards and heuristics for similar future episodes. This process guides expectations and can alter self-attitudes. It is characterized by the reliving of glorious past experiences or fantasies of the "if I had only . . ." variety.

From Intention to Action

Incentive Development

My discussion of the self-regulation model has presumed the prior formation of an intent toward achievement of a given goal. Helping clients to
develop goals and commit themselves to them is frequently the first step
toward change. Figure 1.3 shows a modified version of the motivational
stages, adapted for therapy. The first transformation, from a wish to a want,
signifies a transition from idle fantasy to potential outcomes. The relevance
of the want to the present situation determines whether a commitment is
formed and persists until the goal is attained (Klinger, 1975, 1987). *O*ppor-
tunity for achieving the goal, *T*ime to pursue it, *I*mportance to the person,
*U*rgency for attaining it, and available *M*eans (OTIUM) enhance the probability of a want's becoming an intention (Heckhausen & Kuhl, 1985). The
person's skill repertoire and the presence of obstacles to enacting the intention are among other variables that influence the formation and behavioral
enactment of the intention. Factors that influence the likelihood of making
a commitment may be quite different from those that affect execution of the
intention when the action is imminent (Kanfer, 1975).

Representation of a desired goal state usually sets in motion *prospective
self-regulation.* The person imagines the expected situation, tries out different behaviors, evaluates their relative effectiveness, and eventually decides
on a course of action. During this vicarious trial-and-error learning (Tolman,
1939), the anticipated performance undergoes continuous refinement. The
individual then proceeds with a clearer understanding of possible options or
returns to the previous stage. If he or she continues, a *decision* is formed to
commit resources toward goal attainment. Whether private or public, this act
enhances the individual's current engagement with the proposed goal. Beginning with a *commitment,* which denotes a striving for achieving the goal,
a willingness to assume risks or losses, and an active maintenance of the current intention to achieve the stated goal, the focus shifts to the execution of
behavior. Commitment is enhanced by recognition of the relevance of the
outcome to the person's needs and values, by public declaration of the commitment, and by other factors that reduce the likelihood of renouncing the
earlier decision. At this stage, specific subgoals and instrumental behaviors
are developed in preparation for the next stage, the *behavioral enactment.*

Motivational Stages   Clinical Interventions

Motivational Stages	Clinical Interventions
I. Incentive Development	Persuasion Information exposure Modeling
II. Developing Goal Implementation	Thought experiments Cognitive rehearsal Covert problem solving Anticipatory stress inoculation
III. Decision	Goal/value clarification In vivo exploration of goal states

Predecisional

Postdecisional

IV. Commitment	Goal setting In vivo exploration of action states
II. Behavioral Enactment	Role play Self-confidence Social support Contingency management Desensitization Graduated task assignments
II. Feedforward and Retrospective Self Regulation	Verbalized review Rule development Practice
II. Maintenance	Relapse training Environmental structuring

Figure 1.3. Motivational Stages and Selected Clinical Interventions

A *feedforward stage* follows successful completion of a goal-directed behavior. By facilitating retrieval from memory of cues that signal need for action and by development of algorithms for such actions, the automaticity of behavioral components can be increased in future episodes. *Retrospective self-regulation* is one mechanism by which past experiences are used to set criteria and develop heuristics for future handling of similar situations. Strategies for *maintenance* of motivation are developed in the last stage of treatment.

The clinical procedures described in the following section and illustrated in the right column in Figure 1.3 are used at various points in time to further the specific goals at that moment. The conceptual model thus guides clinical judgment in the selection of strategies to maximize the client's efforts and cooperation. Although only a very small proportion of clients may need help only in implementing a specified change (i.e., they have passed through the earlier portion of the model by themselves or with help), most clients require assistance in moving toward readiness to change. To date, insufficient attention has been given in the formal presentation of therapy methods to these indispensable motivational components, although therapy outcome rests very much on their enlistment toward the desired end state.

CLINICAL IMPLEMENTATION

The analysis of subroutines that contribute to client cooperation and motivation suggests that different methods may be needed to attain the goals of each phase. Methods for behavioral enactment and maintenance represent well-established techniques, whereas techniques for movement toward a commitment have been given less attention and will therefore be discussed in greater detail. In all cases, the underlying approach illustrates the integration of technical knowledge and basic research with clinical data in conceptualizing individual cases (Kanfer, 1987). I have therefore selected examples from well-established clinical interventions and extrapolated laboratory findings.

Generating Incentives

Although symptom removal, resolution of a problem, and amelioration of discomfort are presumed to be the major incentives for treatment, clients present themselves for many other reasons (Kanfer & Schefft, 1988). Many clients hope for a change in the consequences of their actions without change in behavior or hope to find external causes of their plight that would justify shifting responsibility for change to others. Others have been referred and perceive no discrepancy between their current actions and goals and those that would be more efficacious, rewarding, or simply life maintaining in the long run. For example, substance abusers, sexual offenders, paranoids, borderline patients, and others are often motivated to defend the status quo rather than to effectuate a change. A felt discrepancy between current and desired states, a desire to change, is essential for effective therapy. For some clients, dissatisfaction with the current state and a desire for and/or curiosity about better alternatives may have to be created by deliberately increasing any felt discomfort: for example, by emphasis on how the client is missing out on potential pleasures or on the cost of maintaining the status quo and its painful consequences. Clients often do not develop more distant and higher-level goals; rather, they operate on day-by-day or moment-by-moment proximal motives and automatized actions (Semmer & Frese, 1985). Frequently, higher-level goals are described by global, vague, and empty phrases, such as "being healthy," "leading a productive life," "getting along with my partner," or "being secure and self-confident." These vague and vacuous statements do not represent sufficiently clear goal states to motivate specific actions. Often the client's motivation to form an alliance with the therapist is the earliest incentive for engaging in a therapy process. The methods described here can be used to foster the therapeutic relationship and to work toward specific goals.

Incentive development implies that the client becomes interested in the positive aspects of a therapy goal rather than remaining focused solely on the reduction of current distress. At this stage, the task is to animate the client to "dream new dreams," to consider the possibility that the current situation can be changed and that therapy sessions may be beneficial. Out of this work, a tentative problem definition can be achieved (Kanfer & Busemeyer, 1982). The main incentive for developing a therapeutic alliance is the expectation of understanding, acceptance, and competent assistance toward relief and problem resolution.

For many clients, one has to begin with information of *how* their life could change. Can a client with a long history of alcohol abuse who feels comfortable only when intoxicated, spends much of his or her leisure time in taverns, and has social contacts only when inebriated imagine what life would be like without alcohol? Would one expect an agoraphobic who has not left the house for a decade to become enthusiastic about the prospect of battling city traffic or crowds in shopping malls? Can one expect a woman who has been married for a dozen years and for whom the financial arrangements for major purchases, such as a car or a major appliance, have been made by a spouse to go forth alone to find an apartment and a job and to deal with insurance agents and high-pressure sales personnel?

At this stage, changes in attitudes and beliefs about the feasibility of the desired behavior must be activated. Information about positive aspects of the aspired goal state must be given to counter the fear of change. The literatures on attitude changes, persuasion, and modeling provide rich sources of ideas for clinical interventions to achieve this. For example, Fishbein and Ajzen (1975), in their theory of reasoned action, proposed that *personal attitudes* (positive or negative evaluations) toward the behavior and *subjective norms* determine a person's intention to perform an action. When there is no obstacle to implementing the intended action, stating the intention enhances the probability of its execution (Fishbein, 1966; Kanfer & Duerfeldt, 1968; Sherman, 1980). Ajzen (1985) proposed that planning to *attempt* execution of behavior enhances intention. In our model, dealing with clients' beliefs that they are capable of executing the behavior is deliberately postponed to a later stage. At this stage, observation of other persons, collection of information, discussion of positive consequences, and exposure to messages about the goal state are among the methods used. The experienced freedom to explore alternatives, asserting that things do not *have* to be as they are, can represent the first hesitant step toward change.

Work by Fazio (1986) suggests that the formation of a motive is affected by the manner in which information is presented and processed. Fazio (1986) distinguished between *automatically activated attitudes,* which occur when a situation results in "spontaneous activation of the attitude upon mere observation of the attitude object" (p. 237) after strong bonds have been developed, and *controlled process attitudes,* which result from a deliberate reasoning process. When automatic activation does not occur and controlled deliberation is not stimulated, the attitude cannot be expected to influence behavior. Direct experience and repeated expression of the attitude enhance the probability of automatic activation, strengthening the link between attitude and behavior.

From a similar perspective, Petty and colleagues (Cacioppo, Petty, & Stoltenberg, 1985; Petty & Cacioppo, 1986) distinguished between two types of attitude changes in their *elaboration likelihood model* (ELM) of persuasion. The first type results from careful consideration of relevant information, a processing of persuasive information that takes a *central route*. It results in enduring attitudes with adoption of new cognitions. The second, via the peripheral route, uses simple decision rules, forming attitudes with minimal cognitive effort. Effects are superficial and yield only temporary attitude changes, in the form of some momentary agreement with the therapist. To support formation of a stable intention, an attitude change must be developed by the central route.

The ELM model has been applied to clinical situations by Stoltenberg and his coworkers (Stoltenberg, 1986; Stoltenberg, Leach, & Bratt, 1989). At the core of the clinical application lies the involvement of the client in critically examining the issues, developing arguments about the merit of the goal, and initially questioning the therapist's statements about goals and their utility. To facilitate "self-persuasion," the client is then encouraged to advocate the goal. Increasing perceived personal relevance of the therapy goal, presenting recommendations as tentative suggestions rather than authoritative prescriptions, and encouraging the client to argue both pro and con positions may enhance client motivation at this stage. Clients who are high in need for cognition, field-independent, and intellectual and who perceive themselves as able to control their emotions are more likely to engage in central-route processing (Stoltenberg et al., 1989).

Numerous other factors have been described in the social psychology literature on the effectiveness of persuasive communications. For example, the use of models and exposure to information has been advocated to increase the formation of an intention. Research on cognitive dissonance and self-consistency theory suggests that information confirming a person's established beliefs is more likely to be perceived and accepted than disconfirmatory evidence. Many attitude researchers assume a strong link between intentions and behavior. The extent of correlation, however, is affected by the complexity of the behavior to be executed, the number of expected and unexpected obstacles encountered, the person's behavioral skills, and the extent to which emotional predisposition or other competing response tendencies might make the execution of the behavior more difficult.

Social facilitation and modeling are techniques for arousing interest and widening the road to intentions. Asking the client to choose social settings and observe (in detail) how others carry out and are reinforced for the targeted behavior can enhance the client's readiness for the next step.

Assignments of visiting a fitness center for a person attempting to lose weight or choosing acquaintances who support assertive behaviors for a person with excessive dependency and passivity can utilize social facilitation and modeling.

Other approaches for developing incentives derive from Bem's self-perception theory (1972). When persons perform some behaviors, such as assertive or fearless acts, and then reflect on the behaviors, they view themselves as assertive and continue to behave as self-perceived. Although many parameters limit the applicability of this theory, asking clients to engage in behaviors that approximate the goal state after these have been reframed or relabeled enhances the likelihood that clients will work toward attaining these behaviors. For example, a nonassertive individual might first observe and then imitate an admired and assertive brother or fellow worker and then reflect and report about that activity in therapy. Initially such assignments focus on the client's increased skill rather than the interpersonal exchange. Later, the therapist emphasizes the client's ability to carry out the behavior, its positive consequences, and its potential for reducing the client's distress or heightening self-esteem. Intention is also heightened by enhancing the client's perception of free choice (Kanfer & Grimm, 1978; Langer, 1983).

Therapists must be careful not to reinforce verbalizations, the sole function of which are to influence a listener. For example, praising a drug-abusing or aggressive client for promising not to engage in this behavior again may have no effect on the behavior and may facilitate the tendency to make such "empty intention statements" (Kanfer, Cox, Greiner, & Karoly, 1974; Karoly & Kanfer, 1974). When the client has begun to view the therapeutic goals as attractive and relevant, the clinician moves to the next stage. Progress to this point is smoothest when the client is helped to delay consideration of such realistic issues as possession of necessary skills, cost of achieving the goal, or availability of simple methods to attain it.

Developing Goal Implementation

Once the client has recognized the attractiveness of a therapeutic goal, the focus shifts to a lower level of self-regulation: a detailed analysis of possible pathways to reach the goal, including the consideration of obstacles and consequences that have to be anticipated. This stage represents a cognitive approximation of the actions in which the client may have to engage later. Possible future behavioral patterns and their outcomes are cognitively rehearsed, necessary effort and costs are examined, and tentative plans are considered for translating the intention into action. The process is iterative. Various options are played out in trial-and-error fashion until a satisfactory one is reached.

A common feature of all techniques at this stage is their contribution of reducing the client's anxiety about enactment of the intended behavior, planning effective approaches for changing the behavior, and providing the clinician with an opportunity for evaluating the client's skills and weaknesses and possible obstacles that may interfere with achievement of the intended goal state. Work by Johnson and her coworkers (e.g., Johnson & Raye, 1981) also suggests that imagined events are often confused with real experiences. Imagining coping scenarios can increase self-efficacy via a deja-vu experience. Imagining a scenario, having to explain a relationship between events, or arguing for an hypothesis usually increases the person's confidence that the event will occur. Taylor and Schneider (1989) summarized the processes of this stage under the heading of "simulation of events" and suggested specific coping functions for such simulations: These processes "(1) seem 'true,' (2) function as plans, (3) prompt affective responses to situations, (4) help to set expectations and (5) lead to behavioral confirmation" (p. 177). These procedures are similar to "thought experiments" that predated empirical science and were carried out by "construction in mind of potential experimental situations, the outcome of which could safely be foretold from previous every day experience" (Kuhn, 1977, p. 42). Anticipatory self-regulation is limited by the degree of experience the client and therapist have with the anticipated situation. Prior experience is needed for accurate selection of parameters of the anticipated events that may actually occur. Thus, "unless he [the scientist] has already had that much experience, he is not yet prepared to learn from thought experiments alone" (Kuhn, 1977, p. 265). The clinician's knowledge and experience should serve as a "reality monitor" in the client's prospective cognitive constructions.

Cognitive rehearsal and covert problem solving must occur in the context of a construction of the environment and an arousal level that is close to the anticipated situation. The approximation to reality can be strengthened first by assigning the client to watch or imagine another person engaging in the behavior and then by modeling the behavior in the session and playing out several variations of the scenario. Guided imagery, covert modeling, and other cognitive-behavioral methods can be applied at this stage. Curiosity and effectance motivation can also be enlisted by stressing the exploratory and nonbinding nature of the exercises. The clinical methods in this stage serve to prepare the individual for the management of affect and to enhance the client's self-efficacy beliefs and perceived control. They also provide the clinician with some indication of the client's capacity and readiness for change.

Decision and Commitment

After these exercises have refined the client's appreciation of the goal state and his or her understanding of what behaviors are necessary and what may be encountered in attaining the goal state, therapy proceeds to the next two overlapping stages that represent the transition from thinking about future actions to fixing a definitive goal and considering pathways and costs of implementing that goal. At the *decision stage,* the client is helped to define a clear end state that is acceptable to the client and to the clinician. This requires an examination of the broader context of potential therapy goals. The goal and value clarification procedure (Kanfer & Schefft, 1988; Koberg & Bagnall, 1976) is essentially based on the idea that people do not habitually examine and prioritize their life goals. Only when confronted with a situation in which concerns about everyday obligations and practical constraints emerge, will therapists find that practical problem-solving, skills training, and training in anxiety reduction may be helpful. In essence, whatever the therapist can do to simplify the task of changing, to highlight positive outcomes of any change, and to strengthen the person's belief in his or her ability to carry out the task will increase the likelihood that the client stays with the therapy program and retains motivation toward goal attainment.

The importance of flexibility in pursuing therapeutic goals has been widely recognized by most therapeutic schools. Utilization of subgoals, support for small changes that trigger other positive changes, proceeding in small steps, and reinforcing success experiences are among the many strategies that prompt continued progress.

Feedforward and Maintenance

Attainment of a goal is satisfying to the client (and therapist). It signals to the client that the complaint has disappeared and that the problem has been resolved, seemingly requiring no further action. The challenge at this stage is to develop sufficient strength of new behaviors and an awareness of potentially stressful situations, together with new ways of coping with them, so that the client does not suffer defeating disappointment when the problem recurs. As the data on therapeutic outcome attest, successful change is more often found right after termination of treatment than on long-term follow-up. Once a symptom has remitted or a few successes have been achieved, the motivational resources provided by the therapist, the continuing positive feedback of small changes during therapy, and the challenge of attaining a goal are no longer as strong.

Two stages can be differentiated in the transition from therapy to the client's later capacity for effective self-regulation: a feedforward stage during treatment and the preparation for later maintenance. The feedforward segment focuses on motivating the client to continue the change process by extending it to new situations and by strengthening the new behavior so that coping responses become automatic. Among facilitating strategies are the verbalized review of the client's experience in sessions so as to commit the client's success experiences to both episodic and semantic memory. Development of verbal rules can enhance generalization of coping skills and reduce the need for renewed problem solving in situations that differ from those in which the behavior change began. Continued practice, with decreasing support from the therapist, development of social support, deliberate application of newly learned strategies in novel situations, and in-session role play can facilitate the feedforward effect. The selection of environments that facilitate maintenance of the newly acquired behaviors, the early recognition of cues that signal dangerous or tempting situations, arising both in situations and within the person, and continuing self-regulatory efforts to control of the original problems (Kirschenbaum & Tomarken, 1982) are among the therapist's tools for post-therapy maintenance of the therapeutic achievement.

Marlatt and his coworkers (Marlatt & Gordon, 1985; Marlatt & Parks, 1982) have emphasized the importance of targeting long-term maintenance of newly acquired behaviors in the description of their relapse model. Although the model was developed from their research with alcoholic patients, their program for relapse prevention is applicable for most clients.

THE ROLE OF EMOTIONS

No discussion of motivation is complete without consideration of the emotions. The central role of emotions in the explanation of behavior has been emphasized by authors of different persuasions. For example, Izard and Blumberg (1985) stated that "the emotions system is viewed as the principal motivational system for human beings. The emotions are seen as adaptive and motivating organizers of experience and behavior" (p. 123). Frijda (1988) emphasized the change in action readiness as a central feature of emotional states: "They can be defined in terms of some form of action tendency or some form of activation or lack thereof" (p. 351). The relationship of emotions to the self-regulation model was described by Schefft, Moses, and Schmidt (1985). Until recently, most schools of therapy, reflecting prevailing attitudes in Western culture, focused almost exclusively on the disorganizing and disruptive effects of emotions. Research dealt mainly with the negative emotions. Therapeutic efforts were directed at control of the presumably irrational and unpredictable aspects of behavior in "emotional illness," in concert with society's support of rational, logical, and "cool" cognitions in opposition to the emotions. In research as in practice, the emotions have been viewed as targets or dependent variables rather than as potential intervention tools or independent variables that could be systematically introduced to motivate activities. Because of their subjective intensity and their characteristic accompanying physiological and expressive patterns, emotions have often been the exclusive focus of attention, even though emotional reactions (like all motivated behavior) are components of episodes that include specific situations, contents, biological and cognitive processes, and action potentials. Their understanding and modification therefore require attention to all the participating components.

If emotions are defined as action dispositions and it is postulated that they "organize behavior along a basic appetite-aversive dimension . . . associated with either a behavioral set covering approaching, attachment and consummatory behavior or a set disposing the organism to avoidance, escape and defense" (Lang, Bradley, & Cuthbert, 1990, p. 377) and if emotions are viewed essentially as an effective evolutionary mechanism for survival (Frijda, 1988; Plutchik, 1990), then the traditional view of their disorganizing function is not tenable. Instead, negative emotions and moods can be perceived as warning signals to the organism that a change from the current state is necessary, whereas positive moods can be perceived as essentially confirming the benefits of the present state. A person who has been trained to recognize the evaluative and action-orienting cues of an emotion is better able to assess current goal priorities and engage in self-regulating action before emotional arousal reaches its peak.

The intensity of initial emotional reactions is often heightened by the experience of strong secondary emotions. These result from a feeling of loss of control, an incongruence between intent and action, guilt over ambivalence (often between personal feelings and socially prescribed norms), or an intense frustration in being blocked from attaining a very desirable goal. These components of anxiety, panic, or obsessive-compulsive disorders exacerbate the client's sense of helplessness and fear. They may also mask the cues for the primary emotion, making it more difficult to assess the original functions of a symptom.

There have been numerous reviews of the growing literature on emotions, including guides for therapy operations on the basis of robust findings from laboratory research (e.g., Greenberg & Safran, 1987; Izard, 1979; Kanfer & Schefft, 1988; Plutchik, 1990; Salovey & Singer, 1991). Apart from the vast literature on the effects of depression on cognition and behavior, the work on the effects of mood on learning and retrieval has been described extensively in connection with the hypotheses of mood-congruent learning, mood-congruent recall, and mood-dependent retrieval in the literature on the relationship between affect and cognition (e.g., among many others, Bower, 1981; Fiedler & Forgas, 1988; Isen, 1984; Izard, Kagan, & Zajonc, 1984). If we assume that moods are milder, more diffuse, and longer-lasting patterns of action dispositions and physiological states, moods may be more easily controlled as therapeutic tools than intense emotions.

Recent investigations have demonstrated effects of emotions and moods on interpersonal behaviors that have direct relevance to the therapy process: For example, clients' willingness to assume risk (Deldin & Levin, 1986; Isen & Patrick, 1983), helping behavior (Cialdini & Kenrick, 1976; Isen, 1970), judgment about future outcomes (e.g., Mayer & Volanth, 1985), and beliefs about their health (Salovey & Birnbaum, 1989) are modifiable by mood. Persons in a negative mood tend to shift attention to themselves (Kanfer & Hagerman, 1987; Pyszczynski & Greenberg, 1987), reduce their self-efficacy estimates (Smith, 1987), and tolerate pain for shorter intervals (Roll, 1990). The role of emotions and feelings as sources of information for both the person and others has also been given attention (e.g., Schwarz & Clore, 1988), and self-generated behavior has been shown to decrease negative mood (Schefft & Biederman, 1990).

In clinical practice, interventions targeting emotions most commonly address one of the following issues:

1. Emotional reactions are appropriate but not expressed (e.g., in clients fearful of intimacy, lacking assertiveness, or fearing censure for showing emotions).
2. Emotional reactions are excessive in intensity (e.g., phobias, anger outbursts, depressive sadness).
3. Conflicting emotional reactions result in poor coping, inaction, or inconsistent, rapidly alternating behaviors as dominant goals shift (e.g., ambivalence between curiosity and escape in a high-risk situation or sexual dysfunction associated with anxiety-arousing situations).
4. Emotional reactions are secondary responses to one's own feeling states or actions that conflict with personal standards or result from anticipation of intense emotional arousal, positive or negative (e.g., guilt over destructive or malicious thoughts, fear of loss of control, "forbidden" sexual feelings, fear of fear).

I limit myself to a few examples of strategies that can be derived from laboratory findings on moods and emotions. An accumulation of clinical research will be needed to develop robust heuristics for use of mood and emotion-related processes in therapy.

First, it has been shown that memories congruent with a person's current mood are more easily accessed than noncongruent memories (Blaney, 1986; Gilligan & Bower, 1984). A constant focus on the client's problems is likely to be associated with negative moods and a pessimistic outlook, exacerbated by heightened recall and attention to negative life events. To counter these deleterious effects (Peterson & Seligman, 1987; Scheier & Carver, 1985), every session should include intervals of recall or anticipation of positive events to enhance optimism. The work of Isen on the effects of positive affect on information processing further suggests the potentials of mood manipulation in enhancing clients' readiness to take small risks, respond to suggestions, and be more flexible and creative (Isen, 1984; Isen & Patrick, 1983). To enhance commitment to a therapeutic task (e.g., to attempt a change in a routine or to be more open to a new perspective), these "positive" intervals should immediately precede presentation of a task or an attempt at restructuring.

Second, in addition to the effects of mood on memory and information processing, a client's action tendency can be enhanced or blocked by induction of various moods. For example, producing anger in a depressive, invoking pride in an anxious client, inducing surprise or joy in an aggressive client, or inducing aggression in a passive client can disrupt prevailing action tendencies and facilitate further therapeutic steps. Research on the effects of facial feedback on subjective experience also suggests that deliberately exaggerating facial expressions of appropriate emotions may serve as a signal for a subjective experience and result in similar changes in actual mood state. Clearly, strategies for mood induction must be cautiously se lected in kind and intensity to suit the individual client. In most cases, relatively small changes in the therapist's focus on the emotional tone or contents of a client's report or a brief change in the quality of the interpersonal relationship is sufficient for mood alteration.

Third, intense emotional states tend to allot the client's resources to the goal path prescribed by the emotion and enlist automatic processing to achieve this. Consequently, intense emotions tend by bypass self-regulatory processes, much as cognitively demanding tasks do (Kanfer & Stevenson, 1985), and can reduce the effectiveness of self-control techniques. Thus therapists work for recognition of early cues of emotional arousal to which new behaviors can be attached before the client progresses to a highly aroused state. These data also suggest the training of highly automatized self-control repertoires, with low cognitive resource demand when targeting control of intense emotions.

Fourth, training in "emotional intelligence" (Salovey, Hsee & Mayer, 1993) facilitates the client's understanding of emotion in self and others, assists in the regulation of emotion-related actions, and can engage mood alterations to motivate adaptive behaviors. Recognized feelings and (correctly labeled) emotions also inform about one's evaluation of situations and current action dispositions (Schwarz & Clore, 1988), just as observation of emotions in others can guide one's actions. Initially the labeling and recognition and later the self-monitoring of incipient emotional arousal disrupt automatic response sequences. They permit introduction of self-controlling strategies at a time when the emotion-driving behavior is not yet at its height and attentional resources are still free for self-regulatory action. Such awareness "can play a significant role in promoting interactional as well as intrapsychic change" (Greenberg & Safran, 1987, p. 195). The disruption of the automatic emotional sequence can be facilitated by focusing on specific subsidiary patterns, such as physical locus of feelings, cognitive content, or action tendencies (urges) and their goals.

Fifth, bringing earlier emotional experiences into awareness has been a central strategy of therapy since the days of Freud. However, recent reexamination of the utility of reexperiencing or reporting an earlier emotional trauma has radically altered the traditional concept of catharsis as a psychic purge or "cleansing" process. In fact, when the expression of affect merely re-capitulates ancient patterns, it may be ineffective or even harmful in strengthening a patient's destructive interpersonal patterns (Smith-Benjamin, 1990). When traumatic experiences are targeted, a different approach is needed for each client. The strategy depends on what is judged to be the most important original deleterious effect of the trauma and the most desirable outcome for the client at this stage of therapy. Merely the opportunity to report an intense emotional experience that may have evoked guilt, shame, misplaced responsibility, and expectation of punishment may be sufficient when the presence of the nonjudgmental therapist helps to extinguish the client's expectations and facilitates later reappraisal of the event. The therapist's sharing and validating of the client's experience and normalizing of the client's feelings and actions can serve to reduce self-reproaches and "secondary emotions" related to the client's assessment of his or her role in the event. The role of the therapist as a "nonpunishing audience" that allows free expression and eventual extinction of self-defeating thoughts and behavior was considered the main function of therapy by Skinner (1953).

In some cases, free communication permits analysis of the client's strong behavioral predispositions, due to emotional arousal, that are often in conflict with other emotions, motives, or attempts at problem solving. With the proper focus, reexperiencing a trauma can help the client understand his or her feelings and thereby lead to more acceptable action plans in future similar situations.

For some clients, reexperiencing intense emotional episodes provides the basis for constructing alternate scenarios, yielding a cognitive reorganization of the context associated with the event. Such restructuring or reframing can then alter the memory and meaning of the event, reducing its distressing impact. Reliving an intense emotional experience may permit the recognition of competing response tendencies, ambivalence, or discrepancies between the person's feelings and socially prescribed standards, such as the experiencing of hate or anger toward a parent or partner who should be loved or feelings of curiosity or sexual arousal in high-risk situations. Recognition of these conflicting action tendencies can result in eventual resolution of the conflict and a feeling of restoration of control over one's emotions.

Finally, techniques for moderating secondary emotions resulting from unsuccessful attempts to suppress unacceptable thoughts have been derived from the extensive analysis and research of the suppression process by

Wegner and his colleagues (Wegner, 1989; Wegner, Shortt, Blake, & Page, 1990). These reports suggest a shift from trying to control strong emotion-laden thoughts to building up a repertoire of alternate responses. Focus on specified distracting thoughts or actions—for example, by breathing exercises, cognitive restructuring of the core element of the episode, or attention to incompatible actions or thoughts—tends to reduce the distress caused by the intrusion of the unwanted or painful memory. Just confiding or even writing about traumatic events has beneficial effects (Pennebaker, Hughes, & O'Heeron, 1987). Research on this writing procedure has led Pennebaker, Colder, and Sharp (1990) to conclude that these effects are due to the informational rather than the cathartic character of the confrontation, giving subjects a better understanding of their own thoughts, moods, and behavior.

These examples point to the rich potential for clinical strategies that can be derived from recent laboratory research. Some are already embedded in traditional methods of various schools; others will require field research to optimize their utility. In any case, the time has come to give the motivational and emotional components of human experiences a more explicit and prominent place in cognitive-behavioral therapy, both as subject matter of treatment and as potential tools for behavior change. Recent attention to the integration of research and practice in this area (e.g., Greenberg & Safran, 1987; Klinger, in press; Lazarus & Lazarus, 1990; Plutchik, 1990) has paved the way for this latest step in giving behavior therapy a comprehensive framework for covering the wide range of human dysfunctions.

REFERENCES

Ajzen, I. (1985). From intentions to actions: A theory of planned behavior. In J. Kuhl & J. Beckman (Eds.), *Action control: From cognition to behavior* (pp. 11-39). New York: Springer-Verlag.

Bandura, A. (1977). *Social learning theory.* Englewood Cliffs, NJ: Prentice Hall.

Bargh, J. A. (1989). Conditional automaticity: Varieties of automatic influence in social perception and cognition. In J. S. Uleman & J. A. Bargh (Eds.), *Unintended thought* (pp. 3-51). New York: Guilford.

Beck, A. T. (1976). *Cognitive therapy and the emotional disorders.* New York: International Universities Press.

Bem, D. J. (1972). Self-perception theory. *Advances in Experimental Social Psychology, 6,* 114-137.

Blaney, P. H. (1986). Affect and memory: A review. *Psychological Bulletin, 99,* 229-246.

Bower, G. (1981). Mood and memory. *American Psychologist, 36,* 129-148.

Cacioppo, J. T., Petty, R. E., & Stoltenberg, C. (1985). Processes of social influence: The elaboration likelihood model of persuasion. *Advances in Cognitive Behavioral Research and Therapy, 4,* 215-274.

Carver, C. S., & Scheier, M. F. (1981). *Attention and self-regulation: A control theory approach to human behavior.* New York: Springer-Verlag.

Cervone, D., & Peake, P. K. (1986). Anchoring, affect, and action: The influence of judgmental heuristics on self-efficacy judgments and behavior. *Journal of Personality and Social Psychology, 50,* 492-501.

Cialdini, R. B., & Kenrick, D. T. (1976). Altruism as hedonism: A social development perspective on the relationship of negative mood state and helping. *Journal of Personality and Social Psychology, 34,* 907-914.

Cofer, C. N., & Appley, M. H. (1964). *Motivation: Theory and research.* New York: John Wiley.

Deldin, P. J., & Levin, I. P. (1986). The effect of mood induction in a risky decision-making task. *Bulletin of the Psychonomic Society, 24,* 4-6.

Duval, S., & Wicklund, R. A. (1972). *A theory of objective self-awareness.* New York: Academic Press.

Dweck, C. (1986). Motivational processes affecting learning. *American Psychologist, 41,* 1040-1048.

Fazio, R. H. (1986). How do attitudes guide behavior? In R. M. Sorrentino & E. T. Higgins (Eds.), *Handbook of motivation and cognition: Foundations of social behavior* (pp. 204-243). New York: Guilford.

Fiedler, K., & Forgas, J. (Eds.). (1988). *Affect, cognition and social behavior.* Toronto: C. J. Hogrefe.

Fishbein, M. (1966). The relationship between beliefs, attitudes, and behavior. In S. Feldman (Eds.), *Cognitive consistency and motivational antecedents* (pp. 92-144). New York: Academic Press.

Fishbein, M., & Ajzen, I. (1975). *Belief, attitude, intention, and behavior.* Reading, MA: Addison-Wesley.

Ford, D. H. (1987). *Humans as self-constructing living systems.* Hillsdale, NJ: Lawrence Erlbaum.

Frijda, N. H. (1988). The laws of emotion. *American Psychologist, 43,* 349-358.

Garfield, S. L. (1986). An eclectic psychotherapy. In J. C. Norcross (Ed.), *Handbook of eclectic psychotherapy* (pp. 132-162). New York: Brunner/Mazel.

Gilligan, S. G., & Bower, G. H. (1984). Cognitive consequences of emotional arousal. In C. E. Izard, J. Kagan, & R. Zagonc (Eds.), *Emotions, cognition, and behavior* (pp. 547-588). New York: Cambridge University Press.

Greenberg, L. S., & Safran, J. D. (1987). *Emotion in psychotherapy: Affect and cognition in the process of change.* New York: Guilford.

Greenberg, L. S., & Safran, J. D. (1990). Emotional change processes in psychotherapy. In R. Plutchik & H. Kellerman (Eds.), *Emotion: Theory, research and experience: Vol. 5. Emotion, psychopathology, and psychotherapy* (pp. 59-85). New York: Academic Press.

Heckhausen, H., Gollwitzer, P. M., & Weinert, F. E. (Eds.). (1987). *Jenseits des Rubikon: Der Wille in den Humanwissenschaften.* Heidelberg: Springer-Verlag.

Heckhausen, H., & Kuhl, J. (1985). From wishes to action: The dead ends and short cuts on the long way to action. In M. Frese & J. Sabini (Eds.), *Goal-directed behavior: The concept of action in psychology* (pp. 134-159). Hillsdale, NJ: Lawrence Erlbaum.

Hudgins, C. V. (1933). Conditioning and the voluntary control of the pupillary light reflex. *Journal of General Psychology, 8*, 3-51.

Hunter, W. (1924). The symbolic process. *Psychological Review, 31*, 478-497.

Isen, A. M. (1970). Success, failure, attention, and reaction to others: The warm glow of success. *Journal of Personality and Social Psychology, 15*, 294-301.

Isen, A. (1984). Toward understanding the role of affect in cognition. In R. Wyer & T. Srull (Eds.), *Handbook of social cognition* (pp. 179-236). Hillsdale, NJ: Lawrence Erlbaum.

Isen, A., & Patrick, R. (1983). The effect of positive feelings on risk-taking: When the chips are down. *Organization Behavior and Human Performance, 31*, 194-202.

Izard, C. E. (Ed.). (1979). *Emotion in personality and psychopathology.* New York: Plenum.

Izard, C. E., & Blumberg, S. H. (1985). Emotion theory and the role of emotions in anxiety in children and adults. In A. H. Tuma & J. D. Maser (Eds.), *Anxiety and the anxiety disorders* (pp. 109-129). Hillsdale, NJ: Lawrence Erlbaum.

Izard, C. E., Kagan, J., & Zajonc, R. B. (1984). *Emotions, cognitions, and behavior.* New York: Cambridge University Press.

Johnson, M. K., & Raye, C. L. (1981). Reality-monitoring. *Psychological Review, 88.*

Kanfer, F. H. (1970). Self-regulation: Research issues and speculations. In C. Neuringer & J. L. Michael (Eds.), *Behavior modification in clinical psychology* (pp. 178-220). New York: Appleton-Century-Crofts.

Kanfer, F. H. (1975). Self-management methods. In F. H. Kanfer & A. P. Goldstein (Eds.), *Helping people change: A textbook of methods* (pp. 309-356). New York: Pergamon.

Kanfer, F. H. (1977). The many faces of self-control or behavior modification changes focus. In R. B. Stuart (Ed.), *Behavioral self-management* (pp. 1-48). New York: Brunner/Mazel.

Kanfer, F. H. (1987). Self-regulation and behavior. In H. Heckhausen, P. M. Gollwitzer, & F. E. Weinert (Eds.), *Jenseits des Rubikon: Der Wille in den Humanwissenschaften* (pp. 286-299). Heidelberg: Springer-Verlag.

Kanfer, F. H. (1988). Beiträge eines Selbstregulations Modells zur psychotherapeutischen Praxis [Contributions of a self-regulation model to clinical practice]. *Praxis der Klinischen Verhaltensmedizin und Rehabilitation, 1*, 289-300.

Kanfer, F. H., & Ackerman, P. L. (1989). Motivational cognitive abilities: An integrative/aptitude-treatment interaction approach to skill acquisition. *Journal of Applied Psychology, 74*, 657-690.

Kanfer, F. H., & Busemeyer, J. R. (1982). The use of problem solving and decision making in behavior therapy. *Clinical Psychology Review, 2*, 239-266.

Kanfer, F. H., Cox, L. E., Greiner, J. M., & Karoly, P. (1974). Contracts, demand characteristics and self-control. *Journal of Personality and Social Psychology, 30*, 605-619.

Kanfer, F. H., & Duerfeldt, P. H. (1968). Age, class-standing and commitment as determinants of cheating in children. *Child Development, 39*, 545-557.

Kanfer, F. H., & Grimm, L. G. (1978). Freedom of choice and behavioral change. *Journal of Consulting and Clinical Psychology, 46*, 873-878.

Kanfer, F. H., & Hagerman, S. (1987). The role of self-regulation. In F. Halisch & J. Kuhl (Eds.), *Motivation, intention, volition* (pp. 293-307). New York: Springer-Verlag.

Kanfer, F. H., & Schefft, B. K. (1988). *Guiding the process of therapeutic change.* Champaign, IL: Research Press.

Kanfer, F. H., & Stevenson, M. K. (1985). The effects of self-regulation on concurrent cognitive processing. *Cognitive Therapy and Research, 9*, 667-684.

Kanfer, R. (1991). Goals and self-regulation: Applications of theory to work settings. *Advances in Motivation and Achievement, 7,* 237-249.

Karoly, P., & Kanfer, F. H. (1974). Effects of prior contractual experience on self-control in children. *Developmental Psychology, 10,* 459-460.

Kirschenbaum, D. S., & Tomarken, A. J. (1982). On facing the generalization problem: The study of self-regulatory failure. *Advances in Cognitive-Behavioral Research and Therapy, 1,* 119-200.

Klinger, E. (1975). Consequences of commitment to and disengagement from incentives. *Psychological Review, 82,* 1-25.

Klinger, E. (1987). Current concerns and disengagement from incentives. In F. Halisch & J. Kuhl (Eds.), *Motivation, intention and volition* (pp. 337-347). Berlin: Springer.

Klinger, E. (in press). Clinical approaches to mood control. In D. M. Wegner & J. W. Pennebaker (Eds.), *Handbook of mental control.* Englewood Cliffs, NJ: Prentice Hall.

Koberg, D., & Bagnall, J. (1976). *The polytechnic school of values: Value tech.* Los Altos, CA: William Kaufmann.

Kuhn, T. S. (1977). *The essential tension.* Chicago: University of Chicago Press.

Lang, P. J., Bradley, M. M., & Cuthbert, B. N. (1990). Emotion, attention, and the startle reflex. *Psychological Bulletin, 97,* 377-395.

Langer, E. J. (1983). *The psychology of control.* Beverly Hills, CA: Sage.

Lazarus, A. A., & Lazarus, C. N. (1990). Emotions: A multimodal therapy perspective. In R. Plutchik & H. Kellerman (Eds.), *Emotion: theory, research and experience: Vol. 5. Emotion, psychopathology, and psychotherapy* (pp. 195-208). New York: Academic Press.

Locke, E. A. (1968). Toward a theory of task motivation and incentives. *Organizational Behavior and Human Performance, 3,* 157-189.

Locke, E. A., Shaw, K. N., Saari, L. M., & Latham, G. P. (1981). Goal-setting and task performance: 1969-1980. *Psychological Bulletin, 90,* 125-152.

Logan, G. D. (1989). Automaticity and cognitive control. In J. S. Uleman & J. A. Bargh (Eds.), *Unintended thought* (pp. 52-74). New York: Guilford.

Marlatt, G. A., & Gordon, J. R. (Eds.). (1985). *Relapse prevention: Maintenance strategies in the treatment of addictive behaviors.* New York: Guilford.

Marlatt, G. A., & Parks, G. A. (1982). Self management of addictive disorders. In P. Karoly & F. H. Kanfer (Eds.), *Self-management and behavior change: From theory to practice* (pp. 443-488). New York: Pergamon.

Mayer, J. D., & Volanth, A. J. (1985). Cognitive involvement in the emotional response system. *Motivation and Emotion, 9,* 261-275.

Miller, W. R. (1985). Motivation for treatment: A review with special emphasis on alcoholism. *Psychological Bulletin, 98,* 84-107.

Murphy, G. (1949). *Historical introduction to modern psychology.* New York: Harcourt Brace.

Nezu, A. M., & Nezu, C. M. (Eds.). (1989). *Clinical decision making in behavior therapy.* Champaign, IL: Research Press.

Pennebaker, J. W., Colder, M., & Sharp, L. K. (1990). Accelerating the coping process. *Journal of Personality and Social Psychology, 52,* 781-793.

Pennebaker, J. W., Hughes, C., & O'Heeron, R. C. (1987). The psychophysiology of confession: Linking inhibitory and psychosomatic processes. *Journal of Personality and Social Psychology, 52,* 781-793.

Peterson, C., & Seligman, M. E. P. (1987). Explanatory style and illness. *Journal of Personality, 55,* 237-265.

Petty, R. E., & Cacioppo, J. T. (1986). *Communication and persuasion: Central and peripheral routes to attitude change.* New York: Springer-Verlag.

Plutchik, R. (1990). Emotions and psychotherapy: A psychoevolutionary perspective. In R. Plutchik & H. Kellerman (Eds.), *Emotion: Theory, research and experience: Vol. 5. Emotion, psychopathology and psychotherapy* (pp. 3-41). New York: Academic Press.

Powers, W. T. (1973). *Behavior: The control of perception.* Chicago: Aldine.

Prochaska, J. O., & DiClemente, C. C. (1982). Transtheoretical therapy: Toward a more integrative model of change. *Psychotherapy: Theory, Research and Practice, 19,* 276-288.

Pyszczynski, T., & Greenberg, J. (1987). Self-regulatory perseveration and the depressive self-focusing style: A self-awareness theory of depression. *Psychological Bulletin, 102,* 122-138.

Roll, C. N. (1990). *Effects of mood and perceived control on the tolerance of pain.* Unpublished honors thesis, University of Illinois-Champaign.

Salovey, P., & Birnbaum, D. (1989). Influence of mood on health-relevant cognitions. *Journal of Personality and Social Psychology, 57,* 539-551.

Salovey, P., Hsee, C. K., & Mayer, J. D. (1993). Emotional intelligence and the self-regulatory affect. In J. D. Wegner & J. W. Pennebaker (Eds.), *Handbook of Mental Control.* Englewood Cliffs, NJ: Prentice Hall.

Salovey, P., & Singer, J. A. (1991). Cognitive behavior modification. In F. H. Kanfer & A. P. Goldstein (Eds.), *Helping people change* (4th ed., pp. 361-395). Elmsford, NY: Pergamon.

Schefft, B. K., & Biederman, J. J. (1990). Emotional effects of self-generated behavior and the influence of resourcefulness and depressed mood. *Journal of Social and Clinical Psychology, 9,* 354-366.

Schefft, B. K., Moses, J. A., Jr., & Schmidt, G. L. (1985). Neuropsychology and emotion: A self-regulatory model. *International Journal of Clinical Neuropsychology, 7,* 219-247.

Scheier, M. F., & Carver, C. S. (1985). Optimism, coping, and health: Assessment and implication of generalized outcome expectancies. *Health Psychology, 4,* 219-247.

Schneider, W., & Schiffrin, R. M. (1977). Controlled and automatic human information processing. 1. Detection, search, and attention. *Psychological Review, 84,* 1-66.

Schwarz, N., & Clore, G. L. (1988). How do I feel about it? The information function of mood. In K. Fiedler & J. Forgas (Eds.), *Affect, cognition, and social behavior* (pp. 230-247). Toronto: C. J. Hogrefe.

Semmer, N. & Frese, M. (1985). Action theory in clinical psychology. In M. Freze & J. Sabini (Eds.), *Goal directed behavior. The concept of action in psychology* (pp. 296-310). Hillside, NJ: Lawrence Erlbaum.

Sherman, S. J. (1980). On the self-erasing nature of errors of prediction. *Journal of Personality and Social Psychology, 39,* 311-221.

Skinner, B. F. (1953). *Science and human behavior.* New York: Macmillan.

Smith, J. R. (1987). *Content dimensions of the Velten mood induction procedure: Multiple routes to negative mood.* Unpublished doctoral dissertation, University of Illinois-Champaign.

Smith-Benjamin, L. (1990). Interpersonal analysis of the cathartic model. In R. Plutchick & H. Kellerman (Eds.), *Emotion: Theory, research and experience: Vol. 5. Emotion, psychopathology and psychotherapy* (pp. 209-229). New York: Academic Press.

Stoltenberg, C. D. (1986). ELM and the counseling process. In F. J. Dorn (Ed.), *The social influence process in counseling and psychotherapy* (pp. 55-64). Springfield, IL: Charles C Thomas.

Stoltenberg, C. D., Leach, M. M., & Bratt, A. (1989). The elaboration likelihood model and psychotherapeutic persuasion. *Journal of Cognitive Psychotherapy: An International Quarterly, 3,* 181-199.

Taylor, S. E., & Schneider, S. K. (1989). Coping and the simulation of events. *Social Cognition, 7,* 174-194.

Tolman, E. C. (1939). Prediction of vicarious trial and error by means of the schematic sowbug. *Psychological Review, 46,* 318-336.

Wegner, D. M. (1989). *White bears and other unwanted thoughts.* New York: Viking.

Wegner, D. M., Shortt, J. W., Blake, A. W., & Page, M. S. (1990). The suppression of exciting thoughts. *Journal of Personality and Social Psychology, 58,* 409-418.

White, R. W. (1959). Motivation reconsidered: The concept of competence. *Psychological Review, 66,* 297-333.

2

Cognitive-Behavioral Approaches
to Anger Reduction

JERRY L. DEFFENBACHER

This chapter focuses on cognitive-behavioral approaches to anger reduction. It begins with a clinical model of anger to which interventions are linked in terms of their therapeutic focus. Then broad cognitive-behavioral intervention strategies are described in terms of their therapeutic goals, research support, therapeutic processes, and suggestions for implementation.

A WORKING MODEL OF ANGER

Conceptual confusion exists in defining and delineating meaningful groups of dysfunctional anger reactions. For example, the third, revised edition of the *Diagnostic and Statistical Manual of Mental Disorders* (*DSM-III-R;* American Psychiatric Association, 1987) provides little help. Anger is a secondary element (i.e., a factor that contributes to a diagnosis but is not

AUTHOR'S NOTE: This chapter was prepared for the 24th Banff International Conference on the Behavioural Sciences. Preparation of this chapter was funded, in part, by the Tri-Ethnic Center for Prevention of Drug Abuse, National Institute of Drug Abuse Grant #P50DA07074.

necessary for diagnosis) in some Axis I disorders, such as dysthymia, post-traumatic stress disorder, and explosive impulse control disorders; some Axis II disorders, such as borderline, passive-aggressive, and antisocial personality disorders; and some Axis III disorders in which it is a contributor to physical illness. However, there is no group of disorders for which anger is the primary defining characteristic (i.e., necessary for a diagnosis), even though there are well-defined groups of anxiety and depressive disorders. For example, a client can have a diagnosable disorder for chronic, moderate worry and anxiety (generalized anxiety disorder) or depression (dysthymia) but not for chronic, moderate anger. Diagnoses are available for situational anxiety reactions (phobias) but not for intense, situational anger reactions (e.g., in response to criticism, a child's misbehavior, or discourteous drivers). Some adjustment disorders are defined by their emotional/mood elements (e.g., adjustment disorder with anxiety, depression, or mixed emotional features). There is, however, no adjustment disorder with angry mood unless it is associated with conduct problems. But what of the adolescent who is very angry at parents for moving him or her to a new city but is not acting out? What of the divorcing adult who is very angry but not aggressive? Perhaps we need specific diagnostic categories for anger problems (e.g., generalized anger disorder, situational anger disorder, and adjustment disorder with angry mood). Nonetheless, the absence of official diagnostic categories does not mean that meaningful anger-based emotional disorders do not exist and are not worthy of treatment.

To amplify this point, a clinical analogue of generalized anger will be described. A high-general-anger clientlike group has been defined by college students who score in the upper quartile of the Trait Anger Scale (Spielberger, 1988) and who describe themselves as having a significant problem with anger and a desire for help with it (i.e., they report more general anger than their peers and want help for the problem). When compared to low-anger students (students in the lower quartile on the Trait Anger Scale who indicate no personal problem with anger), high-anger students (see Deffenbacher, 1992, for a review) (a) report significantly more intense anger across a wide range of situations and anger indices; (b) experience more frequent and intense daily anger; (c) experience more intense anger-related physiological arousal; (d) show general tendencies to suppress anger and to express it outwardly in negative, less controlled ways; (e) experience more frequent and sometimes more serious anger consequences (e.g., bodily damage to self and others, property damage, disrupted interpersonal relationships, and lowered self-esteem); (f) report more anger than university counseling center clients in general and more anger than those who did not report anger as a reason for seeking counseling; (g) are generally anxious; (h) cope poorly with common stressors; (i) report lower self-esteem; and (j) are more likely to abuse alcohol (e.g., drink more frequently, consume more when drinking, and experience more negative alcohol-related consequences, such as impact on school work, damaged relationships, and physical injury to self and others). Thus this group reflects a meaningful mild to moderate pathology group representing perhaps 4% to 7% of students.

Loss of clarity in defining anger has also resulted from conceptual confusion with aggression (Spielberger, 1988; Spielberger, Jacobs, Russell, & Crane, 1983). *Anger* refers to internal affective experience that may vary in intensity and chronicity and can refer both to the experience of the moment (state anger) and to the propensity to experience state anger across time and situations (trait and situation-specific anger). *Aggression*, however, refers to behavior that does or could lead to some kind of damage to a person, object, or social system. Anger and aggression can go hand in hand. When angered, some individuals physically and/or verbally assault others, objects, and/or themselves. However, these are not the only behaviors commonly seen. Some individuals, especially when anger is mild, become assertive and active problem solvers. Others suppress their behavioral responding, showing little outward expression, but experience considerable internal turmoil and arousal, which may eventuate in increased somatic involvement. Others withdraw and distance themselves from the source of provocation. Still others become anxious and engage in defensive maneuvers such as denial, projection, intellectualization, and reaction formation. Still others pout and sulk. Simply, anger is not synonymous with aggression. Problematic anger can and should be separated from the behaviors to which it is related and should be conceptualized, assessed, and treated on its own merit.

To aid in the conceptualization of and treatment planning for anger problems, a working model of anger is introduced. This model (see Figure 2.1) is an integration of others' work, such as Lazarus's (1991) work on stress and emotions, Novaco's (1979) application of Lazarus's concepts to anger, the work of cognitive theorists such as Ellis (1977) and Beck (1976), and Meichenbaum's (1985) work on stress inoculation. Although neurological, temperament, endocrine, and other physiological processes may influence anger, anger results from complex interactions between (a) one or more eliciting stimuli; (b) the individual's preanger state, both momentary and endur-

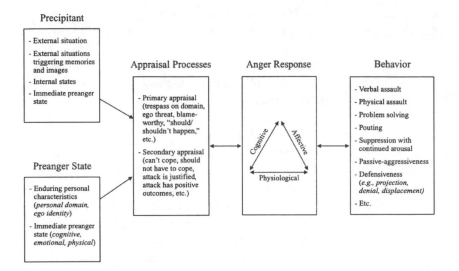

Figure 2.1.   Model of Anger

ing characteristics; and (c) appraisal processes. Anger, in turn, is an internal experience composed of emotional, physiological, and cognitive components that rapidly interact with and influence each other such that they are often experienced as a relatively unitary state. Anger, however, is separate from behaviors with which it is associated. Moreover, although the model appears somewhat static, anger is influenced by rapid interactions and recyclings of personal and environmental variables over time.

Precipitants of Anger

Anger seems to be elicited or influenced by four types of stimuli. These sources of anger elicitation are not mutually exclusive, for more than one type may be present in a given anger reaction. In some cases, anger appears to be elicited straightforwardly by some definable external situation. Such situations vary from person to person and may involve specific circumstances (e.g., being cut off in traffic or company policies at work), behavior of others (e.g., children, spouse, coworker), specific objects (e.g., a car that will not start), impersonal events (e.g., events in the newspaper, the weather), or the person's own behavior and characteristics (e.g., doing poorly in an interview, being overweight). That is, a relatively clear, specifiable event or condition appears to elicit anger. Furthermore, individuals can often easily identify the precipitant of anger (e.g., "X makes me really angry").

Other anger is also reliably related to external events, less by direct provocation and more through the eliciting of anger-related memories and images. Strong reactions of this type are seen in post-traumatic stress disorders. For example, a woman who was raped may experience intense anger and rage at hearing about a rape on the television, or a victim of incest may become angered by his or her partner's sexual approach because of some similarity to the incest. Less dramatic but clinically relevant examples abound. For example, anger at one's child for poor athletic performance may reflect memories of being ridiculed and embarrassed for poor athletic ability as a child, or a supervisor's feedback may trigger anger mediated, in part, by memories of a hated parent. Clinically, such anger may take more time and patience to treat. Often the individual is unaware or only partially aware of important memories and images being elicited, and the memories may also be associated with anxiety that elicits cognitive avoidance mechanisms. Exploration of not only current situations that elicit anger but also situations in the past in which the individual felt the same, self-monitoring that includes attention to self-dialogue and imagery, and imagery or simulation assessments in which internal experiences are fully explored may help elucidate memory components that are partial prompts of anger. Additional therapeutic time may also be needed to deal with other emotions and issues connected to earlier events.

In other cases, anger appears elicited more by internal stimuli. For example, an individual becomes angry when worrying, brooding, or ruminating about some event (e.g., an upcoming performance review or an interaction with an ex-spouse). Anger may also be elicited by other emotions such as hurt, rejection, or anxiety. In either case, anger is secondary to and heavily influenced by other internal emotional and cognitive processes. These processes need clarification so that intervention can be targeted to them appropriately. The degree of insight into these sources of anger, however, can vary considerably. Some clients are relatively clear that they become angry when thinking about or feeling certain things. Progress with these clients may be more rapid and smooth because they can learn to monitor the internal prompts and apply interventions when the prompts are experienced. Other clients, however, may have little awareness of the internal prompts of anger. Again, patient exploration (e.g., interviewing, self- monitoring, imagery recall, reactions to simulations, interpretation) may be needed to clarify these internal connections and link them to treatment.

A fourth anger-eliciting or influencing condition is the individual's immediate preanger state: namely, what the individual is feeling and thinking at the time. For example, prior anger is an important factor. If an individual is angry or frustrated, the probability, intensity, and perhaps duration of subsequent anger may increase dramatically compared to the person's reaction if he or she were in a calm, relaxed state. That is, excitation from prior anger arousal seems to transfer (Zillman, 1971; Zillman & Bryant, 1974), even when subsequent events bear little resemblance to the prior provocation. Such transfer effects, however, are not limited only to anger. Nearly any aversive state (e.g., being ill, anxious, stressed, fatigued) seems to increase the probability and intensity of anger (Berkowitz, 1990). That is, aversive experience seems to increase the presence and salience of aversive images and memories, which in turn lower the threshold for anger reactions. Clients whose anger is influenced significantly by their preanger state often report overreacting to minor frustrations and provocations or becoming angry in situations in which they normally do not. This response variability often holds the key to understanding the influence of the preanger state. Exploration of why the individual responded relatively calmly on one occasion and angrily on another may reveal that anger was heavily influenced by already being tired, stressed, or ill. Monitoring of and intervening to reduce these aversive states can therefore become an important focus of intervention.

Preanger State

The preanger state is composed of two parts, enduring personal characteristics and the momentary physical-emotional-cognitive state. Relevant personal characteristics may be subsumed under Beck's (1976) concept of the personal domain—those things the person believes in, cares about, and values—or Lazarus's (1991) parallel concept of ego identity. Anger arises from trespass on the personal domain (Beck, 1976), from a perceived violation of personal rules for living (Beck, 1989; Dryden, 1990; Ellis, 1977), or from a blameful attack on ego identity (Lazarus, 1991). Individuals with dysfunctional anger, however, often have extensive and rigid boundaries to their personal domain. Values are no longer flexible, personal preferences for living become rigid dogma to be imposed on the world, rules of conduct become commandments, promises and expectations become sanctified and written in stone, personally defined freedoms become absolute, and goal-directed behavior becomes imperative. The nature and structure of the personal domain or ego identity, therefore, are important to assess, as they may suggest areas of vulnerability in need of intervention.

As noted in the prior section on precipitants, anger is also influenced by the immediate state of the person. If he or she is relatively calm or experiencing a positive state, he or she is much less likely to become angered by an event than if he or she is in an aversive state. This area too should be assessed and perhaps targeted for intervention.

Appraisal Processes

Precipitants interact with and are appraised in light of the individual's enduring and temporary state. Primary appraisal processes involve an evaluation of the precipitating source. Typically, this involves encroachment on the personal domain, violation of expectations and rules for living, and/or blockage of goal-directed behavior. In essence, something happens that "should not." Anger increases if the precipitating source is perceived as intentional (i.e., someone or something purposefully directing the event toward the person), preventable (i.e., something that could be controlled), unjustified (i.e., judged as unwarranted and unfair, a violation of a sense of social justice), and/or blameworthy and punishable (i.e., judged as culpable and deserving to suffer; Hazaleus & Deffenbacher, 1985; Lohr, Hamberger, & Bonge, 1988; Zwemer & Deffenbacher, 1984). Secondary appraisal processes involve an evaluation of the person's capacity to cope. The person may not feel able to cope, and the primary appraisal processes channel him or her toward anger and perhaps aggressive behavior because of the sense of infringement and blame. Anger is also likely to be elevated when the individual favors attack as a mode of coping and has a positive outcome expectancy for attack (Lazarus, 1991). Even when the individual possesses adequate coping skills, anger may ensue because of a secondary appraisal that the individual "should not" have to experience or put up with the precipitating source. That is, the individual invokes a narcissistic rule that he or she should not be subject to frustration, pain, disappointment, inconvenience, and the like and therefore should not have to deal or cope with the event—an appraisal dimension described by rational-emotive therapists as low tolerance for frustration (Dryden, 1990; Ellis, 1977). In essence, the individual has experienced or may experience something he or she believes should not happen (primary appraisal) and for which he or she is not adequately prepared, for which he or she believes attack is appropriate, or to which he or she does not believe he or she should be subject (secondary appraisal).

Anger Response

Anger-engendering appraisals activate physiological, emotional, and cognitive response systems. Although it is important to separate these systems for assessment and treatment planning, it should be noted that response systems are at least somewhat correlated and influence each other. Physiologically, anger is marked by heightened sympathetic arousal, increased tone in skeletal and facial muscles, and release of adrenal hormones. Although these are relatively temporary physiological aspects of anger arousal, anger may sometimes be inferred from an increase of anger-related physical or disease processes (e.g., an increase in the frequency or intensity of migraines, gastritis, dermatitis, or bruxism). Emotionally, anger is experienced affectively along a continuum from mild annoyance, irritation, and frustration to fury and rage. Cognitively, anger is often a "moral" emotion resulting from the appraisal of trespass and sometimes retribution if blaming processes are activated. As will be discussed later in the section on cognitive restructuring, cognitive processes in dysfunctional anger often involve biased appraisals, information processing, attributions, self-dialogue, and imagery.

Generally, anger will be judged dysfunctional or problematic if it shows high frequency, intensity, or duration and/or results in more frequent and severe negative consequences (Deffenbacher, 1994; Novaco, 1979). Moreover, greater dysfunction is suggested when more response components (cognitive, affective, and physiological), parameters (frequency, intensity, and duration), and consequences (frequency and severity) are involved over greater periods of time. It is suggested that dysfunctional anger, much like anxiety and depression, can be defined as a significant emotional disorder primarily in terms of its experiential qualities and their consequences and that dysfunctional anger is an understandable, assessable, treatable problem.

Anger-Related Behavior

As noted earlier, the individual may behave in adaptive (e.g., assertion, problem solving, limit setting, appropriate withdrawal) or maladaptive (e.g., verbal or physical assault, passive aggressive behavior, defensiveness) ways when angry. These are conceptually and clinically separable from the internal experience of anger. Anger-related behavior and its consequences should be carefully mapped and targeted for intervention as needed.

COGNITIVE-BEHAVIORAL INTERVENTION STRATEGIES FOR ANGER REDUCTION

Several cognitive-behavioral interventions will be presented. With the working model above as a guide, the site or target of intervention will be described first because different interventions theoretically focus on different aspects of anger elicitation and experience. Then, where available, research literature related to that strategy will be reviewed. This will be followed by a description of procedures and additional clinical suggestions.

Enhanced Personal Awareness

Focus

In a sense, this intervention strategy targets the whole anger experience as it targets a deautomatization of anger reactions. For many angry clients, anger is a highly automatic, habitual response pattern of which they are relatively unaware and over which they feel relatively little control. Anger is something that just "happens." In enhancing personal awareness of anger, the individual is trained to be a careful observer of the internal and external prompts of anger, of appraisal processes, and of the experience of anger and its consequences. In so doing, he or she no longer experiences anger as an automatic response but as one that becomes somewhat more predictable and potentially more modifiable. Often, as clients become more aware of anger, they initiate improved coping as they employ skills and strategies already available but previously unused. They often report enhanced self-efficacy because they understand better what is happening to them and can do something about it. Enhanced awareness also provides the basis for implementing many other interventions (e.g., perception of increased emotional arousal serving to cue cognitive or relaxation coping skills).

Research

No research which has focused strictly on enhanced self-awareness and self-monitoring; however, all interventions include some emphasis on enhanced self-awareness.

Intervention

Although there are many ways to enhance awareness, self-monitoring is probably the most versatile and consistently yields the greatest amount of information. That is, the client and therapist collaboratively develop a recording system, and the client observes and records his or her experience in vivo. Self-monitoring is clarified, honed, and made more complex over time as the client gains greater self-understanding and experience in self-monitoring.

Self-awareness within the session can be enhanced through imagery and simulation procedures. The client imagines or role-plays an anger-provoking event and attempts to create "hot" emotions and cognitions because these seem to be state dependent and assessment is improved if the person is in the state at the time (Persons & Miranda, 1991). After the simulation or imagery experience, the client explores the thoughts, feelings, images, physical reactions, and so forth experienced, and these are linked to other elements of self-understanding. Sometimes the therapist may offer his or her observations, and in group settings other clients may be involved in simulations and offer feedback. If available, simulations can be augmented by audio and video recording. Subsequently tapes are reviewed, and client reactions at different places are explored (e.g., "What were you experiencing right there when she raised her voice and made that swipe with her hand?"). In some cases, it may be possible for clients to audiotape naturally occurring events such as family discussions or other problematic events (e.g., one businessman activated his pocket-size dictation equipment when he approached his teenage son about issues of responsibility). Such tapes can be reviewed in the next session.

On occasion, the therapy session itself may present opportunities for enhanced awareness. Three examples occur with some frequency. First, the client may become angry while recalling and describing some event. Immediate reactions (e.g., how the client is thinking, feeling, and planning) can be explored. Second, the client may come to the session angered by external events or simply in an angry mood. This too can be worked as an in vivo sample. Third, the client may become angry with the therapist (e.g., over a bill or something the therapist said or implied). Although it is probably unwise to provoke such anger purposefully, it is appropriate to explore it as a natural example of anger, as well as to clarify relationship issues.

Self-understanding can also be facilitated by the use of various anger inventories. For example, a client may get a general, normative sense of general anger from a review of his or her score on the 10-item Trait Anger Scale (Spielberger, 1988; Spielberger et al., 1983). This scale also provides items assessing angry temperament (e.g., hotheadedness) and anger in common situations (e.g., being slowed by others). Informal analyses of these items may suggest a general irritability or more specific situations in which to monitor anger. Situational provocation can be clarified by the use of one of the scales that assess anger situationally. For example, Novaco's (1975) Anger Inventory asks clients to rate the degree of anger evoked by 90 different situations. Exploring situations in which greatest anger is elicited may elucidate types of situations to which the individual is most vulnerable. Further exploration may lead to greater awareness of the types of appraisals and cognitive themes that tie them together. The Anger Expression Inventory (Spielberger, 1988) may also assist the client in understanding his or her style of expressing anger. This questionnaire contains three eight-item indices of general anger expression style: (a) suppressing or holding anger in; (b) expressing it outwardly and negatively through behaviors such as throwing things and cursing; and (c) expressing it in controlled, socially acceptable ways such as being patient and calm. Exploration of these scales may not only suggest the most preferred style but also clarify the situational and intrapersonal factors that influence selection of one style over another and may also suggest assets to be included in treatment and areas in need of remediation.

Whatever the means employed, the client should be assisted to be more aware of his or her anger reactions, the events that provoke them, and their course. It is from this increased awareness that the client can begin to make anger reactions less automatic and to establish greater choice and control.

Additional clinical suggestions are as follows:

1. Start enhanced awareness early, and maintain it throughout therapy. It provides an early basis for therapeutic collaboration, an increased sense of control and self-efficacy, and information from which to modify or maintain intervention.
2. Integrate self-awareness with other strategies (e.g., perception of anger arousal prompting a time-out, relaxation, or problem solving).
3. If self-monitoring is employed, make it simple, flexible, and reviewed. Self-monitoring is an unusual behavior for most clients. Making the recording system simple at the beginning and adding complexity over time increases compliance. Developing a monitoring system that fits the client also enhances compliance. Diaries and logs are excellent, but tallies and checklists may be more fitting at times. Perhaps it should go without saying, but self-monitoring should not be given a low priority. To fail to do a quality review may lead the client to discontinue self-monitoring, as well as undermining the working alliance and the value of homework generally. Where feasible, arrange for the client to drop off self-monitoring so it may be reviewed prior to the session.

Stimulus Control and
Response Disruption Strategies

Focus

These strategies target anger prompts and immediate preanger state variables that elicit or continue to prompt anger. That is, these strategies either (a) remove or reduce the saliency of anger prompts or (b) actively disrupt anger responding so that it cannot continue. Anger is reduced because it is not elicited or because the change of cuing provides an opportunity for the individual to cool down and engage in alternative activities.

Research

Many interventions touch on these strategies, but no studies use them as the primary form of intervention. However, because they can be very useful and often easily employed, a variety of strategies will be described.

Intervention

It may be appropriate to engage in *planned avoidance of provocation*. This is particularly appropriate for repetitive sources of anger that can be dealt with in another way and/or for some aversive preanger states. For example, a working mother made an agreement with her children that they would not make requests of her when she was on the phone or within the first 10 minutes of arriving home, both of which had been explosive points. In another family, the husband agreed to discuss budget matters but not when he was tired (a preanger state that increased the probability of anger), and his wife signaled the presence of perimenstrual tension and irritability by placing a red sticker on the refrigerator. In such cases, important issues and requests are not avoided altogether but are dealt with in places and under conditions that are less conducive to anger arousal.

Other interventions involve *physically distancing the individual from provocative cues* once they are presented. One way is to remove provoking cues, as in asking a surly child to go to his or her room or asking an obnoxious guest to leave a party. If the provocation cannot be easily removed, then the person can remove him- or herself. For example, the person may quietly exit or may state why he or she is leaving (e.g., "I'm getting really mad about this and don't want to say things I'll regret. So I'm going downstairs for a while, and we can discuss it later."). A useful variant in social systems is "negotiated time-outs" in which members of the system (e.g., parents and children, spouses, teachers and students at school, coworkers) agree that members may take a time-out to prevent anger or aggression. Negotiated time-outs may be bilateral, with all parties removing themselves, as when spouses go to separate rooms, or unilateral, as when a child goes to a delegated area at school. An individual may strike a similar contract with him- or herself. For example, a graduate student who became angry and resentful when working on his thesis, sometimes tearing up work, exiled himself to sitting for 30 minutes in an uncomfortable straight-backed chair in the basement before returning to work.

Another strategy is *temporally distancing the individual from provocative cues*. One way to do this is to seek a delay between the presence of something that is angering and one's response. For example, the individual might indicate that he or she needed time to think the issue over (e.g., "Let me think it over and get back to you") or to gather information prior to responding (e.g., "Let me check into that and get back to you later today"). The person might also gain a delay by seeking an alternative mode of expression and review prior to initiating a direct response. For example, the individual might write down or dictate his or her thoughts or talk to a friend prior to responding. A variant on this theme for frequent anger is an adaptation of Borkovec's (Borkovec, Wilkinson, Folensbee, & Lerman, 1983) stimulus control program for worry. First, the individual sets a consistent time and place for his or her "anger session." Second, through awareness enhancement activities, the individual learns to monitor his or her arousal. Third, when the individual perceives anger arousal during the day, he or she makes a note of it and consciously delays dealing with it until the appointed time. On arrival at the appointed time and place, he or she explores the issue(s) for at least 30 minutes, focusing not only on angry feelings but also on problem solving.

Other interventions involve *physical, mental, or behavioral disruption of anger arousal*, in which new stimuli are introduced that are strong enough to interrupt at least temporarily current cuing and recuing of anger. At a physical level, the individual may self-administer an aversive stimulus (e.g., snap of a rubber band on the back of the hand or pressing fingers together tightly) sufficient to disrupt anger. For example, an impatient company executive would put his hand under the table, place a pencil between his middle finger and thumb, and press very firmly to disrupt anger and associated hostile comments. At a mental level, thought stopping can be useful. The person covertly shouts a loud "Stop!" or other phrase such as "Cut it out!" or "Knock it off!" to disrupt anger. Visual imagery may also be disruptive at a cognitive level. For example, some individuals find a visual version of thought stopping helpful—for example, visualizing a red and white octagonal stop sign or, like one client, seeing the stop sign as hitting oneself in the forehead. Others find aversive, anger-related imagery helpful, as did an angry businessman who visualized his coronary arteries full of plaque, the fearfulness of his children when he stormed about, and himself unemployed and looking for work because of his anger. Another cognitive variant is to engage in mentally distracting activities such as meal planning or planning a trip. Anger may also be disrupted by engaging in anger-incompatible, distracting behavior. For example, when angry, a parent consciously did laundry or grocery shopping rather than talk to her teenager when angry, and another person worked on cleaning and straightening the basement rather than responding to his spouse.

A final set of strategies attempt to change the overall stimulus complex by adding *physical, mental, and emotional palliatives*. That is, even if some of the provocative cues cannot be eliminated, addition of palliatives may elicit anger-incompatible affect, prompt endurance of aversive events, and/or mobilize other coping strategies. For example, the person might engage in palliative self-dialogue (e.g., "Bad things happen to good people," "Shit happens, but I have a choice about how I respond," "This too shall pass," "I've had open heart surgery, comparatively this is insignificant," or "No use dying over it") or imagery that evokes relaxation or converts portions of the provocation (e.g., visualizing oneself as a turtle with a tough shell letting things bounce off, or as a duck in the rain of harassment, with the hassles just dripping off). Palliative activities might include calming activities such as drinking a favorite cup of tea or taking a hot shower. Palliatives rarely will resolve provocation, but they may allow the person to endure with less anger and to regain a sense of control.

Additional clinical suggestions are as follows:

1. Consider stimulus control/response disruption strategies early in therapy. Even though they are rarely sufficient in and of themselves, they can be relatively easy to implement and often provide rapid improvement and a sense of control and self-efficacy.

2. Tailor the intervention to the nature of the individual's presenting problem. For example, planned avoidance only works for predictable events, whereas thought stopping may be appropriate for anger-engendering rumination.

3. Integrate these with other interventions. For example, a father who was angry with his child removed himself from negative interactions and initiated relaxation coping, cognitive restructuring, and problem-solving activities before returning to deal with his child.

4. Attend to and resolve issues that may interfere with successful deployment of these strategies. For example, some clients may need to develop permission-giving attitudes and self-dialogue (e.g., "I'm starting to get really pissed now. It's important to step back and get my act together before I respond"). This is especially important if they believe that they should not back away from provocation, label themselves negatively for doing so (e.g., "weak," "wimp," "coward"), and make negative interpretations of such activities (e.g., "rolling over," "giving in"). These issues need cognitive restructuring (see later section), or it is unlikely that the client will follow through.

5. Finally, there is the issue of calling time-in and reinitiating coping. Distance from or disruption of provocation does not mean the source of provocation has been removed. If the client has taken a time-out or distance from the provocation, then he or she has responsibility for calling time-in and facing the issues. Therapists should be alert to the possibility that clients are not doing this and that inappropriate avoidance and passive-aggressive behavior are being encouraged.

Relaxation Interventions

Focus

Relaxation interventions target heightened emotional and physiological arousal. As relaxation replaces arousal, the client gains a sense of calmness and control over disruptive emotional-physiological arousal. This may free him or her to gain a different cognitive perspective and employ other coping skills.

Research

Two early studies (Hearn & Evans, 1972; Rimm, deGroot, Boord, Heiman, & Dillow, 1971) applied desensitization to anger and reported significant anger reduction compared to control conditions. One 6-month follow-up study (Evans & Hearn, 1973) revealed maintenance of anger reduction. Both studies, however, were marred by methodological problems. The subjects in the Hearn and Evans study were student nurses without significantly elevated anger, calling into question any generalization of findings. Subject selection in the Rimm et al. study was improved by selecting males who reported anger while driving; however, little evidence supported the clinical relevance of their anger. Moreover, both studies could have employed more extensive measurement, especially the Rimm et al. study. Thus, although weakened by methodological issues, these studies suggested that relaxation may be helpful when delivered in a desensitization format.

In an extensive, well-controlled study of general anger reduction, Novaco (1975) did a component analysis of stress inoculation training in which cognitive (cognitive restructuring and attention focusing) and relaxation (modified desensitization) conditions were compared to their combination (stress inoculation) and an attentional control. Stress inoculation revealed the greatest anger reduction, with the cognitive condition nearly as effective. Relaxation, however, differed from the control only on reactions to imaginally presented provocation and was less effective than cognitive and stress inoculation conditions on several measures. Thus it appeared that the cognitive component was the primary effective ingredient in stress inoculation and that although relaxation was somewhat effective, its efficacy alone was questionable.

Deffenbacher and his colleagues (Deffenbacher, Demm, & Brandon, 1986; Deffenbacher & Stark, 1992; Hazaleus & Deffenbacher, 1986), however, suggested that relaxation effects in Novaco's (1975) study may have been underestimated due to issues in intervention design and implementation. For example, the treatment rationale emphasized active self-control, whereas treatment was in a passive counterconditioning format. This may have confused subjects and undermined efficacy. There may have been insufficient time and attention to develop relaxation coping skills. For example, specific relaxation coping skills and methods of training were not specified; progressive relaxation was practiced only once prior to beginning its use in desensitization; home practice of relaxation was apparently not employed; no assignments for in vivo application of relaxation were apparently given; and the brief, 3-week treatment interval may have been insufficient for relaxation skill development. Any or all of these issues may have mitigated the effectiveness of self-managed relaxation. To overcome these issues, anxiety management training (Suinn, 1977, 1990; Suinn & Deffenbacher, 1988) was adapted to anger reduction. This relaxation coping skills procedure provides (a) a consistent self-control rationale and training procedure, (b) consistent relaxation coping skill development within and between sessions, and (c) training of application of relaxation for active anger reduction within and between sessions. In the first study (Deffenbacher et al., 1986), relaxation subjects, compared to controls, showed significant anger reduction on a number of indices, results that held up at 5-week and 1-year follow-ups. Furthermore, relaxation effects appeared to be stronger than those achieved in Novaco's study. Two subsequent studies (Deffenbacher & Stark, 1992; Hazaleus & Deffenbacher, 1986) replicated the short- and long-term effects of this relaxation condition and showed it to be as effective as cognitive-only and combined cognitive-relaxation conditions. In addition, Nakano (1990), employing this condition for anger reduction, reported significant reductions of Type A behavior in Japanese businessmen, and Schlichter and Horan (1981), employing a somewhat similar self-managed relaxation condition, reported significant anger reduction in adjudicated juvenile delinquents. Thus relaxation is effective when procedures provide sufficient time and attention to the development of quality relaxation coping skills, to active anger reduction within sessions, and to the transfer and maintenance of anger management in the face of real-life provocations.

Intervention

Although many different relaxation approaches are available, it is suggested that the adaptation of anxiety management training be adopted in most cases. It is the most empirically supported relaxation strategy, and detailed procedural descriptions are available (Suinn, 1990; Suinn & Deffenbacher, 1988). It has perhaps the greatest flexibility in groups of individuals with different anger concerns because it employs individualized anger scenes for anger arousal within sessions. It also may be effectively combined with other interventions such as cognitive restructuring and social skills training (e.g., Deffenbacher, McNamara, Stark, & Sabadell, 1990a, 1990b; Deffenbacher & Stark, 1992; Deffenbacher, Story, Brandon, Hogg, & Hazaleus, 1988; Deffenbacher, Story, Stark, Hogg, & Brandon, 1987; Deffenbacher, Thwaites, & Wallace, 1993).

Applied relaxation skills are developed in 6 to 10 sessions once emotional and physiological arousal are targeted. The first three sessions are devoted to a self-control rationale, progressive relaxation, and specific relaxation coping skills, including (a) relaxation without tension (focusing on muscle groups and releasing them without tension exercises), (b) breathing-cued relaxation (taking three to four deep breaths and relaxing on each breath out), (c) cue-controlled relaxation (repeating slowly a calm word or phrase such as "relax," "chill," or "calm control"), (d) relaxation imagery (visualizing a personal relaxing experience), and (e) unobtrusive adaptations of tension-release exercises (tensing and letting go key muscle groups in ways that are unnoticed). Usually, a client is exposed to all coping skills but develops one or two with which he or she is most proficient. Homework in these sessions involves (a) self-monitoring with attention to situational, emotional, and physiological cues; (b) daily progressive relaxation practice; (c) in vivo application of relaxation coping skills in nonstressful situations, such as riding on a bus; and (d) identification of initial anger scenes.

At about the fourth session, the emphasis shifts to application of relaxation for anger control within and between sessions and for the reduction of other disquieting emotional and physical states (e.g., anxiety, physical discomfort). At the beginning of each session, homework is discussed. Successful application is clarified and supported, and plans to circumvent difficulties are outlined. The rest of the session is devoted to eliciting anger and deploying relaxation for anger reduction. Typically, anger is elicited by visualization of provocative images, but simulation (e.g., applying relaxation in role plays of criticism or discussing rule violations with a teenager) should be considered where possible, particularly in later sessions as part of transfer activities. Anger-evoking images should be based on real-life experiences and should include sufficient clear, concrete situational cues and emotional, physiological, and cognitive response detail to elicit anger arousal. Scenes in early sessions are selected to elicit mild to moderate anger and increase in anger intensity over sessions as clients demonstrate ability to reduce anger actively. Also, the level of therapist assistance decreases with increased client control. In early sessions, the therapist controls exposure to anger imagery and actively assists in relaxation retrieval but fades to minimal assistance over sessions. In latter sessions, clients visualize highly angering scenes and initiate relaxation coping skills while continuing to visualize the scene, turning the scene off when they have brought anger under control. When clients demonstrate good control within sessions, attention is directed to in vivo applications in naturally occurring events and predictable provocations (e.g., dealing with a difficult coworker). Homework involves in vivo application of relaxation skills for control of anger and other negative emotional and physical states.

Additional clinical suggestions are as follows:

1. If relaxation is to be employed, start it early in the course of treatment. It is a commonsense intervention that fits well with many clients' conceptualization of problems—that is, the need to calm down. Relaxation thus facilitates the working alliance and therapeutic relationship without prematurely confronting clients in ways that might breed unnecessary reactance and resistance. Moreover, clinical experience in two studies (Deffenbacher et al., 1988; Hazaleus & Deffenbacher, 1986) suggested that preceding cognitive interventions with relaxation made them more acceptable and easier to implement. If both cognitive and relaxation interventions are to be employed, consider beginning the relaxation intervention first, say by two to four sessions.

2. Target application of relaxation to aversive preanger physical (e.g., pain, physical tension, fatigue) and emotional (embarrassment, anxiety, stress) states to reduce their contribution to anger arousal. That is, clients monitor preanger states covarying with anger arousal and employ relaxation skills to reduce them.

3. Integrate relaxation skills with other interventions as appropriate (e.g., applying relaxation during a time-out, combining relaxation and cognitive coping skills).

Cognitive Change Interventions

Focus

Cognitive change strategies target biased, anger-engendering information processing: that is, cognitive content, process and product errors, underlying negative schemas, and cognitive deficiencies (Kendall, 1992). These interventions most appropriately focus on dysfunctional primary and secondary appraisal processes, some enduring personal characteristics, and the cognitive components of the anger response. As clients become aware of "hot" cognitions and replace them with "cooler," less distorting, more problem-oriented styles of thinking, they perceive provocations in more realistic ways. This reduces emotional-physiological arousal and facilitates problem-solving and coping strategies.

Research

Novaco's (1975) component analysis of stress inoculation revealed significant effects for a cognitive-restructuring and attention-refocusing intervention, effects that were generally superior to relaxation and control conditions and nearly as effective as the combination of cognitive and relaxation conditions. Several studies since have supported the effectiveness of cognitive interventions. For example, a rational-emotive therapy for anger in Type A university faculty was superior to a no-treatment control condition in the reduction of anger and Type A behavior, with effects holding up at 1-year follow-up (Thurman, 1985b). In a study with hypertensives, Achmon, Granek, Golomb, and Hart (1989) found that compared to a no-treatment control condition, cognitive therapy (cognitive-restructuring and task-oriented self-instruction elements of stress inoculation) for anger reduction and heart rate biofeedback for stress management both reduced hypertension. Blood pressure reductions were, however, significantly greater for biofeedback, whereas anger reduction was significantly greater for the cognitive condition, perhaps reflecting their differential targets of intervention. Similarly constructed cognitive coping skills interventions have proven effective with generally angry college students (Deffenbacher et al., 1988; Hazaleus & Deffenbacher, 1986; Moon & Eisler, 1983), and these effects have been maintained at 12- to 15-month follow-ups (Deffenbacher et al., 1988; Hazaleus & Deffenbacher, 1986). Moon and Eisler (1983) also reported significant anger reduction effects for another cognitive intervention: namely, a social problem-solving procedure. Moreover, cognitive interventions are generally as effective as relaxation (Hazaleus & Deffenbacher, 1986), social skills (Moon & Eisler, 1983), combined cognitive-relaxation (Deffenbacher et al., 1988), and combined cognitive-assertion training (Thurman, 1985a) conditions. In summary, cognitive interventions produce significant, lasting effects roughly equivalent to those of other interventions.

Intervention

Cognitive change procedures often involve one or more related but conceptually distinct interventions of cognitive-restructuring, humor, and task-oriented, problem-solving self-instruction. Each will be discussed sepa rately, although they follow similar steps and are often integrated.

Restructuring of cognitive distortions involves five overlapping stages, with multiple strategies employed at each stage. For example, the first two therapeutic tasks consist of helping clients to become more aware of cogni tive processes and to accept that they influence affect and behavior. Neither of these may be obvious to angry clients. Many angry clients are not highly self-observant. Anger may seem to be an automatic reaction to external events or a mood that wells up inexplicably from within. Self-monitoring and tracking of self-dialogue and imagery during interviews, simulations, and imagery recall procedures help clients become more aware of their cognitions and how these are patterned together. However, it is often a contrast of reactions to the same situation that points up the influence of cognitions. That is, having clients explain why they reacted differently to similar situations leads them to indicate that they had a different perspective on separate occasions. This provides a basis for a cognitive treatment rationale, linking a perspective (cognitive) change to lowered anger.

In the next therapeutic phase, the therapist and client elucidate the errors and distortions involved in client thought processes. Seven different anger-engendering cognitive processes occur with frequency in dysfunctional anger and may need attention.

The first process is *misestimation of event probabilities*. Many angry individuals overestimate the probability of negative events (e.g., unfair treatment, rejection) and underestimate positive events and personal and environmental resources, increasing the sense of trespass and violation (primary appraisal) and of inability to cope effectively (secondary appraisal). Clients making this error need to explore probabilities on logical and experiential-empirical grounds and arrive at more accurate appraisals of self and the world.

The second process is *misattribution*. Many angry individuals jump quickly to egocentric, negative conclusions and attributions, even when situations are ambiguous or when information would suggest alternative, more benign possibilities. Their causal attribution systems often are marked by automaticity, hostility, personalization, and mind-reading qualities (Beck,

1989). That is, such individuals unthinkingly and uncritically accept attributions as true and explain events in negative, attacking ways that are coded as directed intentionally toward themselves. Individuals employing such attributions "know" what others are thinking and the motivations for their behavior. For example, they quickly "know" that another purposefully did something to get back at and hurt them or because he or she does not care about them. They then react as if their attributions are valid, whether or not they are. Even where there may be validity to their attributions, they tend to respond stereotypically with anger, defensiveness, and potentially attack, without entertaining other cognitive or behavioral options. Clients making this type of error need to explore the automatic attributional processes, entertain other plausible interpretations, and actively seek confirming and disconfirming information.

The third process is *demandingness and dictatorial thinking*. Anger often involves a violation of rigid, absolutistic rules and expectations and the elevation of one's preferences to "moral" dictates or demands of self, others, or events. The sense of affront, injustice, and frustration escalates as one's "shoulds" and "expectations" are not met. Such demands and dictates need to be replaced with realistic personal preferences and values, ones that the individual owns and pursues actively but does not impose.

The fourth process is the assuming of *catastrophic implications*. Many angry clients, ipso facto, code negative events, especially unmet demands, in dramatic, dire terms (e.g., "awful," "terrible," "can't stand it"). Clients making this error need to ask themselves realistically how bad conditions are and to label events in realistically negative but often less extreme terms (e.g., "annoying," "frustrating," "sad," "disappointing"). These are conditions with which most individuals can cope.

The fifth process is *inflammatory thinking*. This is a pattern of thinking that is highly salient in many anger reactions. It involves labeling things in connotatively highly negative, often obscene ways (e.g., "jerk," "slimeball," "ass"). These words have an incendiary quality of cognitive gasoline as the individual responds to the emotive meaning of the label rather than the reality at hand. Clients need to replace these colorful terms with realistic, situation-specific appraisals.

The sixth process is *overgeneralization*. Broad, sweeping conclusions about time (e.g., "always," "never") or people, including self, (e.g., "idiot," "worthless," "worst ever seen") often elevate the sense of trespass and damage. As with inflammatory labels, once events are so coded, the person responds to the meaning of the construction rather than the specifics of reality. Correction of this process error involves becoming more of a situational thinker—focusing on the specifics of the given situation and basing affect and behavior on those.

The seventh process is *black-white thinking*. Anger may also eventuate from dichotomous, either-or processing. When an individual construes reality in highly polarized (e.g., good/bad, winner/loser, love me/hate me) terms, anger may result when the positive coding is not confirmed (i.e., because there is some bad news, it's all bad). Clients engaging in this type of thinking need to employ qualifying adjectives, adverbs, and phrases (e.g., *a little bit, somewhat*) that allow shades of gray and to discriminate complexity (e.g., being good at some things and not others rather than being a winner/loser).

In the next phase of therapy, the client and therapist collaboratively explore the errors and distortions in the client's cognitions. Strategies are tailored to the client and his or her cognitions. One of the most basic interventions is Socratic questions through which the client explores the logical and emotional limits of his or her thinking. For example, questions such as "What's another way of looking at that?" may increase the range of attributions and interpretations. Questions such as "And how does that follow?" may press the limits of catastrophic thinking, misattributions, and probability estimates, as may a series of "And then what would happen?" questions that lead the individual to clarify how he or she would actually feel and deal with negative realities. Questions such as "Why shouldn't bad things happen to you?" may help elucidate demandingness. In addition, the style of questions can vary from fairly gentle inquiries such as those above to quite confrontational inquiries (e.g., "And who appointed you God?" in dealing with demandingness). Cognitive modeling, in which the therapists thinks aloud alternative ways of looking at situations, provides not only contrasts with the client's thinking but also different ways of coding and interpreting situations (e.g., "I guess it's really frustrating, but hardly total shit" in dealing with catastrophic, inflammatory labeling). Behavioral experiments in which clients empirically evaluate their cognitions can also be very powerful. For example, a businessman who became angry at any subordinate who questioned his authority actively asked, over a week's time, for input on and criticism of his plans, and a person who was consistently angered by other people's lateness interviewed 10 friends to find out how they thought about and dealt with others' lateness. Role reversal can also be adapted (e.g., the therapist plays the role of a friend who is angry, and the client tries to help him or her become less angry, thereby accessing appropriate cognitions that can be related to the client's issues). Whatever the strategy, the goal is for the client to explore actively and challenge his or her habitual thinking style.

The next therapeutic step is to convert the understanding of errors and distortions into new, concrete, functional cognitions with which to replace the prior dysfunctional ones. These new images and self-dialogue are refined over time until the client has a flexible set of believable, realistic cognitive counter-responses for anger, responses that are nondemandingly anchored in his or her values and preferences.

The final stage involves rehearsal and transfer activities. Anger-related cognitive sets are often highly overlearned, and reliable anger control requires considerable overlearning of new cognitions. Rehearsal and transfer strategies described for relaxation interventions can be adapted. For example, clients may employ cognitive counter-responses to reduce anger induced by anger imagery, simulations, or role plays. When cognitive restructuring is established within sessions, in vivo experiments and application to naturally occurring provocations are employed to ensure transfer and maintenance of cognitive restructuring.

Humor is another cognitive change procedure that has considerable relevance to anger. It lowers anger by introducing anger-incompatible affect, by assisting clients in gaining cognitive distance or perspective shift, and by providing alternative interpretations and attributions.

Before examples of humorous interventions are provided here, four things should be noted about the use of humor. First, clients are not encouraged simply to laugh off and deny difficulties. To the contrary, they are encouraged to develop humor as a way of gaining a brief emotional release and change in perspective so that they can better think through and cope with difficulties. Second, humor should be of the silly type. Hostile and sarcastic humor have little place in anger reduction and may actually increase anger and dysfunctional means of expressing it. Third, humor interventions follow the stages noted previously for cognitive restructuring: that is, becoming aware of the impact of humor and developing, rehearsing, and transferring new humorous self-dialogue and imagery for anger control. Fourth, some clients initially react negatively to humor, thinking that they are being laughed at or made fun of. Humor generally should be introduced when the therapeutic relationship is strong or the therapist assesses that the client can handle humor.

A relatively simple, yet powerful form of humor is concretizing inflammatory and catastrophic constructs. First, clients are asked to literally and concretely define colorful terms such as "bitch," "asshole," or "slime bucket." After verbal definition, they may be asked to draw a picture of the term. For example, this has led to pictures of buttocks emitting dollar bills for "rich asshole," a baseball with a screw stuck into it for "screwball," and buttocks in front of classrooms for "asses" who teach university courses. Humorous drawings and images can also relate to demandingness (e.g., a client might draw a picture of him- or herself as god, king or queen, or emperor). Humorous hyperbole and exaggeration may also prove helpful, especially for changing perspective and attributions. For example, clients who are angered by putdowns, labels, and rejection might be exposed to exaggerated putdowns. Often this seems ludicrous, yet their nonangry reaction can be contrasted with their angry reaction to lesser insult. Humorous reattributions may also counteract anger. For example, absentmindedness might be attributed to "brain damage" rather than being seen as a personalized insult, or another's constant complaining might be attributed to being "totally constipated" rather than to intentional harassment.

Interventions such as these typically bring a momentary laugh and change of perspective in the therapy session. However, with repetition, clients often indicate that they can no longer code events in the same ways without laughing and changing perspective. Effective humorous images and self dialogue can then be rehearsed to further strengthen their coping value.

Humor and cognitive restructuring tend to focus on changing anger-engendering cognitions. However, some clients show cognitive deficits in initiating and maintaining appropriate task-oriented cognitions and guides for behavior. Task-oriented self-instruction and problem-solving interventions (Meichenbaum, 1985; Moon & Eisler, 1983) address these deficits, reducing anger as the individual codes events as problems to be solved and initiates calm, effective problem-solving activities rather than anger-engendering cognitions and behavior.

Specific self-instructions should be tailored to the client and the nature of cognitive deficits involved and should not be derived prescriptively from a therapist-generated list. With this caveat in mind, Meichenbaum and

Deffenbacher (1988) suggested several classes of potentially relevant self-instructions.

1. *Cool, calming thoughts* elicit relaxation skills, provide emotional palliatives, and focus attention in nonangering ways (e.g., "Big, slow deep breaths. . . . Stay focused now. This too shall pass").

2. *Orienting to anger as a problem* involves instructing one's self to see anger as a hassle or problem and to cue up problem solving (e.g., "Ok, it's not an awful mess, just a problem to solve. Let's focus on that. Getting all mad doesn't help").

3. When anger results from multiple sources, clients may benefit from *breaking anger down* into component sources or smaller units (e.g., "Break it down. I can handle the little hassles one at a time").

4. *Planning and problem-solving* self-instructions initiate (e.g., "Ok, develop a plan. So what is it that I need to do?"), implement (e.g., "Ok, this seems like a good plan. I am going to start by . . ."), and evaluate (e.g., "So let's take a look at the outcome. How's it going so far?") planning and potential solutions.

5. Even though every source of anger does not have a good solution, some clients angrily press on, insisting on finding a solution. They may benefit from self-instruction to *terminate problem solving when no good solution is apparent* (e.g., "Looks like no good solution here. No use getting all pissed and acting dumb. Best thing I can do is back away and think about it later").

6. *Ultimate control and escape* self-instruction (e.g., "Bottom line, I'm in control. If I feel like hitting, I'm going to hit the road") is particularly appropriate for clients who react with rapid, intense anger and/or who are confronting intense, explosive situations.

7. *Self-reward/self-efficacy* self-instructions reward positive coping, nurture coping attempts, self-attribute gains, and provide realistic, positive expectations of future anger management (e.g., "Great. I kept my cool. I'm getting better at chilling out").

Additional clinical suggestions are as follows:

1. As implied earlier, cognitive interventions may require a strong therapeutic alliance and relationship. Thus, if multiple interventions are employed, consider delaying cognitive interventions until a few sessions into therapy.

2. Integrate cognitive interventions with other interventions (e.g., initiating relaxation followed by cognitive-restructuring and problem-solving self-instruction).

3. Be ready to deal with at least two types of resistance. First, in dealing with demandingness, therapists should not avoid the issue of values. Some clients dismiss the therapist as valueless when he or she works to have clients explore

implicit and explicit demands. The importance of personal values and standards, of being committed to and working hard to achieve them, and of inevitable frustrations and disappointments in their pursuit should be underscored. However, the therapist should be equally persistent in helping the client to see how he or she creates anger and misery by elevating personal preferences to moral dictates. Second, particularly in dealing with catastrophization and misattributions, the therapist may encounter clients who insist that the world really is as bad or malevolent as they claim and, by implication, that their anger is appropriate and they should not have to change. This issue deserves careful assessment. On further exploration, the therapist and client may decide that the situation is toxic or abusive enough to shift toward crisis intervention, advocacy, assisting the client in extricating him- or herself from the environment, and/or behavioral limit setting. The therapist also should remain open to the possibility that negativity is exaggerated and be ready to address the implicit demand that negative events should not be experienced and/or that difficult decisions should not have to be made.

Behavioral Skill Building

Focus

Some individuals lack the behavioral skills and strategies with which to handle inevitable interpersonal conflict. Anger and conflict escalate as their poor responses further antagonize others and inflame the situation. Skill enhancement interventions target these behavioral deficiencies and thereby secondary appraisal processes, and anger is reduced as the individual deploys skills that enhance interactions and defuse conflict.

Research

Indirectly, many different literatures are relevant to anger reduction. For example, assertion training may enhance nonaggressive interpersonal skills, parent training may increase child management skills in angry parents, communication and negotiation skills may help angry partners and spouses, and supervisory training programs may assist angry managers. However, relatively little literature has directly approached anger reduction from a behavioral skill-building perspective. Three different social communication skills programs (Deffenbacher et al., 1987, 1993; Moon & Eisler, 1983) revealed significant anger reduction that was as great as that of cognitive, cognitive-relaxation, and social problem-solving interventions. Effects were maintained at year follow-up as well (Deffenbacher, 1988).

Intervention

Intervention formats vary widely depending on the nature of the skill deficit and therefore will not be discussed here.

Additional clinical suggestions are as follows:

1. Assess contributing skill deficits and target them for intervention as needed through treatment or referral.
2. If behavioral skill training is included as part of a complex program, consider delaying it until later sessions. This allows for other interventions to reduce anger that may interfere with skill training and time to see what skills and competencies emerge when the client is better able to manage anger.

Combined Interventions

Focus

Following the logic outlined for focused programs, interventions that combine treatment components target multiple sites for intervention. Anger, therefore, should be lowered through various components targeted.

Research

Perhaps the single best researched anger reduction intervention is the combination of cognitive and relaxation skills. A series of studies have documented effectiveness with generally angry community volunteers (Novaco, 1975), anger-involved occupational groups such as probation (Novaco, 1980) and police (Novaco, 1977) officers, incarcerated juvenile delinquents (Schlichter & Horan, 1981), and generally angry college students (Deffenbacher et al., 1987, 1988, 1990b, 1993; Deffenbacher & Stark, 1992). Followups of a year or more show that effects are well maintained (Deffenbacher, 1988; Deffenbacher et al., 1988, 1990b; Deffenbacher & Stark, 1992). Comparative outcomes are equivalent to relaxation (Deffenbacher & Stark, 1992), cognitive (Deffenbacher et al., 1988), social skill (Deffenbacher et al., 1987, 1993), and process group (Deffenbacher et al., 1990b) interventions, with some studies (Novaco, 1975; Schlichter & Horan, 1981) suggesting greater effects than relaxation interventions. Thus the combination of cognitive and relaxation coping skills is a robust, empirically validated approach that has wide applicability and may be the treatment of choice for heterogeneous groups (Deffenbacher et al., 1987). In addition, programs combining cognitive and social skills (Thurman, 1985a) and cognitive, relaxation, and social skills interventions (Deffenbacher et al., 1990a) are effective.

Intervention

Interventions involve an integration of individual components (see earlier sections).

Additional clinical suggestions are as follows:

1. Be careful to guard against combining too many components at the expense of rehearsal. Practice of skills within and between sessions appears very important to bringing about lasting change. If program components are judged important, then allow sufficient time, by extending either the number or the length of sessions, to ensure their adequate coverage and rehearsal.
2. If all treatment components were combined into a comprehensive program, they might, for reasons outlined in earlier sections, be sequenced roughly in the following manner: (a) awareness enhancement; (b) relaxation and stimulus control/response disruption; (c) cognitive restructuring and humor; and (d) task-oriented, problem-solving self-instructions and behavioral skill enhancement.
3. Target transitory preanger-state variables as appropriate. Their influence is often overlooked. Four interventions are often helpful. First, as part of awareness enhancement, train clients to monitor these states and use this information to initiate other interventions. Second, relaxation may be employed to reduce some of the contributing emotional and physical states. Third, cognitive restructuring and problem solving may be appropriate in altering unrealistic expectations and reallocating resources limited by these conditions. Finally, simple assertion and communication skills letting others know of these transitory preanger states and their impact can be helpful (e.g., "I am feeling really tired and have a splitting headache. I feel that if we discuss that now, it's going to be really tough for me not to be unreasonably angry. Can we arrange to discuss it tomorrow?").

CONCLUDING COMMENTS

In summary, there now is a rudimentary arsenal of empirically documented, clinically effective, cognitive-behavioral interventions that can be delivered effectively in individual therapy or in small, mixed-sex groups led by a single therapist. These interventions, however, focus on anger reduction, not anger elimination. It is simplistic to think that anger can, or perhaps should, ever be eliminated. Quite simply, injustice, frustration, hurt, loss, pain, and disagreement are parts of life. People will continue to become ill and sometimes die, important relationships will end, economies will shift and jobs will be lost, and others will violate our values and fail to meet our expectations. Even when individuals cope with and manage anger well, a level of mild anger (e.g., frustration, annoyance, disappointment) and other emotions (sadness, loss, hurt) is appropriate as difficult choices and adaptations remain. However, learning to maintain coping efforts despite these difficulties is one of the basic existential and developmental tasks of life. Cognitive-behavioral anger management interventions such as those described in this chapter may help clients reduce anger and free coping resources to cope with and enjoy life, a life that inevitably will be frustrating, disappointing, and painful at times.

REFERENCES

Achmon, J., Granek, M., Golomb, M., & Hart, J. (1989). Behavioral treatment of essential hypertension: A comparison between cognitive therapy and biofeedback of heart rate. *Psychosomatic Medicine, 51*, 152-164.

American Psychiatric Association. (1987). *Diagnostic and statistical manual of mental disorders* (3rd. ed., Rev.). Washington, DC: Author.

Beck, A. T. (1976). *Cognitive therapy and the emotional disorders*. New York: International Universities Press.

Beck, A. T. (1989). *Love is never enough*. New York: Harper & Row.

Berkowitz, L. (1990). On information and regulation of anger and aggression: A cognitive-neoassociationistic analysis. *American Psychologist, 45*, 494-503.

Borkovec, T. D., Wilkinson, L., Folensbee, R., & Lerman, C. (1983). Stimulus control applications to the treatment of worry. *Behaviour Research and Therapy, 21*, 247-251.

Deffenbacher, J. L. (1988). Cognitive-relaxation and social skills treatments of anger: A year later. *Journal of Counseling Psychology, 35*, 234-236.

Deffenbacher, J. L. (1992). Trait anger: Theory, findings, and implications. *Advances in Personality Assessment, 9*, 177-201.

Deffenbacher, J. L. (1994). Anger reductions: Issues, assessment and intervention strategies. In A. W. Siegman & T. W. Smith (Eds.), *Anger, hostility and the heart* (pp. 239-269). Hillsdale, NJ: Lawrence Erlbaum.

Deffenbacher, J. L., Demm, P. M., & Brandon, A. D. (1986). High general anger: Correlates and treatment. *Behaviour Research and Therapy, 24*, 481-489.

Deffenbacher, J. L., McNamara, K., Stark, R. S., & Sabadell, P. M. (1990a). A combination of cognitive, relaxation, and behavioral coping skills in the reduction of general anger. *Journal of College Student Development, 31*, 351-358.

Deffenbacher, J. L., McNamara, K., Stark, R. S., & Sabadell, P. M. (1990b). A comparison of cognitive-behavior and process oriented group counseling for general anger reduction. *Journal of Counseling and Development, 69,* 167-172.

Deffenbacher, J. L., & Stark, R. S. (1992). Relaxation and cognitive-relaxation treatments of general anger. *Journal of Counseling Psychology, 39,* 158-167.

Deffenbacher, J. L., Story, D. A., Brandon, A. D., Hogg, J. A., & Hazaleus, S. L. (1988). Cognitive and cognitive-relaxation treatments of anger. *Cognitive Therapy and Research, 12,* 167-184.

Deffenbacher, J. L., Story, D. A., Stark, R. S., Hogg, J. A., & Brandon, A. D. (1987). Cognitive-relaxation and social skills interventions in the treatment of general anger. *Journal of Counseling Psychology, 34,* 171-176.

Deffenbacher, J. L., Thwaites, G. A., & Wallace, T. (1993). *Social skill and cognitive-relaxation approaches to general anger reduction.* Unpublished manuscript, Department of Psychology, Colorado State University-Fort Collins.

Dryden, W. (1990). *Dealing with anger problems: Rational-emotive therapeutic interventions.* Sarasota, FL: Practitioner's Resource Exchange.

Ellis, A. (1977). *Anger: How to live with and without it.* New York: Reader's Digest Press.

Evans, D. R., & Hearn, M. T. (1973). Anger and systematic desensitization: A follow-up. *Psychological Reports, 32,* 569-570.

Hazaleus, S. L., & Deffenbacher, J. L. (1985). Irrational beliefs and anger arousal. *Journal of College Student Personnel, 26,* 47-52.

Hazaleus, S. L., & Deffenbacher, J. L. (1986). Relaxation and cognitive treatments of anger. *Journal of Consulting and Clinical Psychology, 54,* 222-226.

Hearn, M. T., & Evans, D. R. (1972). Anger and reciprocal inhibition therapy. *Psychological Reports, 30,* 943-948.

Kendall, P. C. (1992). Healthy thinking. *Behavior Therapy, 23,* 1-11.

Lazarus, R. S. (1991). *Emotion and adaptation.* New York: Oxford University Press.

Lohr, J. M., Hamberger, L. K., & Bonge, D. (1988). The relationship of factorially validated measures of anger proneness and irrational beliefs. *Motivation and Emotion, 12,* 171-183.

Meichenbaum, D. H. (1985). *Stress inoculation training.* New York: Pergamon.

Meichenbaum, D. H., & Deffenbacher, J. L. (1988). Stress inoculation training. *Counseling Psychologist, 16,* 69-90.

Moon, J. R., & Eisler, R. M. (1983). Anger control: An experimental comparison of three behavioral treatments. *Behavior Therapy, 14,* 493-505.

Nakano, K. (1990). Effects of two self-control procedures on modifying Type A behavior. *Journal of Clinical Psychology, 46,* 652-657.

Novaco, R. W. (1975). *Anger control.* Lexington, MA: DC Heath.

Novaco, R. W. (1977). A stress inoculation approach to anger management in training of law enforcement officers. American *Journal of Community Psychology, 5,* 327-346.

Novaco, R. W. (1979). The cognitive regulation of anger and stress. In P. C. Kendall & S. D. Hollon (Eds.), *Cognitive-behavioral interventions: Theory, research, and procedures* (pp. 241-285). New York: Academic Press.

Novaco, R. W. (1980). Training of probation counselors for anger problems. *Journal of Counseling Psychology, 27,* 385-390.

Persons, J. B., & Miranda, J. (1991). Treating dysfunctional beliefs: Implications of the mood-state hypothesis. *Journal of Cognitive Psychotherapy, 5,* 15-26.

Rimm, D. C., deGroot, J. C., Boord, P., Heiman, J., & Dillow, P. V. (1971). Systematic desensitization of anger response. *Behaviour Research and Therapy, 9,* 273-280.

Schlichter, K. J., & Horan, J. J. (1981). Effects of stress inoculation on the aggression management skills of institutionalized juvenile delinquents. *Cognitive Therapy and Research, 5*, 359-365.

Spielberger, C. D. (1988). *State-Trait Anger Expression Inventory*. Orlando, FL: Psychological Assessment Resources.

Spielberger, C. D., Jacobs, G. A., Russell, S. I., & Crane, R. J. (1983). Assessment of anger: The State-Trait Anger Scale. *Advances in Personality Assessment, 3*, 112-134.

Suinn, R. M. (1977). *Manual: Anxiety management training (AMT)*. Fort Collins, CO: Rocky Mountain Behavioral Sciences Institute.

Suinn, R. M. (1990). *Anxiety management training*. New York: Plenum.

Suinn, R. M., & Deffenbacher, J. L. (1988). Anxiety management training. *Counseling Psychologist, 16*, 31-49.

Thurman, C. W. (1985a). Effectiveness of cognitive-behavioral treatments in reducing Type A behavior among university faculty. *Journal of Counseling Psychology, 32*, 358-362.

Thurman, C. W. (1985b). Effectiveness of cognitive-behavioral treatments in reducing Type A behavior in university faculty—One year later. *Journal of Counseling Psychology, 32*, 445-458.

Zillman, D. (1971). Excitation transfer in communication-mediated aggressive behavior. *Journal of Experimental Social Psychology, 7*, 419-434.

Zillman, D., & Bryant, J. (1974). Effect of residual excitation on the emotional response and delayed aggressive behavior. *Journal of Personality and Social Psychology, 30*, 782-791.

Zwemer, W. A., & Deffenbacher, J. L. (1984). Irrational beliefs, anger and anxiety. *Journal of Counseling Psychology, 31*, 391-393.

3

Common Change Processes
in Cognitive-Behavioral Therapies
for Depression

KEITH S. DOBSON

SUSAN JACKMAN-CRAM

Clinical depression (American Psychiatric Association, 1994) is the single most common psychiatric disorder seen by mental health professionals. The prevalence of this disorder is such that it has been referred to as the "common cold of mental illness" in the popular press (Gelman, 1987). It has been estimated that more than 100 million people worldwide develop clinically significant depression each year and that this number is likely to rise.

In the past two decades, there has been a proliferation of theoretical and empirical work directed at understanding and treating depression. One of the most dominant orientations in depression research and theory has been the cognitive approach. Volumes of research have examined the cognitive correlates of depression (e.g., Alloy, 1988; Ingram, 1990), and it has now been well established that depression is characterized by dysfunctional cognitions (see Haaga, Dyck, & Ernst, 1991, for a review). A variety of cognitive and cognitive-behavioral interventions have been developed and have proved efficacious for the treatment of depression. In general, such programs of treatment have reported about a 67% success rate in treating patients with diagnosable major depressive disorder (e.g., Dobson, 1989; Hollon, Shelton, & Davis, 1993). Relapse rates, although still uncomfortably high, compare favorably to other treatment modalities. It is notable that the success of cognitive-behavioral therapies has been a major driving force in the sustained interest in cognitive models of depression (Haaga et al., 1991; Robins & Hayes, 1993).

In the present chapter, we focus on an examination of the common change processes in cognitive-behavioral therapies. We begin with a review of historical formulations regarding cognition and behavior in depression, followed by a discussion of contemporary cognitive-behavioral formulations and treatment programs. We then review evidence related to the hypothesis that behavior change may account for the major proportion of change in cognitive-behavioral therapies and offer potential reasons for this observation. We conclude with suggestions for future theory building and research.

COGNITIVE-BEHAVIORAL FORMULATIONS
OF DEPRESSION IN HISTORY

Clinical descriptions of depression are evident in approximately two millennia of medical writings (Jackson, 1986). Depression, known historically as melancholia, was in fact noted as a distinct disease in Hippocratic writings as early as the fifth and fourth centuries B.C. (Jackson, 1986). Although there have been some shifts and changes, there has also been a remarkable consistency in the clinical content of depressive disorders over the centuries. From the Hippocratic writings to the present, dysfunctional cognitions and reduced behavioral activation have been cardinal features in the clinical description of depression. Soranus of Ephesus (Jackson, 1986), writing during the second century A.D., and as translated by Galen, provided the following description of melancholy:

> Mental anguish and distress, dejection, silence, animosity toward members of the household, sometimes a desire to live and at other times a longing for death, suspicion on the part of the patient that a plot is being hatched against him, weeping without reason, meaningless muttering, precordial distention, especially after eating, coldness of the limbs, mild sweat, a sharp pain in the oesophagus or cardia . . . , heaviness of the head, complexion greenish-black

or somewhat blue, body attenuated, weakness, indigestion with belching that
has a foul odor, intestinal cramps, vomiting, sometimes ineffectual and at other
times bringing up yellowish, rust, or black matter. (p. 34)

Soranus's description contains clear reference to negative cognition, including the pessimism and dejection associated with modern formulations of
depression. Also consistent with contemporary descriptions is his noting of
the behavioral manifestations of depression, including withdrawal, silence,
and irritability (American Psychiatric Association, 1994). Rufus of Ephesus,
another second-century A.D. Greek physician, wrote that melancholia was
caused by much thinking and sadness, implying that activity of the mind was
the direct cause of melancholia (Jackson, 1986). Rufus further wrote that
melancholics tended to turn from the company of others and to seek solitude.

Dysfunctional cognition and retardation of physical activity continued to
be viewed as aspects of the clinical description of melancholia in medieval
medical thought. In the 11th century, Constantinus Africanus (1020?-1087)
described melancholia as an illness that produced gloomy ideas and caused
patients to fear imaginary things that they believed were real (Jackson,
1986). For Constantinus, black bile produced the pathological effects seen
in melancholia, corrupting the understanding such that it did not function as
it ordinarily would. Avicenna's (980-1037) *Canon of Medicine,* a highly
influential work of the medieval era, indicated that melancholia included
sadness, proneness to anger, a preference for solitude, and casting the worst
interpretation on things.

There was no significant change in how melancholia was described in the
transition from the medieval era to the Renaissance (Jackson, 1986). Medical
writings on melancholia essentially consisted of more elaborated versions of
earlier statements. Felix Potter (1536-1614), for example, one of the Renaissance medical authorities, described melancholy as

> a kind of mental alienation (*mentis alienatio*) in which imagination and
> judgement are so perverted that without cause the victims become very sad
> and fearful. For they cannot adduce any certain cause of grief or fear except
> a trivial one or a false opinion which they have conceived as a result of dis-
> turbed apprehension. . . . They have solitude and flee the company of others.
> (Jackson, 1986, p. 91)

Early in the 19th century, Esquirol (1772-1840) reduced the clinical content of melancholia and sharpened its outlines (Jackson, 1986). A state of

dejected mood, together with distressed preoccupation and slowing of cognition and physical function, became increasingly viewed as the descriptive core (Jackson, 1986). Modern-day descriptions of depression continue to capture the cognitive and behavioral symptoms of dejection, pessimism, hopelessness, psychomotor retardation, and lethargy that have been described in the medical writings throughout the history of melancholy.

Given the critical role that behavioral and cognitive features played in the nosology of depression, it is hardly surprising that early treatments included attention to cognitive and behavioral symptoms. Hippocratic writers advised measures to correct patients' thinking (Jackson, 1986). Pleasant company was recommended to guard against patients' tendency toward solitude. Physical diversions were recommended to treat patients' inclinations to inactivity. Celsus, for example, writing in the first century A.D., indicated that

> the motions are to be kept very soft, causes of fright excluded, good hope rather put forward; entertainment sought by story-telling, and by games, especially by those with which the patient is wont to be attracted when sane; work of his, if there is any, should be praised, and set out before his eyes; his depression should be gently reproved as being without cause; he should have it pointed out to him now and again how in the very things which trouble him there may be the cause of rejoicing rather than of solitude. (Jackson, 1986, pp. 299-301)

With minor variations, these recommendations continued to be included within the treatment regimen for melancholia for over the next 1,500 years (Jackson, 1986).

In the still Galenic medicine of the 17th century, reference is again found to moderate exercise, diverting preoccupations, and company. Robert Burton (1557-1640), the well-known expert on melancholy, urged, "Be not solitary, be not idle" (Jackson, 1986, p. 99) to guard against melancholia. From Pitcairn in the late 17th century to Cullen in the late 18th century, remarkable consistency in therapeutic themes continued (Jackson, 1986). Exercise was frequently advised, along with diverting the melancholic from his fixed line of thought. There was growing attention to psychological management and interventions for the treatment of melancholia in the 18th and 19th centuries. At the beginning of the 19th century, Pinel (1745-1826), for example, emphasized the importance of "forcibly agitating the system; of interrupting the chain of gloomy ideas, and of engaging [patients'] interest by powerful and continuous impressions on their external senses" (Jackson, 1986, p. 393). In the 20th century, psychological measures—for example, cognitive therapy—have come to be used increasingly in the treatment of depression. Prominent contemporary cognitive treatment models, presented in the next section, continue to highlight the importance of cognitive and behavioral variables in understanding depression.

CONTEMPORARY VIEWS OF COGNITION AND BEHAVIOR IN DEPRESSION

The enthusiasm for the cognitive-behavioral approach to depression is evidenced by the number of major theoretical models that have appeared. The most prominent models include Lewinsohn's behavioral theory (e.g., Lewinsohn & Arconad, 1981); Beck's cognitive theory (e.g., Beck, Rush, Shaw, & Emery, 1979); Seligman's learned helplessness theory (Seligman, 1975), which was reformulated by Abramson, Seligman, and Teasdale (1978) and Abramson, Alloy, and Metalsky (1990); and the self-control theory (e.g., Rehm, 1977). In recent years, these major theoretical models have evolved as new research has been generated and new findings emerged. Revised statements of theory have most often involved the incorporation of more cognitive constructs. Cognitive revisions to major theories have also been accompanied in the literature by the appearance of new theoretical positions that derive more from modern cognitive theory (e.g., Derry & Kuiper, 1981; Ingram, 1990; Teasdale, 1988).

Contemporary cognitive-behavioral theories and therapies share with their historical forebears and among themselves features related to cognitive and behavioral symptoms. The critical and common features of the most prominent cognitive-behavioral therapies are described below.

Lewinsohn's Behavioral Approach

Lewinsohn's treatment of depression, particularly in its formative stages (e.g., Lewinsohn, Biglan, & Zeiss, 1976; Lewinsohn & Graf, 1973), drew on reinforcement theory (Ferster, 1973). A low rate of response-contingent positive reinforcement was assumed to constitute a critical antecedent for the occurrence of depression. The guiding principle for treatment was to restore an adequate schedule of reinforcement through altering the level, quality, and range of the patient's activities and interactions.

Lewinsohn's treatment approach had a sequential system for the assessment and treatment of depression. In the assessment phase, the model recommended three areas for consideration. First, the availability of reinforcers was to be assessed. This availability in part depended on the activity level of patients because patients who increased their activity level were more likely to encounter sources of reinforcement. The second area for assessment was that of skills deficits (e.g., assertiveness, social skills) because patients who possessed adequate skills were more likely to attain positive reinforcement from their environment than those without such skills. Finally, Lewinsohn recommended an assessment of how the depressed person interpreted reinforcement because patients who underestimated either the frequency of reinforcers or the valence of reinforcement potentially deprived themselves of available reinforcement. Thus, within Lewinsohn's model, interpersonal behavior and cognitive factors played an important role.

Lewinsohn and his colleagues developed a structured model of treatment based on the above principles (e.g., Lewinsohn & Arconad, 1981; Lewinsohn, Sullivan, & Grosscup, 1982). Therapy involved a series of predictable stages:

1. *Differential diagnosis:* ascertaining the problem using self-report instruments and clinical interview
2. *Functional analysis of the role of activity:* pinpointing specific person-environment interactions and events related to the individual's depression by using the Pleasant Events Schedule (PES; MacPhillamy & Lewinsohn, 1975) and the Unpleasant Events Schedule (UES; Lewinsohn, 1975)
3. *Social learning tactics:* focusing on changing environmental conditions and on teaching depressed patients the skills necessary to modify detrimental patterns of interaction with the environment (e.g., self-change methods, social skills, and cognitive skills)

For Lewinsohn, cognitions and feelings were most effectively influenced by behavior change. Consequently, a graduated goal-oriented behavioral focus was established early in treatment and continued throughout the course of therapy. Over the years, Lewinsohn has expanded on the cognitive module present in his treatment approach. In addition, a revised statement of theory (Lewinsohn, Hoberman, Teri, & Hautzinger, 1985) has proposed a new integrative model of depression that significantly builds on the cognitive component.

Rehm's Self-Control Model

The self-control model of depression (Rehm, 1977, 1981, 1988) emphasizes deficits in self-monitoring, self-evaluation, and self-reinforcement as causes of depression. Rehm suggested that depressed individuals attend to more negative information about themselves, tend to make more frequent negative evaluations, and are less likely to reinforce adequate performance. More recently, Rehm's original model was revised (Rehm & Naus, 1990) to propose a memory model of emotion in which emotionally biased information processing in depression was emphasized.

Rehm's self-control therapy program aimed to remedy the various deficits specified in the model in a systematic way. Therapy consisted of a sequence of self-monitoring, self-evaluation, and self-reinforcement modules that focused on the depressed behavior associated with each phase of self-control (Rehm, 1981). Recognizing that mood was related to activity and that gaining control over activity was a means of controlling depression was fundamental to the overall self-control treatment program. Carrying out self-monitoring exercises of activity was a crucial first step in treatment. "The homework assignment at the end of the first session was to record daily participation in positive activities" (Rehm, 1981, p. 77). The focus of therapy later shifted to self-evaluation and self-reinforcement components designed to facilitate cognitive change.

Of particular relevance to this chapter are studies that have attempted to examine the mechanism of change in self-control therapy. In a study by Kornblith, Rehm, O'Hara, and Lamparski (1983), subjects were randomly assigned to engage in either behavioral assignments or self-reinforcement. There were no significant differences in the outcomes between these two groups, and although the small number of subjects renders this finding somewhat tentative, it suggests that self-reinforcement may not be the critical element of change in this therapy program.

Another study conducted by Rehm and his colleagues (Rehm, Kaslow, & Rabin, 1985) attempted to determine whether behavioral or cognitive targets (or their mixture) could be selectively modified with a self-control therapy. In a well-designed study with a good number of subjects, it was found that all treatment groups evidenced increases in the number of positive events and cognitions, as well as decreases in negative events and cognitions. These results were taken to reflect a reciprocal model of behavior and cognition in which each influenced the other.

Seligman's Learned-Helplessness Model

Abramson, Seligman, and Teasdale (1978) reformulated the learned-helplessness theory (Seligman, 1975) to incorporate attributional constructs: Individuals who made stable, global, and internal attributions for negative life events were hypothesized as the most likely to become depressed. The attributional reformulation was recently refined (e.g., Abramson et al., 1990) to emphasize the importance of hopelessness as a proximal and sufficient cause of depression. The hopelessness model stressed the distal contributory nature of attributional style in the chain of events leading to depression. According to the hopelessness theory, an individual's attributional style, interacting with a negative life event, resulted in particular attributions for that event. To the extent that the attribution was global and stable, it led to hopelessness, which in turn potentially led to depression.

A structured program of treatment has not been derived from the hopelessness model. Abramson et al. (1990), however, suggested that any therapeutic strategy that undermined hopelessness and restored hopefulness would be effective in the treatment of depression. The authors further noted that modifying depressogenic attributions, the hopelessness-inducing environment, and the person's behavior would be important therapeutic goals.

Beck's Cognitive Theory

According to Beck's theory (Beck, 1967), the depression-prone individual has enduring maladaptive cognitive schemas or structures containing negative information about the self in relation to the world and the future. These schemas consist of representations of past experiences that are stored in memory and serve as a screen against which incoming information is perceived and encoded. They can be activated by relevant life stressors and when activated begin to dominate the individual's information processing. The dominance of these negative schemas leads to systematic biases in the perception and interpretation of information. The motivational, behavioral, and physical manifestations of depression are rooted in dominance of these cognitive schemas.

Beck's cognitive therapy (e.g., Beck, 1993; Beck et al., 1979; Beck & Weishaar, 1989; Robins & Hayes, 1993) is a structured problem-solving approach aimed at modifying the faulty information processing that characterizes depression. Both behavioral and cognitive procedures are used to realize treatment goals. Cognitive functioning is addressed at a product, processing, and schema level (Clark & Beck, 1990). Therapy begins with the provision of a treatment rationale and instruction in the specifics of the cognitive model. Beck's cognitive therapy recognizes that experience is the most effective way to change existing thoughts and beliefs (Clark & Beck, 1990). Of note, behavioral tasks are frequently used at the beginning of therapy, especially for the severely depressed, to mobilize to activity. Behavioral activation strategies include weekly activity scheduling, graded task assignments, and pleasure/mastery rating assignments. Cognitive techniques are presented to train the patient to identify, evaluate, and correct the faulty thinking that distorts reality. Patients are taught to identify and reevaluate automatic thoughts through the use of the three-column technique. Therapy shifts toward modification of faulty assumptions during the middle and later stages. Behavioral tasks are assigned to test specific assumptions against experience. Such behavioral experiments are presented in a collaborative, hypothesis-testing manner, usually as part of a homework assignment. By emphasizing an empirical hypothesis-testing approach, maladaptive beliefs are disconfirmed, and more adaptive thinking is verified.

Common Elements of Cognitive-Behavioral Therapies

All of the above cognitive-behavioral treatment programs are complex packages, and the rationales and the theories behind them vary considerably. However, examination of the therapeutic strategies involved reveals considerable overlap across programs. To begin with, all the treatment programs reviewed are highly structured, with well-defined sequences of steps. All programs include efforts to assess and modify both behavioral and cognitive features of depression, and, of particular note, the format of all programs is such that the early focus is behavioral. Uniformly, these treatment approaches target behavioral inaction as requiring early modification and promote activities with positive hedonic tone. Once a patient is engaged with the environment, the focus shifts toward assessment and modification of the problematic cognitions that depressed persons exhibit during that engagement. This treatment sequencing is critical, we believe, in suggesting common pathways out of depression.

CHANGE PROCESSES IN DEPRESSION

Where does the change in depression during cognitive-behavioral therapies occur? In a study of depressed outpatients receiving a standard research protocol of 20 sessions of cognitive therapy (Murphy, Simons, Wetzel, & Lustman, 1984; Simons, Murphy, Levine, & Wetzel, 1986), it was reported that approximately half of the change in Beck Depression Inventory (BDI) scores occurred in the first five sessions. The results of Murphy et al. (1984) are consistent with data from the National Institute of Mental Health collaborative study on the treatment of depression (Elkin et al., 1989), which showed that BDI scores declined 40% in the first five sessions of cognitive therapy. Indeed, there is general recognition that most of the improvement in the severity of depression is achieved early in therapy (see Hollon et al., 1993; Persons, 1989).

It is notable that the early phase of cognitive-behavioral therapies is dominated by behavioral assessment and therapy interventions. The suggestion that most patient change in cognitive therapy occurs early in the process, at a stage when the focus of therapy is largely behavioral, suggests that the most powerful techniques in these treatments may be those related to behavior change. In this section, we examine the idea that behavior change, without any explicit focus on cognitive assessment or modification, can enhance mood.

The Mood-Enhancing Effect of Exercise

One source of data relevant to the potency of behavior change for improving mood is related to the treatment of depression through exercise programs. Although the number of controlled studies that have directly examined the impact of exercise regimens on clinical depression is small, there is growing and consistent evidence that such regimens can significantly reduce depression.

In one of the best of the studies examining the effect of exercise on depression, Doyne and her colleagues (Doyne, Chambless, & Beutler, 1983; Doyne et al., 1987; Ossip-Klein et al., 1989) randomly assigned clinically depressed female patients to a running, weight-lifting, or delayed-treatment condition. Treatments consisted of monitored exercise at least three times a week (four times weekly was promoted, three was the minimum accepted), with a focus on ensuring aerobic activity in the running condition and anaerobic conditioning in the weight lifting condition. Patients in the study were assessed before, during, and after therapy and for up to a year after the end of therapy.

The findings of the Doyne studies showed that both forms of exercise led to significantly improved scores on depression and that both groups of these subjects were considerably better than those in the delayed-treatment condition. Further, patients who were assessed at the follow-up periods continued to show significant changes from their pretreatment levels of depression, although this effect was clearly modulated by whether the patient had continued with any form of exercise. This study's results are, of course, subject to the possibility of a nonspecific treatment effect in that both forms of treatment involved attention and an increase in personal control that the delayed treatment group would not experience.

The results of the Doyne et al. study are not isolated. A study by Sexton, Maere, and Dahl (1989) showed that 8-week-long walking or running programs significantly reduced depression. This study also reported both greater aerobic gain and more dropouts in the running group, leaving the true nature of the results somewhat clouded. The fact that there was no control condition also limits the value of this study for making conclusions about the benefit of exercise on depression.

Another study concerning the impact of exercise on depression is that by Klein et al. (1985). In this study, group psychotherapy was directly contrasted with one of three self-selected exercise programs chosen by a group of outpatient depressed subjects. The data showed that although both treatments were effective, no significant differences between the two treatment groups existed at the end of therapy. This study unfortunately suffers from some methodological problems, such as weak assessment, a vaguely defined form of psychotherapy, no control group, and inadequate follow-up, but is again suggestive of the impact of exercise on depression.

Although the above studies suggest the power of behavior change on depression, there are, of course, problems in making a strong interpretation. First, it is not clear from the descriptions of the above studies how the issue of patients' conceptualization and interpretation of their exercise programs was handled. If patients were encouraged to conceptualize these activities as positive, as methods to build self-esteem, or as sources of accomplishments, the studies cannot adequately measure the role of activity in the treatment of depression because their results reflect both behavioral change and cognitive modification.

It is also known that exercise not only increases behavior rates but also modifies body chemistry. Aerobic exercises in particular are associated with increases in bodily endorphins, which may themselves be mood altering. The fact, however, that both aerobic and anaerobic exercise resulted in improved mood (Doyne et al., 1987; Ossip-Klein et al., 1989) to some extent mitigates this concern.

Another reason for caution in making a strong statement from the above research is that much of it suffers from similar methodological problems: subjects who may or may not have met criteria for clinical depression, nonexistent or limited follow-up assessments, and poor attention to issues of nonspecificity of treatment effects.

Isolating Cognitive and Behavioral Therapy Effects

A less contaminated manner in which to study the relative antidepressant effects of behavior change and cognitive change is to design treatment components that specifically target behavioral or cognitive features of depression, in an attempt to isolate cognitive and behavioral therapy effects.

It was previously noted that a dismantling study of Rehm's self-control therapy (Kornblith et al., 1983) revealed no significant difference in the effects of behavioral assignments or self-reinforcement strategies. A more recent study has explicitly attempted a component analysis of Beck's cognitive therapy of depression (Jacobson et al., 1995; see also Sweet & Loizeaux, 1991, for a discussion of the same issue). For the purposes of the study, three components of cognitive therapy were identified:

1. *Behavioral activation:* a focus on activity levels, the functional relationship between activity and mood, behavioral assignments, rehearsal of activities, mastery and pleasure analyses of activities, and graduated task assignments
2. *Automatic thought interventions:* the assessment of dysfunctional thinking and cognitive distortions, psychoeducational efforts to teach the relationship between cognition and mood, training in the assessment of negative cognitions, challenging of negative cognitions through rational alternative or evidence-based examination

3. *Assumptive work:* review of patterns of negative thinking, early experiences and their role in establishing negative beliefs and assumptions, and efforts to modify beliefs and assumptions through such techniques as examining the short- and long-term consequences of alternative assumptions and trying to behave according to different, more functional assumptions and beliefs

The design of the component analysis study was additive, and subjects were randomly assigned to 20 sessions in one of three conditions: (a) behavioral activation alone, (b) behavioral activation plus automatic thought interventions, or (c) the complete treatment package with all three treatment components. A treatment manual was created for each of the components, and a group of experienced cognitive therapists was trained to provide differentially the treatment conditions. Outcomes were assessed using multiple measures, and correlates of change were also assessed to determine potential mechanisms of change.

The results of this study are important for understanding change processes in depression because of the careful control of the interventions provided. If behavioral interventions alone effectively led to depression change, the idea that cognitive assessment and change are critical therapeutic processes would be challenged. If the two conditions that involve cognitive assessment and change both led to comparable outcomes, both of which were better than the behavioral condition, this finding would support a cognitive mediation model but would suggest that the assessment and modification of beliefs or assumptions were not critical to that process. Finally, if the full package had the best outcomes, this finding would provide support for the full complement of cognitive therapy techniques and the cognitive model of depression (see Segal, 1988).

The results of this study did not support the cognitive therapy model for depression. All three conditions were associated with significant decreases in BDI and Hamilton Rating Scale for Depression (HRSD) scores. These results were not significantly different among the treatment conditions, nor were there any treatment-by-phase-of-study interactions. The BDI and HRSD results were further reinforced by an examination of the diagnostic status of patients at the end of treatment. The percentages of subjects who no longer met criteria for major depression (American Psychiatric Association, 1987) at the end of the study were not significantly different across the three treatment conditions. These results suggest the potent impact of behavior change on depression because the addition of cognitive interventions did not further contribute to change in depression compared to behavioral interventions alone.

Despite no significant differences at posttest assessment, it is possible that the full treatment package would differentially be associated with better follow-up status. Indeed, such a prediction would be made from the cognitive model (Beck et al., 1979) because it is only the change in underlying assumptions that putatively changes the underlying cognitive vulnerability to depression. Although the results of this part of the study are not yet complete, follow-up assessments of study subjects continue to reveal nonsignificant differences among subjects in the three treatment groups. Further, relapse is comparable across treatment groups, suggesting that the stated theoretical importance of addressing underlying assumptions as causal agents of future depression (Beck et al., 1979) may not be warranted. Most significantly, these results suggest that addressing behavior change alone is as important as any of the other treatment interventions in cognitive therapy.

One of the limits of the Jacobson et al. (1995) study is its omission of a no-treatment or other control condition. Although the outcomes associated with the full-treatment package were comparable to those results reported in other studies of cognitive therapy (e.g., Dobson, 1989; Hollon et al., 1993), the lack of a no-treatment control makes it possible that there was something about this sample that would have yielded positive results in any event. It is also important that in addition to providing behavioral interventions, all three treatment conditions rested on a therapeutic relationship. It is possible that the nonspecific therapy factors, including the provision of a supportive, nonevaluative relationship, rather than (or in addition to) behavior change, created change in depression.

Summary

It appears that modifying activity in depressed patients is antidepressant. This is not a new finding, and it is not surprising that all cognitive-behavioral therapies have integrated techniques to modify behavior into their treatments. The fact that behavioral interventions are at the earliest stages of therapy, when most of the apparent change in depression takes place, does, however, suggest that perhaps these techniques are in fact the most powerful. It has further been shown that exercise programs alone can significantly improve depression and in one study did so as much as group psychotherapy. The further finding, in the University of Washington study, that behavioral interventions led to the same outcome as behavioral and cognitive interventions lends weight to the hypothesis that most of the efforts of therapists treating depression ought to be devoted to behavior change strategies.

If behavior change is the most powerful technique for modifying depression, does this finding mean that it does so directly, without any necessary change in cognition? Even further, does it mean that therapists should limit themselves to behavior change and assume that effects in other domains will occur through other reactive processes? The answer to both of these questions is at present indeterminate.

Before examining whether behavior change directly modifies depression, it should be noted that several potential linkages between cognition and depression exist. Hollon, DeRubeis, and Evans (1987) suggested three different potential perspectives on the role of cognitive mediation in the treatment of depression,[1] which they labeled *strong, partial,* and *nonmediational.* The strong model is that cognitive interventions directly affect cognitive processes, which then lead to changes in depression. The partial model is that there are both strong effects and direct effects of treatment on depression (i.e., treatment affects depression both directly and through its effects on cognitive processes). Finally, the nonmediational model posits that treatment directly affects depression, which then indirectly affects cognitive processes (i.e., cognitive changes are epiphenomenal aspects of change in depression). The idea that behavior change directly affects depression, which then indirectly changes cognitions, is an example of a nonmediational model.

Research reveals that the nonmediational model is highly untenable. It is clear, for example, that cognition is correlated with depression (Haaga et al., 1991). Indeed, in the development and validation of cognitive assessment measures, one of the cardinal features of such measures has been their strong correlation with depression. Community studies also reveal linkages between cognition and depression. Lewinsohn and his colleagues (Lewinsohn, Steinmetz, Larson, & Franklin, 1981) showed that significant changes in depression-related cognitions were correlated with changes in depression status. Finally, studies of behavior therapy of depression have shown that even though cognitions are not the focus of therapy, they do change (Kornblith et al., 1983; Nezu & Perri, 1989; Shaw, 1977).

Whether the strong or partial models of mediation best describe change in depression is not clear at present. Recognizing that cognitions and depression are correlated does not invalidate the importance of the behavior-depression linkage. As has been argued above, the relationship between behavior change and depression is generally as strong as that between cognition and depression, and this relationship has been observed for several hundred years. Thus both cognitive and behavioral aspects of depression appear related to each other, as well as to the overall phenomenon of depression.

One of the central issues addressed in this chapter has been the importance of behavior change in treating depression. It has been argued that behavior change may be a necessary part of cognitive-behavioral therapy for depression. To say that behavior change is critical for the treatment of depression is not to say, however, that *any* change in behavior will suffice. One of the understudied phenomena in the behavioral activation phase of cognitive-behavioral therapy is the process of how therapists and patients select their activities for early attention. Aside from choosing activities with "pleasantness" or positive hedonic tone, most cognitive-behavioral theorists do not focus on how to select activities. It is possible that there is actually an elaborate causal model in most therapists' minds when they assign behavioral activation tasks, in that they conjecture, before making such assignments, about the patient's likely interpretations of their change in activity relative to their beliefs about themselves and the world. Indeed, until therapists know how a given patient will interpret different behaviors, most will not assign any random task just to increase activation (see also Kanfer, Chapter 1 of this volume).

Just as effective therapists predict the interpretation of behavior change before it is instituted, they also ensure that antidepressant interpretations are placed on behavior change once it occurs: that patients are not, for example, minimizing their accomplishment or saying that the task really did not have relevance to their lives. Thus, although we may grant some partial direct antidepressant properties to activities themselves, the bulk of this effect may be through the indirect effect of interpretation.

What has been stated is not an argument for a strong cognitive mediational model. The role of behavior change and its interpretation is critical for cognitive interventions to succeed. Further, it has been previously suggested that some activities such as exercise may have direct, perhaps physiological effects on mood. Thus it is the convergence of cognitive and behavioral change that represents the needed modification for the effective treatment of depression. In this model, cognition and behavior reciprocally influence each other. Thus these two correlated aspects of human functioning may also, either directly or through their reciprocal influence, affect depression.

CONCLUSION

This chapter has argued that behavior processes are at least as important as cognitive processes in the understanding of depression. We have cited historical referents to show that behavioral components of melancholia and depression have been recognized for centuries. We have shown that cognitive-behavioral models all include significant degrees of attention to behavioral processes and interventions. We have examined the role of direct behavior change in the form of exercise on mood and have finally shown that the few studies that have tried to identify the effective ingredients of cognitive-behavioral therapy have not been able to show an additive value to cognitive over behavioral interventions. Consequently, we submit that behavior change, the association between behavior and cognition, and the potentially reciprocal impact of behavior and cognition on depression deserve more attention than is currently the case.

Critics will note that most of the data that have been drawn on are outcome data and that such data do not maximally speak to process issues in treatment. It is an unfortunate reality that until relatively recently, the focus of the depression therapy literature has been on establishing treatment outcomes. An outcome perspective carries with it a major focus on pre- and post-treatment assessment, but usually relatively less of a focus on process measures. The field is beginning to examine different response domains within a variety of treatment modalities; however, knowledge to date is limited. Analyses of the causal pathways between behavioral, cognitive, and other aspects of depression, within both clinically depressed, treated samples and community samples, are clearly needed before we can assert with confidence which of the potential mechanisms of change is maximally ecologically valid.

Studies that examine the change processes in other forms of therapy are also needed. Does pharmacotherapy, for example, exert its influence through increasing the potential for activation, through energizing patients, who can then begin to engage with their world as they were previously unable to do? Studies of cognitive and behavioral aspects of pharmacotherapy would help to address this type of issue.

Until our understanding of the processes of depression becomes more validated, we can certainly take pride in the knowledge that our treatments for depression are highly efficacious for a large number of individuals (Dobson, 1989). Knowing why these treatments work and which subgroups of patients will respond best will be the next important focus of research.

NOTE

1. Their article focused on pharmacotherapy versus cognitive mediation, but the perspective on mediation also holds with respect to behavior change and cognitive mediation. See also Barnett and Gotlib (1988) for a related discussion.

REFERENCES

Abramson, L. Y., Alloy, L. B., & Metalsky, G. I. (1990). Hopelessness and depression: An empirical search for a theory-based subtype. In R. E. Ingram (Ed.), *Contemporary psychological approaches to depression: Theory, research and treatment* (pp. 37-58). New York: Plenum.

Abramson, L. Y., Seligman, M. E. P., & Teasdale, J. (1978). Learned helplessness in humans: Critique and reformulation. *Journal of Abnormal Psychology, 87,* 49-59.

Alloy, L. B. (Ed.). (1988). *Cognitive processes in depression.* New York: Guilford.

American Psychiatric Association. (1987). *Diagnostic and statistical manual of mental disorders* (3rd ed., Rev.). Washington, DC: Author.

American Psychiatric Association. (1994). *Diagnostic and statistical manual of mental disorders* (4th ed.). Washington, DC: Author.

Barnett, P. A., & Gotlib, I. H. (1988). Psychosocial functioning and depression: Distinguishing among antecedents, concomitants, and consequences. *Psychological Bulletin, 104,* 97-126.

Beck, A. T. (1967). *Depression: Causes and treatment.* Philadelphia: University of Pennsylvania Press.

Beck, A. T. (1993). Cognitive therapy: Past, present and future. *Journal of Consulting and Clinical Psychology, 61,* 194-198.

Beck, A. T., Rush, A. J., Shaw, B. F., & Emery, G. (1979). *Cognitive therapy of depression.* New York: Guilford.

Beck, A. T., & Weishaar, M. (1989). Cognitive therapy. In A. Freeman, K. M. Simon, L. E. Beutler, & H. Arkowitz (Eds.), *Contemporary handbook of cognitive therapy* (pp. 21-36). New York: Plenum.

Clark, D. A., & Beck, A. T. (1990). Cognitive therapy of anxiety and depression. In R. E. Ingram (Ed.), *Contemporary psychological approaches to depression: Theory, research and treatment* (pp. 155-167). New York: Plenum.

Derry, P. A., & Kuiper, N. A. (1981). Schematic processing and self-reference in clinical depression. *Journal of Abnormal Psychology, 90,* 286-297.

Dobson, K. S. (1989). A meta-analysis of the efficacy of cognitive therapy for depression. *Journal of Consulting and Clinical Psychology, 57,* 414-419.

Doyne, E. J., Chambless, D. L., & Beutler, L. E. (1983). Aerobic exercise as a treatment for depression in women. *Behavior Therapy, 14,* 434-440.

Doyne, E. J., Ossip-Klein, D. J., Bowman, E. D., Osborn, K. M., McDougall-Wilson, I. B., & Neimeyer, R. A. (1987). Running versus weight lifting in the treatment of depression. *Journal of Consulting and Clinical Psychology, 55,* 748-754.

Elkin, I., Shea, M. T., Watkins, J. T., Imber, S. D., Sotsky, S. M., Colins, J. F., Glass, D. R., Pilkonis, P. A., Leber, W. R., Docherty, J. P., Fiester, S. J., & Parloff, M. B. (1989).

NIMH Treatment of Depression Collaborative Research Program: I. General effectiveness of treatments. *Archives of General Psychiatry, 46,* 971-982.

Ferster, C. B. (1973). A functional analysis of depression. *American Psychologist, 28,* 857-870.

Gelman, D. (1987, May 4). Depression. *Newsweek,* 48-52, 54-57.

Haaga, D. A. F., Dyck, M. J., & Ernst, D. (1991). Empirical status of cognitive theory of depression. *Psychological Bulletin, 110,* 215-236.

Hollon, S. D., DeRubeis, R. J., & Evans, M. D. (1987). Causal mediation of change in treatment for depression: Discriminating between nonspecificity and noncausality. *Psychological Bulletin, 102,* 139-149.

Hollon, S. D., Shelton, R. C., & Davis, D. D. (1993). Cognitive therapy for depression: Conceptual issues and clinical efficacy. *Journal of Consulting and Clinical Psychology, 61,* 270-275.

Ingram, R. E. (Ed.). (1990). *Contemporary psychological approaches to depression: Theory, research and treatment.* New York: Plenum.

Jackson, S. W. (1986). *Melancholia and depression.* New Haven, CT: Yale University Press.

Jacobson, N. S., Dobson, K. S., Truax, P. A., Addis, M. E., Koerner, K., Gollan, J. K., Gortner, E., & Prince, S. E. (1995). *A component analysis of cognitive behavioral treatment for depression.* Unpublished manuscript, University of Washington.

Klein, M. H., Greist, J. H., Gurman, A. S., Neimeyer, R. A., Lesser, D. P., Bushnell, N. J., & Smith, R. E. (1985). A comparative outcome study of group psychotherapy vs. exercise treatments for depression. *International Journal of Mental Health, 13,* 148-177.

Kornblith, S. J., Rehm, L. P., O'Hara, M. W., & Lamparski, D. (1983). The contribution of self-reinforcement training and behavioral assignments to the efficacy of self-control therapy for depression. *Cognitive Therapy and Research, 7,* 499-527.

Lewinsohn, P. M. (1975). The behavioral study and treatment of depression. In M. Hersen, R. M. Eisler, & P. M. Miller (Eds.), *Progress in behavior modification* (pp. 52-75). New York: Academic Press.

Lewinsohn, P. M., & Arconad, M. (1981). Behavioral treatment of depression: A social learning approach. In J. F. Clarkin & H. I. Glazer (Eds.), *Depression: Behavioral and directive intervention strategies* (pp. 33-67). New York: Garland STPM.

Lewinsohn, P. M., Biglan, T., & Zeiss, A. (1976). Behavioral treatment of depression. In P. O. Davidson (Ed.), *The behavioral management of anxiety, depression and pain* (pp. 91-146). New York: Brunner/Mazel.

Lewinsohn, P. M., & Graf, M. (1973). Pleasant events and depression. *Journal of Consulting and Clinical Psychology, 41,* 261-268.

Lewinsohn, P. M., Hoberman, H. M., Teri, L., & Hautzinger, M. (1985). An integrative theory of depression. In S. Reiss & R. Bootzin (Eds.), *Theoretical issues in behavior therapy* (pp. 64-89). New York: Academic Press.

Lewinsohn, P. M., Steinmetz, J. L., Larson, D. W., & Franklin, J. (1981). Depression-related cognitions: Antecedent or consequence? *Journal of Abnormal Psychology, 90,* 213-219.

Lewinsohn, P. M., Sullivan, J. M., & Grosscup, S. J. (1982). Behavioral therapy: Clinical applications. In A. J. Rush (Ed.), *Short-term psychotherapies for depression: Behavioral, interpersonal, cognitive, and psychodynamic approaches* (pp. 50-87). New York: Guilford.

MacPhillamy, D., & Lewinsohn, P. M. (1975). *Manual for the Pleasant Events Schedule.* Eugene: University of Oregon, Department of Psychology.

Murphy, G. E., Simons, A. D., Wetzel, R. D., & Lustman, P. J. (1984). Cognitive therapy and pharmacotherapy, singly and together in the treatment of depression. *Archives of General Psychiatry, 41,* 33-41.

Nezu, A. M., & Perri, M. G. (1989). Social problem-solving therapy for unipolar depression: An initial dismantling investigation. *Journal of Consulting and Clinical Psychology, 57,* 408-413.

Ossip-Klein, D. J., Doyne, E. J., Bowman, E. D., Osborn, K. M., McDougall-Wilson, I. B., & Neimeyer, R. A. (1989). Effects of running or weight lifting on self-concept in clinically depressed women. *Journal of Consulting and Clinical Psychology, 57,* 158-161.

Persons, J. (1989). *Cognitive therapy in practice: A case formulation approach.* New York: Norton.

Rehm, L. P. (1977). A self-control model of depression. *Behavior Therapy, 8,* 787-804.

Rehm, L. P. (1981). A self-control therapy program for treatment of depression. In J. F. Clarkin & H. I. Glazer (Eds.), *Depression: Behavioral and directive intervention strategies* (pp. 68-110). New York: Garland STPM.

Rehm, L. P. (1988). Self-management and cognitive processes in depression. In L. B. Alloy (Ed.), *Cognitive processes in depression* (pp. 143-176). New York: Guilford.

Rehm, L. P., & Naus, N. J. (1990). A memory model of emotion. In R. E. Ingram (Ed.) *Contemporary psychological approaches to depression: Theory, research, and treatment.* New York: Plenum Press (pp. 23-35).

Rehm, L. P., Kaslow, N. J., & Rabin, A. S. (1985). Cognitive and behavioral targets in a self-control therapy program for depression. *Journal of Consulting and Clinical Psychology, 55,* 60-67.

Robins, C. J., & Hayes, A. M. (1993). An appraisal of cognitive therapy. *Journal of Consulting and Clinical Psychology, 61,* 205-214.

Segal, Z. V. (1988). Appraisal of the self-schema construct in cognitive models of depression. *Psychological Bulletin, 103,* 147-162.

Seligman, M. E. P. (1975). *Helplessness: On depression, development and death.* San Francisco: W. H. Freeman.

Sexton, H., Maere, A., & Dahl, N. H. (1989). Exercise intensity and reduction in neurotic symptoms: A controlled follow-up study. *Acta Psychiatrica Scandinavica, 80,* 231-235.

Shaw, B. F. (1977). Comparison of cognitive therapy and behavior therapy in the treatment of depression. *Journal of Consulting and Clinical Psychology, 45,* 543-551.

Simons, A. D., Murphy, G. E., Levine, J. E., & Wetzel, R. D. (1986). Cognitive therapy and pharmacotherapy for depression: Sustained improvement over one year. *Archives of General Psychiatry, 43,* 43-49.

Sweet, A. A., & Loizeaux, A. L. (1991). Behavioral and cognitive treatment methods: A critical comparative review. *Journal of Behavior Therapy and Experimental Psychiatry, 22,* 159-185.

Teasdale, J. D. (1988). Cognitive vulnerability to persistent depression. *Cognition and Emotion, 2,* 247-274.

4

Cognitive Factors in Chronic Pain and Disability

DENNIS C. TURK

PAIN: THE MAGNITUDE OF THE PROBLEM

Pain has been the focus of philosophical speculation and scientific attention for centuries, yet it continues to remain one of the most challenging problems for the sufferer, health care providers, and society. For the individual experiencing chronic pain, there is a continuing quest for relief that often remains elusive and leads to feelings of demoralization, helplessness, hopelessness, and outright depression. The health care provider shares these feelings of frustration as his or her patients' reports of pain continue despite the health care provider's best efforts and at times in the absence of pathology that is sufficient to account for the pain reported. On a societal level, pain creates a major burden in lost productivity and disability benefits. Third-party payers are confronted with escalating medical costs, disability payments, and frustration when patients remain disabled despite extensive treatment and rehabilitation efforts.

In short, pain is a major health problem in society that affects millions of people and costs billions of dollars in health care and lost productivity. Table 4.1 contains some representative statistics from the United States to support the magnitude of the problem.

TABLE 4.1   Magnitude of the Problem

Pain is the primary reason for visiting physicians, accounting for over 70 million (80%) of all office visits to physicians each year (National Center for Health Statistics, 1986).

Almost 10% of all individuals in the United States have pain symptoms more than 100 days/ year (Osterweis, Kleinman, & Mechanic, 1987).

Over 30 million Americans suffer from back pain alone, with 11.7 million significantly disabled by it (Holbrook, Grazier, Kelsey, & Staufer, 1984).

More than 37 million Americans have arthritis, with 1 million new cases diagnosed each year (Lawrence et al., 1989).

More than 11 million Americans suffer from migraine headaches, with 4.5 million experiencing one or more attacks each month (Stewart, Lipton, Celentano, & Reed, 1991).

Social security disability pays out $110 billion annually, and workers' compensation pays out another $6 billion annually for pain-related disability (Osterweis et al., 1987).

In 1984, an estimated $7.2 billion was spent on compensation and medical payments for occupationally related back disorders alone (Frymoyer & Cats-Baril, 1987).

The cost of pain to American society in lost productivity is estimated to be $55 billion (Frymoyer & Cats-Baril, 1987).

$1 million is paid out each working day for compensable back injury alone (Antonakes, 1981).

A national survey conducted in 1985 revealed that over 4 billion days for all Americans and 550 million workdays for Americans in the workforce are lost each year due to pain (Taylor & Curran, 1985).

With such astronomical figures, it is all too easy to lose sight of the incalculable human suffering accompanying chronic pain for both the individual and his or her family.

The amount of attention devoted to pain has been disproportionately small given the magnitude of the problem. One difficulty with pain is that it is a symptom associated with many diseases and syndromes and may result from diverse sources of pathology or trauma. Moreover, pain may be reported even in the absence of identified physical pathology. For example, in up to 80% of cases the cause of back pain is un- known (Deyo, 1986), and in the case of the majority of persistent headaches there is no identifiable physical pathology. Persistent pain and recurrent episodes of acute pain are particularly frustrating problems in health care despite the tremendous advances in biomedical knowledge and technology.

Chronic pain, by definition, extends over long periods of time. The average duration of pain noted for patients treated at pain clinics exceeds 7 years, with durations of 20 to 30 years not uncommon. The emotional distress that is prevalent in a majority of chronic pain patients may be attributed to a variety of factors, including inadequate or maladaptive coping resources, iatrogenic complications, overuse of tranquilizers and narcotic medication, inability to work, financial difficulties, prolonged litigation, disruption of usual activities, inadequate social support, and sleep disturbance. Moreover, the experience of "medical limbo"—that is, the presence of a painful condition that eludes diagnosis and carries the implication of psychiatric causation, malingering, or an undiagnosed life-threatening disease—is itself the source of significant stress and can initiate psychological distress or aggravate a premorbid psychiatric condition.

In sum, chronic pain is a demoralizing situation that confronts the individual not only with the stress created by pain but with a cascade of ongoing stressors that compromise all aspects of the life of the sufferer. Living with chronic pain requires considerable emotional resilience and tends to deplete one's emotional reserves. It taxes not only the individual but also the capacity of family, friends, coworkers, and employers to provide support.

UNDERSTANDING PERSISTENT PAIN AND DISABILITY: ALTERNATIVE CONCEPTUALIZATIONS

Biomedical Model

The traditional biomedical view of pain dates back several hundred years and is based on a simple linear view that assumes a close correspondence between a biological state and symptom perception. From the traditional view, the extent of pain severity is presumed to be directly proportionate to the amount of tissue damage.

There are several perplexing features of persistent pain complaints that do not fit within the traditional biomedical model. For example,

1. Patients with objectively determined equivalent degrees and types of tissue pathology vary widely in their reports of pain severity.
2. Asymptomatic individuals often reveal objective radiographic evidence of structural abnormalities.

3. Conversely, patients with minimal objective physical pathology often complain of severe pain.

4. Surgical procedures designed to inhibit symptoms by severing neurological pathways believed to be subserving the reported pain may fail to alleviate pain.

5. Patients with objectively equivalent degrees of tissue pathology and treated with identical interventions respond in widely disparate ways.

6. There are only low to modest correlations among physical impairment, physical functioning, pain report, disability, and response to rehabilitation.

Psychogenic Model

As is frequently the case in medicine, when physical explanations prove inadequate to explain symptoms, psychological alternatives are entertained. If the pain reported is disproportionate to objectively determined physical pathology or if the complaint is recalcitrant to "appropriate" treatment, it is assumed that psychological factors must be involved, even if not causal. Several variants of psychogenic etiologic models have been proposed. For example, a model of a "pain-prone" personality originally proposed by Engel (1959) and extended and championed by Blumer and Heilbronn (1982) suggests that persistent pain complaints occur in individuals who are *predisposed* to experience pain because of family history and specific, long-standing personality characteristics. The American Psychiatric Association (1987) has created a psychiatric diagnosis, somatoform pain disorder, that is based on the absence of specific physical pathology or other psychiatric disorders in the presence of reports of pain.

These psychogenic views are posed as alternatives to purely physiological models. Put quite simply, dichotomous reasoning is invoked. If the patient's report of pain occurs in the absence of or is "disproportionate" to objective physical pathology, the pain reports have, ipso facto, a psychological basis.

Motivational View

A variation of the dichotomous organic versus psychogenic views is a conceptualization held by many third-party payers. They suggest that if there is insufficient physical pathology to justify the report of pain, the complaint is invalid, the result of symptom exaggeration or outright malingering. The assumption is that reports of pain without adequate biomedical evidence are motivated by financial gain. This belief has resulted in a number of attempts to "catch" malingerers using surreptitious observation methods and sophisticated biomechanical machines geared toward identifying inconsistencies in functional performance. It has been suggested by Koplow (1990) that fear of malingering drives the entire American social security disability system. There are, however, no studies that have demonstrated dramatic improvement in pain reports subsequent to the receiving of disability awards.

Operant Conditioning Model

As an alternative to the more traditional causal biomedical and psychogenic views of pain described above, a conceptualization based on operant conditioning (Fordyce, 1976) has been proposed and has received a good deal of attention. This model proposes that when an individual is exposed to a stimulus that causes tissue damage, the immediate response is withdrawal and attempts to escape from noxious sensations. This may be accomplished by avoiding activity believed to cause or exacerbate pain, seeking help to reduce symptoms, and so forth. These behaviors are observable and thus subject to the principles of operant conditioning. The operant conditioning model does not concern itself with the initial cause or report of pain. Rather, it considers pain to be an internal subjective experience that may be maintained even after the initial physical cause of pain has resolved. The operant conditioning model focuses on overt manifestations of pain and suffering— "pain behaviors"—such as limping, moaning, and avoiding activity. Emphasis is placed on the communicative function of these behaviors.

According to the operant conditioning model, positive reinforcement such as attention gained by avoidance of undesirable or feared activities may serve to maintain the pain behaviors even in the absence of noxious sensory input. In this way, respondent behaviors that occur following an acute injury may be maintained by reinforcement after any tissue damage has resolved.

A particularly important feature of conditioning models of pain is pain avoidance. Fordyce, Shelton, and Dundore (1982) hypothesized that avoidance behavior does not necessarily require intermittent sensory stimulation from the site of bodily damage, environmental reinforcement, or successful avoidance of aversive social activity may be sufficient to account for the maintenance of pro- tective movements. They suggested that protective behaviors could be maintained by *anticipation* of aversive consequences based on prior learning because ongoing occurrence of pain is a powerful reinforcer.

Operant factors can have a direct effect on pain. This can be observed when an individual is negatively reinforced for an abnormal gait pattern (e.g., limping). Eventually the maladaptive response patterns that develop may lead to nociception arising from myofascial syndromes that are a consequence of compensatory activity of muscle associated with the distorted gait.

The operant principle of stimulus generalization is also important in that patients may come to avoid more and more activities that they believe are similar to those that previously produced pain. Reduction of activity leads to greater physical deconditioning, more activities eliciting pain, and consequently even greater disability. Moreover, it is quite probable that the deconditioning resulting from reinforced *in*activity can result directly in increased noxious sensory input. Muscles that were involved in the original injury generally heal rapidly, but due to underuse they become weakened and subject to noxious stimulation when called into action.

Several studies have provided evidence that supports the underlying assumptions of the operant model. For example, Cairns and Pasino (1977) and Doleys, Crocker, and Patton (1982) demonstrated that pain behaviors could be decreased and "well behaviors" (e.g., activity) increased by verbal reinforcement. Block, Kremer, and Gaylor (1980) demonstrated that pain patients reported differential levels of pain in an experimental situation depending on whether they thought they were being observed by their spouses or ward clerks. The operant model has also generated what has proven to be an effective treatment for select samples of chronic pain patients (for a review, see Keefe & Williams, 1989).

The operant model has, however, received some criticism (Kotarba, 1983; Schmidt, Gierlings, & Peters, 1989; Turk & Flor, 1987; Turk & Matyas, 1992; Turk & Rudy, 1990). Table 4.2 summarizes the major concerns raised.

A fundamental problem with the operant approach is the emphasis on pain behavior rather than pain per se because behaviors that are observed are then used as the basis to infer something about the internal state of the individual—that the behaviors are communications of pain (Turk & Matyas, 1992). This is an indirect method, and there is no way of determining from the behavior whether it results from pain or from a structural abnormality. Limping, for example, is viewed from the operant perspective as a pain behavior, but this is an inference. It is quite possible that limping may result from physical pathology and have no direct association with pain, distress, or suffering.

TABLE 4.2   Concerns About the Operant Conditioning Perspective

1. Questionable validity of the pain behavior construct

2. Lack of specificity and overinclusiveness of the pain behavior construct

3. Assumed maladaptiveness and inappropriateness of the observed behaviors

4. Potential detrimental consequences of underreporting pain in certain circumstances

5. Patients' lack of acceptance of the operant treatment or dissatisfaction with treatment goals

6. Exclusive reliance on motor behavior

7. Problems of generalization and maintenance of behaviors following successful treatment

To underscore the distinction between pain behavior as a communication and as a result of physical perturbation, two recent studies reported by Keefe et al. (1990a, 1990b) can be considered. These investigators failed to find a reduction of pain behavior in osteoarthritic knee pain patients following a coping skills training program, but the program did produce a reduction in pain and disability. Alteration of specific behaviors that result from structural pathology is not likely to result from coping skills training. Thus calling these behaviors pain behaviors is open to question (Turk & Flor, 1987; Turk & Matyas, 1992).

A related concern about the pain behavior construct is captured by the emphasis on the communicative role of these behaviors. Recent attempts to operationalize the pain behavior construct have broadened to the point that any behavior can be subsumed under the rubric of pain behaviors. For example, Vlaeyen, Van Eek, Groenman, and Schuerman (1987) asked nurses to observe pain patients and to enumerate behaviors that they felt communicated pain. Some of the behaviors identified included the failure of the patient to take initiative, insomnia, falling asleep during the day, querulousness, and boredom. Philips and Jahanshahi (1986) created a "pain behavior checklist" that included "self-help" strategies and "distraction."

Boredom, querulousness, fatigue, distraction, or other self-help strategies can readily be imagined to have causes and effects other than communication of pain. Boredom can result from an unstimulating environment, querulousness may be a premorbid characteristic of the individual, fatigue may be a consequence of vigorous exercise, and lying down during the day may indicate compliance with recommendations to practice relaxation exercises or appropriate pacing behaviors. Importantly, distraction and other self-help strategies can clearly have adaptive functions above and beyond any communicative function.

Each of the views described above is based on the validity of a fundamental assumption: namely, a cause-effect relationship from pathology to pain report. If the physical basis is not identified or if the pain reported is deemed to be disproportionate to the extent of pathology identified, psychogenic, motivational, or operant factors are invoked.

Despite the apparent reasonableness of the dichotomous model—physical-psychological (motivational)—in chronic pain, there is a substantial literature that challenges its validity. Current clinical tests and sophisticated diagnostic imaging procedures often offer few clues to the precise source of pain. As noted earlier, in the case of chronic low back pain it has been reported that the cause of pain is unknown in up to 80% of patients. Similarly, in the case of persistent headaches the cause is rarely known despite numerous medical examinations and tests. Should it be assumed that the symptoms of the large majority of back pain sufferers and the millions of migraine sufferers are caused and maintained by psychological factors, or that these people are consciously fabricating?

Moreover, the clinical significance of identifiable structural abnormalities has been challenged by a number of studies. For example, several investigators have found that spinal radiographic abnormalities based on plain x-rays (Deyo, 1986), CAT scans (Wiesel, Tsourmas, & Feffer, 1984), and magnetic resonance imagining (MRI; Boden, Davis, Dina, Patronas, & Wiesel, 1990) believed to be associated with pain can be identified in a significant number of asymptomatic patients and therefore cannot be used to validate the legitimacy of pain reports.

SEARCH FOR ALTERNATIVE
CONCEPTUALIZATIONS OF CHRONIC PAIN

The inadequacies of the biomedical, psychogenic, operant, and motivational models have instigated attempts to reformulate thinking about the complex and subjective phenomenon of pain. As noted, health care providers, laypersons, and third-party payers have long considered pain as synonymous with physical pathology. It is important, however, to make a distinction between nociception (peripheral sensory stimulation that is capable of being perceived as pain), pain, suffering, and disability.

Nociception is associated with sensory stimuli that are *capable* of being perceived as painful. *Pain,* because it involves conscious awareness, selective abstraction, appraisal, ascribed meaning, and learning, is best viewed as a perceptual rather than a purely sensory process. *Suffering* includes interpersonal disruption, economic distress, occupational problems, psychological distress, and myriad other factors associated with the individual perception of the impact of pain on one's life. *Disability* is a complex phenomenon that incorporates the tissue pathology, the individual response to that physical insult, and environmental factors that can serve to maintain the disability and associated pain even after the initial physical cause has resolved. From this description, it should be apparent that there is no direct link between nociception and disability or pain and suffering. Rather, the extent of pain, suffering, and much of the disability observed is associated with an interpretive process.

As implied by the term *chronic,* it is important to recognize that chronic pain persists over an extended period of time. Thus pain has an impact on all domains of the individual sufferer's life: vocational, familial, social, and psychological as well as physical. Although in most cases biomedical factors appear to instigate initial reports of pain, over time psychosocial and behavioral factors may serve to exacerbate and maintain levels of pain, influence adjustment, and modulate disability. Moreover, as will be discussed below, secondary physical factors not present in acute pain may come to play an important role in chronic pain.

A MULTIDIMENSIONAL MODEL
OF PERSISTENT PAIN AND DISABILITY

The variability of patient responses to nociceptive stimuli and treatment is somewhat more understandable when we consider that pain is a personal experience influenced by attention, anxiety, prior learning history, the meaning of the situation, and other physiological and environmental factors, as well as physical pathology. Biomedical factors, in the majority of cases, appear to instigate the initial report of pain. Over time, however, psychosocial and behavioral factors may serve to maintain and exacerbate levels of pain, influence adjustment, and aggravate disability. Consequently, pain that persists over time should not be viewed as either solely physical or solely psychological. Rather, the experience of pain is maintained by an interde pendent set of biomedical, psychosocial, and behavioral factors. Although this view may appear intuitively obvious, it is of relatively recent origin.

Gate Control Model

Melzack and his colleagues (Melzack & Casey, 1968; Melzack & Wall, 1965) proposed the gate control theory of pain, emphasizing the modulation of pain by peripheral as well as central nervous system processes. This model provides a physiological basis for the role of psychological factors in chronic pain. Melzack and Casey (1968) differentiated three systems related to the processing of nociceptive stimulation—motivational-affective, cognitive-evaluative, and sensory-discriminative—all thought to contribute to the subjective experience of pain.

Although the physiological details of the gate control model have been challenged (Nathan, 1976; Price, 1987), it has had a substantial impact on basic research and in generating a wide range of treatment modalities. The gate control model was developed as a static, cross-sectional model; consequently, it has not incorporated the role of reinforcement and learning factors that are especially salient when one takes more dynamic, longitudinal view of pain.

Cognitive-Behavioral Perspective

As suggested by the preceding sections of this chapter, a comprehensive model of chronic pain, suffering, and disability needs to incorporate the mutual relationships among physical, psychosocial, and behavior factors and the changes that occur among these relationships over time (Flor, Birbaumer, & Turk, 1990; Turk & Rudy, 1991). A model that focuses on only one of these three core sets of factors will inevitably be incomplete.

If one accepts that chronic pain is a complex, subjective phenomenon that is uniquely experienced by each individual, then knowledge about idiosyncratic beliefs, appraisals, and coping repertoires become critical for optimal treatment planning and for accurately evaluating treatment outcome. This view is nicely demonstrated in a study reported by Reesor and Craig (1988). They showed that the primary difference between chronic low back pain patients who were referred because of the presence of many "medically incongruent" signs and those who did not display these signs was *maladaptive thoughts*. Interestingly, there were no significant differences between these groups on the number of surgeries, compensation, litigation status, or employment status. These maladaptive cognitive processes may amplify or distort patients' experiences of pain and suffering. Thus the cognitive activity of chronic pain patients may contribute to the exacerbation, attenuation, or maintenance of pain, pain behavior, affective distress, and dysfunctional adjustment to chronic pain (Turk & Rudy, 1986, 1992).

Biomedical factors that may have initiated the original report of pain play less and less of a role in disability over time, although secondary problems associated with deconditioning may exacerbate and serve to maintain the problem. Inactivity leads to increased focus on and preoccupation with the body and pain, and these cognitive-attentional changes increase the likelihood of misinterpreting symptoms, overemphasizing symptoms, and perceiving oneself as disabled. Reduction of activity, fear of reinjury, pain, loss of compensation, and an environment that perhaps unwittingly supports the "pain patient role" can impede alleviation of pain, successful rehabilitation, reduction of disability, and improvement in adjustment. As we shall see, cognitive factors may not only affect patients' behavior and indirectly their pain but actually have a direct effect on physiological factors believed to be associated with the experience of pain.

The most important focus of the cognitive-behavioral model, as of the operant model, is the patient, rather than symptoms and pathophysiology. Unlike the operant model, however, the cognitive-behavioral model places a great deal of emphasis on the patient's thoughts and feelings because these will influence behavior. Conversely, the cognitive-behavioral model acknowledges that environmental factors can also influence behavior and that behavior can affect the patient's thoughts and feelings. Bandura (1978) referred to this as a process of *reciprocal determinism*. From this perspective, assessment of and consequently treatment of the patient with persistent pain requires a strategy broader than those based on the previous dichotomous models described—a strategy that examines and addresses the entire range of psychosocial and behavioral factors in addition to biomedical ones (Turk & Rudy, 1989, 1991).

Individuals respond to medical conditions in part on the basis of their subjective representations of illness and symptoms (schemas). When confronted with new stimuli, the individual engages in a "meaning analysis" that is guided by the schemas that best match the attributes of the stimulus (Cioffi, 1991). It is on the basis of patients' idiosyncratic schemas that incoming stimuli are interpreted, labeled, and acted on.

People build fairly elaborate representations of their physical state, and these representations provide the basis for action plans and coping (Turk, Rudy, & Salovey, 1986). Beliefs about the meaning of pain and one's ability to function despite discomfort are important aspects of cognitive schemas about pain (Slater, Hall, Atkinson, & Garfin, 1991). These representations are used to construct causal, covariational, and consequential information from one's symptoms. For example, a cognitive schema that one has a very serious, debilitating condition, that disability is a necessary aspect of pain, that activity is dangerous, and that pain is an acceptable excuse for neglecting responsibilities is likely to result in maladaptive responses (Schwartz, DeGood, & Shutty, 1985; Williams & Thorn, 1989). Similarly, if patients believe they have a serious condition that makes them quite fragile and puts them at high risk for reinjury, they may fear engaging in physical activities (Philips, 1987a). Through a process of stimulus generalization, patients may avoid more and more activities, becoming more physically deconditioned and more disabled.

Patients' beliefs, appraisals, and expectations about their pain, their ability to cope, their social supports, their disorder, the medicolegal system, the health care system, and their employers are all important in that these may facilitate or disrupt patients' sense of control and ability to manage pain. These factors also influence patients' investment in treatment, acceptance of responsibility, perceptions of disability, adherence to treatment recommendations, support from significant others, expectancies for treatment, and acceptance of treatment rationale (Slater et al., 1991; Turk & Rudy, 1991).

Cognitive interpretations also will affect how patients present symptoms to significant others, including health care providers and employers. Overt communication of pain, suffering, and distress will enlist responses that may reinforce the pain behaviors (overt communications of pain such as limping, moaning, ambulating in a guarded or distorted fashion) and impressions about the seriousness, severity, and uncontrollability of the pain. That is, complaints of pain may lead physicians to prescribe more potent medications, order additional diagnostic tests, and in some cases perform surgery. Family members may express sympathy, excuse the patient from usual responsibilities, and encourage passivity, thereby fostering further physical deconditioning. It should be obvious that the cognitive-behavioral perspective integrates the operant conditioning emphasis on external reinforcement and corresponding view of learned fear and avoidance within the framework of information processing.

From the cognitive-behavioral perspective, people with chronic pain, like all individuals, are active processors of information. They have negative expectations about their own ability and responsibility to exert any control over their pain. Moreover, they often view themselves as helpless. Such negative, maladaptive appraisals about their conditions, situations, and personal efficacy in controlling their pain and problems associated with pain serve to reinforce their experience of demoralization, inactivity, and overreaction to nociceptive stimulation. Such cognitive appraisals are posed as having an effect on behavior, leading to reduced effort, reduced perseverance in the face of difficulty and activity, and increased psychological distress.

The specific thoughts and feelings that patients experience prior to exacerbations of pain, during an exacerbation or intense episode of pain, and following a pain episode can greatly influence the experience of pain and subsequent pain episodes. Moreover, the methods patients use to control their emotional arousal and symptoms have been shown to be important predictors of both cognitive and behavioral responses (Flor & Turk, 1988; Reesor & Craig, 1988). Several interrelated sets of cognitive variables have been examined, including thoughts about the controllability of pain, attributions about one's own ability to use specific pain coping responses, expectations concerning the possible outcomes of various coping efforts, and common erroneous beliefs about pain and disability. Although these different cognitive constructs are highly related, they will be discussed separately for ease of presentation.

Direct Effects of Psychological Factors on Pain Experience and Disability

Psychological factors may act directly on pain and disability by reducing physical activity and consequently reducing muscle flexibility, strength, tone, and endurance. Fear of reinjury, fear of loss of disability compensation, and job dissatisfaction can also influence return to work.

Beliefs About Pain

Clinicians working with chronic pain patients are aware that patients having similar pain histories and reports of pain may differ greatly in their beliefs about their pain. The cognitive-behavioral perspective suggests that behavior and emotions are influenced by interpretations of events rather than solely by objective characteristics of the events themselves. Thus when pain is interpreted as signifying ongoing tissue damage and consequently greater disability and incapacity, it is likely to produce considerably more suffering and behavioral dysfunction than when it is viewed as the result of a stable problem that may improve, although the amount of nociceptive input in the two cases may be equivalent.

Certain beliefs may lead to maladaptive coping, increased suffering, and greater disability. Patients who believe their pain is likely to persist may be quite passive in their coping efforts and fail to make use of cognitive strategies or behavioral strategies to cope with pain. Patients who consider their pain to be an unexplainable mystery may negatively evaluate their own abilities to control or decrease pain and may be less likely to rate their coping strategies as effective in controlling and decreasing pain (Williams & Keefe, 1991; Williams & Thorn, 1989). A person's cognitions (beliefs, appraisals, expectancies) regarding the consequences of an event and his or her ability to influence them or cope with them are hypothesized to affect functioning in two ways. They may have a direct influence on mood and an indirect influence through their impact on coping efforts.

In a set of studies, Schmidt (1985a, 1985b) found evidence that low back pain patients demonstrated poor behavioral persistence in various exercise tasks and that their performance on these tasks was independent of any physical parameters or actual self-reports of pain. These patients appeared to have a negative view of their abilities and expected increased pain if they performed physical exercises. Thus the rationale for their avoidance of exercise was not the presence of pain but their *anticipation* of heightened pain. The physical arousal that accompanied anticipation might exacerbate pain and reinforce patients' beliefs regarding the pervasiveness of their disability. These results are consistent with the hypothesis of Fordyce et al. (1982) cited earlier. Schmidt postulated that patients' negative perceptions of their capabilities for physical performance produced a vicious circle, with the failure to perform activities reinforcing the perception of helplessness and incapacity.

The persistence of avoidance of specific activities will reduce disconfirmations that are followed by corrected predictions (Rachman & Arntz, 1991). The prediction of pain promotes pain avoidance behavior, and overpredictions of pain promote excessive avoidance behavior, as demonstrated in the Schmidt (1985a, 1985b) studies. Insofar as pain avoidance succeeds in preserving the overpredictions from repeated disconfirmation, the predictions will continue unchanged (Rachman & Lopatka, 1988). By contrast, repeatedly engaging in behavior that produces significantly less pain than was predicted will be followed by adjustments in subsequent predictions, which also become more accurate. These increasingly accurate predictions of pain will be followed by increasingly appropriate avoidance behavior, up to and including elimination of all avoidance if that is appropriate. These observations add support to the importance of physical therapy, with patients progressively increasing their activity levels despite fear of injury and discomfort associated with renewed use of deconditioned muscles.

Chronic pain patients tend to believe that they have limited ability to exert control over their pain. Such negative, maladaptive appraisals about the situation and personal efficacy may reinforce the experience of demoralization, inactivity, and overreaction to nociceptive stimulation commonly observed in chronic pain patients (Biederman, McGhie, Monga, & Shanks, 1987).

A cognitive schema that views disability as a necessary aspect of pain, activity despite pain as dangerous, and pain as an acceptable excuse for neglecting responsibilities is likely to increase disability (Smith, Follick, Ahern, & Adams, 1986). In support of the importance of patients' cognitive schemas, Slater et al. (1991) reported that patients' beliefs about their pain and disability were significantly related to actual measures of disability but not to physicians' ratings of disease severity.

In addition to beliefs about capabilities to function despite pain, beliefs about pain per se appear to be important for understanding response to treatment, compliance, and disability. For example, Schwartz et al. (1985) presented patients with information about the role of cognitive, affective, and behavioral factors in the rehabilitation process. They found that patients who rated the information as applicable to their pain condition had much better treatment outcomes. Those who disagreed with the concepts presented were found at follow-up to have higher levels of pain, lower levels of activity, and a high degree of dissatisfaction.

Schwartz et al. (1985) suggested that the psychological dimension that appears most relevant to treatment planning is the patients' ability and willingness to understand and accept a cognitive model of chronic pain, along with its implications for rehabilitation. The results of several studies suggest that when successful rehabilitation occurs, there is an important cognitive shift from beliefs about helplessness and passivity to beliefs about resourcefulness and ability to function regardless of pain.

In an observation consistent with the central role of a cognitive shift in rehabilitation, Herman and Baptiste (1981) noted that successes and failures in their treatment program could be distinguished most prominently on the basis of changed versus unchanged thought patterns relative to the prospect of living a useful life despite pain. Williams and Thorn (1989) found that chronic pain patients who believed that their pain was an "unexplained mystery" reported high levels of psychological distress and pain and also showed poorer treatment compliance than patients who believed that they understood their pain.

In an innovative process study designed to evaluate the direct association between patients' beliefs and pain symptoms, Newton and Barbaree (1987) used a modified thought-sampling procedure to evaluate the nature of patients' thoughts during and immediately following headache both before and after treatment. Results indicated significant changes in certain aspects of headache-related thinking in the treated groups compared to the control group. Reduction in negative appraisal and increase in positive appraisal ("It's getting worse," "There is nothing I can do") revealed a significant shift in the thoughts of treated subjects in comparison with untreated, indicating that treated subjects were evaluating headaches in a more positive fashion. Treated patients reported experiencing significantly fewer headache days per week and lower intensity of pain than untreated controls. Correlational analyses suggested that complaints of more intense pain were associated with more negative appraisals of headache episodes. In similar results reported by Flor and Turk (1988), back pain and rheumatoid arthritis patients' negative thoughts predicted pain, disability, and physician visits. Newton and Barbaree noted that patients who reported the largest positive shift in appraisal also reported the greatest reduction in headache intensity.

The results of the Newton and Barbaree (1987) study support the argument that changes in cognitive reactions to headache may underlie headache improvement (see also Blanchard, 1987; Holroyd & Andrasik, 1982). There appears to be strong evidence pointing toward a reduction in negative appraisal as representing the potential change mechanism in many pain treatment outcome studies. In considering the efficacy of biofeedback for back pain patients, Nouwen and Solinger (1979) concluded that

> simultaneous accomplishment of muscle tension reduction and lowering reported pain convinced patients that muscle tension, and subsequently pain, could be controlled. . . . As self-control could not be demonstrated in most

patients, it seems plausible that the feeling of self-control, rather than actual control of physiological functions or events, is crucial for further reductions. (p. 110)

In other words, it appears that the extent to which voluntary control over muscles has been achieved dictates the outcome, which is not, however, necessarily accompanied by lasting reductions in muscular reactivity.

Blanchard (1987), much like Nouwen and Solinger (1976), speculated that for headache patients the maintenance of treatment effects endures despite almost universal cessation of regular home practice of biofeedback because the self-perpetuating cycle of chronic headache has been broken. The experience of headache serves as a stressor to cause, partially, a future headache. It may also serve to maintain improper analgesic medication consumption, the cessation of which can also lead to "rebound headache." By the end of treatment, when the patient has experienced noticeable headache relief, it is as if the patient redefines him- or herself as someone able to cope with headaches. As a consequence, one source of stress is removed, and the patient copes with recurrences more adaptively.

Clearly, it appears essential for patients with chronic pain to develop adaptive beliefs about the relationships among impairment, pain, suffering, and disability and to deemphasize the role of experienced pain in their regulation of functioning. In fact, results from numerous treatment outcome studies have shown that changes in pain level do not parallel changes in other variables of interest, including activity level, medication use, return to work, rated ability to cope with pain, and pursuit of further treatment (e.g., see a meta-analysis reported by Flor, Fydrich, & Turk, 1992).

Self-Efficacy

A central cognitive construct of particular importance seems to be self-efficacy (Bandura, 1977): individuals' perception of their ability to exert any control over their plight generally and their pain more specifically. A self-efficacy expectation is defined as a personal conviction that one can successfully execute a course of action (perform required behaviors) to produce a desired outcome in a given situation.

Bandura (1977) suggested that given sufficient motivation to engage in a behavior, an individual's self-efficacy beliefs determine the choice of activities that the individual will initiate, the amount of effort that will be expended, and how long the individual will persist in the face of obstacles and aversive experiences. Efficacy judgments are based on the following four sources of information regarding one's capabilities, in descending order of impact: (a) one's own past performance at the task or similar tasks; (b) the performance accomplishments of others who are perceived to be similar to oneself; (c) verbal persuasion by others that one is capable; and (d) perception of one's own state of physiological arousal, which is in turn partly determined by prior efficacy estimation. Performance mastery experience can be created by encouraging patients to undertake subtasks that are increasingly difficult or close to the desired behavioral repertoire. From this perspective, the occurrence of coping behaviors is conceptualized as being mediated by the individual's beliefs that situational demands do not exceed his or her coping resources.

Converging lines of evidence from investigations of both laboratory and clinical pain indicate that perceived self-efficacy operates as an important cognitive factor in the control of pain (e.g., Bandura, O'Leary, Taylor, Gauthier, & Gossard, 1987; Holroyd et al., 1984; Lorig, Chastain, Ung, Shoor, & Holman, 1989; Shoor & Holman, 1984), adaptive psychological functioning (e.g., Affleck, Tennen, Pfeiffer, & Fifield, 1987; Keefe et al., 1987; Lorig et al., 1989; Rosensteil & Keefe, 1983; Spinhoven, Ter Kuile, Linssen, & Gazendam, 1989; Turner & Clancy, 1986), disability (e.g., Dolce, Crocker, & Doleys, 1986; Lorig et al., 1989), impairment (e.g., Lorig et al., 1989), and treatment outcome (e.g., O'Leary, Shoor, Lorig, & Holman, 1988; Philips, 1987b). The greatest amount of attention has been given to the importance of self-efficacy beliefs in headache, back pain, and rheumatoid arthritis patients. Thus the role of self-efficacy in several illustrative studies for these three populations will be considered.

Headache.   Holroyd et al. (1984) and Gauthier, Cote, and Drolet (1985) both reported that self-efficacy expectancies are predictive of response by headache patients to biofeedback treatment. In the Holroyd et al. study, recurrent tension headache patients were randomly assigned to four electromyographic (EMG) biofeedback conditions. Half of those patients received feedback for reducing frontalis EMG levels, and half received feedback for increasing EMG levels. All subjects, however, were told that they were learning to decrease muscle tension. In addition, half of the subjects in each of these groups received bogus feedback indicating high levels of success, and half received feedback reflecting only minor success.

Despite the direction of the EMG feedback received, patients given high success feedback reported significantly higher self-efficacy ratings and significantly greater reductions in headache activity than did those who received the lower success information. Furthermore, higher self-efficacy ratings were observed to correlate significantly with larger reductions in headache activity scores, whereas actual EMG levels failed to be associated with headache activity. Similar results were reported by Gauthier et al. (1985) with migraine headache patients. Again, self-efficacy expectancies were found to be significant predictors of treatment, but there was no association between psychophysiological change and headache relief.

Chronic Back Pain.   Research by Dolce and colleagues (Dolce, Crocker, Molettcire, & Doleys, 1986) has focused on the important associations among concern about the performance of exercises, actual performance of exercise, and self-efficacy in back pain patients. Exercise quotas were shown to increase levels of previously avoided exercises. In addition, when quotas were implemented, self-efficacy ratings were observed to increase and patients' ratings of concern to diminish. Self-efficacy expectancies were found to parallel closely increases in exercise levels during treatment. The high degree of association observed between self-efficacy ratings and actual exercise levels provides strong support for the self-efficacy theory postulate that success experiences are effective means of increasing self-efficacy expectancies.

In another study, Dolce et al. (1986) observed that chronic pain patients' post-treatment self-efficacy ratings correlated significantly with exercise levels, reduction in medication use, and work status at follow-up periods ranging from 6 to 12 months. Dolce et al. suggested that if self-efficacy expectancies are related to improvement, then patients who do not increase their perceptions of self-efficacy following treatment, despite other post-treatment advances, are likely candidates for relapse.

Council, Ahern, Follick, and Kline (1988) reported similar results to those of Dolce et al. (1986). They noted that actual physical performance of back pain patients was best predicted by self-efficacy ratings, which appeared to be determined by pain response expectancies. These results suggest that daily pain experience determines pain response expectancies for specific movements. Furthermore, pain response expectancies appear to influence performance and associated pain behavior through their effects on efficacy expectancies. These findings also indicate that pain response expectancies associated with specific movements are based on generalized expectancies drawn from daily experiences and suggest that chronic pain patients have well-established ideas that are incorporated in their schemas as to how much pain they will experience in different situations. As noted earlier, anticipation of pain can greatly inhibit actual behavioral performance and thereby contribute to disability.

Rheumatoid Arthritis (RA).   Lorig et al. (1989) found that pretreatment scores on self-efficacy for pain functioning and on symptoms were associated negatively with pain, disability, and depression for RA patients at a 4-month follow-up. Increases in self-efficacy beliefs also correlated with improvement in pain, disability, and depression.

Perceptions of helplessness are similar to those of low self-efficacy. Several authors have suggested that the seemingly unpredictable and uncontrollable waxing and waning of physical symptomatology of some chronic pain conditions (i.e., RA) and its impact on functional capabilities may induce feelings of helplessness, with the associated behavioral and emotional consequences (Bradley, 1985; Nicassio, Wallston, Callahan, Herbert, & Pincus, 1985).

Several studies support the association of helplessness, impairment, and disability. Plant, Button, and Cawley (1984) found that functional impairment of RA patients was associated with negative feelings and helplessness. These results are consistent with those cited earlier of Newton and Barbaree (1987) for headache patients and Flor and Turk (1988) for back pain and RA patients.

In a longitudinal study, Stein and his colleagues (Stein, Wallston, & Nicassio, 1988; Stein, Wallston, Nicassio, & Castner, 1988) found that changes in helplessness across a period of 2 years were associated with changes in depression, pain, use of passive coping strategies, and global health status. They also reported that initial levels of hopelessness predicted subsequent depression, passive coping, global health rating, pain severity, psychosocial impairments, and arthritis symptoms severity up to 2 years later.

The studies reviewed all suggest that self-efficacy plays a particularly important role in perception of and adjustment to pain and subsequent disability. What are the mechanisms that account for the observed association between self-efficacy and behavioral outcome? Cioffi (1991) suggested that at least four psychological processes could be responsible: (a) As perceived self-efficacy decreases anxiety and its concomitant physiological arousal, the patient may approach the task with less potentially distressing physical information to begin with; (b) the efficacious person is able willfully to distract attention from potentially threatening physiological sensations; (c) the efficacious person perceives and is distressed by physical sensations but simply persists in the face of them (such item), and (d) physical sensations are neither ignored nor necessarily distressing but rather are relatively free to take on a broad distribution of meanings (changing of interpretations).

There are several ways in which perceived coping efficacy can bring relief from pain. People who believe they can alleviate suffering are likely to mobilize whatever ameliorative skills they have learned and to persevere in their efforts. Those who doubt their coping efficacy are likely to give up readily in the absence of quick results. A sense of coping efficacy also reduces distressing anticipations that create aversive physiological arousal and bodily tension, which only exacerbate pain sensation and discomfort. Bandura (1977) further suggested that the techniques that enhance mastery experiences the most will be the most powerful tools for bringing about behavior change. He proposed that cognitive variables are the primary determinants of behavior but that these variables are most effectively influenced by performance accomplishments. The research on headache, back pain, and RA cited above appears to support Bandura's prediction.

Cognitive Errors

In addition to specific efficacy beliefs, a number of investigators have suggested that a common set of cognitive errors will affect perceptions of pain and disability. A cognitive error may be defined as a negatively distorted belief about oneself or one's situation.

Lefebvre (1981) developed a Cognitive Errors Questionnaire (CEQ) to assess cognitive distortion in back pain patients. Lefebvre found that chronic low back pain patients were particularly prone to cognitive errors such as "catastrophizing" (self-statements, thoughts, and images anticipating negative outcomes or aversive aspects of an experience or misinterpreting the outcome of an event as extremely negative; characterized by lack of confidence and control and an expectation of negative outcome); "overgeneralization" (assuming that the outcome of one event necessarily applies to the outcome of future or similar events); "personalization" (interpreting negative events as reflecting personal meaning or responsibility); and "selective abstraction" (selectively attending to negative aspects of one's experience).

Dufton (1989) reported that persons experiencing chronic pain had a tendency to make cognitive errors related to the emotional difficulties associated with living with pain rather than to the pain intensity alone and that those who made such errors were more depressed.

As was the case with self-efficacy, specific cognitive errors and distortions have been linked consistently to depression (e.g., Gil, Williams, Keefe, & Beckham, 1990; Lefebvre, 1981; Slater et al., 1991; Smith, Aberger, Follick, & Ahern, 1986), self-reported pain severity (e.g., Gil et al., 1990; Flor & Turk, 1988; Keefe & Williams, 1990), and disability (e.g., Flor & Turk, 1988; Smith, Follick, et al., 1986) in chronic pain patients. Such negative thoughts (a) predict long-term adjustment to chronic pain, (b) may mediate a portion of the relationship between disease severity and adjustment, and (c) make a unique contribution (over and above other cognitive factors) to the prediction of adjustment (Smith, Peck, & Ward, 1990).

Catastrophizing.   Catastrophizing appears to be a particularly potent way of thinking that greatly influences pain and disability. Several lines of research, including experimental laboratory studies, of acute pain with normal volunteers and field studies with patients suffering clinical pain, have indicated that "catastrophizing"—extremely negative thoughts about one's plight—and adaptive coping strategies are important in determining one's reaction to pain. Two findings from laboratory studies are particularly important. Individuals who spontaneously used less catastrophizing self-statements and/or more adaptive coping strategies rated experimentally induced pain as lower and tolerated painful stimuli longer than those who indicated that they engaged in more catastrophizing thoughts (Heyneman, Fremouw, Gano, Kirkland, & Heiden, 1990; Spanos, Horton, & Chaves, 1975).

Individuals who spontaneously used less catastrophizing self-statements reported more pain in several clinical studies (Keefe & Williams, 1990; Martin, Nathan, Milech, & Van Keppel, 1989; Romano, Turner, Syrjala, & Levy, 1987; Turner & Clancy, 1986). Rosensteil and Keefe (1983) found that cognitive coping and suppression (adaptive strategies) and catastrophizing were predictive of adjustment.

Turner and Clancy (1986) showed that during cognitive-behavioral treatment, reductions in catastrophizing were significantly related to reductions in pain tolerance and physical impairment. They reported that the simple correlation between catastrophizing and psychosocial impairment on the

Sickness Impact Profile was .48. They showed that reduction of catastrophizing following cognitive-behavioral treatment related to reduction of pain intensity and physical impairment. Flor and Turk (1988) found that in low back pain sufferers and arthritis patients, between 32% and 60% of the variance in pain and disability respectively was accounted for by cognitive factors labeled as *catastrophizing, helplessness, coping,* and *resourcefulness.* In both the low back pain and the arthritis groups, the cognitive variables of catastrophizing and helplessness had substantially more explanatory power than did disease variables and measures of impairment.

Some concerns with viewing catastrophizing as an independent cognitive variable have recently been raised. Sullivan and D'Eon (1990) reported a statistically significant association between catastrophizing and depression. This suggests that catastrophizing indexes the cognitive and affective components of dysphoria rather than measuring a distinct aspect of pain-related cognition. In other words, the catastrophizing is conceptually and operationally confounded with depression. The authors suggested that depression might entirely explain the relationship between the use of coping strategies and disability. Additional research is needed to address directly the links between catastrophizing and depression.

Coping Strategies

Self-regulation of pain and its impact depends on the individual's specific ways of dealing with pain, adjusting to pain, and reducing or minimizing pain and distress caused by pain: that is, their coping strategies. Coping is assumed to be manifested by spontaneously employed purposeful and intentional acts and can be assessed in terms of overt and covert behaviors. Overt behavioral coping strategies include rest, medication, and the use of relaxation. Covert coping strategies include various means of distracting oneself from pain, reassuring oneself that the pain will diminish, seeking information, and problem solving. Coping strategies are thought to alter both the perception of intensity of pain and one's ability to manage or tolerate pain and to continue everyday activities (Turk, Meichenbaum, & Genest, 1983).

Studies have found active coping strategies (efforts to function despite pain, e.g., by engaging in activity, or to distract oneself from pain, e.g., by ignoring it) to be associated with adaptive functioning, and passive coping strategies (depending on others for help in pain control and restricting activities) to be related to greater pain and depression (Brown & Nicassio,

1987; Brown, Nicassio, & Wallston, 1989; Lawson, Reesor, Keefe, & Turner, 1990). However, beyond this, there is no evidence supporting the greater effectiveness of any one active coping strategy compared to any other (Fernandez & Turk, 1989). It seems likely that different strategies will be more effective than others for some individuals at some specific times but not necessarily for all individuals all of the time.

In a number of studies it has been demonstrated that when patients are instructed in the use of adaptive coping strategies, their ratings of intensity of pain decrease and their tolerance of pain increases (for a review, see Fernandez & Turk, 1989). The most important factor in poor coping appears to be the presence of catastrophizing rather than differences in the nature of specific adaptive coping strategies (e.g., Heyneman et al., 1990; Martin et al., 1989). Turk et al. (1983) concluded that "what appears to distinguish low from high pain tolerant individuals in their cognitive processing, catastrophizing thoughts and feelings that precede, accompany, and follow aversive stimulation" (p. 197).

Direct Effects of Psychological Factors on Physiology

Up to this point, the discussion of cognitive factors in pain and disability has focused on the impact of various cognitive variables on reports of pain and responses to pain and disability. Several studies have suggested that cognitive factors may actually have a direct effect on physiological parameters associated more with the production or exacerbation of nociception. Psychological factors, through cognitive interpretations and affective arousal, may have a direct effect on physiology by increasing or decreasing autonomic sympathetic nervous system arousal (Bandura, Taylor, Williams, Meffort, & Barchas, 1985), endogenous opioid (endorphins) production (Bandura et al., 1987), and levels of muscle tension (Flor, Turk, & Birbaumer, 1985; Rudy, 1990).

Effects of Thoughts on Sympathetic Arousal

Circumstances that are appraised as potentially threatening to safety or comfort are likely to generate strong physiological reactions. For example, Rimm and Litvak (1969) demonstrated that subjects exhibit physiological arousal when they merely think about or imagine a painful stimulus. Barber and Hahn (1962) showed that subjects' self-reported discomfort and physiological responses (frontalis electromyographic activity [EMG], heart rate, skin conductance) were similar when they imagined taking part in a cold pressor test (a laboratory pain-induction task) as compared to actually participating in it. In patients suffering from recurrent migraine headaches, Jamner and Tursky (1987) observed increase in skin conductance related to the processing of words describing migraine headaches.

Chronic increases in sympathetic nervous system activation known as increased skeletal muscle tone may set the stage for hyperactive muscle contraction and possibly for the persistence of a contraction following conscious muscle activation. Excessive sympathetic arousal and maladaptive behaviors are viewed as the immediate precursors of muscle hypertonicity, hyperactivity, and persistence. These in turn are the proximate causes of chronic muscle spasm and pain. It is not unusual for people in pain to exaggerate or amplify the significance of their problem and needlessly "turn on" their sympathetic nervous system (Ciccone & Grzesiak, 1984). In this way, cognitive processes may influence sympathetic arousal and thereby predispose the individual to further injury or otherwise complicate the process of recovery.

Several studies support the direct effect of cognitive factors on muscle tension. For example, Flor et al. (1985) demonstrated that for back pain patients, discussing stressful events and pain produced elevated levels of EMG activity localized to the site of pain. The extent of abnormal muscular reactivity was best predicted by depression and cognitive coping style rather than by pain demographic variables (e.g., number of surgeries or duration of pain). Rudy (1990) reported similar results for patients with temporomandibular disorders. For this group, imagery reconstruction of episodes and pain produced elevated muscle tension in the facial muscles.

Although "causal," pain-eliciting psychophysiological mechanisms (e.g., elevated EMG) may exist, only one recent longitudinal study has been reported that directly tested the causal relationship. It found no consistent muscle hyperactivity during headache attacks compared to a pain-free baseline, no differences in EMG activity between tension-type headache patients and controls, and no covarying of EMG with stress, negative affect, or pain (Hatch et al., 1991). Moreover, the natural evolution and course of many chronic pain syndromes is unknown. At present, it is probably more appropriate to refer to abnormal psychophysiological patterns as antecedents of chronic pain states or to view them as consequences of chronic pain that subsequently maintain or exacerbate the symptoms rather than to assign them any etiological significance.

Effects of Thinking on Biochemistry

Bandura et al. (1987) examined the role of central opioid activity in cognitive control of pain. They provided 30 minutes of training in cognitive control of pain, in which subjects received instructions and practice in using different cognitive strategies for alleviating pain, including attention diversion from pain sensations to other matters, vivification of engrossing imagery, dissociation of the limb in pain from the rest of the body, transformation of pain to nonpain sensations, and self-encouragement of coping efforts. They demonstrated (a) that self-efficacy increased with cognitive training, (b) that self-efficacy predicted pain tolerance, and (c) that naloxone blocked the effects of cognitive control. The latter result directly implicates the effects of thoughts on the endogenous opioids.

O'Leary et al. (1988) provided cognitive-behavioral stress management treatment to RA patients. RA is an autoimmune disease that may result from impaired functioning of the suppressor T-cell system. Degree of self-efficacy (expectations about the ability to control pain and disability) enhancement was correlated with treatment effectiveness. Those with higher self-efficacy and greater self-efficacy enhancement displayed greater numbers of suppressor T-cells (a direct effect of self-efficacy on physiology). Significant effects were also obtained for self-efficacy, pain, and joint impairment. Increased self-efficacy for functioning was associated with decreased disability and joint impairment.

Much more research is required before there can be confidence in the direct role of thoughts on physical mechanisms inducing nociception. However, the large body of research in psychoneuroimmunology attests to the direct role of psychological factors on the body's immune system. On the basis of the results of the handful of studies available, it would seem that further research examining the direct effects of thoughts on the physiology known to be associated with pain—namely, sympathetic nervous system activity and the endorphins—would be a fruitful endeavor.

CONCLUSION

The studies reviewed above provide a good deal of support for the cognitive-behavioral alternative model for understanding chronic pain and disability. Many cognitive variables and constructs appear to have an indirect effect on nociception as well as pain and disability. A limited number of studies have suggested that there may also be a direct effect of patients' thoughts on the physiology associated with nociception.

Patients come to treatment with diverse sets of attitudes, beliefs, and expectancies. What the research reviewed suggests is the importance of addressing these subjective factors as they are likely to influence patients' self-presentation and responses to treatments offered. Viewing all patients with the same medical diagnosis as similar is likely to prove unsatisfactory. It would seem prudent (a) to attempt to identify pain patients' idiosyncratic beliefs, (b) to address beliefs that are inaccurate and potentially maladaptive, and (c) to match coping strategies with patients' individual differences.

A word of caution seems appropriate. There has been a proliferation of cognitive measures. There seems to be an implicit assumption that what may be related measures are actually assessing different constructs. This assumption may not be warranted. To date, no studies have examined the overlap that is quite likely. No research has yet demonstrated the effectiveness of matching treatments to patient characteristics (Turk, 1990). What is greatly needed are studies that identify groups of patients who differ on specific cognitive measures and that evaluate interventions customized to these differences. For example, studies might directly test the effectiveness of the following interventions: (a) providing patients who believe their pain is a mystery with sound objective information about the nature of their pain and about coping skills that have worked well for others and (b) teaching patients who believe that their pain is enduring that different coping strategies can be used as a means of managing flare-ups. In both these instances, the most effective way to accomplish behavioral changes would consist of verbal persuasion and actual performance accomplishment, with the latter being most likely to bring about lasting behavioral change. The research reviewed in this chapter would suggest that such approaches would be more effective than providing all patients with standard treatment packages. Whether this is the case remains to be demonstrated.

REFERENCES

Affleck, G., Tennen, H., Pfeiffer, C., & Fifield, J. (1987). Appraisals of control and predictability in adapting to chronic disease. *Journal of Personality and Social Psychology, 53,* 273-279.

American Psychiatric Association. (1987). *Diagnostic and statistical manual* (3rd ed., Rev.). Washington, DC: Author.

Antonakes, J. A. (1981). Claims cost of back pain. *Best's Review, 9,* 36.

Bandura, A. (1977). Self-efficacy: Toward a unifying theory of behavior change. *Psychological Review, 84,* 191-215.

Bandura, A. (1978). The self-system in reciprocal determinism. *American Psychologist, 33,* 344-359.

Bandura, A., O'Leary, A., Taylor, C. B., Gauthier, J., & Gossard, D. (1987). Perceived self-efficacy and pain control: Opioid and nonopioid mechanisms. *Journal of Personality and Social Psychology, 53,* 563-571.

Bandura, A., Taylor, C. B., Williams, S. L., Meffort, I. N., & Barchas, J. D. (1985). Catecholamine secretion as a function of perceived coping self-efficacy. *Journal of Consulting and Clinical Psychology, 53,* 406-414.

Barber, T., & Hahn, K. W. (1962). Physiological and subjective responses to pain producing stimulation under hypnotically-suggested and waking-imagined "analgesia." *Journal of Abnormal and Social Psychology, 65,* 411-418.

Biederman, H. J., McGhie, A., Monga, T. N., & Shanks, G. L. (1987). Perceived and actual control in EMG treatment of back pain. *Behaviour Research and Therapy, 25,* 137-147.

Blanchard, E. B. (1987). Long-term effects of behavioral treatment of chronic headache. *Behavior Therapy, 18,* 375-385.

Block, A. R., Kremer, E. F., & Gaylor, M. (1980). Behavioral treatment of chronic pain: Variables affecting treatment efficacy. *Pain, 8,* 367-375.

Blumer, D., & Heilbronn, M. (1982). Chronic pain as a variant of depressive disease: The pain-prone disorder. *Journal of Nervous and Mental Disease, 170,* 381-406.

Boden, S. D., Davis, D. O., Dina, T. S., Patronas, N. J., & Wiesel, S. W. (1990). Abnormal magnetic-resonance scans of the lumbar spine in asymptomatic subjects. *Journal of Bone and Joint Surgery, 72A,* 403-408.

Bradley, L. A. (1985). Psychological aspects of arthritis. *Bulletin of the Rheumatic Diseases, 35,* 1-12.

Brown, G. K., & Nicassio, P. M. (1987). Development of a questionnaire for the assessment of active and passive coping strategies in chronic pain patients. *Pain, 31,* 53-62.

Brown, G. K., Nicassio, P. M., & Wallston, K. A. (1989). Pain coping strategies and depression in rheumatoid arthritis. *Journal of Consulting and Clinical Psychology, 57,* 652-657.

Cairns, D., & Pasino, J. (1977). Comparison of verbal reinforcement and feedback in the operant treatment of disability of chronic low back pain. *Behavior Therapy, 8,* 621-630.

Ciccone, D. S., & Grzesiak, R. C. (1984). Cognitive dimensions of chronic pain. *Social Science and Medicine, 19,* 1339-1345.

Cioffi, D. (1991). Beyond attentional strategies: A cognitive-perceptual model of somatic interpretation. *Psychological Bulletin, 109,* 25-41.

Council, J. R., Ahern, D. K., Follick, M. J., & Kline, C. L. (1988). Expectancies and functional impairment in chronic low back pain. *Pain, 33,* 323-331.

Deyo, R. A. (1986). The early diagnostic evaluation of patients with low back pain. *Journal of General Internal Medicine, 1,* 328-338.

Dolce, J. J., Crocker, M. F., & Doleys, D. M. (1986). Prediction of outcome among chronic pain patients. *Behavior Research and Therapy, 24,* 313-319.

Dolce, J. J., Crocker, M. F., Moletteire, C., & Doleys, D. M. (1986). Exercise quotas, anticipatory concern and self-efficacy expectancies in chronic pain: A preliminary report. *Pain, 24,* 365-375.

Doleys, D. M., Crocker, M., & Patton, D. (1982). Response of patients with chronic pain to exercise quotas. *Physical Therapy, 62,* 1112-1115.

Dufton, B. D. (1989). Cognitive failure and chronic pain. *International Journal of Psychiatry in Medicine, 19,* 291-297.

Engel, G. L. (1959). "Psychogenic" pain and the pain-prone patient. *American Journal of Medicine, 26,* 899-918.

Fernandez, E., & Turk, D. C. (1989). The utility of cognitive coping strategies for altering perception of pain: A meta-analysis. *Pain, 38,* 123-135.

Flor, H., Birbaumer, N., & Turk, D. C. (1990). The psychobiology of chronic pain. *Advances in Behaviour Research and Therapy, 12,* 47-84.

Flor, H., Fydrich, T., & Turk, D. C. (1992). Efficacy of multidisciplinary pain treatment centers: A meta-analytic review. *Pain, 49,* 221-230.

Flor, H., & Turk, D. C. (1988). Chronic back pain and rheumatoid arthritis: Predicting pain and disability from cognitive variables. *Journal of Behavioral Medicine, 11,* 251-265.

Flor, H., Turk, D. C., & Birbaumer, N. (1985). Assessment of stress-related psychophysiological responses in chronic back pain patients. *Journal of Consulting and Clinical Psychology, 53,* 354-364.

Fordyce, W. E. (1976). *Behavioral methods for chronic pain and illness.* St. Louis: C. V. Mosby.

Fordyce, W. E., Shelton, J., & Dundore, D. (1982). The modification of avoidance learning pain behaviors. *Journal of Behavioral Medicine, 4,* 405-414.

Frymoyer, J. W., & Cats-Baril, L. (1987). Predictors of low back pain disability. *Clinical Orthopedics and Related Research, 221,* 89-98.

Gauthier, J., Cote, L., & Drolet, M. (1985). Migraine and blood volume pulse biofeedback: How does clinical improvement related to perceived self-efficacy? *Canadian Psychology, 26,* Abstract No. 167.

Gil, K. M., Williams, D. A., Keefe, F. J., & Beckham, J. C. (1990). The relationship of negative thoughts to pain and psychological distress. *Behavior Therapy, 21,* 349-352.

Hatch, J. P., Prihoda, T. J., Moore, P. J., Cyr-Provost, M., Borcherding, S., Boutros, N. N., & Seleshi, E. (1991). A naturalistic study of the relationship among electromyographic activity, psychological stress, and pain in ambulatory tension-type headache patients and headache-free controls. *Psychosomatic Medicine, 53,* 576-584.

Herman, E., & Baptiste, S. (1981). Pain control: Mastery through group experience. *Pain, 10,* 79-86.

Heyneman, N. E., Fremouw, W. J., Gano, D., Kirkland, F., & Heiden, L. (1990). Individual differences in the effectiveness of different coping strategies. *Cognitive Therapy and Research, 14,* 63-77.

Holbrook, T. L., Grazier, K., Kelsey, J. L., & Staufer, R. N. (1984). *The frequency of occurrence, impact and cost of selected musculoskeletal conditions in the United States.* Park Ridge, IL: American Academy of Orthopaedic Surgeons.

Holroyd, K. A., & Andrasik, F. (1982). Do the effects of cognitive therapy endure? A two-year follow-up of tension headache sufferers treated with cognitive therapy or biofeedback. *Cognitive Therapy and Research, 6,* 325-333.

Holroyd, K. A., Penzien, D. B., Hursey, K. G., Tobin, D. L., Rogers, L., Holm, J. E., Marcille, P. J., Hall, D. R., & Chila, A. G. (1984). Change mechanisms in EMG biofeedback training: Cognitive changes underlying improvements in tension headache. *Journal of Consulting and Clinical Psychology, 52,* 1039-1053.

Jamner, L. D., & Tursky, B. (1987). Syndrome-specific descriptor profiling: A psychophysiological and psychophysical approach. *Health Psychology, 6,* 417-430.

Keefe, F. J., Caldwell, D. S., Queen, K. T., Gil, K. M., Martinez, S., Crisson, J. E., Ogden, W., & Nunley, J. (1987). Pain coping strategies in osteoarthritis patients. *Journal of Consulting and Clinical Psychology, 55,* 208-212.

Keefe, F. J., Caldwell, D. S., Williams, D. A., Gil, K. M., Mitchell, D., Robertson, C., Martinez, S., Nunley, J., Beckham, J. C., Crisson, J. E., & Helms, M. (1990a). Pain coping skills training in the management of osteoarthritis knee pain: A comparative approach. *Behavior Therapy, 21,* 49-62.

Keefe, F. J., Caldwell, D. S., Williams, D. A., Gil, K. M., Mitchell, D., Robertson, C., Martinez, S., Nunley, J., Beckham, J. C., Crisson, J. E., & Helms, M. (1990b). Pain coping skills training in the management of osteoarthritis knee pain. II. Follow-up results. *Behavior Therapy, 21,* 435-447.

Keefe, F. J., & Williams, D. A. (1989). New directions in pain assessment and treatment. *Clinical Psychology Review, 9,* 549-568.

Keefe, F. J., & Williams, D. A. (1990). A comparison of coping strategies in chronic pain patients in different age groups. *Journal of Gerontology: Psychological Sciences, 45,* P161-P165.

Koplow, D. A. (1990, November). *Legal issues.* Paper presented at the annual scientific session of the American Academy of Disability Evaluating Physicians, Las Vegas.

Kotarba, J. A. (1983). *Chronic pain: Its social dimensions.* Beverly Hills, CA: Sage.

Lawrence, R. C., Hochberg, M. C., Kelsey, J. L., McDuffie, F. C., Medsger, T. A., Felts, W. R., & Shulman, L. E. (1989). Estimates of the prevalence of selected arthritis and musculo-skeletal diseases in the U.S. *Journal of Rheumatology, 16,* 427-441.

Lawson, K., Reesor, K. A., Keefe, F. J., & Turner, J. A. (1990). Dimensions of pain-related cognitive coping: Cross validation of the factor structure of the Coping Strategies Questionnaire. *Pain, 43,* 195-204.

Lefebvre, M. F. (1981). Cognitive distortion and cognitive errors in depressed psychiatric low back pain patients. *Journal of Consulting and Clinical Psychology, 49,* 517-525.

Lorig, K., Chastain, R. L., Ung, E., Shoor, S., & Holman, H. R. (1989). Development and evaluation of a scale to measure perceived self-efficacy in people with arthritis. *Arthritis and Rheumatism, 32,* 37-44.

Martin, P. R., Nathan, P., Milech, D., & Van Keppel, M. (1989). Cognitive therapy vs. self-management training in the treatment of chronic headaches. *British Journal of Clinical Psychology, 28,* 347-361.

Melzack, R., & Casey, K. L. (1968). Sensory, motivational and central control determinants of pain: A new conceptual model. In D. Kenshalo (Ed.), *The skin senses* (pp. 423-443). Springfield, IL: Charles C Thomas.

Melzack, R., & Wall, P. D. (1965). Pain mechanisms: A new theory. *Science, 50,* 971-979.

Nathan, P. W. (1976). The gate control theory of pain: A critical review. *Brain, 99,* 123-158.

National Center for Health Statistics. (1986). *The management of chronic pain in office-based ambulatory care: National Ambulatory Care Survey* (Advance Data From Vital and

Health Statistics No. 123, DHHS Pub. No. PHS 86-1250). Hyattsville, MD: U.S. Public Health Service.

Newton, C. R., & Barbaree, H. E. (1987). Cognitive changes accompanying headache treatment: The use of a thought-sampling procedure. *Cognitive Therapy and Research, 11,* 635-652.

Nicassio, P. M., Wallston, K. A., Callahan, L. F., Herbert, M., & Pincus, T. (1985). The measurement of helplessness in rheumatoid arthritis: The development of the Arthritis Helplessness Index. *Journal of Rheumatology, 12,* 462-467.

Nouwen, A., & Solinger, J. W. (1979). The effectiveness of EMG biofeedback training in low back pain. *Biofeedback and Self-Regulation, 4,* 103-111.

O'Leary, A., Shoor, S., Lorig, K., & Holman, H. R. (1988). A cognitive-behavioral treatment for rheumatoid arthritis. *Health Psychology, 7,* 527-544.

Osterweis, M., Kleinman, A., & Mechanic, D. (1987). *Pain and disability: Clinical, behavioral, and public policy perspectives.* Washington, DC: National Academy Press.

Philips, C., & Jahanshahi, M. (1986). Validating a new technique for the assessment of pain behavior. *Behaviour Research and Therapy, 24,* 35-42.

Philips, H. C. (1987a). Avoidance behaviour and its role in sustaining chronic pain. *Behaviour Research and Therapy, 25,* 273-279.

Philips, H. C. (1987b). The effects of behavioural treatment on chronic pain. *Behaviour Research and Therapy, 25,* 365-377.

Plant, R. D., Button, E. J., & Cawley, M. I. D. (1984). Belief and illness: A study of patients with rheumatoid arthritis. *British Journal of Rheumatology, 22,* 143-145.

Price, D. D. (1987). *Psychological and neural mechanisms of pain.* New York: Raven.

Rachman, S., & Arntz, A. (1991). The overprediction and underprediction of pain. *Clinical Psychology Review, 11,* 339-356.

Rachman, S., & Lopatka, C. (1988). Accurate and inaccurate predictions of pain. *Behaviour Research and Therapy, 26,* 291-296.

Reesor, K. A., & Craig, K. (1988). Medically incongruent chronic pain: Physical limitations, suffering and ineffective coping. *Pain, 32,* 35-45.

Rimm, D. C., & Litvak, S. B. (1969). Self-verbalizations and emotional arousal. *Journal of Abnormal Psychology, 74,* 181-187.

Romano, J. M., Turner, J. A., Syrjala, K. L., & Levy, R. L. (1987). Coping strategies of chronic pain patients: Relationship to patient characteristics and functioning. *Pain, 21* (Suppl. 4), S416 (Abstract No. 802).

Rosensteil, A. K., & Keefe, F. J. (1983). The use of coping strategies in chronic low back pain patients: Relationship to patient characteristics and current adjustment. *Pain, 17,* 33-44.

Rudy, T. E. (1990). Psychophysiological assessment in chronic orofacial pain. *Anesthesia Progress, 37,* 82-87.

Schmidt, A. J. M. (1985a). Cognitive factors in the performance of chronic low back pain patients. *Journal of Psychosomatic Research, 29,* 183-189.

Schmidt, A. J. M. (1985b). Performance level of chronic low back pain patients in different treadmill test conditions. *Journal of Psychosomatic Research, 29,* 639-646.

Schmidt, A. J. M., Gierlings, R. E. H., & Peters, M. L. (1989). Environment and interoceptive influences on chronic low back pain behavior. *Pain, 38,* 137-143.

Schwartz, D. P., DeGood, D. E., & Shutty, M. S. (1985). Direct assessment of beliefs and attitudes of chronic pain patients. *Archives of Physical Medicine and Rehabilitation, 66,* 806-809.

Shoor, S. M., & Holman, H. R. (1984). Development of an instrument to enhance psychological mediators of outcome in chronic arthritis. *Transactions of the Association of American Physicians, 97,* 325-331.

Slater, M. A., Hall, H. F., Atkinson, J. H., & Garfin, S. R. (1991). Pain and impairment beliefs in chronic low back pain: Validation of the Pain and Impairment Relationship Scale (PAIRS). *Pain, 44,* 51-56.

Smith, T. W., Aberger, E. W., Follick, M. J., & Ahern, D. L. (1986). Cognitive distortion and psychological distress in chronic low back pain. *Journal of Consulting and Clinical Psychology, 54,* 573-575.

Smith, T. W., Follick, M. J., Ahern, D. L., & Adams, A. (1986). Cognitive distortion and disability in chronic low back pain. *Cognitive Therapy and Research, 10,* 201-210.

Smith, T. W., Peck, J. R., & Ward, J. R. (1990). Helplessness and depression in rheumatoid arthritis. *Health Psychology, 9,* 377-389.

Spanos, N. P., Horton, C., & Chaves, J. F. (1975). The effects of two cognitive strategies on pain threshold. *Journal of Abnormal Psychology, 84,* 677-681.

Spinhoven, P., Ter Kuile, M. M., Linssen, A. C. G., & Gazendam, B. (1989). Pain coping strategies in a Dutch population of chronic low back pain patients. *Pain, 37,* 77-83.

Stein, M. J., Wallston, K. S., & Nicassio, P. M. (1988). Factor structure of the Arthritis Helplessness Index. *Journal of Rheumatology, 15,* 427-432.

Stein, M. J., Wallston, K. A., Nicassio, P. M., & Castner, N. M. (1988). Correlation of clinical classification schema for the Arthritis Helplessness subscale. *Arthritis and Rheumatism, 31,* 876-881.

Stewart, W. F., Lipton, R. B., Celentano, D. D., & Reed, M. L. (1991). Prevalence of migraine headache in the United States: Relation to age, income, race, and other sociodemographic factors. *Journal of the American Medical Association, 267,* 64-69.

Sullivan, M. J. L., & D'Eon, J. L. (1990). Relation between catastrophizing and depression in chronic pain patients. *Journal of Abnormal Psychology, 99,* 260-263.

Taylor, H., & Curran, N. M. (1985). *The Nuprin pain report.* New York: Louis Harris & Associates.

Turk, D. C. (1990). Customizing treatment for chronic pain patients: Who, what, and why. *Clinical Journal of Pain, 6,* 255-270.

Turk, D. C., & Flor, H. (1987). Pain > pain behaviors: The utility and limitations of the pain behavior construct. *Pain, 31,* 277-295.

Turk, D. C., & Matyas, T. A. (1992). Pain-related behaviors > communications of pain. *American Pain Society Journal, 1,* 109-111.

Turk, D. C., Meichenbaum, D., & Genest, M. (1983). *Pain and behavioral medicine: A cognitive-behavioral perspective.* New York: Guilford.

Turk, D. C., & Rudy, T. E. (1986). Assessment of cognitive factors in chronic pain: A worthwhile enterprise? *Journal of Consulting and Clinical Psychology, 54,* 760-768.

Turk, D. C., & Rudy, T. E. (1989). An integrated approach to pain treatment: Beyond the scalpel and syringe. In C. D. Tollison (Ed.), *Handbook of chronic pain management* (pp. 222-237). Baltimore: Williams & Wilkins.

Turk, D. C., & Rudy, T. E. (1990). Neglected topics in the treatment of chronic pain patients: Relapse, noncompliance, and adherence enhancement. *Pain, 44,* 5-28.

Turk, D. C., & Rudy, T. E. (1991). Persistent pain and the injured worker: Integrating biomedical, psychosocial, and behavioral factors. *Journal of Occupational Rehabilitation, 1,* 159-179.

Turk, D. C., & Rudy, T. E. (1992). Cognitive factors and persistent pain: A glimpse into Pandora's box. *Cognitive Therapy and Research, 16,* 99-122.

Turk, D. C., Rudy, T. E., & Salovcy, P. (1986). Implicit models of illness: Description and validation. *Journal of Behavioral Medicine, 9,* 453-474.

Turner, J. A., & Clancy, S. (1986). Strategies for coping with chronic pain: Relationship to pain and disability. *Pain, 24,* 355-364.

Vlaeyen, J. W. S., Van Eek, H., Groenman, N. H., & Schuerman, J. A. (1987). Dimensions and components of observed chronic pain behaviour. *Pain, 11,* 66-73.

Wiesel, S. W., Tsourmas, N., & Feffer, H. (1984). A study of computer-assisted tomography. I The incidence of positive CAT scans in an asymptomatic group of patients. *Spine, 9,* 549-551.

Williams, D. A., & Keefe, F. J. (1991). Pain beliefs and the use of cognitive-behavioral coping strategies. *Pain, 16,* 185-190.

Williams, D. A., & Thorn, B. E. (1989). An empirical assessment of pain beliefs. *Pain, 36,* 251-258.

5

Cognitive Therapy of Anxiety Disorders

DIANNE L. CHAMBLESS

MARTHA M. GILLIS

In a seminal paper, Beck, Laude, and Bohnert (1974) demonstrated that anxious clients report characteristic patterns of thinking, such that increments in anxiety are accompanied by thoughts and images of social or physical harm, or both. The results of this early report have proved consistent with an emerging body of self-report and laboratory experimental findings concerning the cognitive psychopathology of anxiety disorders (see review by Chambless, 1988). Analysis of the content of anxiety clients' thoughts provides some support for Beck and Emery's (1985) hypothesis of disorder specificity in anxious cognitions. Thus clients with panic disorder (PD), with

AUTHORS' NOTE: This chapter is adapted by permission of the American Psychological Association from "Cognitive Therapy of Anxiety Disorders," by D. L. Chambless & M. M. Gillis, 1993, *Journal of Consulting and Clinical Psychology, 61,* pp. 248-260. Copyright 1993 by the American Psychological Association.

We wish to thank David A. F. Haaga for his valuable comments on a draft of this manuscript and the following individuals for providing data for this chapter: Aaron T. Beck, Thomas Borkovec, Gillian Butler, David Clark, Jurgen Margraf, Larry Michelson, and Lars-Goran Ost. Preparation of this manuscript was supported by NIMH Grant #R01-MH44190-03 to Gail Steketee and Dianne Chambless.

or without agoraphobia, are primarily concerned with harm to their physical well-being caused by panic symptoms (part of the process dubbed "fear of fear" by Goldstein & Chambless, 1978), whereas clients with social phobia are more concerned with social failure (see, e.g., Chambless & Gracely, 1989; Hope, Rapee, Heimberg, & Dombeck, 1990). The concerns of clients with generalized anxiety disorder (GAD) are more diffuse, involving thoughts of loss of control (e.g., Chambless & Gracely, 1989) and heightened vigilance for threats of both a social and a physical nature (e.g., MacLeod, Mathews, & Tata, 1986). The centrality of this diffuse pattern of worry for GAD clients has been so well documented (see review by Borkovec, Shadick, & Hopkins, 1991) that the criteria of the *Diagnostic and Statistical Manual of Mental Disorders* have been changed to require excessive worry for assignment of the generalized anxiety disorder diagnosis (see third edition [*DSM-III*] vs. third, revised edition [*DSM-III-R*]; American Psychiatric Association, 1980, 1987).

A variety of approaches have been used to modify cognitions of anxious clients, most commonly rational emotive therapy (RET; Ellis, 1962), self-instructional training (SIT; Meichenbaum, 1975), and Beck and Emery's (1985) model of cognitive therapy. Therapy components include teaching clients to identify and label irrational thoughts and to replace them with positive self-statements or to modify them by challenging their veracity. The cognitive modification approaches are often combined with behavioral treatments such as exposure or relaxation training. The behavioral components are viewed either as important in their own right or as vehicles for practicing cognitive techniques. Hence we will use the term *cognitive-behavioral therapy* (CBT) in this review.

For this brief review, we surveyed the results of cognitive therapies for three anxiety disorders for which a substantial body of treatment research on clinical samples is available: generalized anxiety disorder, panic disorder with and without agoraphobia, and social phobia. For a descriptive summary, we have converted treatment findings into effect sizes when authors provided means and standard deviations for the measures across treatment. We calculated two types of effect sizes using Smith and Glass's delta (1977). To include the many studies in which the effects of one treatment were compared, not to a waiting list control or placebo group, but only to another treatment, we first computed crude pretest-posttest and pretest follow-up effects, using the following formula: $(M_{pretest} - M_{posttest})/SD_{pretest}$. Second, for those studies with waiting list or placebo controls, we calculated controlled

TABLE 5.1   Effect Sizes for Reduction in Anxiety Following Cognitive
Therapy for Generalized Anxiety Disorder

Study	Treatment	Pre-Post Effect Size	Pre-Follow-up Effect Size	Follow-up Length
Borkovec et al., 1987	CBT	1.59	—	—
Borkovec & Costello, 1993	CBT	1.81	1.26	1 yr.
Borkovec & Mathews, 1988	CBT	1.67	1.53	1 yr.
Butler, Cullington, et al., 1987	AMT	1.68	2.15	6 mo.
Butler et al., 1991	CBT	1.67	1.79	6 mo.
Power et al., 1989	CBT	5.48	—	—
Power et al., 1990	CBT	4.29[a]	—	—
Weighted average		1.69[b]	1.95	—

NOTE: CBT = cognitive-behavioral treatment; AMT = anxiety management training.
a. Outlier.
b. Outlier deleted from average.

effect sizes contrasting the posttest or follow-up scores of treatment groups to those of control groups, using the formula $(M_{control} - M_{treatment})/SD_{control}$. When multiple measures of a construct were used, we averaged effect sizes for that construct within each study.

GENERALIZED ANXIETY DISORDER

We located nine clinical trials for generalized anxiety disorder in which clients were selected according to *DSM-III* or *DSM-III-R* criteria (American Psychiatric Association, 1980, 1987) or Research Diagnostic Criteria, thus enhancing the probability of reasonably homogeneous samples.[1] In seven of these studies, data necessary for inclusion in a meta-analytic summary were published or provided by the authors (see Table 5.1). Measures included in this analysis were interview (typically the Hamilton Anxiety Scale; Hamilton, 1959) and self-report questionnaires (e.g., Zung Self-Rating of Anxiety, Zung, 1971, and Beck Anxiety Inventory, Beck & Steer, 1990).

In almost all trials, Beck and Emery's (1985) version of CBT was combined with one or more additional behavioral techniques, most commonly progressive relaxation training, and more rarely self-control desensitization or electromyogram biofeedback. The exception was the study by Butler, Fennell, Robson, and Gelder (1991), who seem to have used Beck-Emery

CBT alone. The one study not based on the Beck and Emery manual was that by Butler, Cullington, Hibbert, Klimes, and Gelder (1987), who examined the effects of an anxiety management training package including positive self-talk, relaxation, exposure, and pleasant events scheduling, as well as challenging of irrational thoughts.

Is CBT for Generalized Anxiety Disorder Effective?

The uncontrolled pretest-posttest effect sizes in Table 5.1 indicate that CBT consistently has a substantial impact on anxiety measures. The effect sizes for the studies by Power and colleagues (Power, Jerrom, Simpson, Mitchell, & Swanson, 1989; Power et al., 1990) are unusually large; however, the placebo response effect sizes are also very high for these studies, yielding controlled effect sizes comparable to those for other investigations. Although the reasons for these investigators' discrepant findings are not clear, the brief duration of their clients' disorder (3 or 4 months on average) may be related to an especially powerful response to any intervention.[2] When compared with the effects of control groups, the average effect sizes for CBT (including the Power et al. data) continue to be quite large ($M = 1.54$).

Figure 5.1 depicts the results of five studies in which CBT was compared to one of several control conditions: pill placebo (Power et al., 1989, 1990), nondirective therapy (Borkovec & Costello, 1993), or waiting list (Butler, Cullington, et al., 1987; Butler et al., 1991). Not shown (requisite data were not available), but also including nondirective therapy and/or waiting list control groups, are studies by Barlow et al. (1984) and Blowers, Cobb, and Mathews (1987). In all seven investigations, CBT was more effective than waiting list or pill placebo at posttest.

The results of the two studies using nondirective therapy to control for nonspecific treatment effects are conflicting, despite some collaboration between the two research groups. Whereas Borkovec and Costello (1993) found CBT superior to nondirective therapy, Blowers et al. (1987) did not. However, in the latter study CBT was superior to a waiting list control when nondirective therapy, yielding an intermediate response rate, was not. A number of methodological differences between the two studies might account for the discrepant findings. In the more recent study, Borkovec and Costello included a number of important methodological refinements that

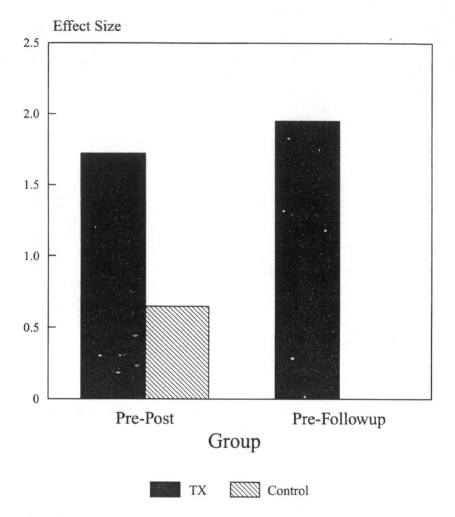

Figure 5.1. Average Effect Sizes of Five Studies Comparing Cognitive-Behavioral Therapy for Generalized Anxiety Disorder to Waiting List, Nondirective Therapy, or Pill Placebo

should reduce variance and give a cleaner picture of the results. In addition, Borkovec and Costello provided subjects with 50% more treatment sessions (12 vs. 8), including slower and more thorough training in relaxation, and they added self-control desensitization to their treatment package.

Do CBT Effects Persist Once Treatment Has Ended?

Examination of the uncontrolled pretest-follow-up effect sizes in Table 5.1 demonstrates that treatment effects were maintained or augmented over 6 to 12 months of follow-up. The large effect size for the Borkovec and Costello (1993) study is particularly impressive in that the data reported are for subjects who received no further treatment during the follow-up period. Comparison of CBT to control groups at follow-up is problematical in that, for ethical reasons, control subjects generally receive treatment after post-test. Thus the only controlled follow-up contrasts are from the two trials comparing CBT with nondirective therapy. In the Blowers et al. (1987) study, CBT and nondirective therapy continued to be equivalent at 6 months after treatment. Borkovec and Costello (1993) also found no differences between treatments at follow-up, but these long-term outcome data were confounded in that, due to their poor initial treatment response, significantly more nondirective therapy clients received additional treatment during the follow-up period (61% of nondirective clients vs. 16% of CBT clients).

Is CBT More Effective Than Behavioral
Treatments for Generalized Anxiety Disorder?

Borkovec and colleagues compared CBT plus relaxation to nondirective therapy plus relaxation in studies with a sample of college students with generalized anxiety disorder (Borkovec et al., 1987) and with a more severely anxious community sample (Borkovec & Mathews, 1988). Despite the similarity in the protocols and high level of methodological refinement in both studies, the results are conflicting. Only with the student sample was CBT superior to nondirective therapy plus relaxation; for the clinical sample, effects of the two treatments were similar at posttest and 12-month follow-up. However, these differences may be more apparent than real. The superiority of CBT for the student sample was found only for self-report questionnaires. The effect sizes (ES) for comparison of CBT and nondirective therapy plus relaxation on the assessor-rated Hamilton Anxiety Scale are comparable and modestly, if not statistically significantly, in favor of CBT in both investigations (student ES = 0.32; clinical ES = 0.43). Hence these discrepancies may reflect the sampling variance associated with test of modest effects at low power. Nevertheless, on the basis of this research, one cannot safely conclude that the CBT effects depicted in Table 5.1 and Figure

5.1 reflect more than simple nonspecific treatment effects in combination with relaxation training.

More complete behavioral treatment programs were used by Borkovec and Costello (1993) and Butler et al. (1991). The former compared a CBT package to an applied relaxation treatment in which clients were taught to identify early signs of anxiety and apply their relaxation skills to dampen incipient arousal. CBT and applied relaxation were similar in their effects, with both being superior to nondirective therapy at posttest. Butler et al. (1991) compared 4 to 12 sessions of pure CBT (without relaxation) to behavior therapy consisting of progressive relaxation, exposure, graded task assignments, and pleasurable activities to combat demoralization. Improvements with CBT were greater than those with behavior therapy on several, but not all, anxiety measures at posttest and at 6-month follow-up; differences were apparent on the most extensively validated anxiety measures employed (Hamilton Anxiety Scale, Beck Anxiety Inventory). At long-term follow-up (11-24 months), significantly more behavior therapy clients than CBT-treated clients were found to have sought extensive additional treatment. Because both studies were methodologically sophisticated, there are no obvious reasons for the discrepant findings. It is possible that the pure and thorough approach taken to CBT by Butler et al. (1991) yields more effective results in a short-term treatment than more complex treatment packages. Only 10 to 15 minutes per session were devoted to cognitive therapy in the Borkovec and Costello CBT program.

Effects on Depression

Clients with generalized anxiety disorder frequently complain of depression, with perhaps one third meeting criteria for dysthymia (e.g., de Ruiter, Rijken, Garssen, van Schaik, & Kraaimaat, 1989). Does CBT benefit their depression as well as their anxiety? Clients with severe or primary depression were generally excluded from the studies reviewed, but less severe depressive symptomatology was common. The three studies providing data comparing CBT with other psychological treatments yield mixed results. Butler et al. (1991) found CBT to have greater impact on depression than behavior therapy, and Borkovec and Costello (1993) determined CBT was superior to nondirective therapy but not to applied relaxation. In contrast, Borkovec et al. (1987) found no significantly superior CBT effects for depression among treatment completers. However, the low levels of pretreatment depression in this student sample may have made the detection of differential treatment effects unlikely. In all three studies, the authors reported having to drop clients from the nondirective, applied relaxation, or behavior therapy conditions because of increased depression; no such losses occurred in the CBT groups. Thus CBT may have an added benefit in addressing mixed anxiety and depression among generalized anxiety disorder clients. Given the considerable comorbidity of anxiety and depression, this question warrants further study.

Effects on Cognitive Measures

Only three of the studies here reviewed included an examination of cognitive changes. In the earliest effort, Blowers et al. (1987) assessed self-report of the perceived controllability and intensity of cognitive symptoms of anxiety. Both nondirective and CBT groups reported greater reduction in intensity than the waiting list group, but only the CBT group reported significantly enhanced control over cognitive symptoms compared to the waiting list group. Butler et al. (1991) used five measures of anxious cognition. Pure CBT yielded better results than behavior therapy on two measures at posttest and on all five measures at 6-month follow-up. Using the Penn State Worry Questionnaire (Meyer, Miller, Metzger, & Borkovec, 1990), Borkovec and Costello (1993) found that CBT led to greater reductions in worry than did nondirective therapy; applied relaxation and CBT were equivalent in their effects. Laboratory measures of thoughts and imagery also showed that treatment responders in this study became more like normal subjects in their mentation, regardless of therapy type (Borkovec & Inz, 1990). Thus a variety of treatment procedures may lead to change on cognitive measures; CBT may result in greater cognitive change than other therapies only when it is the more effective treatment for the clients' overall symptoms.

PANIC DISORDER AND AGORAPHOBIA

Although dichotomizing clients with panic disorder into those with and without agoraphobia belies a continuum of avoidance, we will follow this convention because (a) samples are described in this fashion, and (b) severity of phobic avoidance may have some effect on outcome (Clum, 1989). Studies included in our meta-analysis all follow *DSM-III* or *DSM-III-R* criteria for selection. Samples in some earlier studies on agoraphobia described here were selected on the basis of clinical interviews, whereas later studies relied on structured, reliable diagnostic interviews.

Because the effects of exposure on phobic features of panic disorder are well documented and have already been summarized in meta-analytic form (see reviews by Jansson & Ost, 1982; Trull, Nietzel, & Main, 1988) and because studies with cognitive therapy omitting exposure are rare, we did not focus on avoidance behavior in our meta-analytic summary. Rather, we prepared effect size summaries of data on generalized anxiety, diary-rated panic frequency, and fear of fear. Measures of fear of fear included the Agoraphobic Cognitions Questionnaire (Chambless, Caputo, Bright, & Gallagher, 1984), the Panic Belief Questionnaire (Greenberg, 1989), and the Body Sensation Interpretation Questionnaire (Clark et al., 1991), all of which measure catastrophic misinterpretation of panic symptoms or fear of interoceptive cues associated with panic. Also, we noted the percentage of subjects reporting themselves to be panic-free after treatment.

Cognitive Therapy for Agoraphobia

Is Cognitive Therapy Effective for Agoraphobia?

There are no trials of CBT as a sole treatment for agoraphobia that include control groups. Rather, the research question has been whether CBT can equal or surpass the established treatment of choice, in vivo exposure. In two studies, Emmelkamp and colleagues (Emmelkamp, Brilman, Kuiper, & Mersch, 1986; Emmelkamp, Kuipers, & Eggeraat, 1978) compared the efficacy of SIT or RET alone to exposure. In each case, brief cognitive interventions (five or six sessions over a 1- or 3-week period) failed to equal the success of equivalent amounts of the benchmark exposure treatment.

Does Cognitive Therapy Add to the Effects of Exposure for Agoraphobia?

Investigators comparing cognitive modification plus exposure with exposure alone have used a variety of approaches: paradoxical intention, SIT, RET, and Beck-Emery CBT (Emmelkamp & Mersch, 1982; Michelson, Marchione, & Greenwald, 1989; Michelson, Mavissakalian, & Marchione,

TABLE 5.2 Treatment of Agoraphobia and Panic Disorder by Interoceptive or in Vivo Exposure Plus Various Cognitive Techniques: Pretest-Posttest Effect Sizes

			Effect Sizes			
Study	Sample	No. of Sessions	Anxiety	No. of Panics	Fear of Fear	% Panic-Free
Barlow et al., 1989	PD	15	1.11	0.20	—	87
Chambless et al., 1986	AG	10	—	0.33	0.52	43
Klosko et al., 1990	PD	15	1.31			87
Margraf & Schneider, 1991	PD	15	0.90	0.88	1.77	75
Michelson et al., 1989	AG	16	1.22	0.89	1.34	68
Michelson et al., 1990	PD	13	1.08	1.31	1.10	—
Ost et al., 1993	AG	12	—	0.91	—	—
Weighted average			1.14	0.63	1.03	66

NOTE: PD = panic disorder with no to moderate avoidance; AG = agoraphobia.

1988; Ost, Westling, & Hellstrom, 1993; Williams & Rappoport, 1983). Pretest-posttest effect sizes are depicted in Table 5.2; the subset from studies comparing combined treatments with a control group are shown in Figure 5.2. Combined treatments were consistently more effective than waiting list control groups, but in only one investigation did combined treatment exceed the effects of exposure alone.

In that study, Michelson et al. (1989) found that adding Beck-Emery CBT to exposure for agoraphobia led to significantly better results on some measures of phobia and panic and on a composite measure of high end-state functioning at follow-up. Michelson et al.'s data may be unique because these authors are the only investigators to have combined Beck-Emery CBT with exposure for agoraphobics (all cognitive therapies may not be created equal). Another important factor may be the longer treatment (16 sessions) Michelson et al. provided.

Cognitive Therapy for Panic Disorder

CBT for panic disorder, following Clark and Salkovskis's (1995) model (an adaptation of Beck-Emery CBT specifically devised for this disorder), has now been tested in six trials conducted in four nations (see Table 5.3). In all studies, CBT yielded very large effect sizes for fear of fear, generalized anxiety, and panic frequency; these effect sizes were maintained or enhanced

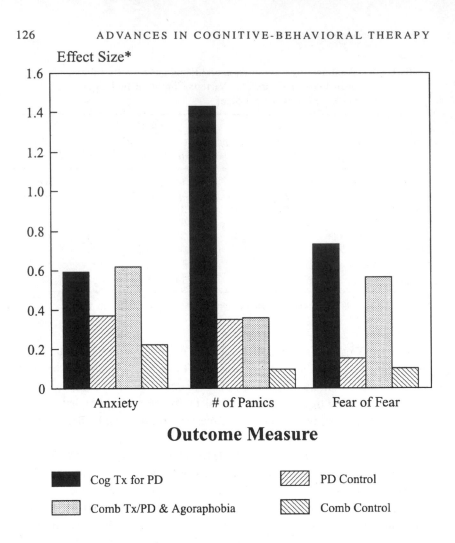

Figure 5.2. Average Effect Sizes of Three Studies Comparing Beck-Emery/Clark-Salkovskis Model Cognitive Therapy for Panic Disorder to Waiting List or Supportive Therapy and of Four Studies Comparing Cognitive-Behavioral Therapy for Panic Disorder With and Without Agoraphobia to Waiting List or Pill Placebo
NOTE: *Weighted average by outcome measure.

at follow-up of 1 to 12 months' duration (effect sizes at follow-up averaged 1.00-1.73). An average of 85% of the clients at posttest and 88% at follow-up were panic-free.

TABLE 5.3 Cognitive Therapy for Panic Disorder: Pretest-Posttest Effects of Studies Using the Beck & Emery/Clark & Salkovskis Model

Study	No. of Sessions	Effect Sizes			% Panic Free
		Anxiety	No. of Panics	Fear of Fear	
Beck et al., 1992	12	1.50	1.05		94
Clark et al., 1991	12	2.04	2.20	1.26	90
Margraf & Schneider, 1991	15	1.18	1.00	1.00	90
Newman et al., 1990	12-16	1.63	0.51	2.29	83
Ost & Westling, 1991	12	2.13	1.21	1.55	75
Sokol et al., 1989	15 (aver.)	1.69	0.80	—	100
Weighted average		1.68	0.98	1.75	85

Comparisons With Control Groups

For three of the six studies described, control group data are available for either a waiting list period or response to supportive psychotherapy (Beck, Sokol, Clark, Berchick, & Wright, 1992; Clark et al., 1991; Margraf & Schneider, 1991; see Figure 5.2). The controlled effect sizes are very large for all three variables (weighted mean ranges from 1.12-1.71). An average of 83% of CBT clients were panic-free at posttest, compared with 12% of the control subjects.

Comparisons to Other Treatments

Three groups of investigators have compared the Clark and Salkovskis (1995) CBT model to another modality: applied relaxation (Clark et al., 1991; Ost & Westling, 1991) or exposure to body sensations associated with panic (interoceptive exposure; Margraf & Schneider, 1991). In only one case did CBT clients improve more than clients in the behavioral treatments (Clark et al., 1991). The discrepancy between the Clark et al. and Ost and Westling studies is puzzling given the similarity of the studies and the cross-fertilization between the two research groups. Investigator effects may play a role in that Clark's group is most closely identified with CBT, whereas Ost has been prominent in the development of applied relaxation. Investigator allegiance may affect the quality and enthusiasm of treatment interventions; however, in the absence of comparative therapist competency ratings for these two studies, such an explanation is speculative.

Data from Barlow's research group (Barlow, Craske, Cerny, & Klosko, 1989; Craske, Brown, & Barlow, 1991) suggest that a treatment package of CBT plus exposure may more successfully retain clients in treatment than relaxation-based therapies; however, there was no differential treatment dropout in the Clark et al. (1991) and Ost and Westling (1991) studies. Thus, although more evidence attests to the efficacy of CBT for panic disorder than for any other psychosocial treatment approach, CBT has not been clearly established as more effective than other panic-focused behavioral treatment programs.

Combination Treatment Approaches
to Agoraphobia and Panic Disorder

Table 5.2 shows the results of six studies in which some form of systematic in vivo exposure or exposure to panic-related interoceptive cues related to panic was used concurrently with a variety of cognitive strategies.[3] It is difficult to draw meaningful conclusions from this set because of the heterogeneous interventions used and the sample variability. The effect sizes indicate consistently strong effects for generalized anxiety, with more variable findings for panic and fear of fear. In particular, the effect sizes seem to be lower for the Chambless, Goldstein, Gallagher, and Bright (1986) study, the only trial in which the cognitive component was not Beck-Emery CBT. These investigators used a combination of paradoxical intention and attention manipulation procedures.

Figure 5.2 depicts the results for the four studies of panic disorder or panic disorder with agoraphobia samples in which CBT plus exposure was compared to a waiting list control or to pill placebo. These effects are similar to, although slightly lower than, those for uncontrolled studies (weighted mean = 0.49-1.07). An average of 72% of clients receiving combined treatment were panic-free at posttest versus 25% in control groups. In each study, CBT was associated with more change than a waiting period. Although Klosko, Barlow, Tassinari, and Cerny (1990) did not find CBT to yield better results than pill placebo, with the exception of the CBT clients' greater achievement of panic-free status, posttest comparisons of completer samples in this study are compromised by the significantly higher placebo group dropout rate.

In the one study to compare the effects of cognitive therapy plus exposure (interoceptive) to Clark-Salkovskis cognitive therapy alone (carefully eschewing behavioral interventions), Margraf and Schneider (1991) observed no additional benefit for the combined treatment package with their panic disorder clients. Similarly, Barlow and colleagues (Barlow et al., 1989; Craske et al., 1991) found that adding relaxation to their Beck-Emery CBT plus interoceptive exposure package for panic disorder provided no better results than Beck-Emery CBT + interoceptive exposure alone. At posttest and 6-month follow-up, the groups getting CBT and interoceptive exposure, alone or in combination, fared better than the relaxation group on a number of measures. Moreover, the relaxation group was more likely to drop out during treatment and to have sought additional treatment by the 2-year follow-up.

Thus, although CBT in combination with behavioral techniques has been established as an effective treatment for panic disorder, it is doubtful that combination treatments are more effective than CBT alone, at least for panic disorder without agoraphobia. For severely phobic cases, the findings might be different; additional research on this question is required.

Cognitive-Behavioral Therapy Effects on Associated Psychopathology

Effects on Depression

Depression is a common feature of panic disorder. For example, Renneberg, Chambless, and Gracely (1992) found 15% of panic disorder clients to suffer from current major depression and 27% from dysthymia. Comparisons to waiting list control groups demonstrate that depressed mood is ameliorated by CBT (Chambless et al., 1986; Clark et al., 1991). However, the available studies do not indicate that CBT's effects are greater than those of other behavioral or supportive treatments (Beck et al., 1992; Clark et al., 1991; Emmelkamp et al., 1978; Margraf & Schneider, 1991; Michelson et al., 1988). Depression among these clients often results from demoralization, and any treatment instilling hope of change or leading to relief from panic may be sufficient. Note, however, that some investigators excluded clients in a major depressive episode (exclusion when depression was the primary problem was typical), and none tested the possible moderating effects of major depression on treatment outcome. Given its success in treatment of depression (see Dobson, 1989), CBT might have superior effects for panic disorder clients with major depression. In light of the frequent comorbidity of these disorders, this hypothesis is worth testing.

Cognitive Change

Comparisons of CBT and waiting list control groups show that the cognitively based treatments are effective in reducing negative cognitions about the disastrous effects of panic as assessed by questionnaires or audiotaped reports of thoughts collected during behavioral avoidance tests (Chambless et al., 1986; Clark et al., 1991; Margraf & Schneider, 1991; Williams & Rappoport, 1983). Tests of treatment effects on laboratory measures of cognitive schemas have yet to be reported.

The positive effects on cognitive measures cannot be said to be exclusive to CBT. In a set of five studies contrasting CBT to other treatments such as exposure alone and applied relaxation (Emmelkamp et al., 1986; Margraf & Schneider, 1991; Michelson et al., 1989; Williams & Rappoport, 1983), only Clark et al. (1991) found CBT to have superior effects on cognitive measures, despite some overlap in the cognitive measures used across investigations. Recall that in the Clark et al. study CBT was the most efficacious treatment on a number of outcome measures.

Normalization of the cognitive responses of panic disorder clients after CBT has been investigated by three research groups, with conflicting results. Although both Chambless et al. (1986) and Williams and Rappoport (1983) found decrements in agoraphobic clients' negative cognitions after treatment, clients still reported higher levels of negative thinking about anxiety than did normal control subjects. On the other hand, Michelson, Schwartz, and Marchione (1992), examining the states of mind (SOM) ratio (number of positive thoughts divided by the number of positive and negative thoughts), found that agoraphobic clients had a lower SOM ratio than normals before treatment but an equivalent ratio after treatment. Although differences could be due to variety in the methodologies used, the lengthier and more thorough Beck-Emery CBT provided in the Michelson et al. study might account for their superior results.

A different but equally important issue is the relationship of cognitive factors to treatment outcome on panic and avoidance. An emerging body of evidence indicates that cognitive measures of catastrophic thinking about panic predict treatment outcome on measures of panic and avoidance regardless of treatment modality (Chambless & Gracely, 1988; Clark et al., 1991; Margraf & Schneider, 1991; Michelson et al., 1989), with greater improvement on cognitive measures being strongly associated with larger decrements in panic and avoidance, and higher levels of negative thinking at pretest predicting poorer treatment response. Indeed, cognitive measures are often the best predictor of treatment outcome. Maintenance of treatment gains may also be related to cognitive variables. Clark et al. found that when symptom severity was controlled for at posttest, clients' clinical status at follow-up was predicted by their cognitive distortions at posttest, whether they had been treated with CDT, applied relaxation, or even pharmacotherapy. Thus, whatever the method of treatment, clients who continued to report thinking that physical symptoms of panic were signs of physical illness or mishap fared poorly at final evaluation. Although they do not prove causality, such data are consistent with the hypothesis that treatment efficacy is mediated by cognitive processes, whether or not the treatment is explicitly cognitive in nature.

SOCIAL PHOBIA

Because symptoms of social phobia overlap with those of other anxiety disorders and avoidant personality disorder and because comorbidity is common, only clinical studies using explicit, standardized diagnostic criteria are included in our statistical analyses. Even so, there are considerable differences among the 10 selected trials in the number of subjects with specific versus generalized social phobias or with additional diagnoses, including avoidant personality disorder. For example, all the subjects included in the Stravynski, Marks, and Yule study (1982) met *DSM-III* criteria for avoidant personality disorder, whereas Mattick and Peters (1988) and Heimberg et al. (1990) excluded subjects meeting these criteria. Such subtype differences may affect treatment outcome (Chambless, 1989).

A variety of interventions have been shown to be effective for social phobia (for reviews, see Agras, 1990; Heimberg, 1989). In the studies reviewed here, cognitive interventions include anxiety management training (relaxation, distraction, and rational self-talk) combined with in vivo exposure (Butler, Cullington, Munby, Amies, & Gelder, 1984), Heimberg's group CBT (Gelernter et al., 1991; Heimberg, Becker, Goldfinger, & Vermilyea, 1985; Heimberg et al., 1990), SIT (Emmelkamp, Mersch, Vissia, & van der Helm, 1985; Jerremalm, Jansson, & Ost, 1986), and RET, whether alone (Emmelkamp et al., 1985; Mattick, Peters, & Clarke, 1989; Mersch, Emmelkamp, Bogels, & van der Sleen, 1989), combined with exposure (Mattick & Peters, 1988; Mattick et al., 1989), or combined with social skills training (SST; Stravynski et al., 1982).

TABLE 5.4   Cognitive-Behavioral Treatment for Social Phobia:
Pre-Post Treatment Effects

Study	Group	Social Phobia	FNE Score	Cognitive Measure
Butler et al., 1984	EXP/GAMT	0.62	0.56	—
Gelernter et al., 1991	CBGT	1.15	—	—
Heimberg et al., 1985	CBGT	1.21	0.78	0.69
Heimberg et al., 1990	CBGT	0.73	0.76	—
Jerremalm et al., 1986	SIT	0.94	—	—
Mattick & Peters, 1988	EXP + CBGT	0.71	0.74	0.47
Mattick et al., 1989	CBGT	0.91	0.57	1.04
	CBGT + EXP	1.79	1.59	1.21
Stravynski et al., 1982	SST + RET	1.53	1.00	0.55
Weighted average		1.00	0.85	0.67

NOTE: CBGT = cognitive-behavioral group treatment; EXP = exposure; GAMT = group anxiety management training; RET = rational-emotive therapy; SIT = self-instructional training; SST = self-statement
training.

Outcome measures included in our summary in Table 5.4 include fear of
negative evaluation (Fear of Negative Evaluation Scale [FNES], Watson &
Friend, 1969), cognitive measures (e.g., the Irrational Beliefs Test [IBT],
Jones, 1969, and the Social Interaction Self Statement Test [SISST], Glass,
Merluzzi, Biever, & Larsen, 1982), and social phobia or anxiety measures
(e.g., the Social Phobia subscale of the Fear Questionnaire, Marks & Mathews,
1979, and the Social Avoidance and Distress Scale, Watson & Friend, 1969).

Is CBT for Social Phobia Effective?

The consistently large pretest-posttest effect sizes reflect substantial and
significant within-group change. Comparisons with waiting list and supportive therapy control groups (Butler et al., 1984; Heimberg et al., 1985, 1990;
Jerremalm et al., 1986; Mattick et al., 1989) indicate that CBT-treated clients
improved significantly more than did control groups on some, if not all,
measures (see Figure 5.3). Weighted average controlled effect sizes are 0.68
and 0.70 for social phobia and fear of negative evaluation respectively.
Because fear of scrutiny and of negative evaluation by others distinguishes
social phobia from related diagnoses and because change on the FNES has
been the best predictor of treatment outcome across a variety of treatments
(Mattick & Peters, 1988; Mattick et al., 1989), results on fear of negative
evaluation bear special attention. CBT has led to consistently large improvements on this variable (Table 5.4).

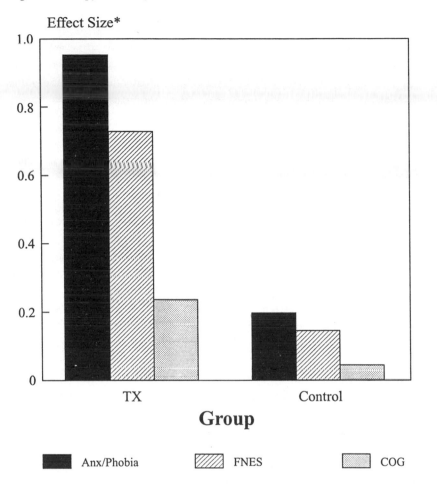

Figure 5.3. Average Effect Sizes of Four Studies Comparing Cognitive-Behavioral Therapy for Social Phobia to Waiting List or Supportive Therapy
NOTE: *Weighted average by outcome measure.

Do Treatment Effects Persist?

Overall, CBT treatment gains are maintained or have increased at 1-to 6-month follow-up. Indeed, Heimberg, Salzman, Holt, and Blendall (1993) found that CBT subjects were still significantly improved 5 years after treatment. Mattick et al. (1989), in comparing CBT, alone or in combination with exposure, to exposure alone, found that both groups of subjects who received CBT required significantly less subsequent treatment than the exposure-only group. Not only do CBT-treated clients maintain their gains after treatment, but in some studies they have continued to improve during the follow-up period (Gelernter et al., 1991; Mattick & Peters, 1988).

Is CBT for Social Phobia More
Effective Than Behavioral Treatment?

Though clearly effective with the socially phobic clinical population, CBT is not consistently superior to behavioral treatments. Investigators comparing applied relaxation, exposure, or SST to CBT have typically found the treatments to be equivalent (Emmelkamp et al., 1985; Gelernter et al., 1991; Jerremalm et al., 1986; Mattick et al., 1989; Mersch et al., 1989; Stravynski et al., 1982). In only two of the eight comparative trials did the effects of combined cognitive-behavioral treatment exceed those of exposure alone (Butler et al., 1984; Mattick & Peters, 1988), although one treatment or another may show superior effects on a given measure. Thus the determination of which treatment is the more effective may be affected by how outcome is assessed, as well as when, but we found no clear association between assessment method and differential treatment effectiveness.

Effects on Depression

Although exclusionary criteria for subjects were not always stated, it appears that about half the studies excluded subjects suffering from current major depression. Comorbidity statistics for clients included in treatment samples were provided only by Gelernter et al. (1991). In that study, 14% of the subjects had a current comorbid diagnosis of dysthymia. Unpublished data from our own laboratory suggest that comorbidity may be as high as 30% for social phobia and depressive disorders. It is therefore an important finding that in the studies reviewed, CBT for social phobia also had a positive impact on depression, with a large controlled effect size of 0.91. These effects were consistently, but not significantly, greater than the comparison group effects.

Conversely, it is troubling that Mersch et al. (1989) and Stravynski et al. (1982) each reported one treatment dropout resulting from increased suicidality. The Mersch et al. (1989) dropout was in the RET treatment group; it is unclear, however, whether the dropout in the Stravynski et al. (1982) study was receiving social skills training alone or with cognitive modification. These reports contrast with the apparent absence of depression-related dropout for CBT-treated clients in studies of panic disorder and generalized anxiety disorder. Note that the socially phobic clients were treated in groups, perhaps making it more difficult to manage depressive episodes before they escalated.

Effects on Cognitive Measures

Not all outcome studies have included measures of cognitive change. The importance of assessing cognition is highlighted by Mattick and Peters's (1988) findings that clients who improved more on the IBT were more likely to have achieved high end-state functioning at both posttest and follow-up.

Using a measure of thoughts collected during a behavioral test, Jerremalm et al. (1986) found that SIT led to significant improvement over a waiting list control group, whereas applied relaxation did not. However, the difference between the two treatment groups reached significance only for the half of the subjects in the SIT treatment classified as cognitive reactors. This classification was made before treatment assignment on the basis of high scores on a measure of negative thoughts following a behavior test and low heart rate reactivity during that test. Because the same measure was used in classifying subjects and in assessing outcome, regression-to-the-mean effects may account for this result. Other investigators found that at posttest, behavioral treatment, supportive/educational therapy, and CBT produced equivalent cognitive change as measured by the IBT, thought listing, or SISST (Emmelkamp et al., 1985; Heimberg et al., 1990; Mattick & Peters, 1988; Mattick et al., 1989; Stravynski et al., 1982). However, both Emmelkamp et al. (1985) and Mattick et al. (1989) found that the clients receiving CBT improved significantly more on cognitive measures after treatment ended than did clients in behavioral treatment groups. Similarly, Heimberg et al. (1990) observed that at follow-up, CBT-treated clients listed significantly fewer negative and more positive thoughts after role plays than did clients in the educational supportive condition.

Thus evidence that CBT is more effective than other treatments in reducing cognitive distortions associated with social phobia is mixed, with differential results most apparent at follow-up. Few studies using laboratory measures of cognitive processes or self-report questionnaire measures specifically tailored to cognitive assessment of social phobia have yet been published. Such research would provide a better test of CBT's effects on the cognitive pathology of these clients.

DISCUSSION

The findings from our review of studies on generalized anxiety disorder, panic disorder/agoraphobia, and social phobia demonstrate that CBT is an effective treatment for these anxiety disorders. Clients in CBT changed significantly more than those who were in waiting list control groups or who received pill placebos. On the whole, CBT's effects have also been found to exceed those of supportive therapy and education, although the differential response rate is not always large or apparent on all measures. Comparisons to focused behavioral treatments yield more mixed results: In general, CBT's effects equal and sometimes surpass those of behavior therapy without explicit cognitive components. The exception appears to be brief CBT excluding exposure instructions for highly avoidant clients with agoraphobia, for whom there is a poor track record.

At follow-up, maintenance of treatment gains is typical of CBT-treated clients. Indeed, an impressive feature of CBT is that clients in a number of studies continued to improve during the follow-up period, as has not typically been the case with behavioral treatments of anxiety. In still other studies, CBT clients were less likely to seek treatment during follow-up than clients in other treatment conditions, suggesting more durable or more generalized treatment effects.

Clients also seem to find CBT an acceptable treatment. Although investigators often did not present dropout rates as clearly as we would have liked, we estimate that CBT has a relatively low rate of premature termination: about 8% for panic disorder, 14% for generalized anxiety disorder, and 13% for social phobia. In several studies of generalized anxiety disorder (Borkovec et al., 1987; Borkovec & Costello, 1993; Butler et al., 1991), CBT's additional effects on depression seem to have enabled investigators to reduce depression-related treatment dropout. Reporting on treatment of panic disorder, Barlow et al. (1989) noted a lower dropout rate for CBT than for behavior therapy alone, although it is not known whether the increased dropout rate with relaxation training was related to depression. On the other hand, in the literature on group CBT of social phobia, there have been one or two reports of dropout associated with increased suicidality. We urge researchers to report comorbidity and dropout data carefully to allow more definitive conclusions to be drawn.

Although investigators have shown that clients change in CBT, they have inadequately assessed or reported the clinical significance of that change. When indices of clinically significant change are reported, comparisons across studies are made difficult by variable and often arbitrary criteria. Estimates of clinically significant change or high end-state functioning range from 7% to 75% for social phobia, 46% to 86% for panic disorder, and 32% to 73% for generalized anxiety disorder. These data suggest that even more powerful treatment interventions are needed. Moreover, end-state functioning criteria based solely on compilations of focused measures for the disorder may obscure remaining psychopathology. For example, on interviewer-rated global assessment of severity, Michelson et al. (1989) found that only 24% of the CBT clients were rated as completely recovered after treatment (although this number had risen to 47% at 3-month follow-up), whereas 86% were rated as having achieved high-end state functioning on the major outcome measures. Thus CBT may be effective, but, as practiced in research trials, it is no panacea.

In the search for more effective treatments, investigators have turned to combinations of treatment components. Given the multiple ways in which anxiety is manifested (physiological arousal, maladaptive cognition, behavioral disturbance or avoidance, and subjective distress), the idea that using different treatments to attack each aspect of the problem would be maximally effective has great intuitive appeal. Unfortunately, our review of the results of studies on combination treatments indicates that this is not uniformly true. The incremental efficacy of combination treatments seems to differ according to diagnosis and the particular outcome measures employed.

There seem to be at least two possible limitations to the utility of combination treatments. First, given a fixed number of sessions, as is typical in research or managed-care settings, introducing a variety of treatment approaches may preclude the client's becoming the master of any of them. Second, a jumble of treatments may prevent the client's having a clear sense of the rationale and direction of the treatment; this is problematical because the rationale itself is an important therapeutic component (Butler, Gelder, Hibbert, Cullington, & Klimes, 1987). Whether combinations could be employed more effectively in lengthier treatments is yet to be explored. If so, it may be necessary to develop strategies for determining the best sequence or integration of treatment elements. Extrapolating from the present set of studies, we suggest that vigorous, systematic exposure instructions in addition to cognitive modification techniques will be required for clients who consistently avoid phobic situations.

We know that CBT works, but does it work in the way it should? Theoretically, CBT should lead to improvement and maintenance of treatment gains via alteration of maladaptive cognitions. Relatively few studies have addressed this issue, and the measures have almost exclusively been limited to self-report of thoughts and attributions. The results indicate that CBT does lead to cognitive change and that cognitive change is related to reduction of anxious symptoms and to the durability of treatment gains at follow-up. In fact, cognitive measures have proved to be the best predictors of outcome in a number of investigations. Nevertheless, CBT is not the only road to cognitive modification. The pattern of results across studies suggests that successful treatment will be accompanied by change on cognitive measures and that cognitive measures predict outcome with a variety of treatment approaches, including pharmacotherapy.

There are a number of possible explanations for such findings; these have been described by Hollon, DeRubeis, and Evans (1987) in the context of the CBT depression literature. At least three explanations seem pertinent here: (a) Cognitive change represents a common mechanism for change with various treatments (Bandura, Adams, & Beyer, 1977) and is necessary for durable benefits; (b) cognition, anxiety, and avoidance are linked so that changing any one aspect of the system leads to changes in other components; or (c) cognitive change covaries with change in anxiety and has no special explanatory properties. The latter explanation becomes less likely in the face of studies such as that by Clark et al. (1990), who controlled for post-treatment severity in anxiety symptoms when demonstrating that cognitive measures predicted outcome on anxiety symptoms at follow-up.

More research using statistical approaches allowing approximation of causal explanations is required (see Baron & Kenny, 1986). Greater attention to cognitive assessment procedures is also necessary (for a review, see Arnkoff & Glass, 1989). Measures often used to assess cognitions in anxiety disorders research, such as the IBT (see Smith & Zurawski, 1983) and the FNES, may not discriminate adequately between anxiety and cognitions. In addition, studies assessing change with laboratory rather than self-report measures are highly desirable. On transparent questionnaires, CBT-treated clients might feel greater pressure to report increased rational thinking after treatment than clients in noncognitive therapies. Moreover, not all important aspects of cognitive psychopathology (e.g., schemas) may be accessible to self-report.

Heterogeneous approaches to cognitive modification were taken in the studies we reviewed, yet few studies have provided comparisons among the types of cognitive treatments. Currently, the most common cognitive treatment used is some form of Beck-Emery (Beck & Emery, 1985) CBT. Michelson and Marchione (1991) suggested that Buck-Emery CBT may prove to be a more powerful approach for anxiety than other cognitive approaches (e.g., SIT) because it is designed to change not only the content of clients' thoughts but also the process and structure of cognition. Indeed, CBT seems to add to the effectiveness of exposure for agoraphobia when RET and SIT do not. However, a variety of cognitive approaches have proved effective for social phobia, including SIT and RET. Hence whether one cognitive treatment is better than another remains an open question, although the documentation of the efficacy of Beck-Emery CBT is more extensive at present. The development of more sophisticated laboratory measurement of cognitive schemas for research on psychopathology of anxiety disorders makes possible a test of whether more explicitly metacognitive therapies (see Hollon & Kriss, 1984) have stronger effects on deeper structures than therapies that rely on distraction or self-statement training. We encourage anxiety researchers to include such tests in their trials on treatment outcome.

In a final point, we note the dearth of studies comparing CBT to psychodynamic therapies. Both psychotherapies rely on introspection and client-therapist verbal interaction for their effects, although the type of insight sought differs. With the current emphasis in CBT on modification of self-schemas, CBT has moved closer to psychodynamic therapy in its goals. These similarities appear to make CBT more acceptable to psychodynamically oriented practitioners than behavior therapy. Given the continued popularity of psychodynamic approaches with American clinical psychologists (Norcross & Prochaska, 1982), controlled comparisons of process and outcome of these approaches would be fruitful.

Notes

1. In two studies (Barlow et al., 1984; Borkovec & Mathews, 1988), clients with panic disorder were included in the sample. These investigations have been retained for this chapter

because in both cases there were no significant differences in treatment response between the generalized anxiety disorder and panic disorder groups.

2. For a diagnosis of generalized anxiety disorder according to *DSM-III-R*, symptoms must have persisted for 6 months, but only 1 month's duration was required under the *DSM-III* scheme.

3. CBT for anxiety disorders often includes some exposure in the form of behavioral experiments or probes for anxious cognitions except when, for theoretical reasons, investigators exclude such interventions (e.g., Margraf & Schneider, 1991). Treatments we are calling combinations differ from CBT alone in the extent to which exposure was provided or assigned by the therapist as an important treatment component in its own right and in the systematic manner in which exposure was performed.

REFERENCES

Agras, W. S. (1990). Treatment of social phobias. *Journal of Clinical Psychiatry, 51,* 52-58.

American Psychiatric Association. (1980). *Diagnostic and statistical manual of mental disorders* (3rd ed.). Washington, DC: Author.

American Psychiatric Association. (1987). *Diagnostic and statistical manual of mental disorders* (3rd ed., Rev.). Washington, DC: Author.

Arnkoff, D. B., & Glass, C. R. (1989). Cognitive assessment in social anxiety and social phobia. *Clinical Psychology Review, 9,* 61-74.

Bandura, A., Adams, N. E., & Beyer, J. (1977). Cognitive processes mediating behavioral change. *Journal of Personality and Social Psychology, 35,* 125-139.

Barlow, D. H., Cohen, A. S., Waddell, M. T., Vermilyea, B. B., Klosko, J. S., Blanchard, E. B., & DiNardo, P. A. (1984). Panic and generalized anxiety disorders: Nature and treatment. *Behavior Therapy, 15,* 431-449.

Barlow, D. H., Craske, M. G., Cerny, J. A., & Klosko, J. (1989). Behavioral treatment of panic disorder. *Behavior Therapy, 20,* 261-282.

Baron, R. M., & Kenny, D. A. (1986). The moderator-mediator variable distinction in social psychological research: Conceptual, strategic, and statistical considerations. *Journal of Personality and Social Psychology, 51,* 1173-1182.

Beck, A. T., & Emery, G. (1985). *Anxiety disorders and phobias: A cognitive perspective.* New York: Basic Books.

Beck, A. T., Laude, R., & Bohnert, M. (1974). Ideational components of anxiety neurosis. *Archives of General Psychiatry, 31,* 319-325.

Beck, A. T., Sokol, L., Clark, D. A., Berchick, B., & Wright, F. (1992). A crossover study of focused cognitive therapy for panic disorder. *American Journal of Psychiatry, 149,* 778-783.

Beck, A. T., & Steer, R. A. (1990). *Manual for the Beck Anxiety Inventory.* San Antonio, TX: Psychological Corporation.

Blowers, C., Cobb, J., & Mathews, A. (1987). Generalized anxiety: A controlled treatment study. *Behaviour Research and Therapy, 25,* 493-502.

Borkovec, T. D., & Costello, E. (1993). Efficacy of applied relaxation and cognitive behavioral therapy in the treatment of generalized anxiety disorder. *Journal of Consulting and Clinical Psychology, 61,* 611-619.

Borkovec, T. D., & Inz, J. (1990). The nature of worry in generalized anxiety disorder: A predominance of thought activity. *Behaviour Research and Therapy, 28,* 153-158.

Borkovec, T. D., & Mathews, A. M. (1988). Treatment of nonphobic anxiety disorders: A comparison of nondirective, cognitive, and coping desensitization therapy. *Journal of Consulting and Clinical Psychology, 56,* 877-884.

Borkovec, T. D., Mathews, A. M., Chambers, A., Ebrahimi, S., Lytle, R., & Nelson, R. (1987). The effects of relaxation training with cognitive or nondirective therapy and the role of relaxation-induced anxiety in the treatment of generalized anxiety. *Journal of Consulting and Clinical Psychology, 55,* 883-888.

Borkovec, T. D., Shadick, R., & Hopkins, M. (1991). The nature of normal and pathological worry. In R. Rapee & D. H. Barlow (Eds.), *Chronic anxiety and generalized anxiety disorders* (pp. 29-51). New York: Guilford.

Butler, G., Cullington, C., Hibbert, G., Klimes, I., & Gelder, M. (1987). Anxiety management for persistent generalised anxiety. *British Journal of Psychiatry, 151,* 535-542.

Butler, G., Cullington, A., Munby, M., Amies, P., & Gelder, M. (1984). Exposure and anxiety management in the treatment of social phobia. *Journal of Consulting and Clinical Psychology, 52,* 642-650.

Butler, G., Fennell, M., Robson, P., & Gelder, M. (1991). Comparison of behavior therapy and cognitive behavior therapy in the treatment of generalized anxiety disorder. *Journal of Consulting and Clinical Psychology, 59,* 167-175.

Butler, G., Gelder, M., Hibbert, G., Cullington, A., & Klimes, I. (1987). Anxiety management: Developing effective strategies. *Behaviour Research and Therapy, 25,* 517-522.

Chambless, D. L. (1988). Cognitive mechanisms in panic disorder. In S. Rachman & J. D. Maser (Eds.), *Panic: Psychological perspectives* (pp. 205-218). Hillsdale, NJ: Lawrence Erlbaum.

Chambless, D. L. (1989, November). *Familial and social factors in simple and social phobias and their treatment.* Paper presented at the National Institute of Mental Health Workshop on Specific Phobias, Bethesda, MD.

Chambless, D. L., Caputo, G. C., Bright, P., & Gallagher, R. (1984). Assessment of fear of fear in agoraphobics: The Body Sensations Questionnaire and the Agoraphobic Cognitions Questionnaire. *Journal of Consulting and Clinical Psychology, 52,* 1090-1097.

Chambless, D. L., Goldstein, A. J., Gallagher, R., & Bright, P. (1986). Integrating behavior therapy and psychotherapy in the treatment of agoraphobia. *Psychotherapy, 23,* 150-159.

Chambless, D. L., & Gracely, E. J. (1988). Prediction of outcome following in vivo exposure treatment of agoraphobia. In I. Hand & H.-U. Wittchen (Eds.), *Panic and phobias: Treatments and variables affecting course and outcome* (pp. 209-220). Berlin: Springer-Verlag.

Chambless, D. L., & Gracely, E. J. (1989). Fear of fear and the anxiety disorders. *Cognitive Therapy and Research, 13,* 9-20.

Clark, D. M., & Salkovskis, P. M. (1995). *Cognitive therapy with panic and hypochondriasis.* Unpublished manuscript, University of Oxford, Department of Psychiatry.

Clark, D. M., Salkovskis, P. M., Hackman, A., Middleton, H., Anastasiades, P., & Gelder, M. (1991, November). *A comparison of cognitive therapy, applied relaxation, and imipramine in the treatment of panic disorder.* Paper presented at the annual meeting of the Association for Advancement of Behavior Therapy, New York.

Clum, G. A. (1989). Psychological interventions vs. drugs in the treatment of panic. *Behavior Therapy, 20,* 429-457.

Craske, M. G., Brown, T. A., & Barlow, D. H. (1991). Behavioral treatment of panic disorder: A two-year follow-up. *Behavior Therapy, 22,* 289-304.

de Ruiter, C., Rijken, H., Garssen, B., van Schaik, A., & Kraaimaat, F. (1989). Comorbidity among the anxiety disorders. *Journal of Anxiety Disorders, 3,* 57-68.

Dobson, K. S. (1989). A meta-analysis of the efficacy of cognitive therapy for depression. *Journal of Consulting and Clinical Psychology, 57,* 414-419.

Ellis, A. (1962). *Reason and emotion in psychotherapy.* New York: Lyle Stuart.

Emmelkamp, P. M. G., Brilman, E., Kuiper, H., & Mersch, P.-P. (1986). The treatment of agoraphobia: A comparison of self-instructional training, rational emotive therapy, and exposure in vivo. *Behavior Modification, 10,* 37-53.

Emmelkamp, P. M. G., Kuipers, A., & Eggeraat, J. (1978). Cognitive modification versus prolonged exposure in vivo: A comparison with agoraphobics. *Behaviour Research and Therapy, 16,* 33-41.

Emmelkamp, P. M. G., & Mersch, P. P. (1982). Cognition and exposure in vivo in the treatment of agoraphobia: Short-term and delayed effects. *Cognitive Therapy and Research, 6,* 77-90.

Emmelkamp, P. M. G., Mersch, P. P., Vissia, E., & van der Helm, M. (1985). Social phobia: A comparative evaluation of cognitive and behavioral interventions. *Behaviour Research and Therapy, 23,* 365-369.

Gelernter, C. S., Uhde, T. W., Cimbolic, P., Arnkoff, D. B., Vittone, B. J., Tancer, M. E., & Bartko, J. J. (1991). Cognitive-behavioral and pharmacological treatments for social phobia: A preliminary study. *Archives of General Psychiatry, 48,* 938-945.

Glass, C. R., Merluzzi, T. V., Biever, J. L., & Larsen, K. H. (1982). Cognitive assessment of social anxiety: Development and validation of a self-statement questionnaire. *Cognitive Therapy and Research, 6,* 37-55.

Goldstein, A. J., & Chambless, D. L. (1978). A reanalysis of agoraphobia. *Behavior Therapy, 9,* 47-59.

Greenberg, R. L. (1989). Panic disorder and agoraphobia. In J. Scott, J. M. G. Williams, & A. T. Beck (Eds.), *Cognitive therapy in clinical practice: An illustrative casebook* (pp. 25-49). London: Routledge & Kegan Paul.

Hamilton, M. (1959). The assessment of anxiety states by rating. *British Journal of Medical Psychology, 32,* 50-55.

Heimberg, R. G. (1989). Cognitive and behavioral treatments for social phobia: A critical analysis. *Clinical Psychology Review, 9,* 107-128.

Heimberg, R. G., Becker, R. E., Goldfinger, K., & Vermilyea, J. A. (1985). Treatment of social phobia by exposure, cognitive restructuring, and homework assignments. *Journal of Nervous and Mental Disease, 173,* 236-245.

Heimberg, R. G., Dodge, C. S., Hope, D. A., Kennedy, C. R., Zollo, L. J., & Becker, R. E. (1990). Cognitive behavioral group treatment for social phobia: Comparison with a credible placebo control. *Cognitive Therapy and Research, 14,* 1-23.

Heimberg, R. G., Salzman, D. G., Holt, C. S., & Blendall, K. (1993). Cognitive behavioral group treatment for social phobia: Effectiveness at five-year follow-up. *Cognitive Therapy and Research, 17,* 325-339.

Hollon, S. D., DeRubeis, R. J., & Evans, M. D. (1987). Causal mediation of change in treatment for depression: Discriminating between nonspecificity and noncausality. *Psychological Bulletin, 102,* 139-149.

Hollon, S. D., & Kriss, M. R. (1984). Cognitive factors in clinical research and practice. *Clinical Psychology Review, 4,* 35-76.

Hope, D. A., Rapee, R. M., Heimberg, R. G., & Dombeck, M. J. (1990). Representations of the self in social phobia: Vulnerability to social threat. *Cognitive Therapy and Research, 14,* 177-189.

Jansson, L., & Ost, L.-G. (1982). Behavioral treatments for agoraphobia: An evaluative review. *Clinical Psychology Review, 2,* 311-336.

Jerremalm, A., Jansson, L., & Ost, L.-G. (1986). Cognitive and physiological reactivity and the effects of different behavioral methods in the treatment of social phobia. *Behaviour Research and Therapy, 24,* 171-180.

Jones, R. G. (1969). A factored measure of Ellis' irrational belief system, with personality and adjustment correlates. *Dissertation Abstracts International, 29,* 4379B-4380B. (University Microfilms No. 69-6443)

Klosko, J. S., Barlow, D. H., Tassinari, R., & Cerny, J. A. (1990). A comparison of alprazolam and behavior therapy in treatment of panic disorder. *Journal of Consulting and Clinical Psychology, 58,* 77-84.

MacLeod, C., Mathews, A., & Tata, P. (1986). Attentional bias in emotional disorders. *Journal of Abnormal Psychology, 95,* 15-20.

Margraf, J., & Schneider, S. (1991, November). *Outcome and active ingredients of cognitive-behavioral treatments for panic disorder.* Paper presented at the annual meeting of the Association for Advancement of Behavior Therapy, New York.

Marks, I. M., & Mathews, A. M. (1979). Brief standard selfrating for phobic patients. *Behaviour Research and Therapy, 17,* 263-267.

Mattick, R. P., & Peters, L. (1988). Treatment of severe social phobia: Effects of guided exposure with and without cognitive restructuring. *Journal of Consulting and Clinical Psychology, 56,* 251-260.

Mattick, R. P., Peters, L., & Clarke, J. C. (1989). Exposure and cognitive restructuring for social phobia: A controlled study. *Behavior Therapy, 20,* 3-23.

Meichenbaum, D. (1975). Self-instructional methods. In F. H. Kanfer & A. P. Goldstein (Eds.), *Helping people change* (pp. 357-391). New York: Pergamon.

Mersch, P. P. A., Emmelkamp, P. M. G., Bogels, S. M., & van der Sleen, J. (1989). Social phobia: Individual response patterns and the effects of behavioral and cognitive interventions. *Behaviour Research and Therapy, 27,* 421-434.

Meyer, T. J., Miller, M. L., Metzger, R. L., & Borkovec, T. D. (1990). Development and validation of the Penn State Worry Questionnaire. *Behaviour Research and Therapy, 28,* 487-495.

Michelson, L. K., & Marchione, K. (1991). Behavioral, cognitive, and pharmacological treatments of panic disorder with agoraphobia: Critique and synthesis. *Journal of Consulting and Clinical Psychology, 39,* 199-114.

Michelson, L., Marchione, K., & Greenwald, M. (1989, November). *Cognitive-behavioral treatments of agoraphobia.* Paper presented at the annual meeting of the Association for Advancement of Behavior Therapy, Washington, DC.

Michelson, L., Marchione, K., Greenwald, M., Glanz, L., Testa, S., & Marchione, N. (1990). Panic disorder: Cognitive behavioral treatment. *Behaviour Research and Therapy, 28,* 141-152.

Michelson, L., Mavissakalian, M., & Marchione, K. (1988). Cognitive, behavioral, and psychophysiological treatments of agoraphobia: A comparative outcome investigation. *Behavior Therapy, 19,* 97-120.

Michelson, L., Schwartz, R. M., & Marchione, K. E. (1992). States-of-mind model: Cognitive balance in the treatment of agoraphobia—II. *Advances in Behaviour Research and Therapy, 13,* 193-213.

Newman, C. F., Beck, J. S., Beck, A. T., & Tran, G. Q. (1990, November). *Efficacy of cognitive therapy in reducing panic attacks and medication.* Paper presented at the annual meeting of the Association for Advancement of Behavior Therapy, San Francisco.

Norcross, J. C., & Prochaska, J. O. (1982). A national survey of clinical psychologists: Affiliations and orientations. *Clinical Psychologist, 35*(3), 1, 4-8.

Ost, L.-G., & Westling, B. E. (1991, September). *Treatment of panic disorder by applied relaxation vs. cognitive therapy.* Paper presented at the annual meeting of the European Association for Behaviour Therapy, Oslo.

Ost, L.-G., Westling, B. E., & Hellstrom, K. (1993). Applied relaxation, exposure in vivo, and cognitive methods in the treatment of panic disorder with agoraphobia. *Behaviour Research and Therapy, 31,* 383-394.

Power, K. G., Jerrom, D. W. A., Simpson, R. J., Mitchell, M. J., & Swanson, V. (1989). A controlled comparison of cognitive behaviour therapy, diazepam and placebo in the management of generalized anxiety. *Behavioural Psychotherapy, 17,* 1-14.

Power, K. G., Simpson, R. J., Swanson, V., Wallace, L. A., Feistner, A. T. C., & Sharp, D. (1990). A controlled comparison of cognitive-behaviour therapy, diazepam, and placebo, alone and in combination, for the treatment of generalised anxiety disorder. *Journal of Anxiety Disorders, 4,* 267-292.

Renneberg, B., Chambless, D. L., & Gracely, E. J. (1992). Prevalence of SCID-diagnosed personality disorders in agoraphobic outpatients. *Journal of Anxiety Disorders, 6,* 111-118.

Smith, M. L., & Glass, G. V. (1977). Meta-analysis of psychotherapy outcome studies. *American Psychologist, 32,* 752-760.

Smith, T. W., & Zurawksi, R. M. (1983). Assessment of irrational beliefs: The question of discriminant validity. *Journal of Clinical Psychology, 39,* 976-979.

Sokol, L., Beck, A. T., Greenberg, R. L., Wright, F. D., & Berchick, R. J. (1989). Cognitive therapy of panic disorder: A nonpharmacological alternative. *Journal of Nervous and Mental Diseases, 177,* 711-716.

Stravynski, A., Marks, I., & Yule, W. (1982). Social skills problems in neurotic outpatients. *Archives of General Psychiatry, 39,* 1378-1384.

Trull, T. J., Nietzel, M. T., & Main, A. (1988). The use of meta-analysis to assess the clinical significance of behavior therapy for agoraphobia. *Behavior Therapy, 19,* 527-538.

Watson, D., & Friend, R. (1969). Measurement of social evaluative anxiety. *Journal of Consulting and Clinical Psychology, 33,* 448-457.

Williams, S. L., & Rappoport, A. (1983). Cognitive treatment in the natural environment for agoraphobics. *Behavior Therapy, 14,* 299-313.

Zung, W. W. K. (1971). A rating instrument for anxiety disorders. *Psychosomatics, 12,* 371-379.

6

Cognitive-Behavioral Approaches
to Panic and Agoraphobia

MICHELLE G. CRASKE

Major advances have been made in recent years with respect to the cognitive-behavioral treatments for panic disorder, with and without agoraphobia. This chapter presents the conceptual basis and implementation of these treatment developments. Until relatively recently, panic attacks were viewed primarily as a form of free-floating anxiety in much the same way as generalized anxiety. However, newer cognitive-behavioral conceptualizations view panic as a very specific fear reaction to very specific types of cues. The newer treatments are based on this conceptualization. Evidence to support the efficacy of such treatments is presented here also.

PHENOMENA OF PANIC AND AGORAPHOBIA

Panic Attacks

According to the fourth edition of the *Diagnostic and Statistical Manual of Mental Disorders* (*DSM-IV;* American Psychiatric Association, 1994), panic disorder is characterized by the recurrent experience of sudden rushes

TABLE 6.1   *DSM-III-R* Panic Attack Checklist

Difficulty breathing
Sweating
Chest pain or discomfort
Unsteadiness, dizziness, or faintness
Feelings of unreality or detachment
Trembling or shaking
Tingling or numbness
Nausea or abdominal distress
Palpitations or tachycardia
Choking or smothering sensations
Hot flashes or cold chills
Fear of dying
Fear of going crazy or losing control

---

of intense fear or discomfort. The diagnostic criteria specify recurrent, unexpected attacks and at least one panic attack followed by at least 1 month of persistent apprehension about the recurrence of panic. A panic attack is defined as a cluster of physical and cognitive symptoms (shown in Table 6.1); the co-occurrence of four or more symptoms defines a full panic attack, and fewer than four symptoms defines a limited symptom attack. Furthermore, the experience of panic is defined as sudden and abrupt, meaning that it is distinct from gradually building anxious arousal and from phobic reactions to clearly discernible, circumscribed external stimuli. Figure 6.1 depicts the physiological profile of a panic attack that was monitored during a regular laboratory recording at the Center for Stress and Anxiety Disorders of the State University of New York at Albany. As can be seen, the subject was undergoing a typical relaxation phase of assessment when, unexpectedly, he or she experienced an abrupt surge of heart rate, muscle tension, and skin temperature, at which time a sense of panic was reported. The figure portrays very clearly the abrupt and intense features of panic.

Some panic attacks are cued by specific external situations, whereas others seem to occur without obvious triggers or cues. Barlow (1988) proposed a 2 × 2 typology of panic, comprising cued/uncued and expected/unexpected dimensions. In this typology, the terms *cued* and *uncued* refer to awareness of a cue in the mind of the sufferer. A cue is an event that has a demonstrated functional relationship with the onset of a panic attack, such

Subject 1

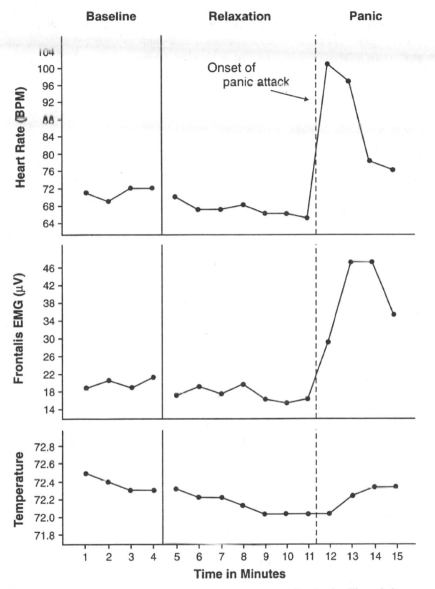

Figure 6.1. Physiological Changes From the Start of the Recording Session Through the
Onset and Peak of a Panic Attack
SOURCE: "The Psychophysiology of Relaxation Association Panic Attacks," by A. S. Cohen,
D. H. Barlow, and E. B. Blanchard, 1985, *Journal of Abnormal Psychology, 94*, p. 98. Copyright
© 1985 by the American Psychological Association, Inc. Reprinted by permission.

as external situations or internal thoughts, images, or bodily sensations. Thus, to the extent that these cues are obvious, the panic attack is cued, and to the extent that cues are not immediately obvious, the panic attack is uncued. *Expected* refers to the degree to which panic is expected to occur on any given occasion, regardless of a specific triggering cue. Accordingly, uncued and unexpected events represent the "out of the blue" or "spontaneous" type of panic attack. Panic attacks that occur without an obvious cue but that are expected because the individual "felt strange all day" and "knew that it was going to happen sometime" represent the uncued-expected type. According to a self-monitoring study conducted by Street, Craske, and Barlow (1989), the most common panic attacks are cued and expected (68%), and the least common are uncued and expected (1.4%). Intermediate to these are cued and unexpected (18%), and uncued and unexpected (or "spontaneous"; 12.5%) attacks.

Agoraphobia

Agoraphobic avoidance is described in *DSM-IV* as avoidance or endurance with dread of situations from which escape might be difficult or help unavailable in the event of a panic attack or paniclike symptoms, such as loss of bowel control. Typical agoraphobic situations include being in a shopping mall, movie theater, crowded restaurant, or crowded store; waiting in line; traveling by car or bus; and being alone. Avoidance behavior varies in terms of degree of restriction on mobility, from mild to severe, with the latter characterizing the truly house-bound agoraphobic.

Although the Epidemiological Catchment Area Study (Myers et al., 1984) reported a high prevalence of agoraphobia without history of panic in the general community, clinical settings rarely detect agoraphobia in the absence of panic attacks. That is, agoraphobia develops after the onset of panic in the majority of clinic cases. The reason for the discrepancy between clinic and community samples is unclear. One possibility is that individuals who panic are much more likely to seek help than persons who are generally anxious and avoidant but who do not experience panic (Boyd, 1986). Alternatively, epidemiological data may vastly overestimate the prevalence of agoraphobic avoidance due to misdiagnosis of specific phobias, generalized anxiety, or "normal" cautiousness about certain situations (e.g., walking in unsafe urban districts) as agoraphobia.

FEATURES OF PANIC AND AGORAPHOBIA

Treatment for panic and agoraphobia is usually sought around the age of 34 years, although the mean age of onset ranges from 23 to 29 (Breier, Charney, & Heninger, 1986; Craske, Miller, Rotunda, & Barlow, 1990; Noyes et al., 1986). A large percentage (approximately 72%; Craske et al., 1990) report the presence of identifiable stressors around the time of the first panic attack. In particular, these stressors include interpersonal and somatic-related events, such as negative drug experiences, disease, or death. However, the number of stressors does not differ from the number experienced by other anxiety groups (Pollard, Pollard, & Corn, 1989; Rapee, Litwin, & Barlow, 1990; Roy-Byrne, Geraci, & Uhde, 1986). Approximately half of persons with panic disorder report having experienced panicky feelings at some time before their first panic, suggesting that panic onset can be either insidious or acute (Craske et al., 1990).

Rarely does the diagnosis occur in isolation from other Axis I and Axis II conditions. Commonly co-occurring Axis I conditions include specific phobia, social phobia, and dysthymia (Sanderson, DiNardo, Rapee, & Barlow, 1990). Several independent investigations have shown that from 25% to 60% of persons with panic disorder (with and without agoraphobia) meet criteria for a personality disorder. Most often, these are avoidant and dependent personality disorders (Chambless & Renneberg, 1988; Mavissakalian & Hamann, 1986; Reich, Noyes, & Troughton, 1987). However, the nature of the relationship between panic disorder and personality disorders remains unclear. For example, comorbidity rates are highly dependent on the method used to establish Axis II diagnosis, as well as the co-occurrence of depressed mood (Chambless & Renneberg, 1988; Alnaes & Torgersen, 1990), and some personality "disorders" remit after successful treatment of panic and agoraphobia (Mavissakalian & Hamann, 1987; Noyes, Reich, Suelzer, & Christiansen, 1991).

CONCEPTUALIZATION OF
PANIC AND AGORAPHOBIA

As mentioned, panic attacks *were* viewed as a form of free-floating anxiety due to the apparent absence of specific triggering cues. Consequently, most theoretical and treatment attention was directed toward agoraphobia. However, several highly convergent conceptualizations of panic have been proposed recently, differing only in their points of emphasis (Barlow, 1988; Clark et al., 1988; Ehlers & Margraf, 1989).

The initial panic attack is conceptualized by Barlow (1988) as a misfiring of the "fear system" under stressful life circumstances in physiologically and psychologically vulnerable individuals. Physiological vulnerability is a topic of much biological research, with no definitive findings as of yet. It is believed to involve autonomic lability, at the very least. Physiological vulnerability is supported by recent evidence examining the construct of temperamental inhibition (Rosenbaum et al., 1988). Temperamental inhibition, or hyperarousal and withdrawal from novelty or challenge, is found with a much higher incidence in children of agoraphobics and social phobics. A physiological vulnerability factor may account for the strong familial concordance for panic disorder (Crowe, Noyes, Pauls, & Slymen, 1983; Moran & Andrews, 1985; Torgersen, 1983).

An isolated panic attack does not necessarily lead to the development of panic disorder. For example, the 10% to 12% prevalence estimate for an unexpected panic attack in the past 12 months (e.g., Norton, Dorward, & Cox, 1986; Telch, Lucas, & Nelson, 1989) is substantially higher than the 2% to 6% prevalence for panic disorder (with or without agoraphobia) in the past 6 months (Myers et al., 1984).

Barlow and others (e.g., Clark et al., 1988; McNally, 1990) speculated that a psychological vulnerability accounts for the development of anxious apprehension about the recurrence of panic, which, in turn, leads to panic disorder. The psychological vulnerability was conceptualized as a set of danger-laden beliefs about bodily sensations (i.e., "I am dying") and about the meaning of emotions in relation to individuals' conceptualization of themselves and their world (i.e., "Events are proceeding uncontrollably and unpredictably"; "I am too weak to control my emotions"). These beliefs were presumed to accrue from various life experiences, including vicarious and informational transmission from significant others about the physical and mental dangers of certain bodily symptoms.

Initial panic attacks can be traumatic, as evidenced by the frequent attendance of panickers at emergency rooms and the vivid recall that individuals have of their first panic many years later. Consequently, fearful associations with the situational context and the symptoms of arousal that were present at the time of the attack are likely to develop. In other words, individuals may learn to be fearful of particular bodily sensations that accompanied the initial panic attack. Learned fearfulness of arousal cues is akin to Razran's (1961) notion of interoceptive conditioning. This is a form of conditioning that is relatively resistant to extinction and is "unconscious." That is, interoceptive conditioned fear responses are not dependent on conscious awareness of triggering cues. According to this model, panic attacks may seem to be uncued or to occur from "out of the blue" because they are triggered by subtle benign alterations in physical state of which the individual is not fully aware. Also, activities that produce bodily sensations similar to the sensations of panic may in turn trigger panic attacks. Examples of these types of activities (that are commonly avoided by persons with panic disorder) are exercise, sexual arousal, quick movement of body posture, and caffeine ingestion.

Furthermore, cognitive misappraisals of danger, such as fears of dying or losing control, are likely to increase fearful arousal, which, in turn, may intensify the cues that are feared. For example, misinterpretation of a racing heart as a sign of heart attack may increase the heart rate. Consequently, a vicious cycle of "fear of fear" is generated and is sustained until the physiological arousal system is exhausted or until disconfirming evidence is obtained (Clark et al., 1988). This cycle is depicted in Figure 6.2.

Hence panic disorder is viewed essentially as a phobia of internal bodily cues. However, in contrast to phobias of external stimuli, internal feared cues tend to be less predictable and less escapable than external feared stimuli, leading to more intense and abrupt fear, less predictable fear, and greater anticipatory anxiety about the recurrence of fear (Craske, 1991). Also, anticipatory anxiety can increase the likelihood of panic because anxious arousal increases availability of sensations that have become conditioned cues for panic and/or increases attentional vigilance for such cues (Barlow, 1988). In this manner, a maintaining cycle is established between panic and anxious apprehension about panic.

The empirical evidence in support of this conceptualization is accruing. For example, persons who panic have stronger beliefs and fears of physical or mental harm arising from specific bodily sensations associated with panic than nonpanickers (Chambless, Caputo, Bright, & Gallagher, 1984; Clark et al., 1988; Holt & Andrews, 1989; McNally & Lorenz, 1987; Van den Hout, Van der Molen, Griez, & Lousberg, 1987). Also, there is partial evidence that persons with panic disorder have heightened awareness of, or ability to detect, bodily sensations of arousal (Antony et al., 1995; Ehlers & Breuer,

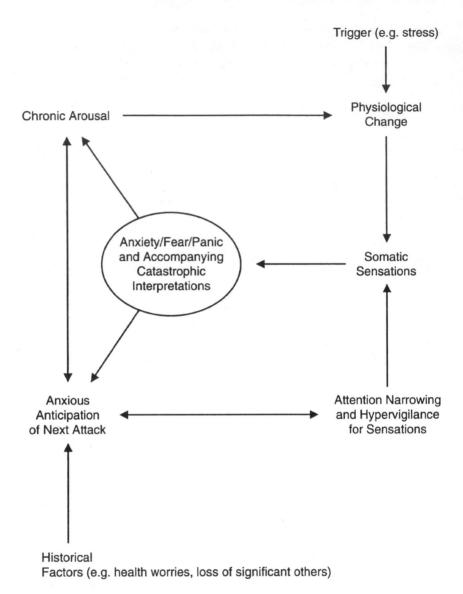

Figure 6.2.   Panic Attack Cycle
SOURCE: From *Mastery of Your Anxiety and Panic–II*. Copyright © 1994 by Graywind
Publications, Inc. Reproduced by permission of publisher, The Psychological Corporation.
All rights reserved.

1995; Ehlers & Margraf, 1989), presumably due to an attentional vigilance mechanism. In addition, persons with panic disorder are fearful of procedures that elicit bodily sensations similar to the ones experienced during panic attacks, including benign cardiovascular, respiratory, and audiovestibular exercises (Zarate, Rapee, Craske, & Barlow, 1988). Furthermore, correcting danger misappraisals about certain bodily sensations seems to lessen fearfulness. For example, considerably less panic is reported when patients are informed that hyperventilation and carbon dioxide inhalations, which produce strong paniclike physical symptoms, are safe and controllable (Rapee, Mattick, & Murrell, 1986; Rapee, Telfer, & Barlow, 1991; Sanderson, Rapee, & Barlow, 1989; Schmidt, Telch, & O'Carroll, 1989).

Though support for the "fear of fear" model is strong, there is insufficient evidence concerning the proposed psychological and physiological predispositional variables. Longitudinal studies of high-risk populations are needed to establish the role of psychological and biological vulnerabilities and the learning that takes place as a result of initial panic attacks.

As mentioned, individuals with agoraphobia who seek treatment almost always report a history of panic that preceded development of their avoidance (Craske et al., 1990; Noyes et al., 1986; Pollard, Bronson, & Kenney, 1989; Swinson, 1986). However, not all persons who panic develop agoraphobic avoidance, and the extent of avoidance that does emerge is highly variable. The reasons for these individual differences are not clear (Craske & Barlow, 1988). Agoraphobia tends to increase as the history of panic lengthens; however, a significant proportion panic for many years without developing agoraphobic limitations. Agoraphobic avoidance is not related to age of onset, panic symptom profiles, proportions of different types of attacks (i.e., cued or unexpected), or frequency of panic (Craske & Barlow, 1988). Gender, however, is significantly related to agoraphobia, with females increasingly predominating the sample as degree of avoidance becomes more severe (Thyer, Himle, Curtis, Cameron, & Nesse, 1985). The male-to-female ratio changes from approximately 45:55 to 10:90 as agoraphobia intensifies. It is believed that sex-role behaviors as well as general style of responding to threat influence the degree to which apprehension about panic leads to agoraphobic avoidance (Craske & Barlow, 1988). For example, males are more likely to use alcohol or drugs in anticipation of panic than to avoid situations (Barlow, 1988). In addition, the likelihood of a concurrent dependent or avoidant personality disorder is greater when agoraphobia is present.

In summary, therefore, agoraphobic avoidance is viewed as one style of coping with the anticipation of panic.

One implication from this conceptualization of panic and agoraphobia is that direct treatment of panic may enhance the treatment of agoraphobic avoidance. The traditional approach of targeting agoraphobic avoidance in behavioral interventions assumed that panic would naturally diminish as approach behavior increased. However, many individuals whose agoraphobic behavior is successfully treated continue to panic (Arnow, Taylor, Agras, & Telch, 1985; Michelson, Mavissakalian, & Marchione, 1985; Stern & Marks, 1973). Furthermore, panic has been linked with agoraphobic relapse (Arnow et al., 1985; Craske, Street, & Barlow, 1989).

For these reasons, efforts have recently concentrated on the development of a cognitive-behavioral approach that targets panic directly. However, before describing that treatment, I will make several comments about the assessment of panic and agoraphobia. According to the conceptualization outlined earlier, the essential measures tap constructs of fearfulness of bodily symptoms, misappraisals of bodily symptoms, vigilance for symptoms of arousal, chronic level of arousal, and agoraphobic avoidance.

ASSESSMENT OF
PANIC AND AGORAPHOBIA

Differential Diagnostic Issues

It is important to note that panic is a ubiquitous phenomenon (Barlow, 1988) occurring across a wide variety of emotional disorders. Therefore it is not uncommon for persons with specific phobias, generalized anxiety disorder, obsessive/compulsive disorder, and post-traumatic stress disorder to report the experience of panic. However, the report of a panic attack does not qualify for the diagnosis of panic disorder. In panic disorder, panic is the primary focus of apprehension. On the other hand, although panic attacks occur often in the circumscribed situations of social phobia and specific phobia, typically the individual is more concerned about negative evaluations from others or dangers inherent in the situation itself, respectively, than about the panic attack. Similarly, generalized anxiety disorder clients frequently report having panic attacks but are less concerned with panic than with external life events. However, if a phobic individual is most concerned with the occurrence of panic, rarely does the panic/worry extend beyond the circumscribed phobic situations. For example, the claustrophobic may be fearful of panicking, but only in the context of closed-in situations. Therefore diagnostic judgments should not be based solely on the self-report of panic attacks.

Diagnostic assessment can be facilitated through the use of structured interviews developed for the purpose of differentially diagnosing different forms of anxiety. These include the Anxiety Disorders Interview Schedule-Revised (ADIS-R; DiNardo & Barlow, 1988), the Schedule for Affective Disorders and Schizophrenia Life-time Version-Anxiety Modified (SADS LA), and the Structured Clinical Interview of Diagnosis (SCID). The ADIS-R was developed at the Center for Stress and Anxiety Disorders and includes the Hamilton Anxiety and Depression scales, as well as screens for psychosis, depressive disorders, and somatoform conditions. The reliability of anxiety disorder diagnoses is generally enhanced by use of structured interviews: For example, it ranges from "satisfactory" to "excellent" when the ADIS-R is used (DiNardo, Moras, Barlow, Rapee, & Brown, 1992).

Medical Conditions

A medical examination is generally recommended because several medical conditions mimic panic attacks and serve as diagnostic "rule-outs." These include thyroid conditions, caffeine or amphetamine intoxication, drug withdrawal, and pheochromocytoma. A useful reference source for medical factors associated with panic disorder, entitled *Panic Disorder in the Medical Setting,* has been published by the National Institute of Mental Health (1989). Furthermore, certain medical conditions can exacerbate panic disorder, although panic would be likely to occur even if the medical condition was alleviated. These include mitrovalve prolapse, asthma, allergies, and hypoglycemia. In reference to the model described earlier, it is understandable that these medical conditions may serve to elicit the types of physical cues the individual has learned to fear due to conditioned associations and/or cognitive misappraisal.

Self-Monitoring

As a general rule, self-monitoring is recommended for assessing panic attack frequency, intensity, type, and symptom profile. Self-monitoring is more effective than retrospective recall for several reasons. First, retrospective recall tends to be inflated (Rapee, Craske, & Barlow, 1990). Indeed, inflation in recall may contribute to apprehension about the recurrence of panic. Furthermore, ongoing self-monitoring is considered therapeutic to the extent that it contributes to the development of an objective self-awareness. Finally, self-monitoring provides feedback about progress. A panic attack record and daily anxiety record are shown in Figure 6.3. Self-monitoring is useful for tracking general anxiety levels and agoraphobic activity levels as well.

Difficulties with self-monitoring include noncompliance and fearfulness of self-monitoring. Clients sometimes dislike self-monitoring because it increases their awareness of "how bad they feel." Instruction about objective self-monitoring and reassurance that the task becomes easier with practice are helpful strategies under these conditions.

Self-Report

Several standardized self-report inventories provide useful information for treatment planning and are sensitive measures of treatment change. These include the Chambless Mobility Inventory (Chambless, Caputo, Jasin, Gracely, & Williams, 1985), the Anxiety Sensitivity Index (Reiss, Peterson, Gursky, & McNally, 1986), the Agoraphobia Cognitions Questionnaire, and the Body Sensations Questionnaire (Chambless et al., 1984). Norms are available for determining the degree to which an individual scores within clinical or non-clinical ranges on these instruments. State and trait anxiety measures typically used include the State-Trait Anxiety Inventory (Spielberger, Gorsuch, & Lushene, 1970) and the Beck Anxiety Inventory (Beck, Epstein, Brown, & Steer, 1988).

Behavioral Approach Tests

Finally, behavioral approach tests are useful for assessing degree of behavioral avoidance. They involve attempts to confront various items from the individual's own hierarchy or from a standardized hierarchy of avoided situations. Unfortunately, behavioral tests are subject to demand influences, so that individuals may complete tasks that are usually avoided. Nevertheless, they provide useful information. For example, maladaptive safety signals or coping strategies of which the individual is not fully aware may become apparent through behavioral tests. Examples include remaining in close proximity to a phone, carrying certain "lucky" objects or unused medication containers, or relying on structural supports for fear of falling. These maladaptive coping strategies are important targets for treatment intervention.

COGNITIVE-BEHAVIORAL
TREATMENT OF PANIC

What follows is a description of the components to the cognitive-behavioral treatment approach developed at the Center for Stress and Anxiety Disorders at Albany. This treatment is detailed in a manual called *Mastery of Your Anxiety and Panic* (Barlow & Craske, 1989) and in the *Therapist's Guide for Mastery of Your Anxiety and Panic* (Craske & Barlow, 1990). As mentioned earlier, several similar treatment protocols exist, including work by David Clark at Oxford, Aaron Beck in Philadelphia, and Jurgen Margraf in Germany. Obviously, the standardized protocol described below should be tailored to meet individual needs in a clinical setting.

The treatment is conducted in either an individual or a group format. Groups typically include three to five patients and two therapists. The treatment sessions are scheduled once a week, extending to once every 2 weeks toward the end of treatment to facilitate consolidation of learning and generalization. The sessions last 1 hour for individual treatment and 90 minutes for group treatment. Although there are a limited number of treatment sessions (ranging from 9 to 12 in this protocol, depending on the degree of agoraphobic avoidance), "self-treatment" is conducted between sessions through homework assignments.

The treatment is divisible into three components. The first two components involve strategies for managing anxiety and panic, and the third involves exposure to cues that trigger panic.

Cognitive Restructuring

Cognitive treatment focuses on correcting threatening misappraisals of bodily sensations. The first phase involves education about the nature of panic and anxiety. Education serves two main purposes, the first being to develop a scientific-observer model to allow individuals to describe their reactions using three response domains (i.e., cognitive, behavioral, and

Panic Attack Record

Name: _____

Date: _____   Time: _____   Duration: _____ (mins.)

With: Spouse _____   Friend _____   Stranger _____   Alone _____

Stressful Situation: Yes/No   Expected: Yes/No

Maximum Anxiety (Circle)

—0——1——2——3——4——5——6——7——8—
None   Moderate   Extreme

Sensation (Check)

Pounding heart	_____	Sweating	_____	Hot/cold flashes	_____
Tight/painful chest	_____	Choking	_____	Fear of dying	_____
Breathlessness	_____	Nausea	_____	Fear of going crazy	_____
Dizziness	_____	Unreality	_____	Fear of losing control	_____
Trembling	_____	Numbness/tingling	_____		

Figure 6.3. Self-Monitoring Forms

Name: _____   Week ending:_____

Weekly Record of Anxiety and Depression

Each evening before you go to bed please rate your *average* level of anxiety (taking all things into consideration) throughout the day, the *maximum* level of anxiety that you experienced that day, your *average* level of depression throughout the day, and your average feeling of pleasantness throughout the day. Use the scale below. Next, please list the dosages and amounts of any medication you took. Finally, please rate, using the scale below, how worried or frightened you were, on the average, about the possibility of having a panic attack throughout the day.

Level of Anxiety/Depression/Pleasant Feeling

—0—1—2—3—4—5—6—7—8—

| None | Slight | Moderate | A lot | As much as you can imagine |

Date	Average anxiety	Maximum Anxiety	Average Depression	Average Pleasant-ness	Medication type, dose, number (mg)	Fear of panic attack

(continued)

SOURCE: From *Mastery of Your Anxiety and Panic–II*. Copyright © 1994 by Graywind Publications, Inc. Reproduced by permission of publisher, The Psychological Corporation. All rights reserved.

physiological) rather than feeling as if they are victims of an uncontrollable "entity." Each panic attack and episode of heightened anxiety is described in terms of "what one thinks," "what one does," and "what one feels," with special emphasis on the way in which the three systems interact with each other. For example, when sensations are cognitively misinterpreted as dangerous, they may intensify (because fearful arousal elicits stronger sensations), providing further confirmation for the perception of danger and an urgency to escape the situation. In turn, urgency to escape a situation is likely to contribute to accelerating arousal, and so on. Second, the educational information provides an alternative, nonthreatening conceptual framework for understanding panic and anxiety. The panic attack model described earlier is presented to the client.

Next, the physiology of panic is described to correct misperceptions of sensations as being dangerous. For example, contrary to the common belief, fainting is highly unlikely during a panic attack because panic is associated with accelerated sympathetic nervous system activity, which is physiologically incompatible with fainting. The physiological information emphasizes two main points. First, fear and anxiety are natural emotions that are designed to protect the individual by facilitating guardedness and escape should danger become imminent. (Anxiety is conceptualized as the preparatory state when danger is expected to occur sometime in the future, whereas fear or panic is conceptualized as the escape or alarm state when danger appears imminent.) Second, the sensations experienced during panic attacks are based on protective physiological mechanisms. Clients are informed that anxiety and fear produce physiological changes characterized by increased heart rate, increased breathing rate, pupil dilation, sweat gland activity, muscle tension, redirection of the blood flow, and so on. All of these changes are mediated by sympathetic nervous system activity, which is designed to protect the organism. However, certain "symptoms" or "side effects" are experienced as a result, including dizziness, coldness in the periphery, visual distortions, lightheadedness, and sensations of shortness of breath.

The next phase of the cognitive component is more Socratic. It begins with a description of the principles of cognition along the lines described by Beck and Emery (1985). The main point is that the way events are interpreted determines the nature of ensuing emotional reactions. Frequently, anxious individuals misattribute their anxiety to external factors: for example, "The shopping mall made me anxious" or "the humid weather makes me panic." In fact, the cognitive model would suggest that "your interpretation of being trapped and suffocating in the mall leads you to feel anxious" or "your fearfulness of feeling hot and suffocated leads you to panic." The principles of automatic and specific thought processes are described. *Automatic* refers to the fact that thoughts can become habitual and occur "almost automatically" without full conscious awareness. An example is that of immediately searching for exits on entering a movie theater without being fully aware of so doing. Similarly, attentional vigilance to symptoms of arousal may occur at a constant "back burner" level without the individual's being fully aware of it. *Specificity* refers to the fact that thoughts can change from one situation to another, often dependent on the parameters of the situation. For example, the individual may fear embarrassment when in a crowded situation and may fear death when isolated from others.

Errors in thinking are divided into two types: overestimations of probability and catastrophic estimations of consequence. Anxious individuals tend to overestimate the likelihood that an aversive event will occur, particularly to themselves (Butler & Mathews, 1983), as well as to catastrophize the significance of such events. *Catastrophizing* refers to blowing an event out of proportion or viewing it as unmanageable and disastrous. After describing these types of errors in thinking, therapists help clients question their thoughts and categorize them as overestimations or catastrophizations. Once the thoughts have been identified and categorized, clients are taught to question and challenge them by looking at realistic probabilities, gathering evidence, exploring alternative interpretations, and considering realistic consequences and ways of managing or dealing with events should they occur.

Individuals are helped to question their probability judgments by looking at realistic evidence and rating actual probabilities on 0-to-100-point scales. Similarly, with catastrophic thinking, individuals are asked to think of the worst that could happen and imagine how they would actually deal with the situation, rather than to consider only the impending disaster.

The questioning and challenging techniques are extended through hypothesis testing. Hypothesis testing refers to behavioral experiments designed to test predictions and gather more data to disconfirm fearful predictions. For example, an individual may predict that he or she will fall if he or she does not rest against a wall when feeling anxious. The hypothesis-testing experiment would involve standing away from walls the next time he or she felt anxious to determine if he or she would actually fall.

Doubts commonly arise as fearful assumptions are being challenged: for example, "Even though I have never fainted before, it could still happen" (which reflects distorted possibilities), "Even though I've never fainted before, it's only because I've managed to get to safety in time" (which reflects false attribution of safety to escape behavior), or "Even though I've never fainted before, the next time the sensations could become worse than ever and then I would faint" (which reflects false association between intensity of sensations and risk level). Also, doubts arise from reliance on selective information to support fearful appraisals. A typical example is a history of psychosis in the extended family (e.g., second cousin) that the individual uses as evidence that the individual him- or herself will go crazy the next time he or she has a panic attack. Doubts also arise in terms of the negative consequences of avoidance: for example, "I am most afraid of becoming so anxious that I'd leave the classroom and never return." In that case, the key would be to identify the cognition that leads the individual to feel as if he or she must leave (e.g., "I'll go crazy and scream if I don't escape"). Finally, individuals often report that they do not have specific thoughts but rather "can't stand the feelings" of panic. In most cases, careful questioning can identify specific thoughts, such as "I cannot function if I have these feelings" or "These feelings will get progressively worse." For all of these reasons, the therapist must be very skillful in questioning the client's thoughts.

Cognitive restructuring is continued throughout the entire treatment program, using self-monitoring records each week to examine panic and anxiety episodes and associated thoughts. Distraction as a way of coping with fearfulness is discouraged because evidence has shown that distraction is not as effective as confrontation in the long term (Craske et al., 1989), most likely due to interference with cognitive relearning. The key to this approach is not to stop at the "fear of panic," but rather to search for the specific cognitions that led to the experience of panic and then to challenge those cognitions.

Breathing Retraining

The second treatment component is breathing retraining. Several researchers have examined the efficacy of breathing retraining for panic disorder, given that 50% to 60% of panickers describe hyperventilatory symptoms as being very similar to their panic attack symptoms (Holt & Andrews, 1989). However, it is noteworthy that recent research indicates that hyperventilatory symptoms do not necessarily represent actual hyperventilatory physiology (Holt & Andrews, 1989). Nevertheless, the conceptualization of panic that emphasizes hyperventilation views panic attacks as stress-induced respiratory changes that either provoke fear because they are perceived as frightening or augment the fear already elicited by other stimuli (Clark, Salkovskis, & Chalkley, 1985). The purposes of breathing retraining are to decrease symptoms of acute hyperventilation that sometimes occur during panic, reduce vulnerability to such symptoms, and develop a self-control technique.

Breathing retraining begins with a demonstration hyperventilation exercise, in which the individual is asked to stand and breath deeply and fast for approximately 90 seconds. (All individuals, of course, have been medically screened first.) Most often, panickers do not endure this exercise for the 90 seconds because they become fearful of the sensations produced by hyperventilation. Following this demonstration exercise and an assessment of the degree to which hyperventilation induces similar sensations to those experienced during panic attacks, education is provided about the nature of hyperventilation. The educational information serves to correct fear-based interpretations (e.g., "I cannot breathe" or "I will suffocate").

The main points conveyed are as follows: (a) It is natural to overbreathe when anxious or panicky because the body searches for more energy in the form of oxygen in preparation for dealing with danger; (b) if the oxygen is not used at the rate at which it is consumed, a state of hyperventilation can ensue; (c) *hyperventilation* refers to a lowering of the proportion of carbon dioxide to oxygen in the blood, which in turn increases the alkalinity of the blood, the oxygen stickiness of hemoglobin, and constriction of the blood vessels; (d) all of these changes lead to slightly less oxygen getting to the tissues and the resultant sensations of lightheadedness, dizziness, depersonalization, and paresthesias; and (e) these effects are not dangerous.

The next step is to teach "correct" breathing. Individuals are taught to breathe from the diaphragm as opposed to the chest because chest breathing is believed to contribute to hyperventilation. In addition, individuals are instructed to concentrate by counting during inhalation (e.g., "one . . .") and thinking the word "relax" during exhalation, proceeding up to 10 and back down to 1 in a continuous cycle. The first homework exercise is to repeat the diaphragmatic counting exercise for approximately 10 minutes, at least two times a day, for a week. There is no attempt to slow the breathing at this point. Sometimes individuals encounter difficulties breathing diaphragmatically. One aid to diaphragmatic breathing is to lie face down, flat on the floor with the arms stretched out. Once the "feeling" of diaphragmatic breathing is experienced in this position, individuals are instructed to practice in a sitting position, concentrating on filling the lower part of their lungs as if slowly filling a balloon.

After 1 week of practice, slowed breathing is approximated by gradually reaching a 6-second cycle (3 seconds inhalation, 3 seconds exhalation). After another week of slow diaphragmatic breathing practice, individuals begin practicing in distracting environments, such as at work or in the car. The last step is to apply slow breathing as a control strategy at times of anxiety or panic.

One difficulty that can arise with breathing retraining is an overreliance on breathing exercises. The provision of a concrete exercise, particularly one that slows symptoms of arousal, is particularly appealing. Frustration and "desperation" can arise from drastic attempts to use the breathing exercise "at all costs" for fear that if breathing is not slowed, then dreaded events such as fainting or death will actually occur. The most effective use of breathing retraining is in combination with cognitive restructuring principles. Another problem is the experience of dizziness or other feared symptoms during slowed-breathing exercises. Such symptoms arise from fear of breathing due to misappraisals of danger or from chronic hyperventilation that renders the individual vulnerable to exacerbation of symptomatology when breathing patterns are disrupted. In each case, symptoms are likely to subside with practice.

Others have used applied relaxation in place of breathing retraining. This involves training in progressive muscle relaxation until individuals are skilled in the use of cue control procedures, at which point the relaxation skill is applied to practice items from a hierarchy of anxiety-provoking tasks (Ost, 1988).

Interoceptive Exposure

The purpose of interoceptive exposure (as in the case of exposure to external phobic stimuli) is to disrupt or weaken associations between specific bodily cues and panic reactions. The theoretical basis for interoceptive exposure is one of fear extinction, given the conceptualization of panic attacks as conditioned or learned alarm reactions to salient bodily cues. Interoceptive exposure is conducted through procedures that induce paniclike sensations reliably, such as cardiovascular exercises. The exposure is conducted using a graduated format and proceeds from simulated exercises in the clinic setting to more naturalistic activities in the home environment. It is important to provide a credible rationale for interoceptive exposure that explains the apparent conflict between earlier strategies, which emphasized decreasing sensations (through cognitive restructuring and breathing control), and this more confrontational procedure.

First, exercises that produce sensations similar to the ones that occur during panic are identified. Next, exposure to individually relevant sensation-induction exercises is repeated so that clients may learn that aversive consequences do not occur. Exercises include hyperventilation, spinning in a swivel chair, holding one's breath, tensing muscles, and breathing through a small tube. A hierarchy is established in order of anxiety level associated with each exercise. Repeated exposure begins with lower-anxiety-level items. Each item is practiced until the maximum anxiety rating is no more than mild. With each practice, clients are instructed to experience the sensations as fully as possible and to tolerate them for a period of time before terminating the exercise. For example, clients may be asked to hyperventilate until they feel sensations of lightheadedness or dizziness and then to continue the hyperventilation exercise for at least 30 seconds longer. By so doing, the urge to avoid and resist the sensations is broken. With each repetition, clients are encouraged to apply the cognitive strategies and breathing strategies after inducing and tolerating the sensations.

In addition to within-session practices, the exercises are practiced every day between sessions. Homework practice not only consolidates learning but also facilitates generalizations to situations in which the therapist is not present as a safety signal. After the simulated exercises are completed, naturalistic exposure activities are identified, listed in a hierarchy, and practiced in the same way. Naturalistic interoceptive exercises include aerobic classes, running up flights of stairs, steamy showers, humid weather conditions, and caffeine.

Interoceptive exercises are not fear provoking for a certain proportion of clients, due to the immediate attribution of the sensations to the exercise procedure and/or the perceived safety of the circumstances in which the exercise is being conducted. In the former case, cognitive restructuring may be employed to identify misperceptions that sensations that occur without being obviously induced are necessarily more dangerous than sensations induced by interoceptive exercises. In the latter case, clients are instructed to practice on their own at home or in a setting they do not necessarily consider protective, so as to learn to be less fearful even in the absence of safety signals.

In Vivo Exposure

In vivo exposure refers to repeated confrontation with, or approach to, the object or situation that is avoided. In this case, the object of in vivo exposure is the agoraphobic situation. At its most intensive, exposure therapy may be conducted 3 to 5 hours a day, 5 days a week. Long, continuous sessions are generally considered more effective than shorter or interrupted sessions (Chaplin & Levine, 1981; Marshall, 1985; Stern & Marks, 1973). The optimal rate for repeating exposure is unclear. Some have suggested that weekly sessions are less effective than daily sessions in the short term (Foa, Jameson, Turner, & Payne, 1980). Others have suggested that spaced exposure is preferred because dropout rates and relapse rates are generally higher with massed exposures (Barlow, 1988). Recently, Chambless (1990) found that massed and spaced exposure were equally effective in terms of short-term and long-term outcome and in terms of dropout rates and relapse patterns. Therefore the choice for type of exposure may be made by the therapist and client.

Typically, in vivo exposure is conducted in a graduated format progressing from the least to the most difficult items on an individual hierarchy. However, Feigenbaum (1988) found that more intense exposure (i.e., in vivo exposure with the most anxiety-provoking situations first) was markedly more effective over the long term. Five years after treatment, 76% of an intensive group versus 35% of a graded group reported themselves to be completely free of symptoms.

Another dimension to consider is whether exposure should be therapist directed or self-directed. Several researchers have found that structured, manualized programs with minimal therapist contact are as effective as intensive therapist contact (Ghosh & Marks, 1987; Mathews, Gelder, & Johnston, 1981; Jannoun, Munby, Catalan, & Gelder, 1980). However, the results may be less promising with severe, house-bound agoraphobics, who may warrant more therapist-directed in vivo exposure (Holden, O'Brien, Barlow, Stetson, & Infantino, 1983). Family members or significant others have been incorporated into exposure-based treatment programs to facilitate self-directed exposure practice. Involvement of significant others in all aspects of assessment and treatment has been shown to produce results that are superior to those from conditions excluding (willing) significant others (Barlow, O'Brien, & Last, 1984)—a finding that is particularly evident 1 and 2 years following treatment (Cerny, Barlow, Craske, & Himadi, 1987). Spouses are taught to serve as coaches for the design and practice of exposure tasks and the application of anxiety control strategies.

A golden rule of in vivo exposure has been to continue an exposure trial until anxiety reduces (Marks, 1978). Similarly, the emotional processing model outlined by Foa and Kozak (1986) proposes that long-term fear reduction is dependent on activation of fearful arousal plus within-session fear reduction. However, others have noted that exposure is equally effective when a trial is terminated at the point that anxiety reaches unduly high levels (Agras, Leitenberg, & Barlow, 1968; DeSilva & Rachman, 1984; Emmelkamp, 1982; Rachman, Craske, Tallman, & Solyom, 1986), as long as the exposure trial is reinitiated after anxiety levels have reduced.

In vivo exposure is believed to be most functional when attention is directed fully toward the phobic object and internal and external sources of distraction are minimized (Foa & Kozak, 1986). In accord, Craske et al. (1989) found that instructions to distract from bodily sensations and thoughts during in vivo exposure led to a deteriorating trend over the follow-up interval after treatment, whereas instructions to focus objectively on bodily sensations and thoughts did not. Therefore clients are encouraged to rehearse coping with physical and cognitive symptoms they are likely to experience before entering an exposure trial. Also, they are encouraged to experience sensations fully throughout in vivo exposure and to monitor their state objectively the entire time, while questioning and challenging misinterpretations.

TREATMENT EFFICACY

Several independent studies have shown that treatments using the types of procedures described above are very effective. This includes treatments that emphasize primarily somatic procedures, such as breathing retraining, in combination with cognitive restructuring (Clark et al., 1985). In addition, Ost (1988) reported that 100% of a group receiving applied progressive muscle relaxation were panic-free after 14 sessions. Furthermore, their success was maintained for approximately 19 months after treatment completion. More recently, Michelson et al. (1990) combined applied progressive muscle relaxation training, breathing retraining, and cognitive restructuring. By the end of treatment, all subjects were free of spontaneous panics, and all but one were free of panic attacks altogether. Similarly, in an uncontrolled study by Sokol and Beck (1986; cited in Beck, 1988) using primarily cognitive strategies, the results showed that panic attacks were eliminated in 17 patients who did not have additional diagnoses of personality disorder within an average of 17 treatment sessions and that the success rate was maintained 12 months later. More impressive is a preliminary report from Margraf (1989) showing that cognitive strategies conducted in isolation from exposure and behavioral procedures are highly effective. Finally, in the first controlled behavioral study for the treatment of panic disorder (Barlow, Craske, Cerny, & Klosko, 1989), the combination of interoceptive exposure, breathing retraining, and cognitive restructuring was found to eliminate panic attacks in approximately 85% of the subject sample who completed treatment, a result that was maintained for up to 2 years following treatment completion (Craske, Brown, & Barlow, 1991).

On the less positive side, it is generally recognized that although these short-term focused treatments are particularly effective for controlling panic attacks, general anxiety may remain at a relatively moderate level.

Results from the treatment of agoraphobia using primarily in vivo exposure procedures, or the combination of in vivo exposure with cognitive and self-statement instruction, are generally good (Jansson & Ost, 1982). When dropouts are excluded, 60% to 70% of agoraphobics show some clinical improvement, which is maintained on average for 4 years or more. However, 30% to 40% fail to benefit, and of the ones who benefit, a substantial proportion may not attain clinically meaningful levels of functioning. As noted by Jacobson, Wilson, and Tupper (1988), although 50% show statistically reliable improvement, only 25% are no longer agoraphobic. It is for these reasons that attempts have been made to maximize the effectiveness of in vivo exposure by including significant others, by incorporating more developed cognitive restructuring techniques, by teaching focusing of attention as opposed to distraction, and so on. More important, however, it is believed that the inclusion of the recently developed panic control strategies will enhance the effectiveness of agoraphobia treatments overall. Empirical investigation of this question is now underway.

CONCLUSION

In conclusion, the behavioral treatment for panic and agoraphobia continues to develop in concert with advancements in theoretical conceptualizations. One of the most exciting areas is the recent burgeoning of short-term treatments for panic attacks. In an impressive and convergent set of results, independent studies are showing successful control of panic for 80% to 100% of treatment completers. More important, this effect seems to be maintained for at least 2 years following treatment completion. However, the extent to which these short-term treatments affect the more pervasive aspects of anxiety (such as anticipation of the recurrence of panic, vigilance for symptoms of arousal, and so on), the means by which they are best combined with in vivo exposure procedures for agoraphobic avoidance, and the mechanisms of therapeutic action remain unclear and require further investigation.

REFERENCES

Agras, W. S., Leitenberg, H., & Barlow, D. H. (1968). Social reinforcement in the modification of agoraphobia. *Archives of General Psychiatry, 19,* 423-427.

Alnaes, R., & Torgersen, S. (1990). *DSM-III* personality disorders among patients with major depression, anxiety disorders, and mixed conditions. *Journal of Nervous and Mental Disease, 178,* 693-698.

American Psychiatric Association. (1994). *Diagnostic and statistical manual of mental disorders* (4th ed.). Washington, DC: Author.

Antony, M., Brown, T. A., Craske, M. G., Barlow, D. H., Mitchell, W. B., & Meadows, E. (1995). Accuracy of heart beat perception in panic disorder, social phobic, and nonanxious subjects. *Journal of Anxiety Disorders, 9,* 355-371.

Arnow, B. A., Taylor, C. B., Agras, W. S., & Telch, M. J. (1985). Enhancing agoraphobia treatment outcome by changing couple communication patterns. *Behavior Therapy, 16,* 452-467.

Barlow, D. H. (1988). *Anxiety and its disorders: The nature and treatment of anxiety and panic.* New York: Guilford.

Barlow, D. H., & Craske, M. G. (1989). *Mastery of your anxiety and panic.* New York: Graywind.

Barlow, D. H., Craske, M. G., Cerny, J. A., & Klosko, J. S. (1989). Behavioral treatment of panic disorder. *Behavior Therapy, 20,* 261-282.

Barlow, D. H., O'Brien, G. T., & Last, C. G. (1984). Couples treatment of agoraphobia. *Behavior Therapy, 15,* 41-58.

Beck, A. T. (1988). Cognitive approaches to panic disorder: Theory and therapy. In S. Rachman & J. D. Maser (Eds.), *Panic: Psychological perspectives* (pp. 91-109). Hillsdale, NJ: Lawrence Erlbaum.

Beck, A. T., & Emery, G. (1985). *Anxiety disorders and phobias: A cognitive perspective.* New York: Basic Books.

Beck, A. T., Epstein, N., Brown, G., & Steer, R. (1988). An inventory for measuring clinical anxiety. *Journal of Consulting and Clinical Psychology, 56,* 893-897.

Boyd, H. H. (1986). Use of mental health services for the treatment of panic disorder. *American Journal of Psychiatry, 143,* 1569-1574.

Breier, A., Charney, D. S., & Heninger, G. R. (1986). Agoraphobia with panic attacks. *Archives of General Psychiatry, 43,* 1029-1036.

Butler, G., & Mathews, A. (1983). Cognitive processes in anxiety. *Advances in Behaviour Research and Therapy, 5,* 51-62.

Cerny, J. A., Barlow, D. H., Craske, M. G., & Himadi, W. G. (1987). Couples treatment of agoraphobia: A two-year follow-up. *Behavior Therapy, 18,* 401-415.

Chambless, D. L. (1990). Spacing of exposure sessions in the treatment of agoraphobia and simple phobia. *Behavior Therapy, 21,* 217-229.

Chambless, D. L., Caputo, G., Bright, P., & Gallagher, R. (1984). Assessment of fear in agoraphobics: The Body Sensations Questionnaire and the Agoraphobic Cognitions Questionnaire. *Journal of Consulting and Clinical Psychology, 52,* 1090-1097.

Chambless, D. L., Caputo, G., Jasin, S. E., Gracely, E. J., & Williams, C. (1985). The Mobility Inventory for Agoraphobia. *Behaviour Research and Therapy, 23,* 35-44.

Chambless, D. L., & Renneberg, B. (1988, September). *Personality disorders of agoraphobics.* Paper presented at the World Congress of Behavior Therapy, Edinburgh, Scotland.

Chaplin, E. W., & Levine, B. A. (1981). The effects of total exposure duration and interrupted versus continued exposure in flooding therapy. *Behavior Therapy, 12,* 360-368.

Clark, D., Salkovskis, P., & Chalkley, A. (1985). Respiratory control as a treatment for panic attacks. *Journal of Behavior Therapy and Experimental Psychiatry, 16,* 23-30.

Clark, D. M., Salkovskis, P., Gelder, M., Koehler, C., Martin, M., Anastasiades, P., Hackmann, A., Middleton, H., & Jeavons, A. (1988). Tests of a cognitive theory of panic. In I. Hand & H. Wittchen (Eds.), *Panic and phobias: Treatments and variables affecting course and outcome* (pp. 71-90). Berlin: Springer-Verlag.

Craske, M. G. (1991). Phobic fear and panic attacks: The same emotional state triggered by different cues? *Clinical Psychology Review, 11,* 599-620.

Craske, M. G., & Barlow, D. H. (1988). A review of the relationship between panic and avoidance. *Clinical Psychology Review, 8,* 667-685.

Craske, M. G., & Barlow, D. H. (1990). *Therapist's guide for mastery of your anxiety and panic.* New York: Graywind.

Craske, M. G., Brown, T. A., & Barlow, D. H. (1991). Behavioral treatment of panic disorder: A two-year follow-up. *Behavior Therapy, 22,* 289-304.

Craske, M. G., Miller, P. P., Rotunda, R., & Barlow, D. H. (1990). A descriptive report of features of initial unexpected panic attacks in minimal and extensive avoiders. *Behaviour Research and Therapy, 28,* 395-400.

Craske, M. G., Street, L., & Barlow, D. H. (1989). Instructions to focus upon or distract from internal cues during exposure treatment for agoraphobic avoidance. *Behaviour Research and Therapy, 27,* 663-672.

Crowe, R. R., Noyes, R., Pauls, D. L., & Slymen, D. J. (1983). A family study of panic disorder. *Archives of General Psychiatry, 40,* 1065-1069.

DeSilva, P., & Rachman, S. J. (1984). Does escape behavior strengthen agoraphobic avoidance? A preliminary study. *Behaviour Research and Therapy, 22,* 87-91.

DiNardo, P., & Barlow, D. H. (1988). *Anxiety Disorders Interview Schedule—Revised.* Albany: State University of New York-Albany, Phobia and Anxiety Disorders Clinic.

DiNardo, P. A., Moras, K., Barlow, D. H., Rapee, R. M., & Brown, T. A. (1993). Reliability of *DSM-III-R* anxiety disorders categories using the Anxiety Disorders Interview Schedule-Revised (ADIS-R). *Archives of General Psychiatry, 50,* 251-256.

Ehlers, A., & Breuer, P. (1995). Selective attention to physical threat in subjects with panic attacks and specific phobias. *Journal of Anxiety Disorders, 9,* 11-31.

Ehlers, A., & Margraf, J. (1989). The psychophysiological model of panic attacks. In P. M. G. Emmelkamp, W. T. Everaerd, F. W. Kraaimaat, & M. J. Van Son (Eds.), *Fresh perspectives on anxiety disorders* (pp. 1-29). Lise, the Netherlands: Swets & Zeitlinger.

Emmelkamp, P. (1982). *Phobic and obsessive-compulsive disorders: Theory, research, and practice.* New York: Plenum.

Fischer, W. (1988). Long-term effects of imaginal versus guided mastery exposure in agoraphobics. In I. Hand & H. Wittchen (Eds.), *Panic and phobias: Treatments and variables affecting course and outcome* (pp. 149-158). Berlin: Springer-Verlag.

Foa, E. B., Jameson, J. S., Turner, R. M., & Payne, L. L. (1980). Massed vs. spaced exposure sessions in the treatment of agoraphobia. *Behaviour Research and Therapy, 18,* 333-338.

Foa, E. B., & Kozak, M. S. (1986). Emotional processing of fear: Exposure to corrective information. *Psychological Bulletin, 99,* 20-35.

Ghosh, A., & Marks, I. M. (1987). Self-directed exposure for agoraphobia: A controlled trial. *Behavior Therapy, 18,* 3-16.

Holden, A. E. O., O'Brien, G. T., Barlow, D. H., Stetson, D., & Infantino, A. (1983). Self-help manual for agoraphobia: A preliminary report of effectiveness. *Behavior Therapy, 14,* 545-556.

Holt, P., & Andrews, G. (1989). Hyperventilation and anxiety in panic disorder, agoraphobia, and generalized anxiety disorder. *Behaviour Research and Therapy, 27,* 453-460.

Jacobson, N. S., Wilson, L., & Tupper, C. (1988). The clinical significance of treatment gains resulting from exposure-based interventions for agoraphobia: A re-analysis of outcome data. *Behavior Therapy, 19,* 539-554.

Jannoun, L., Munby, M., Catalan, J., & Gelder, M., Jr. (1980). A home-based treatment program for agoraphobia: Replication and controlled evaluation. *Behavior Therapy, 11,* 294-305.

Jansson, L., & Ost, L.-G. (1982). Behavioral treatments for agoraphobia: An evaluative review. *Clinical Psychology Review, 2,* 311-336.

Margraf, J. (1989, June). *Comparative efficacy of cognitive, exposure, and combined treatments for panic disorder.* Paper presented at the annual meeting of the European Association for Behavior Therapy, Vienna.

Marks, I. M. (1978). *Living with fear.* New York: McGraw-Hill.

Marshall, W. L. (1985). The effects of variable exposure in flooding therapy. *Behavior Therapy, 16,* 117-135.

Mathews, A. M., Gelder, M. G., & Johnston, D. W. (1981). *Agoraphobia: Nature and treatment.* New York: Guilford.

Mavissakalian, M., & Hamann, M. (1986). *DSM-III* personality disorder in agoraphobia. *Comprehensive Psychiatry, 27,* 471-479.

Mavissakalian, M., & Hamann, M. (1987). *DSM-III* personality disorder in agoraphobia. II. Changes with treatment. *Comprehensive Psychiatry, 28,* 356-361.

McNally, R. (1990). Psychological approaches to panic disorders: A review. *Psychological Bulletin, 108,* 403-419.

McNally, R., & Lorenz, M. (1987). Anxiety sensitivity in agoraphobics. *Journal of Behaviour Therapy and Experimental Psychiatry, 18,* 3-11.

Michelson, L., Marchione, K., Greenwald, M., Glanz, L., Testa, S., & Marchione, N. (1990). Panic disorder: Cognitive-behavioral treatment. *Behaviour Research and Therapy, 28,* 141-151.

Michelson, L., Mavissakalian, M. Y., & Marchione, K. (1985). Cognitive and behavioral treatments of agoraphobia: Clinical, behavioral, and psychophysiological outcomes. *Journal of Consulting and Clinical Psychology, 53,* 913-925.

Moran, C., & Andrews, G. (1985). The familial occurrence of agoraphobia. *British Journal of Psychiatry, 146,* 262-267.

Myers, J., Weissman, M., Tischler, C., Holzer, C., Orvaschel, H., Anthony, J., Boyd, J., Burke, J., Kramer, M., & Stoltzman, R. (1984). Six-month prevalence of psychiatric disorders in three communities. *Archives of General Psychiatry, 41,* 959-967.

National Institute of Mental Health. (1989). *Panic disorder in the medical setting.* Washington, DC: Government Printing Office.

Norton, G., Dorward, J., & Cox, B. (1986). Factors associated with panic attacks in non-clinical subjects. *Behavior Therapy, 17,* 239-252.

Noyes, R., Crowe, R. R., Harris, E. L., Hamra, B. J., McChesney, C. M., & Chaudry, D. R. (1986). Relationship between panic disorder and agoraphobia: A family study. *Archives of General Psychiatry, 43,* 227-232.

Noyes, R., Reich, J., Suelzer, M., & Christiansen, J. (1991). Personality traits associated with panic disorder: Change associated with treatment. *Comprehensive Psychiatry, 32,* 282-294.

Ost, L.-G. (1988). Applied relaxation vs. progressive relaxation in the treatment of panic disorder. *Behaviour Research and Therapy, 26,* 13-22.

Pollard, C. A., Bronson, S. S., & Kenney, M. R. (1989). Prevalence of agoraphobia without panic in clinical settings. *American Journal of Psychiatry, 146,* 559.

Pollard, C. A., Pollard, H. J., & Corn, K. J. (1989). Panic onset and major events in the lives of agoraphobics: A test of contiguity. *Journal of Abnormal Psychology, 98,* 318-321.

Rachman, S. J., Craske, M. G., Tallman, K., & Solyom, C. (1986). Does escape behavior strengthen agoraphobic avoidance? A replication. *Behaviour Therapy, 17,* 366-384.

Rapee, R. M., Craske, M. G., & Barlow, D. H. (1990). Subject described features of panic attacks using a new self-monitoring form. *Journal of Anxiety Disorders, 4,* 171-181.

Rapee, R. M., Litwin, E. M., & Barlow, D. H. (1990). Impact of life events on subjects with panic disorder and on comparison subjects. *American Journal of Psychiatry, 147,* 640-644.

Rapee, R. M., Mattick, R., & Murrell, E. (1986). Cognitive mediation in the affective component of spontaneous panic attacks. *Journal of Behavior Therapy and Experimental Psychiatry, 17,* 245-253.

Rapee, R. M., Telfer, L., & Barlow, D. (1991). The role of safety cues in mediating the response to inhalations of CO_2 in agoraphobics. *Behaviour Research and Therapy, 29,* 353-356.

Razran, G. (1961). The observable unconscious and the inferable conscious in current Soviet psychophysiology: Interoceptive conditioning, semantic conditioning, and the orienting reflex. *Psychological Review, 68,* 81-147.

Reich, J., Noyes, R., & Troughton, E. (1987). Dependent personality disorder associated with phobic avoidance in patients with panic disorder. *American Journal of Psychiatry, 144,* 323-326.

Reiss, S., Peterson, R., Gursky, D., & McNally, R. (1986). Anxiety sensitivity, anxiety frequency, and the prediction of fearfulness. *Behaviour Research and Therapy, 24,* 1-8.

Rosenbaum, J. F., Biederman, J., Gersten, M., Hirshfield, D. R., Meminger, S. R., Herman, J. B., Kagan, J., Reznick, J. S., & Snidman, N. (1988). Behavioral inhibition in children of parents with panic disorder and agoraphobia. *Archives of General Psychiatry, 45,* 463-470.

Roy-Byrne, P. P., Geraci, M., & Uhde, T. W. (1986). Life events and the onset of panic disorder. *American Journal of Psychiatry, 143,* 1424-1427.

Sanderson, W. S., DiNardo, P. A., Rapee, R. M., & Barlow, D. H. (1990). Syndrome comorbidity in patients diagnosed with a *DSM-III-Revised* anxiety disorder. *Journal of Abnormal Psychology, 99,* 308-312.

Sanderson, W. S., Rapee, R. M., & Barlow, D. H. (1989). The influence of an illusion of control on panic attacks induced via inhalation of 5.5% carbon dioxide enriched air. *Archives of General Psychiatry, 48,* 157-162.

Schmidt, M., Telch, M., & O'Carroll, V. (1989, November). *Role of fear in mediating the effects of voluntary hyperventilation in non-clinical panickers and normal controls.* Poster presented at 23rd annual meeting of the Association for Advancement of Behavioral Therapy, Washington, DC.

Spielberger, C. D., Gorsuch, R. L., & Lushene, R. E. (1970). *Manual for the State-Trait Anxiety Inventory.* Palo Alto, CA: Consulting Psychologists Press.

Stern, R. S., & Marks, I. M. (1973). Brief and prolonged flooding: A comparison of agoraphobic patients. *Archives of General Psychiatry, 28,* 270-276.

Street, L., Craske, M. G., & Barlow, D. H. (1989). Sensations, cognitions and the perception of cues associated with expected and unexpected panic attacks. *Behaviour Research and Therapy, 27,* 189-198.

Swinson, R. P. (1986). Reply to Kleiner. *Behavior Therapist, 9,* 110-128.

Telch, M. J., Lucas, J. A., & Nelson, P. (1989). Nonclinical panic in college students: An investigation of prevalence and symptomatology. *Journal of Abnormal Psychology, 98,* 300-306.

Thyer, B. A., Himle, J., Curtis, G. C., Cameron, O. G., & Nesse, R. M. (1985). A comparison of panic disorder and agoraphobia with panic attacks. *Comprehensive Psychiatry, 26,* 208-214.

Torgersen, S. (1983). Genetic factors in anxiety disorders. *Archives of General Psychiatry, 40,* 1085-1089.

Van den Hout, M., Van der Molen, G. M., Griez, E., & Lousberg, G. (1987). Specificity of interoceptive fear to panic disorders. *Journal of Psychopathology and Behavioral Assessment, 9,* 99-109.

Zarate, R., Rapee, R. M., Craske, M. G., & Barlow, D. H. (1988, November). *Response norms for symptom induction procedures.* Poster presented at the 22nd annual meeting of the Association for Advancement of Behavioral Therapy, New York.

7

Changing Cognitive Schemas

A NECESSARY ANTECEDENT TO CHANGING
BEHAVIORS IN DYSFUNCTIONAL FAMILIES?

JAMES F. ALEXANDER

PENNY BROOKE JAMESON

ROBERT M. NEWELL

DONNA GUNDERSON

When the conference organizers (now editors) asked us to develop our presentation, they suggested a second, also somewhat rhetorical question as a subtitle: "Is there much behavior left in cognitive-behavioral therapy?" We want to begin this presentation by asserting that the answer to this latter question is a definite "yes." In treating dysfunctional families, behavior represents our "bottom line," the "final common pathway" for the myriad variables that might be considered as relevant, the ultimate focus of our change philosophy and technology. So as an initial premise, let us remember that despite the current interest in cognition, attributions, object-relational introjects, neurotransmitters, diatheses, and multicultural differences, it is still behavior that we almost always need to change regardless of our epistemological underpinnings.

Further, in the marital and family therapy outcome literature, interventions that have a behavioral component continue to be the most consistently efficacious with respect to a wide range of difficulties (Alexander, Holtzworth-Munroe, & Jameson, 1993; Shadish, Montgomery, Wilson, & Wilson, 1993). The behavioral component of intervention in our functional family therapy (FFT) model, and other models, also presents some of the most interesting clinical challenges requiring our greatest creativity and technical sophistication. Although behavioral technologies represent productive avenues for creating targeted behavior change, this is less and less a reflection of a "one size fits all" package that is applied somewhat uniformly to a wide variety of relational processes. Instead, it is often more effective to incorporate phenom-enological and at the same time systemic considerations in organizing strategies for intervention, so the techniques we design to change specific patterns of behavior must be individualized in a way that represents an inter- personal payoff for all members of a marital or family system (Alexander & Parsons, 1982).

A BROADENED PERSPECTIVE

If traditional behavioral theory, with its linear, microscopic, and present-centered epistemology and methodology, were sufficient for understanding, describing, and changing complex behavior, there would be no need to include additional phenomena such as cognition and affect. Behavioral theorists do not deny the existence of either cognition or affect; rather, as Baer, Nietzel, and Mitchell (1991) emphasized, the behavioral approach elects to focus on immediate, observable behavior in the interest of precision, parsimony, and replicability. Certainly therapy would be a less complicated endeavor if we could simply teach communication skills or reinforcement programs to the dysfunctional families we see.

Unfortunately, our experience suggests that such teaching does not "take" in many families; negative emotions and defensive processes get in the way. Most families presenting for therapy can be characterized by interpersonal relational behavior sequences that are defensive (Alexander, 1973) and/or coercive (Patterson, 1982) and/or aggressive (Margolin, John, & Gleberman,

1988). These sequences are often cyclical, escalating, and emotionally vola-tile. It is often amazing to clinicians and other individuals outside the system when family members repeatedly engage in such obviously destructive and maladaptive behaviors. It is even more amazing when these same family members are resistant to prescribed behavioral change techniques that would eliminate such dysfunctional interaction patterns. It is our belief that to account adequately for such resistance in dysfunctional families it is neces-sary to expand our analyses of behavior to include the additional phenomena of cognition and affect and to conceptualize all three as operating within a systemic—as opposed to an individual—framework. Only by so doing are we able to understand satisfactorily the meaning of the behavior in relation-ship to its motivational context. So-called dysfunctional interactive behavior is, of course, functional (or reinforcing) in some manner (as was so beauti-fully elucidated in the concepts of "reciprocity and coercion" developed by Patterson and Reid, 1970). This functional value of deviant behavior must be understood before we can develop the appropriate change strategies for each family and must be dealt with therapeutically before the family is ready or able to learn a new way of interacting. As we shall see, emotional and system-based interpersonal processes provide avenues to this understanding, as well as vehicles to energize the change process.

To highlight the basis for our assertions and to prevent our discussion from becoming too abstract and "sanitized," consider some demographic and qualitative characteristics of a sample of families seen recently in our clinic: Nearly 80% of the youth had been previously arrested or hospitalized. Of this group, over 80% had a substance abuse problem as a primary feature of the referral; almost one fifth of the youth had attempted suicide. Over one third of the referred families had experienced documented physical violence in the home, and in over 20% at least one parent was chemically addicted. Most of the families had little or no insurance or had already exhausted their benefits (usually via inpatient treatment). Nearly all family members were described clinically as having low self-esteem and efficacy with respect to changing themselves or each other, and all were described as being at extreme risk for dropout and subsequent clinical and legal problems.

The extreme pathos of the situation of many of these families need not lead us to forget the well-controlled studies in which traditional and strictly behavioral approaches have demonstrated efficacy in changing circum-scribed behavioral patterns. However, in reality clinicians often face so-called multiproblem families that demonstrate a number of complex comorbidity patterns (Kazdin, 1992). In such extreme yet frequently encountered cases, the task of the clinician is often onerous due to family members' poor motivation for change. Thus an expanded clinical perspective of behavior is required to enhance our ability to change these dysfunctional patterns.

The addition of cognition to the traditional behavioral domain represents one such expansion of perspectives, one that is well represented in this volume. In fact, it is the popularity of the cognitive component that led to the initial rhetorical question about the status of behavior in the current zeitgeist of intervention approaches. In the marriage therapy domain, for example, behavioral marital therapy (BMT) evolved into cognitive-behavioral marital therapy (CBMT). And although reviews generally support the overall effectiveness of CBMT when compared to other intervention models, challenges such as issues of "clinical significance" (Jacobson & Truax, 1991) have arisen. In addition, the work of Snyder, Wills, and Grady-Fletcher (1991) and the long-term superiority of their insight-oriented marital therapy (IOMT) as opposed to BMT suggested limitations in the behavioral paradigm (see Alexander, Holtzworth-Munroe, & Jameson, 1993). Interestingly, Jacobson responded to Snyder et al.'s work by asserting that the so-called IOMT program actually comprised a substantial number of elements of BMT and further argued that the behavioral therapy represented in that study was outdated and not indicative of good BMT as it is currently practiced (Jacobson, 1991).

This assertion reflects an additional phenomenon in the field. Specifically, many authors who have published under the mantle of behaviorism (or some hyphenated form thereof) have recognized the need for a wider range of clinical perspectives and activities. However, we have been to some extent stymied by the lack of a comprehensive conceptual model that would fully allow us to describe these activities. At the risk of offending one of our heroes, we refer to Patterson's (personal communication, 1985) use of the word *diddling* when talking about some of the clinical nuances that were not part of the formal behavioral therapy literature a decade or so ago. Since that time, of course, Patterson and his colleagues (see Bank, Marlowe, Reid, & Patterson, 1991; Bank, Patterson, & Reid, 1987; Patterson & Chamberlain, 1994) have developed an impressive program examining the therapeutic process, but the point is that he, like many others, was aware of additional phenomena that we had no vehicle to describe or means to incorporate systematically into our intervention models. A recent article by Kiser, Piercy, and Lipchik (1993) acknowledged the same phenomenon in solution-focused therapy with families as we have acknowledged with respect to functional family therapy (see Jameson, Newell, Robbins, Gunderson, & Alexander, 1992).

In other words, we assert that the addition of the cognitive component to the behavioral component, though representing an important expansion of perspectives, is not sufficient to deal with many of the clinical difficulties we face and is also inaccurate with respect to what many clinicians actually do in therapy. As a result, we and others (see Kanfer's chapter in this volume) also assert the need to include emotion, or affect, as a formal focus in our assessment and behavior change perspectives. This results in a multicomponent ABC (affect, behavior, cognition) framework, not inconsistent with behavioral approaches, that serves to enlarge our conceptual perspective and that facilitates the creative and effective application of traditional behavioral techniques.

Our second major assertion is the necessity of adding a systems perspective. There is mounting evidence that adding such a perspective often increases therapy effectiveness, even with disorders commonly thought of as residing entirely within an individual (see Alexander, 1973; Alexander et al., 1993; Liddle, 1991; Maine, 1991; Minuchin, 1978; O'Farrell, 1992; O'Leary & Beach, 1990; Szapocznik & Kurtines, 1989). In addition, behavioral techniques, when used at the level of the system rather than at the level of the individual to affect problematic processes and adjust internal organization, have been demonstrated to be a powerful tool for decreasing symptomatology in treating delinquent families (e.g., Alexander & Parsons, 1973; Parsons & Alexander, 1973; this effect also has generalized to siblings of referred youth at 3-year follow-up by Klein, Alexander, & Parsons, 1976). Thus a systemic approach that includes the consideration of essential cultural and developmental issues provides a way of understanding the larger pattern of behavioral processes in a family. This expanded perspective then facilitates the identification of specific problem areas and outcome goals for each case.

Seen from a systemic-developmental perspective, a fundamental feature underlying dysfunctional family process is a learning history that has created a present context of shared basic distrust and psychological vulnerability. In this context, conflicts of any sort are dealt with through externalizing or internalizing processes. The functional character of these processes serves to alter control characteristics or interpersonal distance in ways that immediately protect the individual or are otherwise reinforcing; however, the temporary "benefits" are achieved only at the expense of the relationship long term. Again, the early and well-established concepts of reciprocity and coercion (Patterson & Reid, 1967), as well as interactive models of in-home negative processes that generalize to later problems in youth (e.g., Patterson, 1974), identify such processes.

Such a conceptualization of pathology changes the way in which the therapist targets behaviors; symptomatic behaviors are seen as functional adaptations or responses to dysfunctional systemic processes. Within such a context, a family member experiences the defensive, aggressive, or coercive behavior exchange as an immediate necessity that is somehow reinforcing in the context of the immediate interchanges but ultimately aversive in its destructive impact on familial relationships, trust, and hope, as well as on family members' ability to have their dependency and relational needs met.

Thus the systemic and multicomponent ABC frameworks include a descriptive (e.g., identification of recurring patterns, antecedents and consequences, learning history) and an inferential (e.g., motivation) component. As an extension of Bandura's (1978) reciprocal determinism model, we propose that affect and cognition are significant interactive traces of an individual's and a family system's learning history as it relates to present learning situations, particularly motivational state. Of course, for theoretical purity it may be possible to create laboratory situations in which learning history is irrelevant and contingencies are unambiguous in terms of reinforcement quality. Similarly, it may be possible to demonstrate intervention success in cases in which historical influence is likely to be greatly simplified —for example, with individuals manifesting extreme developmental delays, very young children, autistic individuals, and some animal species. But in most therapy cases, an individual's or family's history and the immediate and long-term quality of reinforcement are likely to be important complicating factors. Because this history is a powerful determinant of motivation, it has the potential to enhance the intervention or to interfere with it; the impetus to change can be enhanced if emotional energy can be mobilized in support of change rather than self-protection. If a new way of adapting is to be learned, generalized, and maintained by an individual or family, it is imperative that the adaptive aspect of this learning history as seen in present behavior be understood and dealt with by the clinician as part of the therapy process. The question then becomes whether one can retain a present-centered behavioral therapeutic focus *and* include past and future as part of that present context while still remaining faithful to behavioral theory.

A central tenet of behaviorism is the definition of reinforcement and the motivational state of the organism. *Reinforcement* is any contingent event that alters the likelihood that a particular behavior will be emitted. *Motivation* describes the need state that increases the salience of a particular reinforcement: A hungry rat is more likely to press a bar to obtain food. In the context of therapy, behaviorism does not assert that the same contingent event will be reinforcing for all individuals or at all times for a given individual. Rather, it requires that a therapist identify on a family-by-family basis the unique reinforcement value of contingent events in the context of the motivational state and then use that understanding as the basis for changing behaviors. The crux of our argument is that present emotions and cognitions provide powerful clues and are efficient means of detecting the motivational state and the operative reinforcement structure of a family system. Although this approach may seem nonbehavioral in its reliance on hypothetical constructs rather than observable S-R relationships, the ultimate proof lies in the success of the behavioral interventions. This use of emotion and cognition is thus in the service of a behavior change strategy to the extent that it facilitates the identification of appropriate goals for more effective behavioral interventions.

PAYING ATTENTION TO EMOTION

Over the past few decades, different paradigms have been developed to describe the relationship between cognition and emotion in the psychotherapy change process, none as yet with convincing experimental support, each the foundation of a model of therapeutic intervention, and none incompatible with a behavioral perspective.

For example, Ellis (1962), Beck (1967), and Jacobson and Addis (1993) are among the therapist/researchers who maintain that some degree of cognitive appraisal must precede all emotional experience and who regard emotion as a by-product of cognition. Cognitive-behavioral interventions thus target irrational and nonadaptive beliefs or cognition and presume that changes will be paralleled by changes in behavior and emotion. In this process, awareness of patterns of interpersonal contingencies within a family system may or may not be conscious. For example, native speakers of a language abstract and apply the regularities, or rules, of their language with no explicit awareness of those rules (Bellugi, Poizner, & Klima, 1989). It seems reasonable to assume that "native users" of a particular family system would similarly intuit, not necessarily consciously, the regularities, or rules, governing interpersonal processes in that system. Each family member's behavior is filtered through an attributional process that has intrapersonal and interpersonal aspects (Newman, 1981). The active components of the intrapersonal attributional process are each family member's cognition, emotions, and behaviors. The content of some cognitions and the accompanying emotions will be similar across family members because of shared history, whereas other cognitive/emotional processes and patterns will be quite different across family members due to differences in perceptions or understanding of events as a result of individual characteristics such as developmental level. For the purposes of therapy, the important attributions relate to relational processes, such as how each family member sees his or her role in the family, how that role is affected by other family members, and the meaning of that impact.

Rachman (1981), Clark (1987), and Greenberg and Johnson (1988), as an alternative to the above framework, are among those theorists who assert that emotional experience is not merely a consequence of cognition but may in fact precede or parallel cognitive experience, at times even taking a predominant role over cognition. Greenberg and Johnson (1988) defined a functional relationship connecting cognition, emotion, and the environment. Emotion is fundamentally an adaptive system; emotional experience leads to autonomic nervous system arousal, which serves the purpose of alerting and directing the attention of the individual toward some potentially dangerous or threatening aspect of the environment. Thus emotion underpins the motivational state of the individual, and any behavioral response that reduces the level of autonomic activity (thereby reducing the perception of impending harm) will be reinforced by that corresponding reduction. The corresponding therapeutic model targets the expression and acceptance of, as well as responsivity to, feelings and needs, both of the individual and of the other members of the system.

Thus we propose paying attention to affect, behavior, and cognition and to the contexts in which emphasis on one or another of these seems more effective. Our suspicion is that as the level of pathology in a system increases, it may be increasingly important to include multiple levels of assessment and intervention and to mobilize more systems to produce change. Ultimately we seek to change behavior, and such change is sometimes best facilitated through an emphasis on behavioral processes. Sometimes, however, the initiation of change will be better served through an emphasis on cognitive processes as they relate to behaviors, and sometimes through an emphasis on emotional processes as they relate to cognition and behavior. The assessment performed during initial sessions should give the therapist a sense of the breadth of perspective (i.e., affect, behavior, cognition, learning history, motivation state, etc.) that will be required in working with a given family, as well as the most efficient focus. In addition, a family's cultural background should also be considered during this initial assessment in terms of the impact that cultural and ethnic factors may have on behaviors and on family members' perceptions of problematic behaviors.

PRACTICAL APPLICATIONS

A clinical example might demonstrate our point. The 16-year-old son in a middle-class African American family was referred for auto theft, joyriding, and a previous incident of drunkenness in school. The father in this family was a contractor (the "strong, silent type"); the mother was a highly verbal school teacher. The son was part of a strong peer system, which included a racially mixed group in which he was currently dating a white 15-year-old girl. Other than the specifics indicated in the referral, there had been no incidents of substance abuse (or even use) by this adolescent, who was also doing reasonably well in school. At home, the mother and son typically demonstrated a highly conflicted, ambivalently enmeshed process: He often sought her advice or approval, but frequently these interactions ended in a challenge to her extremely controlling behavior (which he attributed to her "racist attitudes") and her intensely agitated response to what he considered fairly normal teenage behavior. The father spent much more time on his own, typically becoming involved only when the arguing reached an acute level of intensity. Both mother and son verbally expressed extremely angry emotions, although neither had become physically violent. The father (usually tacitly) agreed with his son that the mother overreacted, but did not tell her this openly out of fear of a confrontation. The mother, in turn, felt a vague alienation from her husband, but not knowing the reason for this feeling, she tended to criticize herself for not being a "good enough" parent and for teaching school rather than "taking better care of" her family.

In this case, the therapist's initial efforts to introduce communication training and a behavioral contract were continually blocked by the mother's resistance. It was not until the therapist focused on the strong affect accompanying the mother's resistance that she began to make progress with this family. By enlarging her perspective to include affect, the therapist—and the other family members—discovered that the mother's older brother had been killed at age 16 in a gang-related incident in which he was supposedly an innocent bystander. Although they knew vaguely that he had died in some sort of accident, they had never before known the circumstances or her involvement. Because negative self-disclosure may not have been compatible with the family's cultural background (Sue & Zane, 1987), the mother had never mentioned to anyone that she thought her brother was killed because of his interest in one of her white friends—a relationship she had encouraged. In terms of behavior change, there was no way of dealing with what appeared to be the mother's seemingly irrational response to her son's behavior until the adaptive value of her affect (i.e., her guilt about her brother's death and her fear for her son's safety) was understood and dealt with clinically within the current familial context.

A second example comes from a single-parent family. The mother in this family worked as an assistant office manager in a state government office. She referred her family to the Division of Family Services, stating that she wanted her 14-year-old son (the youngest of four children) removed from the home. The two oldest children were no longer living at home, and the 16-year-old sister had recently returned home after being sent to live with relatives for 2 years. This sister had demonstrated a behavior pattern similar to her younger brother's when she was 14 but was seen by mother as really having "turned around" after being sent away. The son was a member of a loosely formed "gang," which seemed to be more a group of "wannabes" than an actual street gang. Although the son had not been accused of committing any criminal acts, the mother reported that he "comes and goes as he pleases" and "comes out with all this macho bullshit." During the initial family session she stated, "I just don't want to be his mother anymore" and "I'm too tired. . . . He just wears me out." It should be noted that although the son was performing only marginally in school, he was a gifted athlete who excelled on the school track team. He expressed hurt and resentment that his mother was always "too tired" to come to track meets to watch him.

In an attempt to reduce the negativity in the family environment and help the mother gain more control over her son's behavior, a previous therapist had already attempted to institute communication training and negotiation processes, coupled with parent training for the mother and a recommendation that she might want to consult a physician about her "tiredness." However, these more traditional behavioral interventions had produced increasing resistance and the decision by the mother to attempt to have the son removed from the home. She had obviously been rewarded for such a maneuver when she forced her daughter to move away, and it would be naive to presume that this powerful and rewarding learning history, coupled with the powerful emotions and attributions currently operating, could be counteracted solely by the incremental steps involved in the communication training and parent training technologies we currently possess.

Instead, the therapist focused on the cognitive and, more important, the emotional components of the situation. The mother's sense of being "tired" was reframed as a feeling of being totally overwhelmed by the parenting needs of this 14-year-old son. Rather than implying that she was an inept and rejecting mother, the therapist reframed her as trying to "protect" her son from having to deal with her overwhelming sense of being unable to meet his needs. At the same time, the son's gang-related activities and unacceptable in-home behaviors were reframed as a need for feeling that he "belonged" to a group that cared for him coupled with a "secret love test." That is, his behavior was reframed as indicating "Since I'm not important enough to you to come to my track meets, I'll see if I'm important enough for you to control me . . . or will you eventually abandon me just like my father did?" Regardless of whether these reframes represented objective "reality," they were successful in producing an emotional atmosphere in the session that reduced blaming and replaced it with an awareness of the loneliness that both mother and son felt, more empathy from each, and expressions of a desire for a better relationship. In this new atmosphere, the therapist was able to reinstate communication training, but this time focusing less immediately on "person-control" processes and more on "person-validating" processes. The sister was also comfortably brought into this process and was actually sometimes asked to "talk for" both her brother and mother. Interestingly, this gave the sister a more central role in the family; up to this time she had felt she was still "walking on eggs" and did not feel a part of this otherwise intensely interconnected system that had been ongoing while she had been away. As all three members of the family began experiencing each other differently, and as a result communicating differently, the therapist was able to help them target specific behavioral processes that represented problems and develop alternative strategies. One example included a simple contract: Any time the adolescent wanted his mother to observe either a practice session or a track meet, the night before he would come home early enough to help her around the house. The next day not only would she have more energy to watch his athletics (usually for a specified time), but she could also support his being with friends because he had been "so responsible." This simple and very traditional "contract seems not much different than that represented in the very early work of Stuart (1971) and later Alexander and Parsons (1973). However, only by understanding and directly dealing with the systemic nature of the behavioral processes, including their cognitive and emotional components, was this family able to adopt these alternative behaviors.

THERAPIST SKILLS:
DEALING WITH NEGATIVELY BASED
EMOTIONS AND ATTRIBUTIONS

In both of these clinical cases, progress was not realized until therapists expanded their perspective to include the family members' attributions and affect at the level of their own phenomenology. As scientists, most of us have been trained to understand the world in terms of some objective reality—one that can be shared by other independently observing scientists. But as clinicians, we must understand the unique phenomenology of each family member, often not shared by other family members, and the ways these phenomenologies interlock and are mediated by dysfunctional behavioral processes. In the examples above, this expansion of perspective facilitated the understanding of the reinforcing, or adaptive, value of existing dysfunctional family processes. In each case, strong emotions led to the uncovering of learning histories operating in the present context, histories with affective and cognitive derivatives. Although this enlargement of perspective to include an affective and phenomenological focus is not new, it does require additional and unique skills beyond those usually employed in more typically behavioral and/or cognitive models. Uncovering emotional processes that are driving negative behavior in volatile families, and working with these processes in a therapeutic manner, is a difficult, intricate process and one that requires considerable clinical acumen and skill.

For example, in a first session with a highly conflicted family, one of the most dangerous things the therapist can do is to ask, "How do you feel about that?" Ranking a close second in dangerousness is a question along the lines of "Why do you think [he or she] does that?" In other words, our call for the inclusion of emotion and cognition is not a prescription for simply eliciting affect and cognition regardless of their nature. Questions such as those above, which are often very appropriate for individual therapy, are usually disastrous in family therapy. Such naive intrusions can lead to escalated negativity and defensiveness, explosive sessions, partial or complete family dropout, and anything but the building of an effective therapeutic alliance. "Catharsis" belongs elsewhere; our goal is to produce positive, constructive cognition and emotions, not negative and destructive ones.

Although this chapter is not intended to represent a "how-to" manual on therapeutic techniques included in this expanded repertoire, we will briefly introduce some of these techniques, in a sense to "operationalize" our concepts. All these techniques are best used in early sessions (the earlier the better) and are designed not so much to represent specific elements of long-term changes in the families as to create a motivational atmosphere in which such changes can be initiated (Alexander, Barton, Waldron, & Mas, 1983). More complete descriptions of these techniques can be found else-where (Alexander & Barton, 1981; Alexander et al., 1993; Alexander, Mas, & Waldron, 1988; Alexander & Parsons, 1982; L'Abate, Ganahl, & Hansen, 1986; Morris, Alexander, & Waldron, 1988).

Relationship Focus/Sequences

One technique that allows the therapist to retain a focus on behavior, yet avoid escalating negativity, is to take an active role in identifying sequences between people, rather than focusing on the negative behavior of a person. For example, in asking about a negative sequence between family members, the therapist might avoid sequencing two or three questions of the follow-ing nature: "What did he do then? . . . Then what did he do? . . . Uh-hum, and then what?" Instead, the therapist might ask about the interactive nature of the sequence, introducing some new elements: "[To Person 1]: After he did that, how did you attempt to let him know how much emotional pain you were in?" The answer to that question could then be followed with a ques-tion to Person 2: "So that's how she responded to you. How do you feel about what you did next—did your response produce something that you wanted?"

Note that in this sequential focus the therapist avoids asking open-ended questions about feelings. Instead, she asks family members to indicate how they expressed their feelings behaviorally. This sort of question automatically links affect to behavior, allowing the therapist to focus on one, the other, or the relationship between the two.

Directly Interfering With Negativity

Sometimes in the face of powerful negative affect between family members, therapists can appear to be either immobilized, overwhelmed, or "too polite." Negative affect can, of course, provide important diagnostic clues; too much negative affect, on the other hand, elicits forms of defensiveness and rigidity that can become impossible to handle constructively. As a result, therapists must at times be prepared to interrupt negative sequences assertively, identify them for what they are, then provide the message that the therapist is able to provide an alternative:

> [Interrupting] Excuse me for breaking in—I don't mean to be impolite, but it seems that all of you are so frustrated right now, I bet your insides don't feel too good! Let's see if we can back this up, and figure out how we got to this place so we can find a different way to deal with it. It seems that . . . [therapist can then pick some convenient starting point to "slow down" the interaction, identify attributions that were working at the time, and perhaps reframe them (see below)].

Fearless Empathy

We have coined the phrase *fearless empathy* to describe the cognitive (and somewhat emotional) set that therapists must have to deal with negative, helpless, and dysfunctional families. Empathy begins with sending family members the message that the therapist is totally committed to understanding their inner world. It is important for family members, particularly those of different gender, socioeconomic status, religion, ethnicity, and the like, to experience some form of acceptance from the therapist. Empathy allows therapists to send such a message without having to agree with, accept, or like the (sometimes very destructive) ways family members express these inner worlds. It is important, therefore, for the clinician to be aware of the possible biasing influence of his or her own background and to avoid the possibility of "confounding" the values held by the family with their culture/ethnicity (American Psychological Association, 1993; Sue & Zane, 1987). The second ("fearless") component involves sending the message that the therapist is not personally overwhelmed, frightened, or intimidated by the intensity or nature of family members' emotions and attributions. We must send a tacit yet unequivocal message that "I hear your pain, and I will be here with you. We will deal with this together." Imagine, for example, a child who in the session is considering sharing with the therapist the fact that abuse occurs. Then imagine that this child sees the therapist beginning to experience defensiveness, anxiety, or otherwise avoidant reactions to a parent when the parent's negative affect begins to increase in intensity. Certainly such a reaction would not provide the child with a sense of safety and comfort.

As a second example, imagine a response to the depressive ideation of one family member. If the therapist immediately begins talking about hospitalization and/or medication, it certainly does not provide the family with a sense that alternative communication and/or other behavioral strategies are available. Instead, the therapist needs to have nonavoidant ways to deal with intensely negative and disturbing thoughts and feelings. Reframes, already introduced above, provide such ways.

Reframes

We are using the concept of reframes in a very general manner, referring to therapeutic maneuvers that cast a family member's (or members') behaviors and sequences in an alternative (usually more benign) light, one that increases the likelihood of positive change. "Normalizing" behavior represents one such maneuver:

> [To adolescent] You're mad because they yell? I know it can feel like a putdown—and you [to parent] need to know how it feels to him—but you [back to adolescent] also need to know that it is probably abnormal to have a parent who never yells. So it isn't the yelling as much as something else behind all your anger. . . . Do you know what it is, or do you want me to guess?

Note that with this family, the therapist later would target yelling specifically as a behavior to modify. At this point in the intervention, however, a focus on yelling per se would prevent the therapist from focusing on some of the more dynamic processes we have described above. "Normalizing" allowed to therapist to move to these more salient features without sending the adolescent the message of simply ignoring the issue—especially because the therapist retained his focus on the adolescent and his inner world. The therapist at the same time sent the parents the message that they too would be supported in the therapeutic process.

A second technique involves referring to "idealized" memories, simply to confuse and/or "muddy" the singularly negative attribution/emotional schema that is operating. For example,

> Earlier you said she's always been oppositional. Were there ever times when she was little that you found yourself laughing at her in a good-natured way because she made a fool of herself or got herself in trouble because she was so "independent"? I remember when my little girl, who also had a "mind of her own" [note the implicit "normalizing" in this phrase], insisted on wearing some favorite shorts of hers when we rode horses on our vacation. It was cold, and she nearly froze to death before she would admit she was miserable, but I had thrown in some long pants, so the second half of the ride went okay. Did your daughter ever do anything like that?

Note that such a maneuver on its own can act as a positive mood induction, as well as introducing a developmental perspective and letting the adolescent know that you do not see her as a "congenital bad seed."

Reframes most often involve an "interpretation" of motives or patterns of behavior that is different from the severely blaming attributional explanations one or more family members hold. In the single-parent example above, when the son believed that his mother was a rejecting and insensitive person (already having sent away his sister for 2 years), he was not motivated to behave "nicely." Perhaps in other families a threat of being sent away would have produced more compliant behavior, but it did not for this young man. However, when the therapist reframed the mother as "overwhelmed," "frightened," and "protective" of him (in a roundabout way), the son began to experience some sadness and was more motivated to behave in a less confrontational way toward his mother. This, in turn, positively affected her, particularly when his negative behavior was reframed not as a "challenge" that he made to be in control, but as a bid to "see if he is important enough to you to get yourself mobilized as a parent."

CONCLUSION

We have tried to emphasize two major points: Our focus on behavior must include a consideration of affect and cognition, and the focus must be contextualized in terms of the current system in which it is operating. This will require clinical techniques that do not replace the more time-honored behavioral technology (e.g., parent training, contingency management, contingency contracting and negotiation, other forms of communication training). However they do represent essential additions to our therapeutic repertoires because they serve to increase the effectiveness of traditional interventions. Our clients are not "radical behaviorists"; they think and feel as well as behave, and quite often they experience their feelings and thoughts as being powerful and controlling, especially in an interactive family context. We suggest that if we are to respond to such clinical realities, our clinical models must include the same elements.

REFERENCES

Alexander, J. F. (1973). Defensive and supportive communications in family systems. *Journal of Marriage and Family Therapy, 35,* 613-617.

Alexander, J. F., & Barton, C. (1981). Functional family therapy. In A. S. Gurman & D. P. Kniskern (Eds.), *Advances in clinical behavior therapy.* New York: Brunner/Mazel.

Alexander, J. F., Barton, C., Waldron, H. B., & Mas, C. H. (1983). Beyond the technology of family therapy: The anatomy of intervention model. In K. D. Craig & R. J. McMahon (Eds.), *Advances in clinical behavior therapy* (pp. 48-73). New York: Brunner/Mazel.

Alexander, J. F., Holtzworth-Munroe, A., Jameson, P. (1993). Research on the process and outcome of marriage and family therapy. In A. E. Bergin & S. L. Garfield (Eds.), *Handbook of psychotherapy and behavior change* (4th ed., 595-630). New York: John Wiley.

Alexander, J. F., Mas, C. H., & Waldron, H. (1988). Behavioral and systems family therapies or auld lang syne: Should old perspectives be forgot? In R. D. Peters & R. J. McMahon (Eds.), *Social learning and systems approaches to marriage and the family* (pp. 287-314). New York: Brunner/Mazel.

Alexander, J. F., & Parsons, B. V. (1973). Short term behavioral intervention with delinquent families: Impact on family process and recidivism. *Journal of Abnormal Psychology, 81,* 219-225.

Alexander, J. F., & Parsons, B. V. (1982). *Functional family therapy: Principles and procedures.* Carmel, CA: Brooks/Cole.

American Psychological Association. (1993). Guidelines for providers of psychological services to ethnic, linguistic and culturally diverse populations. *American Psychologist, 48,* 45-48.

Baer, R. A., Nietzel, R., & Mitchell, T. (1991). Cognitive and behavioral treatment of impulsivity in children: A meta-analytic review of outcome literature. *Journal of Clinical Child Psychology, 20,* 400-412.

Bandura, A. (1978). The self system in reciprocal determinism. *American Psychologist, 33,* 344-351.

Bank, L., Marlowe, J. H., Reid, J. B., & Patterson, G. R. (1991). A comparative evaluation of parent training interventions for families of chronic delinquents. *Journal of Abnormal Child Psychology, 19*(1), 15-33.

Bank, L., Patterson, G. R., & Reid, J. B. (1987). Delinquency prevention through training parents in family management. *Behavior Analyst, 10*(1), 75-82.

Beck, A. T. (1970). *Depression: Causes and treatment.* Philadelphia: University of Pennsylvania Press.

Bellugi, U., Poizner, H., & Klima, E. S. (1989). Language, mobility and the brain. *Trends in Neurosciences, 12,* 380-388.

Clark, E. (1987). Responses of mothers and fathers on the personality inventory of children. *Journal of Psychoeducational Assessment, 5*(2), 138-148.

Ellis, A. (1962). *Reason and emotion in psychotherapy.* New York: Lyle Stuart.

Greenberg, L. S., & Johnson, S. M. (1988). *Emotionally-focused couples therapy.* New York: Guilford.

Jacobson, N. S. (1991). Behavioral versus insight-oriented marital therapy: Labels can be misleading. *Journal of Consulting and Clinical Psychology, 59,* 142-145.

Jacobson, N. S., & Addis, M. E. (1993). Research on couples and couple therapy: What do we know? Where are we going? *Journal of Consulting and Clinical Psychology, 61,* 85-93.

Jacobson, N. S., & Truax, P. (1991). Clinical significance: A statistical approach to defining meaningful change in psychotherapy research. *Journal of Consulting and Clinical Psychology, 59,* 12-19.

Jameson, P., Newell, R., Robbins, M., Gunderson, D., & Alexander, J. (1992, October). *Decreasing negativity in adolescents' conflicted families.* Paper presented at the annual meeting of the American Association for Marital and Family Therapy, Miami Beach, FL.

Kazdin, A. E. (1992). Child and adolescent dysfunction and paths toward maladjustment: Targets for intervention. *Clinical Psychology Review, 12,* 795-817.

Kiser, D. J., Piercy, F. P., & Lipchik, E. (1993). The integration of emotion in solution-focused therapy. *Journal of Marital and Family Therapy, 19,* 233-242.

Klein, N., Alexander, J. F., & Parsons, B. V. (1976). Impact of family systems intervention on recidivism and sibling delinquency: A model of primary prevention and program intervention. *Journal of Consulting and Clinical Psychology, 45,* 469-474.

L'Abate, L., Ganahl, G., & Hansen, J. C. (1986). *Methods of family therapy.* Englewood Cliffs, NJ: Prentice Hall.

Liddle, H. A. (1991). Empirical values and the culture of family therapy. *Journal of Marital and Family Therapy, 17,* 327-348.

Maine, M. (1991). *Father hunger: Fathers, daughters and food.* Carlsbad, CA: Gurze.

Margolin, G., John, R. S., & Gleberman, L. (1988). Affective responses to conflictual discussions in violent and nonviolent couples. *Journal of Consulting and Clinical Psychology, 56,* 24-33.

Minuchin, S. (1978). *Psychosomatic families: Anorexia nervosa in context.* Cambridge, MA: Harvard University Press.

Morris, S., Alexander, J. F., & Waldron, H. (1988). Functional family therapy: Issues in clinical practice. In I. R. H. Falloon (Ed.), *Handbook of behavioral family therapy* (pp. 107-127). New York: Guilford.

Newman, H. (1981). Communication within ongoing intimate relationships: An attributional perspective. *Personality and Social Psychology Bulletin, 7,* 59-70.

O'Farrell, T. J. (1992). Families and alcohol problems: An overview of treatment research. *Journal of Family Psychology, 5,* 339-359.

O'Leary, K. D., & Beach, R. H. (1990). Marital therapy: A viable treatment for depression and marital discord. *American Journal of Psychiatry, 147,* 183-186.

Parsons, B. V., & Alexander, J. F. (1973). Short term family intervention: A therapy outcome study. *Journal of Consulting and Clinical Psychology, 41,* 195-201.

Patterson, G. R. (1974). Interventions for boys with conduct problems: Multiple settings, treatments and criteria. *Journal of Consulting and Clinical Psychology, 42,* 471-481.

Patterson, G. R. (1982). *Coercive family process.* Eugene, OR: Castalia.

Patterson, G. R., & Chamberlain, P. (1994). A functional analysis of resistance during parent training therapy. *Clinical Psychology: Science and Practice, 1,* 53-70.

Patterson, G. R., & Reid, J. B. (1970). Reciprocity and coercion: Two facets of social systems. In C. Neuringer & J. Michael (Eds.), *Behavior modification in clinical psychology.* New York: Appleton-Century-Crofts.

Rachman, S. (1981). The primacy of affect: Some theoretical implications. *Behaviour Research and Therapy, 19,* 279-290.

Shadish, W. R., Montgomery, L. M., Wilson, P., & Wilson, M. R. (1993). Effects of family and marital psychotherapies: A meta-analysis. *Journal of Consulting and Clinical Psychology, 61,* 992-1002.

Snyder, D. K., Wills, R. M., & Grady-Fletcher, A. (1991). Long-term effectiveness of behavioral versus insight-oriented marital therapy: A four year follow-up study. *Journal of Consulting and Clinical Psychology, 59,* 138-141.

Stuart, R. B. (1971). Behavioral contracting with the families of delinquents. *Journal of Behavior Therapy and Experimental Psychiatry, 2,* 1-11.

Sue, S., & Zane, N. (1987). The role of culture and cultural techniques in psychotherapy: A critique and reformulation. *American Psychologist, 42,* 37-45.

Szapocznik, J., & Kurtines, S. (1989). *Breakthroughs in family therapy with drug-abusing and problem youth.* New York: Springer.

8

Addressing Parent Cognitions in Interventions With Families of Disruptive Children

CHARLOTTE JOHNSTON

Disruptive child behaviors, including inattention, defiance, impulsivity, and aggression, are most characteristic of the disruptive child disorders (i.e., attention deficit hyperactivity disorder, oppositional defiant disorder, and conduct disorder) as defined by the third, revised edition of the *Diagnostic and Statistical Manual of Mental Disorders* (*DSM-III-R;* American Psychiatric Association, 1987). However, disruptive behaviors are also found among children with other diagnoses (e.g., developmental disorders) and among children who do not meet any particular diagnostic criteria. In fact, regardless of diagnostic status, disruptive behaviors characterize a substantial portion of children referred for mental health services (Kazdin, 1987)

AUTHOR'S NOTE: I wish to thank Eric J. Mash and Charles E. Cunningham for their inspiration, direction, and encouragement. Many of their ideas are reflected in this chapter. Thanks also to Kathryn Short, Josie Geller, and Wendy Freeman, who offered useful suggestions on earlier drafts of the chapter. This chapter was prepared while I was supported by grants from the British Columbia Health Research Foundation and the Medical Research Council of Canada.

and are often the impetus for referral (e.g., "He just doesn't listen," "Everything is such a battle with her").

Behavioral models have identified these disruptive child acts as learned responses to environmental contingencies (e.g., vague commands, diminished positive attention, inconsistent punishment). On the basis of these models, interventions to reduce disruptive child behaviors have targeted alterations in environmental factors, in particular parent behavior, as the mechanism for changing child behavior. Although in theory the behavioral approach recognizes that the relationship between parent and child behaviors is reciprocal (Patterson, 1982), pragmatics have pulled for a more unidirectional parent-to-child focus in the design of behavioral parent training (BPT) programs.

Numerous BPT programs have been developed (see Dangel & Polster, 1984). All such programs seek to provide parents with skills to observe and monitor child behavior accurately, to alter environmental stimuli so as to increase appropriate behavior (e.g., using prompts and direct instructions), to reinforce appropriate behavior contingently, and to extinguish or punish inappropriate behavior effectively. On the basis of demonstrations by investigators such as Patterson, Chamberlain, and Reid (1982), Webster-Stratton (1984), and Wells, Forehand, and Griest (1980), recent reviews (Dumas, 1989; Kazdin, 1987) have placed BPT programs high on the list of treatments effective in reducing disruptive child behaviors.

Despite their solid theoretical foundation and demonstrated superiority over placebo or no-treatment conditions, BPT approaches remain limited in their effectiveness (Miller & Prinz, 1990). Social validity research suggests that not all parents are willing to accept behavioral treatments (Cross Calvert & Johnston, 1990) and that among families who do enter treatment, dropout rates hover around 25% (Forehand, Middlebrook, Rogers, & Steffe, 1983). Even when families complete BPT programs, only about half of the children show a significant reduction in disruptive behaviors (Pisterman et al., 1989). Finally, the stability of the changes engendered by BPT programs has not been extensively investigated.

Numerous explanations can be offered for the limited efficacy of BPT programs. First, longitudinal research has revealed that disruptive behavior patterns are often chronic (Loeber, 1990). Thus our definition of successful treatment for disruptive behaviors may need to be modified from that of a cure brought about by relatively short-term interventions to that of longer-term treatment that assists parents in coping with relatively enduring child characteristics (Kazdin, 1987). Second, behavioral treatments may be too narrow given the less than optimal social contexts that often provide a backdrop to disruptive child behaviors (Johnston, 1988; Miller & Prinz, 1990). Poverty, social isolation, multiple family problems, and parental dysfunction are frequent correlates of disruptive child behaviors (McMahon, 1987) and, not surprisingly, interfere with the implementation of BPT programs. Movements to expand BPT programs by adding marital therapy, individual parent therapy, or systemic components have yielded promising results (e.g., Dadds, Schwartz, & Sanders, 1987; Henggeler & Borduin, 1990). A third possible contributor to the limited efficacy of BPT programs is the manner in which such programs are delivered. As early as 1976, Alexander, Barton, Schaivo, and Parsons demonstrated that relationship-building behaviors by therapists were important predictors of whether families of delinquent adolescents completed a behaviorally based treatment. More recently, Patterson and Forgatch (1985) showed that when therapists directly teach or confront parents, resistance to BPT treatment increases. Similarly, Cunningham, Davis, Bremner, Dunn, and Rzasa (1993) found that a treatment format using coping models and problem solving reduced client resistance to the content of behavioral training. In sum, attention to therapy process offers promise for improving the effectiveness of BPT programs.

Existing BPT programs may also be limited by an emphasis on parent behavior to the exclusion of other parent variables. In addition to expanding BPT programs to include extraparental and extrafamilial factors, the focus of treatment might be expanded to encompass nonbehavioral aspects of parenting. Parents' thoughts and feelings about parenting and children, and the interplay of these thoughts and feelings with parent-child behavioral exchanges, are important areas neglected by BPT programs. A combined cognitive-behavioral approach to understanding and treating families of disruptive children deserves exploration. Driven by motivations shared with the field of cognitive-behavioral therapy (Dobson & Block, 1989), adding the cognitions that accompany parent behavior to the behavioral model of child disruptiveness is expected to enhance the power of this model.

This chapter considers parent cognitions and the role they may play in integrated cognitive-behavioral parent training programs. The chapter begins by presenting a cognitive-behavioral model of parenting. This is followed by consideration of four particular forms of parent cognition and evidence suggesting that these cognitions are related to parenting and disruptive child behavior. Potential avenues for exploiting parent cognitions within the context of more traditional BPT programs are also considered. Finally, the chapter offers directions to guide the development of cognitive-behavioral interventions for parents of disruptive children.

A COGNITIVE-BEHAVIORAL
MODEL OF PARENTING

As a context within which to consider parent cognitions in relation to BPT, an elementary model is presented outlining influences on parent cognitions and linking cognitions to parent behavior and, subsequently, to child behavior. The model is intended as a conceptual heuristic to guide the following discussion rather than as a complete or testable set of hypotheses. Reflecting influences from developmental psychology (Dix & Grusec, 1985) and marital therapy (Baucom & Epstein, 1990), and consistent with the premises of cognitive-behavioral therapies (Dobson & Block, 1989), the model places parent cognitions in a mediational role. As outlined in Figure 8.1, parent cognitions are interposed between situational factors and parent behavior and reflect input from characteristics such as parent affect and personality style, as well as from the historical context of parenting (e.g., the parent's investment in parenting, past parent-child interactions). The incompleteness of the model is immediately obvious. Other factors undoubtedly influence parent cognitions (e.g., input from the parenting partner), and, as any parent can testify, recursive arrows are needed to reflect the undeniable effects of children on parents. However, a simplified model was chosen to highlight the paths through which parent cognitions are most likely to be relevant to disruptive child behavior and BPT programs.

Examining this basic mediational model reveals two paths through which parent cognitions may serve to enhance the changes in parent behavior sought in BPT programs. The route between parent cognitions and behavior (Arrow B in Figure 8.1) highlights the role that cognitions may play in motivating or driving parents' actions. Examples of such cognitions would include a parent's skill in monitoring his or her own behavior in caregiving interactions or problem-solving abilities when faced with child-rearing decisions. Research has shown that in comparison to parents of nonproblem children, parents of disruptive children generate fewer problem solutions, disagree more regarding possible solutions, and more often fail to resolve problems (Forgatch, 1984, cited in Chamberlain & Baldwin, 1987). Thus

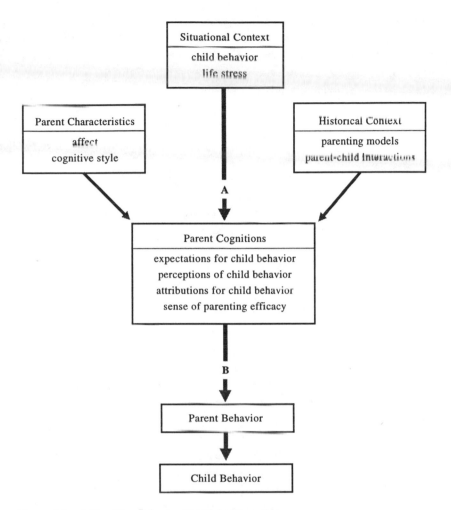

Figure 8.1. A Cognitive-Behavioral Model of Parenting

teaching problem-solving skills may offer one potential method for altering parent cognitions so as to promote more effective parenting (Cunningham, 1990).

The ability of parent cognitions to moderate the impact of external stimuli on parent behavior (Arrow A in Figure 8.1) may also be exploited to enhance BPT programs. Here the focus shifts from cognitions as precursors of behavior to the capacity of cognitions to alter a parent's ability to cope with external stress. Cognitions may either exacerbate or attenuate the disruptive impact of variables such as situational stress on parent behavior. Examples of such moderating cognitions would include parents' interpretations of child behavior or feelings of self-efficacy that create vulnerable or resilient parenting in interactions with difficult children (Bugental & Shennum, 1984; Mash & Johnston, 1990). Enhancing the buffering capacity of such cognitions may serve as a useful adjunct to BPT programs.

TYPES OF PARENT COGNITIONS

The following sections outline four different forms of parent cognitions and how each may act to influence Paths A and/or B in the model.

Expectancies for Child Behavior

Expectancies for child behavior provide an overarching framework within which parents perceive and interpret particular child behaviors. These expectancies are the stable, general beliefs that parents hold regarding how their children will behave. The power of expectancies is revealed in statements such as "I know her, she'll keep whining until I can't take it and give in" or "He's just like his father." Such expectancies function as colored lenses, focusing and tinting how the parent perceives and responds to child behavior.

A recent study by Hoover and Milich (1994) illustrated the importance of parent expectancies. In this study, mothers who had endorsed the common expectancy that sugar causes disruptive child behavior were observed interacting with their children. Some mothers were led to believe that their child had ingested sugar prior to the interaction and others that their child had ingested a placebo substance. In actuality, all children had received placebos. In a manner consistent with their expectancies, mothers who thought their children had received sugar rated their children as more disruptive during the interaction than mothers who thought their children had received a placebo. Mothers expecting sugar were also observed to be more critical and directive with their children. Interestingly, the effects were particularly strong for mothers with rigid rather than flexible cognitive styles. In sum, parent expectancies appear not only to moderate perceptions of child behavior but also to drive parent behavior.

Similar cognitive expectancy effects were reported in a classic study by Brunk and Henggeler (1984). Their study found that adults interacting with disruptive child confederates quickly developed a cognitive set expecting child deviance and that this expectancy led them to act in a controlling manner, even in the absence of actual child misbehaviors. Our research with abusive mothers (Mash, Johnston, & Kovitz, 1983) also suggested the importance of expectancies in guiding parent behavior. Abusive mothers rated their children as extremely deviant on questionnaires and were observed to interact in a directive manner designed to control this expected child deviance. However, observations of child behavior revealed little difficult or deviant behavior; instead, the children were as compliant and responsive as normal controls. As in the previous examples, these mothers appeared to be responding on the basis of cognitive expectancies rather than actual child behavior in the immediate situation.

Perceptions of Child Behavior

With expectancies "setting the stage," parents' perceptions of specific child behaviors represent a second form of cognition that deserves consideration. Research has repeatedly demonstrated that what parents "see" is influenced not only by actual child behavior but also by characteristics of the parent (e.g., affective state) and of the situation (e.g., stress). Wahler and Dumas (1989) suggested that factors such as daily hassles, chronic stress, and affective distress create disruptions in the attentional and surveillance skills of parents. These external and internal stresses detract from parents' attentional capacity, leaving fewer resources to be deployed in observing and monitoring child behavior. Thus, as stress increases and the number of resources decreases, parents' perceptions of child behavior are expected to diminish in accuracy, becoming more influenced by preexisting expectancies than by specific child behaviors.

Regarding the influence of external stress on parents' perceptions of child behavior, several studies have revealed an association between parents' reports of life stress and their perceptions of child behavior as deviant (Mash & Johnston, 1990; Middlebrook & Forehand, 1985). Extending this research, recent work in our lab has demonstrated that mothers' perceptions of child behavior are differentially affected by daily hassles or major life stresses. Using written stimulus materials, Krech and Johnston (1992) found that mothers perceived ambiguous child behaviors as most deviant and deserving of harsh discipline when these behaviors occur in the context of daily hassles. In contrast, mothers' perceptions and responses were significantly less negative in a major life stress context and least negative when the child behaviors were presented in nonstressful contexts.

Consistent with Wahler and Dumas's (1989) model of limited attentional resources, the Krech and Johnston (1992) study found that depressed mood functioned in the same manner as external stress in promoting negative perceptions of child behavior. Mothers experiencing greater dysphoric affect were more likely to perceive the ambiguous child behaviors as deviant and deserving of a punitive response, regardless of the surrounding stress context. This finding corroborates a large body of research that has demonstrated, at least among mothers, a modest but consistent relationship between depressed mood and negative perceptions of child behavior (e.g., Johnston, 1991; Schaughency & Lahey, 1985). In sum, parent perceptions of child behavior appear to be influenced by a host of factors beyond actual child behavior. Following from these findings, adding strategies for reducing life stress or improving parent mood to BPT programs may serve to reduce the potentially devastating effects of negative perceptions on parent-child interactions.

Attributions for Child Behavior

Defined as the explanations offered for *why* individuals behave as they do, interpersonal causal attributions have proven important in marital research (Baucom & Epstein, 1990) and in developmental and child clinical psychology (Bugental, Blue, & Cruzcosa, 1989; Dix & Grusec, 1985). In the context of parent-child interactions, parent attributions are the explanations that parents offer regarding the causes of their children's actions: for example, their answers to questions such as "Why did Johnny wipe his dirty hands on the new towel?" or "Why is Martha standing, arms akimbo, refusing to clean up her toys?" The attributions that parents make in such situations appear to be important moderators of the impact of these child behaviors on subsequent parenting actions.

The child and family research literatures converge to suggest that dysfunctional parenting and disruptive child behavior are both associated with negative parent attributions for child behaviors. In the family area, Mas, Alexander, and Turner (1991) asked both high- and low-conflict families of adolescent delinquents to discuss either satisfying or dissatisfying family events. The results indicated that high-conflict families used dispositional attributions to explain both the positive and negative behavior of each other.

In contrast, low-conflict families used dispositional attributions only in explaining positive behaviors. In the marital literature, Fincham and Grych (1991) found that in contrast to nonproblem families, parents in clinic-referred families viewed the causes of both marital and child problems as more global and pervasive and that their attributions for child behavior in dicated less recognition of developmental constraints. Studies by Gretarsson and Gelfand (1988) and Dix and Lochman (1990) both demonstrated an association between disruptive child behaviors and a parent attributional style that holds children responsible for negative behaviors. Again, this pattern stands in contrast to the positive bias demonstrated by parents of nonproblem children, in which negative behaviors are attributed to factors external to the child and only positive behaviors are seen as reflecting child disposition (Dix & Grusec, 1985). Finally, a study in our lab by Geller and Johnston (1995) found a significant relationship between mothers' attributions for their own and their child's behavior. Consistent with the research on perceptions, this study revealed that depressed mood and expectancies of child deviance were associated with more negative attributions for child behavior. Together, these studies suggest a consistently negative interpersonal attributional style in families of disruptive children.

We have recently extended the study of attributions to consider the match between parent attributions and child intentions. A preliminary study using young adult raters (Johnston, Patenaude, & Inman, 1992) indicated that raters can discriminate between intentional and unintentional child behaviors (e.g., defiance versus distractibility) when these behaviors are presented separately. However, when the behaviors co-occur, the distinctiveness in rater attributions suffers. Thus, when a child displays both intentional and unintentional forms of disruptive behavior (e.g., shows behaviors characteristic of both attention deficit hyperactivity and oppositional defiant disorders), parents may have difficulty matching their attributions to the intentionality of the child's behavior. For example, parents may blame children for unintentional restlessness and, conversely, excuse children for malicious defiance. This line of research clearly illustrates the importance of cognitions as moderators in the link between child behavior and parenting action.

Self-Efficacy in the Parenting Role

In addition to cognitions about child behavior, parents' thoughts about their own functioning in the parenting role contribute to the outcome of parent-child interactions. Consistent with theories of social cognition

(Bandura, 1986) and discoveries in cognitive-behavioral therapies for anxiety disorders (Rachman, 1990), research suggests that feelings of self-efficacy are an important adjunct to and predictor of behavior change. In the realm of parenting, disruptive child behaviors and parents' sense of parenting efficacy appear to share a transactional relationship. Disruptive child behaviors threaten parents' feelings of competence, and a lowered sense of confidence places parents at risk for responding inappropriately to challenging child behaviors.

A program of research by Bugental and colleagues (Bugental, 1989; Bugental et al., 1989; Bugental & Shennum, 1984) has demonstrated that parents who credit themselves with less power than their children in controlling the outcome of caregiving interactions are more likely to be upset by disruptive child behaviors and to react in a negative, coercive style. Our research in both clinic-referred and nonproblem samples has consistently revealed a relationship between disruptive child behavior and diminished feelings of parenting competence (Johnston & Mash, 1989; Mash & Johnston, 1990). Finally, the potential importance of parenting sense of competence in interventions with families of disruptive children is revealed in a recent study by Pisterman et al. (1992). This research found that a BPT program offered to parents of preschoolers with attention deficit hyperactivity disorder resulted in significant and clinically meaningful increases in parent reports of competence in the parenting role. Interesting, these significant cognitive changes did not correlate with observed behavior changes or with measures of treatment compliance. Thus BPT programs appear useful in promoting feelings of efficacy in parents of disruptive children. However, the links between this form of parent cognition and parent and child behavioral outcomes have not yet been elucidated.

TREATMENT IMPLICATIONS
OF A COGNITIVE-BEHAVIORAL
MODEL OF PARENTING

Before parent cognitions are incorporated in BPT programs, efforts must be directed to the assessment of these cognitions. At an informal level, therapists are advised to listen carefully to discern how parents are understanding and interpreting child behaviors, their own parenting efforts, and the enterprise of BPT. For example, posing "why" questions can yield important attributional elaborations on parents' claims regarding which behavioral strategies work or do not work with their child. Unfortunately, beyond this ongoing, informal level of assessment, there are few conceptually or psychometrically solid instruments for measuring parent cognitions in a more formal manner. Although some work has been done in the area of parenting self-efficacy (see the Parent Attribution Test, Bugental & Shennum, 1984, and the Parenting Sense of Competence Scale, Johnston & Mash, 1989), adequate measures of parent cognitions such as expectancies or perceptual accuracy are not currently available. As Holden and Edwards (1989) suggested in their excellent review, most existing measures not only are scientifically poor but lack the dynamic nature and situational specificity needed to tap the cognitions most associated with parent and child behavior.

Beyond issues of assessment, suggestions may still be offered for how the positive aspects of parent cognitions might be exploited in BPT programs and how possible detrimental effects might be avoided. For example, it appears that therapists are wise to avoid directly challenging the strong, negative expectancies for child behavior that parents of disruptive children often voice (Cunningham, 1990; Patterson & Forgatch, 1985). Such confrontations increase parent defensiveness and may motivate parents to search for evidence to confirm or buttress their expectancy, an exercise more likely to entrench than change the negative cognition. In addition to deemphasizing the parents' negative expectancies, there may be value in selectively highlighting parents' positive expectancies. For example, parents may express the expectation that treatment will bring about positive changes in child behavior. If this expectancy can be tempered to reflect the degree and rate of change that is realistically attainable, it may provide a cognitive prompt for the difficult task of persevering with new parenting strategies when confronted with limited evidence of improvement.

In considering the role of perceptions in cognitive-behavioral interventions, one might direct attention to solidifying the link between parents' perceptions and actual child behavior in the immediate context. However, in this enterprise the therapist must remain aware that although factors external to the child do influence perceptions, actual child behavior continues to account for the largest portion of the variance in parents' perceptions (Johnston, 1991; Schaughency & Lahey, 1985). Therefore, when directing parents to identify biases in their perceptions, the therapist must be sensitive to keep from conveying that the parents' perceptions are untruths. Particularly given that disruptive children are likely to respond to the novelty of a clinical assessment with exemplary behavior, parents may be sensitized to any suggestion of doubt regarding their experience of the child as difficult. The analogy of stress and pain tolerance is one example of a nonthreatening framework that may assist parents in identifying how their perceptions are influenced by nonchild stresses.

Wahler and Dumas (1989) developed a process referred to as synthesis review to assist parents in developing perceptions that are closely attuned to child behavior and unencumbered by the influence of external stress. The goal of such exercises is to increase the extent to which parent behavior is driven by accurate perceptions of child behavior rather than by inaccurate perceptions or global expectancies of child deviance. In addition to the suggestions of Wahler and Dumas (1989), many traditional BPT strategies provide avenues for enhancing accurate perceptions of child behavior. For example, observation exercises and chart systems provide cues for parents to monitor child behavior using precise behavioral definitions.

Supporting the use of attributions in cognitive-behavioral parent training, attributional retraining has been incorporated as a component in individual psychotherapy (Beck, 1976), marital therapy (Baucom & Epstein, 1990), and family therapy (Alexander & Parsons, 1982). Cunningham (1990) identified a number of strategies, including the use of errorless learning, problem-solving, and coping models that allow BPT programs to be implemented in a manner that encourages parents to develop social learning attributions for both their own parenting strategy choices and the behavior of their children. For example, when having parents review their successful implementations of behavioral strategies, the therapist may attribute changes in both parent and child behavior to deliberate parent efforts to improve the family environment. Previously reviewed research showing that therapist efforts to teach result in increased resistance (Patterson & Forgatch, 1985) may reflect parents' attempts to resist the attributional implication of such therapist teaching—the implication that the parent is lacking the knowledge or skill to be a good parent. Collaborative and supportive therapist behaviors and a Socratic method of conveying information may allow parents to continue to feel self-efficacious while making the behavioral changes recommended by BPT programs.

A recent qualitative analysis of the process of change that occurs during BPT offers fascinating directions for exploring the interplay between parent cognitions and the process of effective therapy (Spitzer, Webster-Stratton, & Hollinsworth, 1991). This work suggests that individuals in BPT pass through several phases ranging from acknowledging the problem of disruptive child behavior, to experiencing alternating feelings of hope and despair, to coming to terms with the hard work of coping effectively with disruptive child behavior. It is likely that as parents progress through these phases in the therapy process, different cognitions will be central at different times. Discovering the intricacies of which cognitions are best addressed at which therapy stage for which parents stands as an exciting challenge to clinical researchers in this area.

FUTURE DIRECTIONS

Despite the strong intuitive and theoretical appeal of many of the above suggestions for incorporating parent cognitions into BPT programs, empirical validation of these strategies is an essential next step. Although research in this vein is emerging (e.g., Alexander, Waldron, Barton, & Mas, 1989; Cunningham et al., 1993), much more work is needed. Theoretical refinements of the cognitive-behavioral model of parenting must proceed alongside demonstrations of the clinical utility of this model.

The discussion of parent cognitions presented in this chapter has cautiously skirted around the complex issue of the interrelations among parent cognitions, affects, and behaviors. As is increasingly acknowledged, the interplay among these three dimensions of parenting must be addressed in future work (Bugental, 1989; Dix, 1991). If we assume transactional patterns of influence among parent thoughts, feelings, and behaviors, it can be argued that interventions aimed at only one of these components miss the potentially synergistic effects found when the three components are addressed simultaneously. Expanding BPT programs to incorporate parent cognitions is a step in the right direction. However, further work is needed to elaborate the role of affect in the model and to focus on parenting as an integration of cognitions, affects, and behaviors.

In addition to the four types of parent cognitions addressed in this chapter, future work will benefit from considering other dimensions along which cognitions may vary. For example, it has been proposed that parent cognitions can be categorized along a dimension from unaware or automatic to controlled or deliberate (Bugental, 1989; Mash & Johnston, 1990). The automatic-processing end of this continuum would include the dynamic, ongoing interpretations of child behavior that parents construct without purposeful intention. Examples of such cognitions would include the thoughts that accompany the almost instinctive parent behavior elicited when a toddler rushes toward the curb at a busy intersection or when the school-aged child spills his grape juice on the new beige carpet. At the opposite end of the processing continuum lie parent cognitions that are effortful and of which the parent is fully conscious. These more controlled and deliberate cognitions are those to which psychologists are likely to have access via questionnaire measures (Holden & Edwards, 1989). Such cognitions would include parents' statements of child-rearing beliefs (e.g., "Children need firm discipline") or reasoning about the origins and nature of disruptive child behaviors (e.g., seeing attention deficit hyperactivity disorder as biologically based). Viewing parent cognitions along a continuum of effortful processing suggests several potentially promising intervention avenues. For example, the behavioral repetition required through role plays and home practice exercises may allow newly acquired parenting strategies that initially require considerable controlled, effortful processing to shift to a less demanding, more automatic form of cognitive direction. The goal of future work will be to translate these intriguing possibilities into testable research questions.

One last direction in the study of parent cognitions that must be mentioned is the very great need to expand our understanding of fathers and father-child relationships. Most of the research reviewed in this chapter has focused on maternal cognitions, and the little that has included both mothers and fathers suggests potentially important differences (e.g, Johnston 1991; Schaughency & Lahey, 1985). Work on parent cognitions will be far from complete until fathers are represented more fully.

In conclusion, this chapter represents an initial attempt to describe a cognitive-behavioral model of parent training. Empirical findings suggest considerable potential in pursuing the addition of cognitions and affects to a behavioral model of parent-child interaction. The challenge is to continue to garner empirical support for the model and to translate the theory into usable and testable intervention techniques. It is only this final step that will ultimately serve to enhance the effectiveness of treatments offered to families of disruptive children.

REFERENCES

Alexander, J. F., Barton, C., Schaivo, R. S., & Parsons, B. V. (1976). Systems-behavioral intervention with families of delinquents: Therapist characteristics, family behavior, and outcome. *Journal of Consulting and Clinical Psychology, 44,* 656-664.

Alexander, J. F., & Parsons, B. V. (1982). *Functional family therapy*. Monterey, CA: Brooks/ Cole.

Alexander, J. F., Waldron, H. B., Barton, C., & Mas, C. H. (1989). Minimizing blaming attributions and behaviors in conflicted delinquent families. *Journal of Consulting and Clinical Psychology, 57,* 19-24.

American Psychiatric Association. (1987). *Diagnostic and statistical manual of mental disorders* (3rd. ed., Rev.). Washington, DC: Author.

Bandura, A. (1986). *Social foundations of thought and action: A social cognitive theory*. Englewood Cliffs, NJ: Prentice Hall.

Baucom, D. H., & Epstein, N. (1990). *Cognitive-behavioral marital therapy*. New York: Brunner/Mazel.

Beck, A. T. (1976). *Cognitive therapy and the emotional disorders*. New York: International Universities Press.

Brunk, M. A., & Henggeler, S. W. (1984). Child influences on adult controls: An experimental investigation. *Developmental Psychology, 20,* 1074-1081.

Bugental, D. (1989, April). *Caregiver cognitions as moderators of affect in abusive families*. Paper presented at the annual meeting of the Society for Research in Child Development, Kansas City, KS.

Bugental, D. B., Blue, J., & Cruzcosa, M. (1989). Perceived control over caregiving outcomes: Implications for child abuse. *Developmental Psychology, 22,* 723-742.

Bugental, D. B., & Shennum, W. A. (1984). "Difficult" children as elicitors and targets of adult communication patterns: An attributional-behavioral transactional analysis. *Monographs of the Society for Research in Child Development, 49*(1).

Chamberlain, P., & Baldwin, D. V. (1987). Client resistance to parent training: Its therapeutic management. *Advances in School Psychology, 6,* 131-171.

Cross Calvert, S., & Johnston, C. (1990). Acceptability of treatments for child behavior problems: Issues and implications for future research. *Journal of Clinical Child Psychology, 19,* 61-74.

Cunningham, C. E. (1990). A family systems approach to parent training. In R. A. Barkley (Ed.), *Attention deficit hyperactivity disorder* (pp. 432-461). New York: Guilford.

Cunningham, C. E., Davis, J. R., Bremner, R., Dunn, K. W., & Rzasa, T. (1993). Coping modelling problem solving versus mastery modelling: Effects on adherence, in-session process, and skill acquisition in a residential parent training program. *Journal of Consulting and Clinical Psychology, 61,* 871-877.

Dadds, M. R., Schwartz, S., & Sanders, M. R. (1987). Marital discord and treatment outcome in behavioral treatment of child conduct disorders. *Journal of Consulting and Clinical Psychology, 55,* 396-403.

Dangel, F. R., & Polster, R. A. (Eds.). (1984). *Parent training*. New York: Guilford.

Dix, T. (1991). The affective organization of parenting: Adaptive and maladaptive processes. *Psychological Bulletin, 110,* 3-25.

Dix, T., & Grusec, J. E. (1985). Parent attribution processes in the socialization of children. In I. E. Sigel (Ed.), *Parental belief systems* (pp. 201-234). Hillsdale, NJ: Lawrence Erlbaum.

Dix, T., & Lochman, J. (1990). Social cognition and negative reactions of children: A comparison of mothers of aggressive and nonaggressive boys. *Journal of Social and Clinical Psychology, 9,* 418-438.

Dobson, K. S., & Block, L. (1989). Historical and philosophical bases of the cognitive-behavioral therapies. In K. S. Dobson (Ed.), *Handbook of cognitive-behavioral therapies* (pp. 3-38). New York: Guilford.

Dumas, J. E. (1989). Treating antisocial behavior in children: Child and family approaches. *Clinical Psychology Review, 9,* 197-222.

Fincham, F. D., & Grych, J. H. (1991). Explanations for family events in distressed and nondistressed couples: Is one type of explanation used consistently. *Journal of Family Psychology, 4,* 341-353.

Forehand, R., Middlebrook, J., Rogers, R., & Steffe, M. (1983). Dropping out of parent training. *Behavioral Research and Therapy, 21,* 663-668.

Geller, J. & Johnston, C. (1995). Depressed mood and child conduct problems: Relationships to mothers' attributions for their own and their children's experiences. *Child and Family Behavior Therapy, 17,* 19-34.

Gretarsson, S. J., & Gelfand, D. M. (1988). Mothers' attributions regarding their children's social behavior and personality characteristics. *Developmental Psychology, 24,* 264-269.

Henggeler, S. W., & Borduin, C. M. (1990). *Family therapy and beyond: A multisystemic approach to treatment behavior problems of children and adolescents.* Pacific Grove, CA: Brooks/Cole.

Holden, G. W., & Edwards, L. A. (1989). Parental attitudes toward child rearing: Instruments, issues and implications. *Psychological Bulletin, 106,* 29-58.

Hoover, D. W., & Milich, R. (1994). Effects of sugar ingestion expectancies on mother-child interactions. *Journal of Abnormal Child Psychology, 22,* 501-515.

Johnston, C. (1988). A behavioral-family systems approach to assessment: Maternal characteristics associated with externalizing behavior in children. *Advances in Behavioral Assessment of Children and Families, 4,* 161-188.

Johnston, C. (1991). Predicting mothers' and fathers' perceptions of child behavior problems. *Canadian Journal of Behavioural Sciences, 23,* 349-357.

Johnston, C., & Mash, E. J. (1989). A measure of parenting satisfaction and efficacy. *Journal of Clinical Child Psychology, 18,* 167-175.

Johnston, C., Patenaude, R., & Inman, G. (1992). Attributions for hyperactive and aggressive child behaviors. *Social Cognition, 10,* 255-270.

Kazdin, A. E. (1987). Treatment of antisocial behavior in children: Current status and future directions. *Psychological Bulletin, 102,* 187-203.

Krech, K. H., & Johnston, C. (1992). The relationship of depressed mood and life stress to maternal perceptions of child behavior. *Journal of Clinical Child Psychology, 21,* 115-122.

Loeber, R. (1990). Development and risk factors of juvenile antisocial behavior and delinquency. *Clinical Psychology Review, 10,* 1-41.

Mas, C. H., Alexander, J. F., & Turner, C. W. (1991). Dispositional attributions and defensive behavior in high- and low-conflict delinquent families. *Journal of Family Psychology, 5,* 176-191.

Mash, E. J., & Johnston, C. (1990). Determinants of parenting stress: Illustrations from families of hyperactive children and families of physically abused children. *Journal of Clinical Child Psychology, 19,* 313-328.

Mash, E. J., Johnston, C., & Kovitz, K. R. (1983). A comparison of the mother-child interactions of physically-abused and nonabused children during play and task situations. *Journal of Clinical Child Psychology, 12,* 337-346.

McMahon, R. J. (1987). Some current issues in the behavioral assessment of conduct disordered children and their families. *Behavioral Assessment, 9,* 235-252.

Middlebrook, J. L., & Forehand, R. (1985). Maternal perceptions of deviance in child behavior as a function of stress and clinic versus nonclinic status of the child: An analogue study. *Behavior Therapy, 16,* 494-502.

Miller, G. E., & Prinz, R. J. (1990). Enhancement of social learning family interventions for childhood conduct disorder. *Psychological Bulletin, 108,* 291-307.

Patterson, G. R. (1982). *Coercive family process.* Eugene, OR: Castalia.

Patterson, G. R., Chamberlain, P., & Reid, J. B. (1982). A comparative evaluation of a parent-training program. *Behavior Therapy, 13,* 638-650.

Patterson, G. R., & Forgatch, M. S. (1985). Therapist behavior as a determinant for patient noncompliance: A paradox for the behavior modifier. *Journal of Consulting and Clinical Psychology, 53,* 846-851.

Pisterman, S., Firestone, P., McGrath, P., Goodman, J. T., Webster, I., Mallory, R., & Goffin, B. (1992). The effects of parent training on parenting stress and sense of competence. *Canadian Journal of Behavioural Sciences, 24,* 41-58.

Pisterman, S., McGrath, P., Firestone, P., Goodman, J. T., Webster, K., & Mallory, R. (1989). Outcome of parent-mediated treatment of preschoolers with attention deficit disorder with hyperactivity. *Journal of Consulting and Clinical Psychology, 57,* 628-635.

Rachman, S. J. (1990). *Fear and courage* (2nd ed.). New York: W. H. Freeman.

Schaughency, E. A., & Lahey, B. B. (1985). Mothers' and fathers' perceptions of child deviance: Roles of child behavior, parental depression, and marital satisfaction. *Journal of Consulting and Clinical Psychology, 53,* 718-723.

Spitzer, A., Webster-Stratton, C., & Hollinsworth, T. (1991). Coping with conduct-problem children: Parents gaining knowledge and control. *Journal of Clinical Child Psychology, 20,* 413-427.

Wahler, R. G., & Dumas, J. E. (1989). Attentional problems in dysfunctional mother-child interactions: An interbehavioral model. *Psychological Bulletin, 105,* 116-130.

Webster-Stratton, C. (1984). Randomized trial of two parent training programs for families of conduct-disordered children. *Journal of Consulting and Clinical Psychology, 52,* 666-678.

Wells, K. C., Forehand, R., & Griest, D. L. (1980). Generality of treatment effects from treated to untreated behaviors resulting from a parent training program. *Journal of Clinical Child Psychology, 9,* 217-219.

9

Understanding and Treating
Marital Distress From a
Cognitive-Behavioral Orientation

DONALD H. BAUCOM

NORMAN EPSTEIN

LYNN A. RANKIN

CHARLES K. BURNETT

THEORETICAL UNDERPINNINGS

Beginning in the late 1960s and early 1970s, a behavioral formulation of marital distress arose. This behavioral formulation rested on two major theories: social learning theory and social exchange theory. There are several tenets of social learning theory (Bandura, 1977; Rotter, 1954), but the one that most greatly influenced the behavioral understanding of marital distress was the belief that social behavior is governed in large part by its consequences (i.e., operant conditioning) and antecedent discriminative stimuli that signal that particular reinforcement contingencies are operating. Thus the behavioral marital therapist had the task of understanding how a particular couple extinguished or punished certain behaviors that were necessary for the adaptive functioning of the couple and how maladaptive behaviors were perhaps inadvertently reinforced.

Social exchange theory (Thibaut & Kelley, 1959) viewed social relationships such as marriage in economic terms. Each person in the relationship is involved in the exchange of goods, and an individual's satisfaction with the relationship is a function of his or her ratio of benefits received from the relationship relative to costs incurred. Consequently, social exchange theory is consistent with social learning theory in its emphasis on rewards and punishments, or benefits and costs. A number of studies have been conducted to explore whether the numbers of positive and negative behaviors engaged in by distressed and nondistressed couples differ. As anticipated, findings indicate that distressed spouses report more displeasing behaviors and fewer pleasing behaviors from their partners than are reported by nondistressed spouses (Birchler, Weiss, & Vincent, 1975; Jacobson, Follette, & McDonald, 1982; Margolin, 1981). In a related vein, findings indicate that daily fluctuations in marital happiness are related to changes in the frequency of positive and negative behaviors provided by the partner (Christensen & Nies, 1980; Jacobson et al., 1982; Jacobson, Waldron, & Moore, 1980; Margolin, 1981; Wills, Weiss, & Patterson, 1974).

Social exchange theory also postulates that the exchange of goods between partners in an ongoing relationship is reciprocal, such that the level of reinforcement and punishment provided by one partner is influenced by the rewards and punishments of the other. Over time, this process results in a relatively equitable exchange of goods between the two partners. A number of studies have conducted sequential analyses of couples' interaction during a discussion task to evaluate whether one partner's communication seems to influence the other's subsequent communication. The findings do confirm that reciprocity exists among spouses during their interaction and that distressed couples demonstrate greater negative reciprocity (negative communication from one spouse increasing the likelihood of negative communication from the partner) than do nondistressed couples (Billings, 1979; Gottman, Notarius, Markman, et al., 1976; Margolin & Wampold, 1981; Raush, Barry, Hertel, & Swain, 1974; Revenstorf, Hahlweg, Schindler, & Vogel, 1984). Nondistressed couples appear to demonstrate either greater positive reciprocity (Revenstorf et al., 1984) than distressed couples or comparable positive reciprocity to that of distressed couples (Gottman, Notarius, Gonso, & Markman, 1976; Margolin & Wampold, 1981). These findings regarding reciprocity have had a major impact on behavioral interventions with couples in two ways. First, therapists have worked with spouses to help them understand that a major way to increase one's partner's positive behaviors is to increase one's own rate of positive behaviors. Second, therapists have educated couples to the likelihood of negative interaction cycles once a negative behavior has been emitted. Thus the couple must be cautious to avoid the initiation of such negative interactions and learn how to terminate such interaction sequences quickly once they begin.

Stuart (1980) stressed that reciprocity does not necessarily imply symmetry or equality in the exchange of positive and negative behaviors between partners. Instead, it implies that over time the exchange is balanced enough to be seen as fair or acceptable by the two partners. Many couples seem to be satisfied in a relationship in which one partner appears to contribute more to the relationship, but they have established a sense of balance that they view as gratifying. Therefore the therapist's task is not to ensure that all contributions to the marriage are "equal" but rather that the couple functions in a manner that both partners find gratifying and acceptable.

Within social learning and social exchange theory, behaviorists have afforded a special role to communication in marriage. This is probably the case for at least two reasons. First, communication is a major way that adults reward and punish each other during interactions. Thus, assisting couples in increasing the frequency of their positive communication and decreasing the frequency of negative communication is a way to influence a major category of "goods" exchanged between partners. Second, effective communication is a modality through which couples can address other important noncommunication issues in their relationships. That is, effective communication provides the tools for problem solving on issues of importance to the couple. Communication is also a way in which couples can share their thoughts and feelings with each other and increase their sense of understanding and closeness to each other. The importance of communication in marriage is underscored by Geiss and O'Leary's (1981) finding that both couples and therapists identify communication concerns as the most frequent and most destructive problem in distressed marriages.

Behaviorists have largely come to view communication problems in marriage as reflecting skill deficits by one or both partners or by the couple as a system. It would be too simplistic to suggest that distressed couples have no ability to communicate under any circumstances. For example, investigations by Vincent, Weiss, and Birchler (1975) and Birchler, Weiss, and Vincent

(1975) found that distressed spouses did not interact negatively with strangers from distressed marriages, although they continued to communicate negatively with their own partners. Therefore, under certain circumstances, maritally distressed partners can communicate positively with other individuals. From a skills-deficit model, these findings would imply that there is some aspect of the marital system that makes it difficult for the partners to communicate effectively with each other. Thus the skill might need to be assessed within the context of a particular marital system. Also, the couple might cease to communicate effectively under a state of high negative emotional arousal that characterizes marital distress. Of course, an alternative explanation is that marital distress is not necessarily caused by a lack of communication skills. Instead, once spouses become distressed, they may not make efforts to communicate effectively, or they may at times deliberately communicate destructively with their partners.

Despite the complex cause-effect and potential interactive relations that may hold between communication and marital distress, behavioral marital therapists have recognized the communication problems presented by almost all couples by the time they seek marital therapy. Behaviorally oriented therapists have expended a great deal of energy teaching spouses how to communicate and solve problems more effectively with each other.

EFFECTIVENESS OF BEHAVIORAL
MARITAL THERAPY (BMT)

Based on the above theoretical formulations and empirical findings, BMT evolved with a set of interventions that have undergone numerous empirical tests. Although different investigators and therapists have focused on somewhat different behavioral skills and interventions, in the United States primary attention has been given to evaluating the effectiveness of communication training, problem solving, and contracting with distressed couples. In-depth descriptions of these and other behaviorally oriented interventions are available in several clinically oriented volumes (Baucom & Epstein, 1990; Beach, Sandeen, & O'Leary, 1990; Jacobson & Margolin, 1979; Stuart, 1980). Although the criteria differ among studies, most often investigators have evaluated whether BMT is effective in increasing marital adjustment, altering couples' communication, and changing noncommunication behavior.

Perhaps the most basic question is whether BMT is more effective than no-treatment and nonspecific treatment conditions. Overall, the findings indicate that BMT is more effective than waiting list and nonspecific treatment conditions (see Baucom, 1982; Baucom & Lester, 1986; Baucom, Sayers, & Sher, 1990; Hahlweg, Schindler, Revenstorf, & Brengelmann, 1984; Jacobson, 1984; Snyder & Wills, 1989; Turkewitz & O'Leary, 1981). The findings from these investigations indicate that marital distress is a state that most couples do not know how to alleviate without some form of active intervention. For example, Jacobson et al. (1984) concluded that only 14% of distressed couples demonstrate reliable improvement while on a waiting list.

Given that these intervention programs for BMT typically have included more than one intervention, investigators have conducted dismantling studies to attempt to isolate what interventions within a broader intervention program are responsible for couple changes. With rare exception (Jacobson, 1984), the results from these investigations have demonstrated that the various components of BMT are all effective and are equally effective (Baucom, 1982; Emmelkamp, van der Helm, MacGillavry, & van Zanten, 1984; Ewart, 1978; Jacobson, 1978). Because couples were randomly assigned to treatment conditions, these investigation do not address whether specific couples would benefit from particular behavioral interventions. However, the findings suggest that there are probably common properties of the behavioral interventions that lead to their effectiveness. Almost all of the behavioral interventions that have been found to be effective include a focus on skills training, placing the couple in control of making changes, and application of skills to the real world outside of the therapy session.

In addition to dismantling the treatment techniques involved in BMT, investigators have evaluated the effects of altering other treatment parameters. For example, Mehlman, Baucom, and Anderson (1983) evaluated whether single therapists would be as effective as cotherapists in offering BMT. The findings indicated that both treatment modalities were effective, with no differences in effectiveness between the two conditions. This finding is important because it suggests that professional time can be used efficiently in providing treatment. Another cost-effective way to offer BMT is within a group context. Hahlweg et al. (1984) compared the effectiveness of conjoint (both spouses present) BMT with conjoint group BMT, in which several couples were treated together. Although both treatment conditions were effective, conjoint BMT was superior to conjoint group BMT. Thus attempting to treat several distressed couples at the same time appears to dilute the effectiveness of the treatment.

On occasion, couples will desire assistance for their marital problems but due to logistics (e.g., conflict in work schedules), it is difficult to have both spouses present for conjoint treatment. Bennun (1985a, 1985b) compared conjoint BMT to BMT in which only one spouse attended the treatment. Although these two treatment conditions were equally effective, change occurred more quickly for couples receiving conjoint BMT. It is important to note that in Bennun's study both spouses were willing to attend treatment. There are a significant number of instances in which one partner is unwilling to seek marital therapy. Whether working with the willing spouse can result in meaningful marital change is unknown at this point.

Another group of couples warranting special attention are those that are maritally distressed and in which one partner is clinically depressed. Estimates indicate that of couples seeking treatment for marital discord, one half have at least one partner who is depressed (Beach, Jouriles, & O'Leary, 1985; Birchler, 1986). Conversely, Rounsaville, Weissman, Prusoff, and Herceg-Baron (1979) indicated that over half of the individuals in their sample seeking treatment for depression were maritally distressed. Sher, Baucom, and Larus (1990) found that BMT was effective in alleviating depression as well as lowering marital distress for couples experiencing both problems. In investigations focusing on the relative utility of BMT and individual cognitive therapy, Beach and O'Leary (1986) found that individual cognitive therapy reduced depression but did not alter marital distress. On the other hand, BMT was effective in alleviating both depression and marital distress. Similarly, Jacobson, Dobson, Fruzzetti, Schmaling, and Salusky (1991) found that BMT and individual cognitive therapy were equally effective in alleviating depression among wives who were also experiencing marital distress. However, BMT was the only condition to have a significant impact on marital satisfaction among these same depressed/maritally distressed couples. Thus BMT appears to be an efficient way to offer treatment to couples experiencing both of these difficulties concurrently.

Given the success of BMT in alleviating marital distress, investigators have begun to investigate the relative effectiveness of BMT versus marital therapy from other theoretical orientations. The number of such studies is still limited (Boelens, Emmelkamp, MacGillavry, & Markvoort, 1980; Crowe, 1978; Emmelkamp et al., 1984; Girodo, Stein, & Dotzenroth, 1980; Hahlweg, Revenstorf, & Schindler, 1982; Johnson & Greenberg, 1985; Liberman,

Levine, Wheeler, Sanders, & Wallace, 1976; O'Farrell, Cutter, & Floyd, 1983; Snyder & Wills, 1989; Snyder, Wills, & Grady-Fletcher, 1991; Turkewitz & O'Leary, 1981), but the findings generally indicate no significant differences between the various active treatment conditions (Hahlweg & Markman, 1983). Perhaps the major conflicting finding in this regard is a study by Snyder et al. (1991) in which BMT was compared with psychodynamically oriented marital therapy. Although the two treatments appeared equivalent at posttest, at 4-year follow-up the psychodynamic treatment was superior to BMT. This is a potentially important finding, and replication of these results is needed. Caution must be raised in interpreting the overall findings of equivalency among theoretical orientations. Given that couples were randomly assigned to treatment conditions, data still do not exist to clarify whether certain couples would benefit from particular theoretical approaches to marital therapy.

The above findings indicate that BMT is effective in assisting couples who are maritally distressed. However, the issue arises of just how effective BMT is. In their meta-analysis of BMT outcome investigations, Hahlweg and Markman (1983) concluded, on the basis of the results of 17 treatment studies, that BMT has an average effect size of .92, suggesting that the average couple receiving BMT is more improved than 82% of couples placed on a waiting list or receiving a nonspecific treatment condition. Another approach to assessing the magnitude of effects of BMT is to evaluate the proportion of couples who demonstrate significant improvement and the proportion of couples in the nondistressed range at the end of treatment. Jacobson et al. (1984) concluded on the basis of earlier investigations that approximately 35% to 40% of couples treated with BMT were in the nondis-tressed range at the end of treatment. However, more recent investigations (Baucom et al., 1990; Jacobson et al., 1991; Snyder et al., 1991) suggest that at least half of the couples treated with BMT join the ranks of the nondis-tressed by the end of treatment.

SUMMARY AND CONCLUSIONS
REGARDING BMT

Since the late 1960s, a great deal of investigation has been conducted to understand marital distress from a behavioral perspective, and BMT outcome studies have ushered in a new wave of evaluation of the effectiveness of marital therapy. Although BMT clearly is of benefit to many couples, the findings also clearly point out that not all couples move into the nondistressed range by the end of treatment. This lack of universal responsiveness might be due to several factors. First, the criterion for success in these treatment studies has been increased marital adjustment and marital happiness. However, there appear to be many marriages in which the two partners do not bring joy or satisfaction to each other, and ending the marriage might be a preferable outcome from a mental health perspective. Second, there have been almost no matching studies in which a particular couple's needs determine the form and course of treatment, although this is the likely strategy employed in an applied clinical context and although matching couples' needs to treatment might result in an increase in responsiveness to treatment. Third, the behavioral model as applied in the 1960s and 1970s might be too restrictive. Although behaviorists have always acknowledged the importance of cognitions and affect in marital distress, treatment has been predicated on a given logic: Behavior, cognition, and affect are interrelated, so changes in behavior should result in subsequent changes in cognition and affect. Although this logic does at times seem to apply, there are many instances in which behavioral change does not seem to lead to the important cognitive and affective changes needed to assist the couple (Iverson & Baucom, 1990).

ATTENDING TO COGNITIONS IN MARITAL DISTRESS

There appear to be at least three reasons to broaden the behavioral model of treatment of marital discord to include a focus on cognitions. First, without attending to cognitive variables, engineering behavioral changes can result in changes that do not have the desired effect. For example, many distressed wives complain that their husbands do not talk to them as much as the wives would like. In addition, it might be important to a given wife, not just that her husband talks to her, but that he *wants* to talk to her. Therefore working out a contract for the couple in which the husband talks to his wife in exchange for being allowed to watch sports events on the television uninterruptedly might not be beneficial. In this instance, the husband is actually engaging in the behavior that the wife desires—talking to her. However, because she interprets his behavior as resulting not from his desire to interact with her but rather from his preference to watch television without being interrupted, his talking behavior has a different meaning to her and therefore a different effect on the relationship. That is to say, behavior is not merely a set of actions. It has meaning; it occurs within the context of an ongoing relationship. Consequently, the therapist must be attentive to the meaning that behavior change will have for the couple. An emphasis on the couple's cognitions and promoting cognitive change often can ensure that behavioral changes have their intended effects.

Second, attending to cognitive variables is important to facilitate behavioral changes that seem to be important for the couple's well-being. Often by the time couples enter marital therapy, they have experienced marital discord over a long period, and self-initiated efforts to promote adaptive change have been unsuccessful. Consequently, they enter therapy discouraged, hopeless, and with the belief that almost all efforts will be unsuccessful. This set of emotions and cognitions can be destructive and self-fulfilling. That is, believing that nothing will help the couple to improve, spouses may be reluctant to expend the energy and effort that is needed to improve the relationship. Instead, each person makes marginal efforts, seeking confirming evidence that there is little chance that their relationship can improve. With little initiative to improve their relationship and a focus on negative events to demonstrate the hopelessness of their situation, they succeed in proving to themselves that their situation is hopeless. Thus it is important to assist couples in developing the proper mind-set so that they will be willing to try to make the behavior changes needed and to persist in their efforts when they are less than successful.

Third, a direct focus on cognitions is important because certain situations do not always call for behavior change. Instead, helping couples shift their cognitions or how they think about the situation may be much more appropriate. As Baucom and Epstein (1991) noted, the broad notion of acceptance of one's partner typically refers to acceptance of one's partner's behavior as a result of cognitive restructuring. For example, a husband may be quite distressed because he believes that partners should spend all of their free time together, and he may feel frustrated and rejected because his wife wants to spend some of her free time alone. In this instance, helping the husband evaluate his standard that spouses should spend all of their free time together might be the intervention of choice. Such an endeavor might result in no behavior change from his wife, but he might be more satisfied if he moderated his standard to allow for time alone as well as time together. As another example, a wife may feel unloved because her husband comes home from work late, and she may interpret this as resulting from his lack of love for her and his desire to stay away from her. However, if her husband helps her to understand that his longer hours at work result from his anxiety about failing on the job (related to his father's persistent remarks throughout the husband's childhood that the husband would never amount to anything), then the wife may feel more compassion for her husband and no longer feel unloved. Her new understanding of her husband's behavior is what is needed in this instance. Of course, the couple may still wish to decide at some point whether they wish to limit work hours and to focus on helping the husband with his fear of failure.

Consequently, appropriate attention to the cognitions involved in marriage may prove to be useful in expanding the behavioral model and lead to more successful interventions in the future. As a first step in investigating the role of cognitions in marriage, it is important to establish a taxonomy of cognitions relevant to couple functioning. It is too broad and vague to suggest that we wish to assess and perhaps alter couples' thoughts. Instead, a clear delineation of the types of cognitions under consideration is needed to advance the field and provide a framework for understanding how cognition, behavior, and affect interrelate in marital distress.

A TAXONOMY OF MARITAL COGNITIONS

Drawing on the theoretical and empirical literature in the areas of marital interaction, social cognition, and cognitive approaches to psychopathology, Baucom, Epstein, Sayers, and Sher (1989) identified five major categories of cognition that play important roles in marital functioning:

1. The process of *selective perception,* in which an individual idiosyncratically notices a subset of the available data about events occurring in his or her marital interactions
2. The *attributions* that the individual makes about the determinants of relationship events (e.g., inferences about causes of a partner's behavior)
3. Each spouse's *expectancies* or predictions about the occurrence of future events in the marriage
4. *Assumptions* that spouses hold about the characteristics of people and close relationships
5. The *standards* that each person holds about the characteristics that spouses and marriages "should" have

Each of these five categories is likely to include both conscious content and a significant portion of cognitive activity that occurs spontaneously and beyond the individual's conscious awareness (Baucom & Epstein, 1990; Epstein & Baucom, 1993). To date, empirical research on marital perceptions, attributions, expectancies, assumptions, and standards, which is summarized below, has focused on the content of cognitions that spouses are able to identify through conscious reflection. However, the need for alternative approaches to the study of cognitions that are beyond spouses' awareness has been recognized (e.g., Fincham, Bradbury, & Grych, 1990), and the limitations of findings restricted to spouses' reports of conscious cognitions must be kept in mind.

Research on Selective Perception

Marital theorists, clinicians, and researchers have noted that spouses commonly notice particular events in their relationships in a selective and often biased manner, a process referred to by Beck and his associates (e.g., Beck, Rush, Shaw, & Emery, 1979) as *selective abstraction*. Behavioral marital therapists (e.g., Jacobson & Margolin, 1979) have described how members of distressed couples tend to engage in "negative tracking," in which they selectively notice negative partner behaviors and pay less attention to positive behavior. Such a perceptual bias is considered problematic both because it can contribute to a global negative, pessimistic view of the marriage and because spouses who fail to notice their partners' positive behavior changes are unlikely to reinforce those changes.

A number of studies have investigated the degree to which partners agree about the occurrence of specific events in their relationship during 24-hour periods. The results of these studies (Christensen & Nies, 1980; Christensen, Sullaway, & King, 1983; Jacobson & Moore, 1981; Margolin, Hattem, John, & Yost, 1985) indicate only modest agreement between spouses, with the average Kappa calculated between wives' and husbands' reports of marital behaviors as approximately .50. Jacobson and Moore's (1981) calculation of agreement rates indicated that spouses tended to agree less than 50% of the time about the occurrence of particular behaviors. Agreement rates are higher among happy than among distressed couples. Furthermore, Arias and O'Leary (1985) found that distressed spouses were less accurate than happy spouses in predicting their partners' responses on a task that involved choosing definitions of relationship concepts such as commitment.

Studies by Floyd and Markman (1983) and Robinson and Price (1980) also have indicated low levels of agreement between spouses and outside observers in rating the occurrence of positive and negative marital behaviors. The tendency for distressed spouses (especially wives) to report more negative partner behaviors than observers do is consistent with the concept of negative tracking. However, the findings also may indicate that spouses notice behaviors identified as positive by outsiders but experience them as negative due to the idiosyncratic meanings that those behaviors have taken on in the context of their marriages.

Such common discrepancies in partners' perceptions of relationship events have led cognitive-behavioral marital therapists to devote considerable attention to assisting couples in tracking and sharing their perceptions of positive and negative behavioral exchanges. Some important directions for future research include investigations of other types of cognitions (e.g., spouses' standards about the way a marriage should be) that may influence selective perceptions of daily events, as well as studies of the relations between spouses' perceptions and their emotional and behavioral responses to each other during their daily interactions.

Research on Attributions

The large majority of existing empirical studies on marital cognition have focused on the attributions that spouses make about determinants of their own and their partners' behaviors (see reviews by Baucom & Epstein, 1990, and Bradbury & Fincham, 1990). The emphasis on attributions in marital research has stemmed from a number of sources, including the current prominence of attribution theory in social and clinical psychology and the influence of theoretical publications (e.g., Doherty, 1981a; Fincham, Bradbury, & Grych, 1990) applying attribution theory to marital and family conflict.

Although the methods for assessing marital attributions have varied across studies (asking spouses to report attributions about hypothetical versus actual events in their relationship; using spouses' self-reports on standardized questionnaires versus coding attributions from videotaped marital discussions), there has been considerable consistency in findings linking attributions with levels of marital distress. In general, empirical results indicate that distressed spouses are more likely than nondistressed spouses to explain negative relationship events in terms of global and stable (i.e., traitlike) characteristics of their partners, whereas nondistressed spouses are more likely to attribute positive relationship events to such causes. Furthermore, marital distress is associated with the degree to which spouses view each other's negative behaviors as intentional, reflecting negative motives and selfish intent, and worthy of blame (Baucom & Epstein, 1990; Bradbury & Fincham, 1990). Compared to happy couples, distressed spouses also tend to discount positive partner behaviors as less intentional and more due to negative motives. These patterns of attributions can contribute to the maintenance of marital distress because partners who view each other's negative behaviors as evidence of stable negative traits and who see any attempts at positive behavior change as fleeting and selfishly motivated are unlikely to encourage and reinforce constructive change.

A longitudinal study by Fincham and Bradbury (1987) indicated that attributions of the sort described above were not only correlated with spouses' current levels of marital satisfaction but also predictive of future distress (among wives but not husbands) a year later, whereas initial distress level did not predict subsequent attributions. Although these findings do not clearly identify the causal direction in the association between attributions and distress, they are strongly suggestive of a causal role for attributions. It remains for future studies to untangle the causal question, but the consistent correlational findings from the existing research underscore the importance of considering attributions as components of spouses' subjective experiences of their marriages.

Research on Expectancies

In addition to making inferences about causes of past events, individuals routinely make predictions about probabilities that particular events will occur in the future, based on their observations of present events. The ability to form such predictions or expectancies is a highly adaptive cognitive process that allows an individual to maximize rewarding consequences and avoid negative outcomes in daily life. Nevertheless, as is the case with all five types of cognitions under consideration, expectancies may vary in their accuracy as representations of life events.

Theory and research on marital expectancies have drawn heavily on social learning concepts, especially Bandura's (1977) writings on outcome and efficacy expectancies. Whereas an outcome expectancy is an individual's belief that a certain action will produce a particular outcome, an efficacy expectancy is the individual's prediction about his or her ability to carry out that action. For example, spouses may hold an outcome expectancy that communicating more clearly about their personal needs would lead to greater intimacy in their relationship, but they may hold low efficacy expectancies concerning their abilities to communicate in that manner.

Doherty (1981b) proposed that spouses with low efficacy expectancies concerning their own and their partners' abilities to engage in behaviors needed to change their relationship would be less likely to make efforts to bring about change. Thus Doherty predicted more cognitive and behavioral learned-helplessness responses among spouses with low efficacy expectancies regarding conflict resolution. Some support for this prediction was found by Pretzer, Epstein, and Fleming (1991), who used a self-report questionnaire to assess spouses' generalized expectancies for resolving marital problems, as well as to assess their attributions for those problems. Pretzer et al. found that attributing problems more to one's own behavior and less to one's partner's behavior and personality was associated with a higher expectancy that the couple would be able to improve their relationship. Spouses with higher efficacy expectancies also were less depressed and more satisfied with their marriages.

Also consistent with Doherty's (1981b) predictions, studies have indicated that spouses' higher efficacy expectancies concerning their problem-solving efforts are associated with lower rates of helplessness responses such as giving up conflict-resolution efforts, as well as more positive behavioral interactions between spouses during their problem-solving discussions. Vanzetti and Notarius (1991) found that spouses' relationship expectancies predicted both their own ratings of subsequent communication that occurred in a laboratory-based interaction and outside raters' evaluations of that same communication. In addition, couples with poor relationship expectancies made more negative attributions for their partners' communications than did couples with more positive relationship expectancies.

The process of an interaction between two spouses typically unfolds at a rapid pace, and clinical observation suggests that each person's emotional and behavioral responses to the partner are shaped not only by prior events in the interactional "chain" but also by anticipated events. Therefore advancing knowledge about expectancies and how they are related to satisfaction, behavior, and other types of cognitions is an important priority for future marital research.

Research on Assumptions and Standards

Theoretical and clinical literature (e.g., Baucom & Epstein, 1990; Ellis, 1977; Epstein, 1982) commonly has proposed that marital conflict and distress arise when spouses are aware that their marital interactions do not match their assumptions about the characteristics of intimate relationships or their standards about the characteristics such a relationship should have. It has been suggested that conflict and distress can result when (a) an individual spouse holds an assumption or standard that is extreme and therefore unlikely to be met by his or her relationship(s); (b) two partners have incompatible assumptions and standards; or (c) a spouse holds assumptions that are not extreme, but he or she is not satisfied with the degree to which they are met within the current relationship.

Until recently, the only existing measure designed to assess marital assumptions and standards was Eidelson and Epstein's (1982) Relationship Belief Inventory (RBI). The RBI was not designed specifically to differentiate between assumptions and standards, but three of its five subscales (disagreement is destructive to a relationship; partners cannot change themselves or their relationship; conflicts between men and women are due to innate gender differences in personality and needs) tap basic assumptions. The remaining two subscales (partners should be able to mind-read each other's thoughts and emotions; one should perform perfectly as a sexual partner) assess standards against which spouses may evaluate the adequacy of their own relationships. The RBI subscales were not intended to provide a comprehensive assessment of potentially problematic relationship beliefs but were selected as important sources of marital distress based on the marital therapy literature.

Research studies employing the RBI (e.g., Eidelson & Epstein, 1982; Epstein & Eidelson, 1981; Epstein, Pretzer, & Fleming, 1987; Fincham & Bradbury, 1987) have supported theoretical predictions and clinical observations that degree of adherence to assumptions and standards of the sort it assesses is associated with lower marital satisfaction.

Jones and Stanton (1988) administered the RBI, an instrument assessing individually oriented irrational beliefs based on Ellis's rational-emotive therapy model, and measures of marital satisfaction to a sample of community couples. Consistent with Epstein and Eidelson's earlier findings, the RBI was a better predictor of marital distress scores than the measure of individually oriented irrational beliefs. In addition, the more that spouses *perceived* similarity in their relationship beliefs, the more satisfied they were, whereas the degree of actual belief similarity between partners (as well as accuracy in perceptions of each other's beliefs) was not correlated with satisfaction level.

In their longitudinal study, Fincham and Bradbury (1987) found that spouses' RBI scores were significantly correlated with concurrent marital satisfaction but that they did not predict later satisfaction. Given that attributions at Time 1 did predict satisfaction at times, Fincham and Bradbury suggested that beliefs (assumptions and standards) shape attributions, which in turn influence satisfaction. Clearly, the relationships among various types of cognitions and spouses' affective and behavioral responses to each other are complex (see models proposed by Epstein & Baucom, 1993, and by Bradbury & Fincham, 1990), and conclusions concerning causal processes must await the results of future studies.

DIMENSIONS OF
RELATIONSHIP FUNCTIONING

One of the strengths, yet also one of the weaknesses, of research on the role of cognitions in marriage is that to a great extent, most investigations have been based on previous research and theorizing from other areas of psychology. For example, the attribution research in marriage has borrowed greatly from social psychological research on interactions among strangers. It has also borrowed greatly from learned-helplessness research, which is a model of clinical depression (Abramson, Seligman, & Teasdale, 1978). This has the positive effect of allowing comparisons of findings from the marital field with findings from other domains of psychology. At the same time, there may be issues or factors that are focal to long-term, intimate relationships such as marriage that are not pertinent to stranger interactions or clinical depression. Not taking such factors into account in cognitive research has the potential of robbing investigators and clinicians of a fuller understanding of the role of cognitive factors in marital distress.

In response to this concern, Epstein, Baucom, Rankin, and Burnett (1991) proposed three dimensions of intimate relationships that they believed all couples must address in some fashion. Although these three dimensions were not proposed as encompassing all of couples' cognitions, they were seen as themes that frequently interfere with marital functioning and that underlie many specific complaints from spouses. They are (a) boundaries, (b) power or control, and (c) investment in the relationship. *Boundaries* refers to the extent to which partners in a marriage have a preference for togetherness and sharing with each other versus a preference for individual functioning. Consistent with existent literature (Gray-Little & Burks, 1983), *power* or *control* is assessed in terms of two factors: (a) process, or whether a partner attempts to assert his or her will, and (b) outcome, or the extent to which one partner has final say or decision-making authority over some aspect of the relationship. *Investment* involves the ways that a partner contributes or gives to the relationship. Two different types of investment are assessed. First, a spouse can give to the relationship in instrumental ways—that is, by engaging in tasks that need to be accomplished for the relationship (e.g., cooking, making money). Second, a spouse can invest in the relationship in an expressive way, through demonstrating care, concern, or affection for the partner. Therefore, if we include the subdimensions for power and investment, there are a total of five proposed dimensions/subdimensions.

The authors proposed that these five dimensions/subdimensions apply to each of the five types of cognitions and provide a conceptual framework for understanding many distressed spouses' cognitions. Thus a distressed wife might offer attributions that suggest that her husband prefers to read a book in bed at night because he wants to avoid interacting and getting close to her (i.e., boundaries). Or a husband might make an attribution that he and his wife have difficulty selecting a movie to attend because they are engaged in a power struggle. Similarly, spouses have standards about these same relationship dimensions. For example, a husband might believe that each person should spend most of his or her free time with the partner but reserve a portion of it for one's own personal play (i.e., a boundaries standard). Likewise, a wife might have a standard that the two partners in a marriage should have equal say in any decisions that affect both persons (i.e., standard regarding control outcome). Consequently, when one is attempting to understand the role of any cognitive variable in a couple's marriage (e.g., attributions or standards), examining this cognitive variable within the context of important relationship dimensions (e.g., boundaries, control, investment) can provide a meaningful way to provide clarity to what can otherwise appear as myriad disjointed thoughts offered by the couple.

These relationship dimensions could be anticipated to relate to numerous attitudinal and behavioral aspects of marriage. The cognitions about these dimensions that guide partners' evaluations of their relationship can be hypothesized to affect marital satisfaction, communication, and spouse be-havior, as well as other attitudinal aspects of marriage. As a beginning step in exploring the role of cognitions about these dimensions of marriage, a relationship-focused cognitive measure was developed and studied in a large sample of married couples. One of the five cognitive dimensions, relation-ship standards, was selected for this first phase of research. Standards were of particular interest because of evidence from other studies (see Baucom & Epstein, 1989; Bradbury & Fincham, 1990) that suggests that extreme or incompatible cognitions are frequently associated with marital discord.

A measure of standards for marriage, the Inventory of Specific Relation-ship Standards (ISRS; Baucom, Epstein, Rankin, & Burnett, in press), was developed to assess the way spouses think their marital relationships should be. The ISRS is a 60-item, self-report measure of marital relationship stan-dards. The items were constructed to include the five cognitive dimensions described above: (a) boundaries, (b) instrumental investment, (c) expressive investment, (d) process control, and (e) outcome control. Items for each di-mension were written to assess 12 content domains common to measures of premarital and marital relationships that have been found to be related to marital quality: (a) leisure activities, (b) relationships with friends, (c) career and job issues, (d) household tasks and management, (e) religion and philosophy, (f) family of origin, (g) finances, (h) affection, (i) sex, (j) com-municating positive thoughts and feelings, (k) communicating negative thoughts and feelings, and (l) child-rearing/parenting strategies. Thus the ISRS includes one item from each of the content domains for each cognitive dimension, resulting in a total of 60 items (e.g., one item assessing boundary standards for leisure activities, one item assessing instrumental investment for leisure activities). Respondents are asked to rate each ISRS item on a 5-point scale of how often they and their partner believe they should behave according to the standards expressed in the items. Additional questions ask respondents if they are satisfied with the way each standard is met in their relationship and how upsetting it is to them when the standard is not met. An example of an ISRS item is "My partner and I should have the same ideas about how we spend our money." Respondents would indicate (a) how often this should occur in their marriage, (b) if they are satisfied with the way this standard is met (yes or no) in their relationship, and (c) how upsetting it is (on a 3-point scale) when this standard is not met.

To investigate the role of standards in marriage, a study was conducted to evaluate the psychometric properties of the ISRS and to examine correlates of the ISRS in a sample of community couples. In addition to the ISRS, self-report measures of marital satisfaction (Dyadic Adjustment Scale [DAS]; Spanier, 1976), communication (Communication Patterns Questionnaire [CPQ]; Sullaway & Christensen, 1983), beliefs about the relationship (Relationship Beliefs Inventory [RBI]; Eidelson & Epstein, 1982), and desired behavior change in the spouse (Areas of Change Questionnaire [A-C]; Weiss, Hops, & Patterson, 1973) were obtained from both partners. A community sample of 386 married couples was randomly selected from the central North Carolina and the College Park, Maryland, areas. Couples in the sample were reasonably representative of the U.S. population of married couples in terms of race and income. Very young and older couples were somewhat underrepresented in the sample, however.

One aspect of relationship standards suggested by previous research on cognitions in marriage was that standards that were extreme or incompatible between partners would be associated with marital discord. However, neither extreme nor incompatible standards were found to be substantially related to relationship satisfaction (median $r = .10$) for either men or women. These findings indicate that having what appear to be extreme standards is not necessarily detrimental to the relationship, at least among community couples. Because clinicians have noted that unrealistic or extreme standards are problematic for some distressed couples, the ways that distressed couples deal with their extreme standards must be understood more fully. Similarly, clinicians have noted that at times each partner may have what appears to be a reasonable standard for the marriage but that the standards for the two partners are incompatible in that area, thus leading to distress. Again, because the results from the current community sample indicate that degree of incompatibility of standards is not correlated with degree of marital discord, there may be something about the ways that distressed couples deal with or react to differing standards between the spouses that leads to difficulties.

Other findings from this investigation confirm that community couples have found ways to deal with extreme or differing standards between the partners. The results indicate only very small correlations between (a) whether spouses believed their standards were being met and (b) how extreme the standards were or how differing the two partners' standards were. Thus, among community couples, having extreme or incompatible standards does not necessarily mean that couples will believe that their standards are not being met. Understanding how some couples deal successfully with different and extreme standards whereas others do not will be critical for understanding how standards operate in marriage to enhance or diminish marital satisfaction. At the very least, these findings suggest that our initial understanding of relationship standards in marriage was too simplistic. Having what appear to be extreme standards or differing standards between partners does not necessarily imply that the individual's standards will go unmet or that the individual will become disenchanted with the relationship.

The relationships among the standards dimensions and measures of marital satisfaction, communication, behavior, and beliefs were assessed with a series of multiple regression analyses. Considering each partner's responses separately, regression equations were constructed to predict the DAS, CPQ, A-C, and RBI from the standards scores and whether the respondent believed his or her standards were being met. The standards' dimension scores were significant predictors of all of the relationship variables studied in the following manner. Spouses indicated higher levels of marital functioning when they endorsed standards that placed a major emphasis on being relationship focused in an egalitarian manner. That is, couples had higher scores on the various marital outcome measures when their marital standards indicated that their marriage should incorporate the following: (a) more sharing or fewer boundaries between partners; (b) more investment or giving to the relationship, both instrumentally and expressively; and (c) shared decision making, with an attempt to accept the partner's perspective. Couples also had higher marital functioning when they believed these standards were being met in the marriage. Thus a partner's standards and beliefs that his or her standards are being met in the relationship are substantially related to marital satisfaction, communication, requested behavior change, and relationship beliefs.

Interestingly, knowing the partner's degree of upset when his or her standards are not met did not add to the relationship between (a) standards endorsement and whether standards are met and (b) the relationship outcome measures. This finding was unanticipated because it was initially believed that becoming very upset when one's relationship standards are not met could lead to marital distress. However, this finding could reflect the different impacts that being upset about one's standards not being met could have. That is, becoming upset could result in unproductive behaviors, such as directing diffuse anger toward one's partner or sulking and isolating oneself from the partner. On the other hand, distress when one's standards are not being met could motivate an individual to work harder on the relationship. Similarly, not becoming upset when one's standards are not met could reflect either disengagement from the relationship or flexibility and an ability to compromise to get one's needs met. Consequently, whether an individual becomes upset when his or her standards for marriage are not being met could be less important than how an individual channels his or her emotional reaction.

IMPLICATIONS FOR THERAPY

One of the strengths of the cognitive-behavioral approach to treating marital distress is its reliance on basic research findings, the development of intervention techniques to reflect those findings, and the systematic empirical exploration of those intervention strategies. Also, as work in this domain has continued, investigators have not been reluctant to point out the limitations of their models or to acknowledge that significant numbers of couples still are maritally distressed after receiving marital therapy, regardless of the theoretical orientation employed. The importance of communication and noncommunication behavior in marital distress has been well established and has provided a firm base for a behavioral approach to treating marital distress. However, as noted previously, there now is a growing body of empirical investigations that demonstrates that couples' cognitions are a significant factor in marital functioning. Consequently, a major task of cognitive-behavioral marital therapists is to develop a set of intervention techniques that promote the cognitive changes needed to enhance marital functioning or to assist couples in making a reasonable decision to terminate their relationships.

Such efforts are clearly underway, but the field of cognitive interventions with couples is still in a stage of early development. There now are five outcome studies that have evaluated the effectiveness of offering cognitive restructuring in combination with behavioral interventions or cognitive restructuring alone to assist distressed couples (Baucom & Lester, 1986; Baucom et al., 1990; Emmelkamp et al., 1988; Epstein, Pretzer, & Fleming, 1982; Huber & Milstein, 1985). Overall, these investigations demonstrate the effectiveness of these techniques in producing cognitive changes and altering marital discord, but, as presented, these interventions are no more effective than behavioral marital therapy without cognitive interventions. However, these investigations were conducted before the basic research on couples' cognitions in marriage had grown to its current extent. Recent conceptualizations and basic findings would certainly alter future intervention studies.

For example, at the time the above outcome investigations were conducted, there were no clear conceptualizations of the cognitive variables that needed to be addressed in marriage. Recent investigations indicate that the cognitive variables proposed by Baucom, Epstein, Sayers, & Sher (1989) all are important to marital functioning and are probably worthy of attention in treating distressed couples. (Baucom & Epstein, 1990, offered an extensive discussion of cognitive interventions intended to address the cognitive variables discussed in this chapter.) Similarly, early behavioral models viewed marital distress from a rather narrow skills-deficit perspective, and the many concerns and complaints of couples were often treated as discrete behaviors requiring new skills or environmental manipulation. However, as suggested by Epstein et al. (1991), there appear to be important dimensions of relationship functioning (e.g., boundaries, control, investment) that are integral to marital adjustment and that serve as unifying themes for the behavioral complaints and cognitions of distressed couples. The above findings indicate that these dimensions are important in understanding couples' standards and are related to a wide variety of indices of marital functioning. Consequently, as we attempt to understand couples' cognitions, it is essential to clarify whether these relationship dimensions or others are most central in providing a framework for understanding couples' thoughts. Given that couples can have unlimited cognitions about their marriages, providing some way of organizing these cognitions is essential for the therapist's own understanding and for the therapist's ability to provide a framework for the couple to understand their distress.

Furthermore, the results of Epstein et al.'s (1991) investigation point out that the way that cognitions function in marriage is likely to be much more complex than originally anticipated. For example, with regard to standards, many community couples apparently learn to deal with differing standards between the partners in an effective manner such that both individuals believe that their standards are being met. Also, rather than extreme standards being maladaptive per se, it appears that having standards that focus on closeness, giving a great deal to the marriage, and providing an egalitarian and accepting approach to decision making is what is critical to adaptive marital functioning. Such findings from basic research on cognitions must be taken into account in developing new cognitive intervention techniques and must be integrated with our current, effective behavioral techniques in assisting distressed couples.

REFERENCES

Abramson, L. Y., Seligman, M. E. P., & Teasdale, J. (1978). Learned helplessness in humans: Critique and reformulation. *Journal of Abnormal Psychology, 87,* 49-94.

Arias, I., & O'Leary, K. D. (1985). Semantic and perceptual discrepancies in discordant and nondiscordant marriages. *Cognitive Therapy and Research, 2,* 51-60.

Bandura, A. (1977). *Social learning theory.* Englewood Cliffs, NJ: Prentice Hall.

Baucom, D. H. (1982). A comparison of behavioral contracting and problem solving/ communications training in behavioral marital therapy. *Behavior Therapy, 13,* 162-174.

Baucom, D. H., & Epstein, N. (1989). The role of cognitive variables in the assessment and treatment of marital discord. *Progress in Behavior Modification, 24,* 223-251.

Baucom, D. H., & Epstein, N. (1990). *Cognitive behavioral marital therapy.* New York: Brunner/Mazel.

Baucom, D. H., & Epstein, N. (1991). Will the real cognitive-behavioral marital therapy please stand up? *Journal of Family Psychology, 4,* 394-401.

Baucom, D. H., Epstein, N., Rankin, L. A., & Burnett, C. K. (in press). Assessing relationship standards: The Inventory of Specific Relationship Standards. *Journal of Family Psychology.*

Baucom, D. H., Epstein, N., Sayers, S., & Sher, T. G. (1989). The role of cognitions in marital relationships: Definitional, methodological, and conceptual issues. *Journal of Consulting and Clinical Psychology, 57,* 31-38.

Baucom, D. H., & Lester, G. W. (1986). The usefulness of cognitive restructuring as an adjunct to behavioral marital therapy. *Behavior Therapy, 17,* 385-403.

Baucom, D. H., Sayers, S. L., & Sher, T. G. (1990). Supplementing behavioral marital therapy with cognitive restructuring and emotional expressiveness training: An outcome investigation. *Journal of Consulting and Clinical Psychology, 58,* 636-645.

Beach, S. R. H., Jouriles, E. N., & O'Leary, K. D. (1985). Extramarital sex: Impact on depression and commitment in couples seeking marital therapy. *Journal of Sex and Marital Therapy, 11,* 99-108.

Beach, S. R. H., & O'Leary, K. D. (1986). The treatment of depression occurring in the context of marital discord. *Behavior Therapy, 17,* 43-49.

Beach, S. R. H., Sandeen, E. E., & O'Leary, K. D. (1990). *Depression in marriage.* New York: Guilford.

Beck, A. T., Rush, A. J., Shaw, B. F., & Emery, G. (1979). *The Cognitive Theory of Depression.* New York: Guilford Press.

Bennun, I. (1985a). Behavioral marital therapy: An outcome evaluation of conjoint, group and one spouse treatment. *Scandinavian Journal of Behaviour Therapy, 14,* 157-168.

Bennun, I. (1985b). Prediction and responsiveness in behavioral marital therapy. *Behavioural Psychotherapy, 13,* 186-201.

Billings, A. (1979). Conflict resolution in distressed and nondistressed married couples. *Journal of Consulting and Clinical Psychology, 17,* 368-376.

Birchler, G. R. (1986). Alleviating depression with "marital" intervention. In A. Freeman, N. Epstein, & K. M. Simon (Eds.), *Depression in the family* (pp. 101-116). New York: Haworth.

Birchler, G. R., Weiss, R. L., & Vincent, J. P. (1975). Multimethod analysis of social reinforcement exchange between maritally distressed and nondistressed spouse and stranger dyads. *Journal of Personality and Social Psychology, 31,* 349-360.

Boelens, W., Emmelkamp, P., MacGillavry, D., & Markvoort, M. (1980). A clinical evaluation of marital treatment: Reciprocity counseling vs. system-theoretic counseling. *Behavior Analysis and Modification, 4,* 85-96.

Bradbury, T. N., & Fincham, F. D. (1990). Attributions in marriage: Review and critique. *Psychological Bulletin, 107,* 3-33.

Christensen, A., & Nies, D. C. (1980). The Spouse Observation Checklist: Empirical analysis and critique. *American Journal of Family Therapy, 8,* 69-79.

Christensen, A., Sullaway, M., & King, C. (1983). Systematic error in behavioral reports of dyadic interaction: Egocentric bias and content effects. *Behavioral Assessment, 5,* 131-142.

Crowe, M. J. (1978). Conjoint marital therapy: A controlled outcome study. *Psychological Medicine, 8,* 623-636.

Doherty, W. J. (1981a). Cognitive processes in intimate conflict: I. Extending attribution theory. *American Journal of Family Therapy, 9,* (1), 5-13.

Doherty, W. J. (1981b). Cognitive processes in intimate conflict: II. Efficacy and learned helplessness. *American Journal of Family Therapy, 9,* (2), 35-44.

Eidelson, R. J., & Epstein, N. (1982). Cognition and relationship maladjustment: Development of a measure of dysfunctional relationship beliefs. *Journal of Consulting and Clinical Psychology, 50,* 715-720.

Ellis, A. (1977). The nature of disturbed marital interactions. In A. Ellis & R. Grieger (Eds.), *Handbook of rational-emotive therapy* (pp. 170-176). New York: Springer.

Emmelkamp, P., van der Helm, M., MacGillavry, D., & van Zanten, B. (1984). Marital therapy with clinically distressed couples: A comparative evaluation of system-theoretic, contingency contracting, and communication skills approaches. In K. Hahlweg & N. S. Jacobson (Eds.), *Marital interaction: Analysis and modification* (pp. 36-52). New York: Guilford.

Emmelkamp, P. M. G., van Linden van den Heuvell, C., Ruphan, M., Sanderman, R., Scholing, A., & Stroink, F. (1988). Cognitive and behavioral interventions: A comparative evaluation with clinically distressed couples. *Journal of Family Psychology, 1,* 365-377.

Epstein, N. (1982). Cognitive therapy with couples. *American Journal of Family Therapy, 10,* (1), 5-16.

Epstein, N. & Baucom, D. H. (1993). Cognitive factors in marital disturbance. In K. S. Dobson & P. C. Kendall (Eds.), *Psychopathology and Cognition.* San Diego: Academic Press.

Epstein, N., & Eidelson, R. J. (1981). Unrealistic beliefs of clinical couples: Their relationship to expectations, goals, and satisfaction. *American Journal of Family Therapy, 9,* (4), 13-22.

Epstein, N., Baucom, D. H., Rankin, L. A., & Burnett, C. K. (1991, November). *Relationship standards in marriage: Development of a new measure of content-specific cognitions.* Paper presented at the 25th annual meeting of the Association for Advancement of Behavior Therapy, New York.

Epstein, N., Pretzer, J. L., & Fleming, B. (1982, November). *Cognitive therapy and communication training: Comparisons of effects with distressed couples.* Paper presented at the annual meeting of the Association for Advancement of Behavior Therapy, Los Angeles.

Epstein, N., Pretzer, J. L., & Fleming, B. (1987). The role of cognitive appraisal in self-reports of marital communication. *Behavior Therapy, 18,* 51-69.

Ewart, C. K. (1978, November). *Behavioral marriage therapy with older couples: Effects of training measured by the Marital Adjustment Scale.* Paper presented at the annual meeting of the Association for Advancement of Behavior Therapy, Chicago.

Fincham, F. D., & Bradbury, T. N. (1987). The impact of attributions in marriage: A longitudinal analysis. *Journal of Personality and Social Psychology, 53,* 510-517.

Fincham, F. D., Bradbury, T. N., & Grych, D. (1990). Conflict in close relationships: The role of intrapersonal phenomena. In S. Graham & V. S. Folkes (Eds.), *Attribution theory: Application to achievement, mental health and interpersonal conflict* (pp. 161-184). Hillsdale, NJ: Lawrence Erlbaum.

Floyd, F. J., & Markman, H. J. (1983). Observational biases in spouse observation: Toward a cognitive/behavioral model of marriage. *Journal of Consulting and Clinical Psychology, 51,* 430-457.

Geiss, S. K., & O'Leary, K. D. (1981). Therapist ratings of frequency and severity of marital problems: Implications for research. *Journal of Marital and Family Therapy, 7,* 515-520.

Girodo, M., Stein, S. J., & Dotzenroth, S. E. (1980). The effects of communication skills training and contracting on marital relations. *Behavioral Engineering, 6,* 61-76.

Gottman, J., Notarius, C., Gonso, J., & Markman, H. J. (1976). *A couple's guide to communication.* Champaign, IL: Research Press.

Gottman, J., Notarius, C., Markman, H., Bank, S., Yoppi, B., & Rubin, M. E. (1976). Behavior exchange theory and marital decision making. *Journal of Personality and Social Psychology, 34,* 14-23.

Gray-Little, B., & Burks, N. (1983). Power and satisfaction in marriage: A review and critique. *Psychological Bulletin, 93,* 513-538.

Hahlweg, K., & Markman, H. J. (1983, December). *The effectiveness of behavioral marital therapy: Empirical status of behavior techniques in preventing and alleviating marital distress.* Paper presented at the 17th annual meeting of the Association for Advancement of Behavior Therapy, Washington, DC.

Hahlweg, K., Revenstorf, D., & Schindler, L. (1982). Treatment of marital distress: Comparing formats and modalities. *Advances in Behavior Research and Therapy, 4,* 57-74.

Hahlweg, K., Schindler, L., Revenstorf, D., & Brengelmann, J. C. (1984). The Munich marital therapy study. In K. Hahlweg & N. S. Jacobson (Eds.), *Marital interaction: Analysis and modification* (pp. 3-26). New York: Guilford.

Huber, C. H., & Milstein, B. (1985). Cognitive restructuring and a collaborative set in couples' work. *American Journal of Family Therapy, 13*(2), 17-27.

Iverson, A., & Baucom, D. H. (1990). Behavioral marital therapy outcomes: Alternative interpretations of the data. *Behavior Therapy, 21,* 129-138.

Jacobson, N. S. (1978). Specific and nonspecific factors in the effectiveness of a behavioral approach to the treatment of marital discord. *Journal of Consulting and Clinical Psychology, 46,* 442-452.

Jacobson, N. S. (1984). A component analysis of behavioral marital therapy: The relative effectiveness of behavior exchange and communication/problem-solving training. *Journal of Consulting and Clinical Psychology, 52,* 295-305.

Jacobson, N. S., Dobson, K., Fruzzetti, A. E., Schmaling, K. B., & Salusky, S. (1991). Marital therapy as a treatment for depression. *Journal of Consulting and Clinical Psychology, 59,* 547-557.

Jacobson, N. S., Follette, W. C., & McDonald, D. W. (1982). Reactivity to positive and negative behavior in distressed and nondistressed married couples. *Journal of Consulting and Clinical Psychology, 50,* 706-714.

Jacobson, N. S., Follette, W. C., Revenstorf, D., Baucom, D. H., Hahlweg, K., & Margolin, G. (1984). Variability in outcome and clinical significance of behavioral marital therapy. A reanalysis of outcome data. *Journal of Consulting and Clinical Psychology, 52,* 497-504.

Jacobson, N. S., & Margolin, G. (1979). *Marital therapy: Strategies based on social learning and behavior exchange principles.* New York: Brunner/Mazel.

Jacobson, N. S., & Moore, D. (1981). Spouses as observers of the events in their relationship. *Journal of Consulting and Clinical Psychology, 49,* 269-277.

Jacobson, N. S., Waldron, H., & Moore, D. (1980). Toward a behavioral profile of marital distress. *Journal of Consulting and Clinical Psychology, 48,* 696-703.

Johnson, S. M., & Greenberg, L. S. (1985). Differential effects of experiential and problem-solving interventions in resolving marital conflict. *Journal of Consulting and Clinical Psychology, 53,* 175-184.

Jones, M. E., & Stanton, A. L. (1988). Dysfunctional beliefs, belief similarity, and marital distress: A comparison of models. *Journal of Social and Clinical Psychology, 7,* 1-14.

Liberman, R., Levine, J., Wheeler, E., Sanders, N., & Wallace, C. J. (1976). Marital therapy in groups: A comparative evaluation of behavioral and interaction formats. *Acta Psychiatrica Scandinavica, 266,* 1-34.

Margolin, G. (1981). Behavior exchange in happy and unhappy marriages: A family cycle perspective. *Behavior Therapy, 12,* 329-343.

Margolin, G., Hattem, D., John, R. S., & Yost, K. (1985). Perceptual agreement between spouses and outside observers when coding themselves and stranger dyads. *Behavioral Assessment, 7,* 235-247.

Margolin, G., & Wampold, B. E. (1981). Sequential analysis of conflict and accord in distressed and nondistressed marital partners. *Journal of Consulting and Clinical Psychology, 9,* 554-567.

Mehlman, S. K., Baucom, R. H., & Anderson, D. (1983). Effectiveness of cotherapists versus single therapists and immediate versus delayed treatment in behavioral marital therapy. *Journal of Consulting and Clinical Psychology, 51,* 258-266.

O'Farrell, T. J., Cutter, H. S., & Floyd, F. J. (1983). *The Class on Alcoholism and Marriage (CALM) project: Results on marital adjustment and communication from before to after therapy* (Tech. Rep. No. 4-1). Brockton, MA: Brockton West Roxbury Veterans Administration Medical Center.

Pretzer, J. L., Epstein, N., & Fleming, B. (1991). The Marital Attitude Survey: A measure of dysfunctional attributions and expectancies. *Journal of Cognitive Psychotherapy, 5,* 131-148.

Raush, H. L., Barry, W. A., Hertel, R. K., & Swain, M. A. (1974). *Communication, conflict and marriage.* San Francisco: Jossey-Bass.

Revenstorf, D., Hahlweg, K., Schindler, L., & Vogel, B. (1984). Interaction analysis of marital conflict. In K. Hahlweg & N. S. Jacobson (Eds.), *Marital interaction: Analysis and modification* (pp. 159-181). New York: Guilford.

Robinson, E. A., & Price, M. G. (1980). Pleasurable behavior in marital interaction: An observational study. *Journal of Consulting and Clinical Psychology, 48,* 117-118.

Rotter, J. B. (1954). *Social learning and clinical psychology.* Englewood Cliffs, NJ: Prentice Hall.

Rounsaville, B. J., Weissman, M. M., Prusoff, B. A., & Herceg-Baron, R. L. (1979). Process of psychotherapy among depressed women with marital disputes. *American Journal of Orthopsychiatry, 49,* 505-510.

Sher, T. G., Baucom, D. H., & Larus, J. M. (1990). Communication patterns and response to treatment among depressed and nondepressed maritally distressed couples. *Journal of Family Psychology, 4,* 63-79.

Snyder, D. K., & Wills, R. M. (1989). Behavioral versus insight-oriented marital therapy: Effects on individual and interspousal functioning. *Journal of Consulting and Clinical Psychology, 57,* 39-46.

Snyder, D. K., Wills, R. M., & Grady-Fletcher, A. (1991). Long-term effectiveness of behavioral versus insight-oriented marital therapy: A 4-year follow-up study. *Journal of Consulting and Clinical Psychology, 59,* 138-141.

Spanier, G. B. (1976). Measuring dyadic adjustment: New scales for assessing the quality of marriage and similar dyads. *Journal of Marriage and the Family, 38,* 15-28.

Stuart, R. B. (1980). *Helping couples change: A social learning approach to marital therapy.* New York: Guilford.

Sullaway, M., & Christensen, A. (1983). Assessment of dysfunctional interaction patterns in couples. *Journal of Marriage and the Family, 45,* 653-660.

Thibaut, J. W., & Kelley, H. H. (1959). *The social psychology of groups.* New York: John Wiley.

Turkewitz, H., & O'Leary, K. D. (1981). A comparative outcome study of behavioral marital therapy and communication therapy. *Journal of Marital and Family Therapy, 7,* 159-169.

Vanzetti, N. A., & Notarius, C. I. (1991, November). *Relational efficacy: A summary of findings.* Paper presented at the 25th annual meeting of the Association for Advancement of Behavior Therapy, New York.

Vincent, J. P., Weiss, R. L., & Birchler, G. R. (1975). A behavioral analysis of problem solving in distressed and nondistressed married and stranger dyads. *Behavior Therapy, 6,* 475-487.

Weiss, R. L., Hops, H., & Patterson, G. R. (1973). A framework for conceptualizing marital conflict, a technology for altering it, some data for evaluating it. In L. A. Hamerlynck, L. C. Handy, & E. J. Mash (Eds.), *Behavior change: Methodology, concepts, and practice* (pp. 309-342). Champaign, IL: Research Press.

Wills, T. A., Weiss, R. L., & Patterson, G. R. (1974). A behavioral analysis of the determinants of marital satisfaction. *Journal of Consulting and Clinical Psychology, 42,* 802-811.

10

Cognitive Therapy With Nontraditional Populations

APPLICATION TO
POST-TRAUMATIC STRESS DISORDER
AND PERSONALITY DISORDERS

JANICE L. HOWES

T. MICHAEL VALLIS

I n this chapter, conceptual and intervention issues involved in the application of cognitive therapy (CT) to nontraditional patient groups are outlined. We define *nontraditional* patient groups as those different from the patient groups in which the validity and efficacy of CT was established. Several contextual points should be noted before proceeding. First, it must be emphasized that conceptual, as opposed to empirical, issues are the focus of this chapter. Currently, there are no data clearly demonstrating the efficacy of CT with nontraditional populations, such as persons with post-traumatic

AUTHORS' NOTE: The order of authorship is alphabetical. Both authors have contributed equally to this chapter.

stress disorder (PTSD) or personality disorder (PD). In the absence of data one must proceed carefully. Although we do not support the blind application of CT, as currently practiced, to nontraditional populations, CT has progressed to the point at which multiple conceptual models can be identified and a metaperspective on the use of CT advanced. With this metamodel as a framework, the characteristics specific to a nontraditional population (e.g., PTSD or PD) can be matched to specific models of CT. It is our hypothesis that such matching will increase the adaptability, efficacy, flexibility, and acceptance of CT. Future empirical studies must confirm this, however. Second, because the focus of this chapter is on nontraditional applications of CT, *traditional applications* must be defined. Traditionally, CT involves the following characteristics (Beck, Rush, Shaw, & Emery, 1979; Vallis, 1991): (a) It is primarily a phenomenological approach, which involves an empirical focus and heavy reliance on out-of-session therapeutic activities (i.e., homework); (b) it is a short-term approach; (c) the therapist is active and directive; and (d) the therapeutic relationship is based on collaborative empiricism. Further, CT focuses on three levels of cognitive function, which, in order of the amount of therapeutic attention given, are *cognitive content* (e.g., automatic thoughts, self-verbalizations, images), *cognitive process* (e.g., distortions), and *cognitive structure* (e.g., dysfunctional assumptions or schemas). Representative CT-specific interventions in traditional CT include graded task assignment, activity scheduling, behavioral rehearsal, role play, exposure, education, verbal challenging, self-monitoring, distraction, imagery, decatastrophization, examining evidence, logical analysis, and designing and carrying out experiments (Beck et al., 1979; Hawton, Salkovskis, Kirk, & Clark, 1989). Finally, the traditional CT patient groups are those for which there is considerable data to support cognitive conceptualization and intervention. These include unipolar, nonsuicidal depressed outpatients (Beck, Hollon, Young, Bedrosian, & Budenz, 1985; Blackburn, Bishop, Glen, Whalley, & Christie, 1981; Elkin et al., 1989; Murphy, Simons, Wetzel, & Lustman, 1984; Rush, Beck, Kovacs, & Hollon, 1977), panic disorder patients (Barlow, 1988; Beck, 1988; Clark, Salkovskis, & Chalkley, 1985), generalized anxiety disorder patients (Borkovec et al., 1987; Butler, Cullington, Hibbert, Klimes, & Gelder, 1987; Rapee & Barlow, 1991), and eating disorder patients (anorexia nervosa and bulimia nervosa), although there is more conceptual than empirical work in this area (Fairburn & Cooper, 1989; Garner & Bemis, 1985).

A CONCEPTUAL FRAMEWORK
FOR ADAPTING COGNITIVE THERAPY

Given that traditional CT has become one of the most respected forms of psychotherapy, on the basis of its demonstrated efficacy, its acceptance by patients, and its highly operationalized nature, one might question why it needs to be adapted at all. Both clinical realities and recent theoretical developments are producing the need for change. The clinical realities include the fact that as CT becomes more well known, referral sources and patient presentations are becoming more varied (e.g., symptom issues are not the targets of change for all patients or referring agents). Further, not all patients respond to traditional CT interventions (Fennell & Teasdale, 1987; Rush & Shaw, 1983). Finally, not all patients report clear cognitive dysfunctions, and this limits therapeutic interventions focused on cognitive content (the area in which there are the greatest number of CT-specific interventions). Recent conceptual developments also call for adaptations to CT. These involve the role of affect in cognition (Greenberg & Safran, 1987), the importance of interpersonal processes in CT (Safran & Segal, 1990), techniques for using the therapeutic relationship to promote cognitive change (Jacobson, 1989; Rothstein & Robinson, 1991), criticism of the adequacy of the information-processing model (which has been the conceptual backbone of CT; Safran, 1988), and the recent movement toward psychotherapy integration (Goldfried, 1982).

Adapting CT for nontraditional populations involves two related tasks: first, identification of generic, non-population-specific adaptations required to produce sufficient conceptual and technical flexibility to deal with patient issues different from the traditional concerns presented; and second, identification of specific cognitive characteristics of a given nontraditional population as therapeutic targets of change. Both of these tasks are addressed in this chapter. With respect to specific adaptations, PTSD and PD are discussed. These populations have been chosen for several reasons. Trauma-related difficulties and long-standing characterological problems are frequently encountered in clinical practice. Although there is clear demand for treatment of these problems, few treatments have been demonstrated to be effective. Finally, we have chosen to examine CT for PTSD and PD because together they illustrate the need for a metamodel of CT.

COGNITIVE THERAPY: A METAMODEL

We are at a stage in the natural history of CT at which differentiation among the various forms of CT and integration of new theoretical developments must occur (Mahoney, 1988; Vallis, 1991). This requires the explicit development of a metaperspective on CT. Historically, we can trace the development of CT along three paths, each with its own theoretical orientation. The three paths can be labeled as the behavior therapy, cognitive therapy, and psychotherapy paths. Figure 10.1 illustrates this development.

The center area of Figure 10.1 illustrates the work of Beck and Ellis, who have advocated cognitively based approaches to psychotherapy for some time. Somewhat independent from this work, behavioral therapists began to apply behavioral principles to cognitive phenomena in the 1970s (cognitive-behavioral modification; the left side of Figure 10.1). In the late 1970s, Beck and his colleagues explicitly merged his cognitive approach with mainstream cognitive-behavioral modification techniques to produce a protocol-based model of CT (Beck et al., 1979). It is this model of CT that has been subjected to the most thorough empirical evaluation. More recently, long-established psychotherapy principles, based on work by Kelly (1955) and Bowlby (1985), among others (Mahoney & Freeman, 1985; the right side of Figure 10.1), have been integrated to form what has become known as constructivist-based CT (Guidano & Liotti, 1983; Mahoney, 1988).

Constructivist-based models offer great potential for developing a metaperspective on CT. In this regard, three issues, and their implications, deserve attention: constructivism, developmentalism, and interpersonal focus. Guidano and Liotti (1983) provided an excellent model of a constructivist-developmental approach to CT. Their approach relied heavily on developmental theory and structural models of knowledge. They differentiated tacit from explicit knowing and highlighted the central role of self-knowledge in emotional dysfunction and well-being. Attachment was seen as playing a major role in the development of self-knowledge.

Guidano and Liotti (1983), as well as others (Meichenbaum & Gilmore, 1984; Safran, Vallis, Segal, & Shaw, 1986) differentiated core from peripheral cognitive events. *Core cognitive events* were defined as central to the experience of the self, whereas *peripheral cognitive events* were defined as noncentral (see Safran et al., 1986). As such, changes in core cognitive processes were thought to lead to greater and more lasting clinical change. Interventions designed to alter core cognitive structure included in-depth

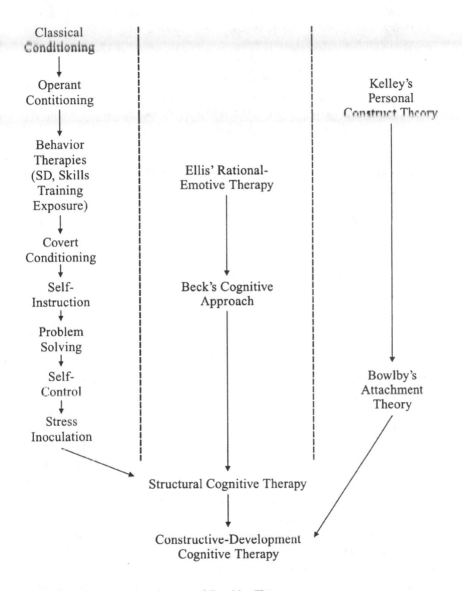

Figure 10.1. Historical Development of Cognitive Therapy

examination/reconstruction of the developmental stages leading to the formation of deep-structure self-knowledge (Guidano & Liotti, 1983), emotional exploration to produce decentering and cognitive differentiation (Safran & Segal, 1990), and the use of the therapeutic relationship to promote cognitive change (Rothstein & Robinson, 1991).

Mahoney (1988) drew an explicit distinction between *rationalist* and *constructivist-developmental* approaches to cognitive therapy. In the rationalist view, reality is external and stable (something that can be confirmed and validated), whereas in the constructivist view, reality is entirely subjective and idiosyncratic. Further, according to a rationalist perspective, knowledge is validated by logic and reason, with priority given to thought over emotion, whereas from a constructivist perspective, knowledge is an integrated cognitive-behavioral-affective experience. Rationalist and constructivist perspectives also differ in their notions of human change. From a rationalist perspective, change proceeds according to cause-and-effect relationships, characterized by associationism. From a constructivist viewpoint, change involves structural differentiation such that mental representations are transformed and refined in an evolutionary fashion (Mahoney, 1988).

Another recent theoretical development that has stimulated adaptation in cognitive therapy is illustrated by Safran's work on cognitive-interpersonal approaches (Safran, 1984, 1988; Safran & Segal, 1990). Safran emphasized the interpersonal nature of an individual's functioning and distress and developed therapeutic interventions directed toward facilitating change, at a core level, in interpersonal schemas. Many of these interventions were based on detailed exploration of the patient-therapist interaction and its relationship to the patient's distress and self-schemas.

In summary, cognitive therapy has been marked by a series of developmental stages. There are currently several different theoretical frameworks within which to develop cognitive conceptualization and from which to plan interventions. As a result, an explicit metamodel of CT can be identified, with rationalist-based and constructivist-based theories as its theoretical guideposts (Vallis, 1991). This metamodel can provide therapists with systematic choices about which cognitive conceptualization to follow in a specific case (Howes & Parrott, 1991).

Figure 10.2 illustrates the multiple available conceptual frameworks within CT for use with nontraditional populations. These frameworks involve conceptualizations based on cognitive content alone, cognitive content versus cognitive process versus cognitive structure (labeled the *tripartite*

Hierarchical Approach

Cognitive Content

↓

Tripartite
(Cognitive Content, Structure, and Process)

↓

Core-Peripheral Beliefs

↓

Developmental Analysis

↓

Interpersonal Context
(Interpersonal Factors, Therapeutic Relationship)

Movement From One Level to the Next Is *Not* Always Sequential and Consecutive.

Movement Is Based on Patient's Progress, His/Her Response to Therapeutic Strategies, and Intervention Targets.

Not All Levels Are Necessary for All Patients; Emphasis on Individualized Conceptualization (Howes & Parrott, 1991).

Figure 10.2. Conceptual Frameworks Within Cognitive Therapy

conceptualization), core versus peripheral cognitive processes, constructivist and developmental processes, and cognitive-interpersonal processes.

In content-based conceptualizations, the focus is on the accessible content of the patient's experience. As noted above, there is considerable empirical support for the efficacy of interventions targeted at cognitive content (Elkin, Parloff, Hadley, & Autry, 1985; Hollon & Najavits, 1989). Conceptualizing at a cognitive content level has a number of advantages. First, immediate material that directly influences affect and behavior can be identified in a way that the patient can easily relate to. Second, content-based conceptualizations are largely descriptive, thus allowing the construction of an idiosyncratic model of a patient's phenomenology. This is a particular advantage when working with nontraditional populations, for whom a priori cogni- tive models do not exist. The major limitation of content-based conceptualizations is that they do not address nonaccessible cognitive processes or structures. Cognitive psychology (e.g., Craik & Tulving's 1975 depth-of-processing model) and CT (e.g., Goldfried, Padawer, & Robins, 1984) research indicates that nonaccessible cognitive processes play a role in emotional and behavioral disorders.

The tripartite conceptualization, which focuses on cognitive content, process, and structure, developed from interest in the role of information processing in psychopathology and in patient change (Hollon & Kriss, 1984). Beck et al. (1979) distinguished between automatic thoughts, faulty information-processing styles, and dysfunctional assumptions, whereas Hollon and Kriss (1984) differentiated cognitive factors into products, structures, and processes. This tripartite conceptualization advances our understanding of patients' problems in that cognitive content, structure, and process interact and interventions at any level may be appropriate. Further, this approach encourages therapists to look beyond cognitive content, to identify deeper-level cognitive factors, and to employ interventions focused directly on process and structure. Despite these strengths, tripartite conceptualizations are limited because they do not help the therapist decide which are the most important cognitive factors to address in interventions and because developmental and interpersonal factors are not specifically addressed (Howes & Parrott, 1991).

The core conceptualization has developed from attention to cognitive structures and, more specifically, self-schemas. This has resulted in cognitive therapists' differentiating between surface-level (peripheral) and deeper-level (core) cognitions (Guidano & Liotti, 1983; Safran et al., 1986). Core cognitions differ from peripheral cognitions in that they can be used to predict a patient's emotional/behavioral responses across situations. Attempts to change core or central beliefs are assumed to create greater anxiety but longer-lasting change (Guidano & Liotti, 1983; Safran et al., 1986). Although this type of conceptualization appears to be clinically useful (Safran et al., 1986), there is very little empirical research addressing it. However, there is some support for the notion that memory performance is superior under self-referent conditions, due to the integration of the to-be-processed information into a structure of self-related concepts (Rogers, Kuiper, & Kirker, 1977). Further, Louisy (1989) presented data that partially support the core-peripheral distinction. To access core cognitive structures clinically, the therapist attends to the patient's automatic thoughts, looks for patterns, constructs hypotheses about core constructs based on accessible cognitions, and then tests these hypotheses. Hypotheses are altered as needed when confronted with confirmatory or disconfirmatory evidence (see Safran et al., 1986). Core conceptualizations appear to facilitate assessment and treatment by identifying those cognitive structures that may serve an organizing function for the individual and are most likely to produce lasting change. This approach may be useful in guiding treatment with more difficult patient populations, given its idiosyncratic focus. Disadvantages of this approach include the following: Accessing core cognitive structures is time consuming and may not be suitable in some therapy situations; core beliefs are hypothetical constructs (i.e., tentative); and the reliability of a core-peripheral distinction may be questionable given the current lack of empirical validation of this approach (Howes & Parrott, 1991).

As mentioned above, Guidano and Liotti (1983) have been instrumental in advancing a developmental-constructivist conceptualization in CT. In this approach, deep structures are viewed as having a developmental basis. That is, early developmental events contribute to core cognitive structures. Thus it is important to focus on the patient's cognitive, as well as emotional, development in assessment and treatment.

Advocates of the interpersonal-based conceptualization, such as Safran (Safran, 1984; Safran & Segal, 1990) highlighted the value of Sullivan's (1953) interpersonal theory to CT. Safran emphasized the importance of the "cognitive-interpersonal cycle," stating that cognitive, interpersonal, and interactional factors (i.e., "me-you patterns") are linked and that information processing in the real world involves "hot cognitions" (i.e., emotionally laden cognitions; see Safran & Greenberg, 1982, 1986). Jacobson (1989) also advocated the use of the therapeutic relationship to evaluate, test, and help the patient change core beliefs. An interpersonal-based conceptualization tends to result in greater attention being paid to the patient's cognitions, behaviors, and affect during the therapy session, as well as to the therapist's feelings and responses that the patient evokes (Jacobson, 1989). The therapeutic relationship can be helpful in identifying core cognitions but can also become a means to develop healthier interpersonal relationships. The therapist may focus more specifically on the "here and now," may employ more Gestalt techniques to help deal with "hot cognitions," and may utilize behavioral strategies such as modeling and role playing within the context of the relationship, as well as more standard cognitive techniques (see Rothstein & Robinson, 1991; Safran & Segal, 1990).

The availability of multiple frameworks allows the therapist to approach conceptualization in a flexible manner by selecting the framework that best applies to the patient's individual difficulties. Howes and Parrott (1991) outlined guidelines that can be helpful in the process of choosing an appropriate cognitive conceptual framework in clinical practice. A hierarchical approach to conceptualization is recommended, in which movement from one level to the next is based on the patient's progress, his or her response to therapeutic strategies, and intervention targets (i.e., movement is not necessarily sequential or consecutive, although it may often be). In this approach, it is suggested that the therapist begin by conceptualizing problems at the cognitive content level. When cognitive strategies targeted at this level fail, or when the patient has apparently gained as much as he or she can from content-focused interventions, the therapist should move to a tripartite conceptualization. This level of analysis is more time consuming but may well produce a deeper understanding of a patient's difficulties (i.e., by differentiating cognitive content from cognitive structure from cognitive process and by exploring the relevance of the difficulties to self-schemas). If the tripartite level of analysis is not sufficient to understand and resolve the patient's problems fully, differentiating core from peripheral beliefs may further advance treatment. Once the therapeutic value of this framework has been exhausted, incorporating a developmental analysis and examining relevant interpersonal factors (both within and outside of the therapeutic relationship) should provide the most complete and flexible cognitive approach. At the same time, specific patient presentations that suggest a specific conceptual model should be identified. For instance, long-standing difficulties that have interfered with a patient's ability to form relationships suggest that a developmental/constructivist approach may be useful. Evidence of difficulty forming trust in the early sessions should alert the therapist to consider interpersonal models of CT. In situations in which patient problems are generalized across multiple situations/contexts, investigation of core cognitive processes may be necessary. Finally, in situations in which the patient presents with circumscribed problems that are recent in onset, a content or tripartite model of CT may well be sufficient.

COGNITIVE THERAPY WITH
POST-TRAUMATIC STRESS DISORDER

Diagnosis, Incidence, and Formation

Post-traumatic emotional reactions have been recognized and treated by clinicians for many years, but the disorder of PTSD was not introduced until the third edition of the *Diagnostic and Statistical Manual of Mental Disorders* (*DSM-III;* American Psychiatric Association, 1980). In the past, multiple terms such as *war neurosis, battle fatigue, rape syndrome*, and *post-Vietnam syndrome* were used to describe the emotional aftermath and symptom presentation displayed by victims and survivors of specific traumas (see Trimble, 1985).

The diagnostic criteria for PTSD in the third, revised edition of the *Diagnostic and Statistical Manual* (*DSM-III-R;* American Psychiatric Association, 1987) are as follows. First, the individual must experience "an event that is outside the usual range of human experience and that would be markedly distressing to almost anyone" (p. 250). This criterion has raised questions about whether low-magnitude traumas qualify for diagnosis (Davidson & Foa, 1991). However, some attempt is made in *DSM-III-R* to focus on victims' appraisal of the trauma. Second, the traumatic event is persistently reexperienced through recurrent flashbacks, intrusive recollections, nightmares, and anniversary reactions. These reexperiencing phenomena are the disorder-specific symptoms for PTSD. The third criterion involves avoidance of stimuli associated with the trauma and "numbing of general responsiveness." The fourth criterion is persistent symptoms of increased arousal. Finally, a duration of at least 1 month is required for diagnosis (see Davidson & Foa, 1991, who discussed data supporting these diagnostic criteria).

Much of the data focusing on incidence of PTSD comes from the literature on Vietnam veterans. Reported incidence rates vary from 5% of active-duty Vietnam veterans to 18% to 54% of veterans now in the civilian community (Stretch, Vail, & Maloney, 1985) to 55% of Canadian Vietnam veterans (Stretch, 1991). These data have been interpreted to reflect the role of support as a moderating variable in the maintenance of PTSD, but selection biases need to be ruled out as an alternative moderating factor.

The incidence of PTSD in non-Vietnam populations is difficult to estimate due to problems in accessing these populations and a failure to recognize symptom presentation. However, Helzer, Robins, and McEvoy (1987) reported epidemiological data to suggest a 1% prevalence rate in the general population. On the basis of a sample of women, 75% of who had been crime victims, Kilpatrick, Saunders, Amick-McMullan, Best, Veronen, & Resnick (1989) reported that 28% of the victims met criteria for PTSD. Similarly, Bownes, O'Gorman, and Sayers (1991) reported that 70% of a sample of rape victims displayed PTSD. Given the high incidence of violence against women (e.g., Brickman & Briere, 1984, reported that in a general sample of Canadian women, 6% had been raped and 21% had been sexually assaulted), post-traumatic distress, if not full-blown PTSD, is likely. Other studies have suggested that PTSD can develop following chronic stress (e.g., following the Three-Mile Island nuclear accident; see Davidson & Baum, 1986).

The most frequently employed conceptual model of the formation of PTSD is the behavioral model. Within this model, the trauma is viewed as the unconditioned stimulus and associated physiological arousal as the unconditioned response (Keane, Fairbank, Caddell, Zimering, & Bender, 1985). Coexisting external and internal stimuli elicit physiological responses through higher-order conditioning, producing generalization to similar stimuli.

Information-processing models have also been proposed and are receiving increased clinical as well as research interest. Horowitz (1976, 1986) presented a psychodynamic model of PTSD in which the traumatic event is processed and integrated into existent self-schemas through a "completion tendency." Repetitive recollections and reexperiencing phenomena are viewed as part of the assimilation process. Peterson, Prout, and Schwarz (1991) used this model to describe adaptive resolution, as well as maladaptive resolution (i.e., based on generalization of fear, anger, withdrawal, or dissociation) of PTSD. Litz and Keane (1989) highlighted a number of information-processing variables thought to be involved in the production and maintenance of PTSD. Storage, retrieval, attentional bias, arousal, and symptom formation were described as central factors. Litz and Keane suggested that fear-related (traumatic) information is organized in a way that facilitates response to threat cues, as well as in a way that leads to a bias to attend to trauma-related stimuli. Other information-processing models include those by Foa and Chemtob (cited in Jones & Barlow, 1990).

Finally, biological models have been proposed, highlighting the role of biochemical-neurochemical changes, as well as biological vulnerability in the development of PTSD (Kolb, 1987; van der Kolk, Boyd, Krystal, & Greenberg, 1984, cited in Jones & Barlow, 1990). Although potentially useful, biological models fail to address important psychosocial variables such as appraisal of trauma, social supports, and extent and severity of trauma (Jones & Barlow, 1990; Parrott & Howes, 1991). Jones and Barlow (1990) presented an integrative model of the etiology of PTSD, in which "Post-Traumatic Stress Disorder develops out of the complex interaction between biological and psychological pre-dispositions, the occurrence of stressful events and alarms, the development of anxiety, and the adequacy of coping strategies and social supports" (p. 324).

Regardless of the etiological model one adopts in assessing and treating PTSD, lack of extinction (despite repeated reexperiencing of at least some aspects of the trauma) must be addressed. Multiple factors to account for this have been suggested (see Keane et al., 1985; Parrott & Howes, 1991). Primary factors in the lack of extinction include cognitive and emotional processing of the trauma as well as the role of reminders of the trauma.

Cognitive Therapy

Cognitive therapy has been successfully used to treat other anxiety disorders much as panic disorder with or without agoraphobia (see Barlow, 1988, Beck & Emery, 1985). Thus extending CT to PTSD, another anxiety disorder, is logical. Much of the treatment literature on PTSD has focused on behavioral treatment, specifically implosive techniques and relaxation training (e.g., Hickling, Sison, & Vanderploeg, 1986; Keane, Fairbank, Caddell, & Zimering, 1989; Keane & Kaloupek, 1982; McCaffrey & Fairbank, 1985; Rychtarik, Silverman, Van Landingham, & Prue, 1984). The reported use of other treatment modalities with PTSD has increased and has included techniques such as hypnosis and psychodynamic psychotherapy with Vietnam veterans (Eichelman, 1985; Grigsby, 1987), group psychotherapy for rape and incest survivors (Roth, Dye, & Lebowitz, 1988), and behavioral as well as psychodynamic psychotherapy for PTSD following bereavement, acts of violence, and traffic accidents (Brom, Kleber, & Defares, 1989; see also Dye & Roth, 1991, for a review of the treatment literature).

Recently, cognitive therapy has begun to be used more widely by clinicians as a means to treat individuals with PTSD. Although conceptual frameworks for the application of CT to PTSD have been proposed (e.g., Parrott & Howes, 1991), there are few systematic empirical studies of CT with PTSD. A recent and promising exception is a study by Foa, Rothbaum, Riggs, and Murdoch (1991). In this study, the efficacy of stress inoculation training, prolonged exposure, and supportive counseling in PTSD rape victims was assessed (a wait-list control condition was also included). Stress inoculation training was most effective in reducing PTSD symptoms in the short term (5 weeks), but prolonged exposure was most effective at 3-month follow-up. Clearly, further empirical studies are needed.

Cognitive Issues

Regardless of which CT model one adopts, the central feature common to all approaches is the assessment and treatment of cognitive content, process, and structure. Application of CT to PTSD requires not only an understanding of the formation and maintenance of the disorder but an understanding of the central cognitive issues unique to this population (see Janoff-Bulman, 1985; Parrott & Howes, 1991). Four specific cognitive factors have been proposed by Parrott and Howes (1991) to be central to PTSD following a range of traumas (including work injuries, crimes, incest, motor vehicle accidents, and disasters).

The first cognitive factor is *appraisal of trauma*. Here the focus is on the victim's, not the clinician's or significant other's, appraisal of the event. The victim's appraisal is central to whether the event is interpreted as traumatic, an essential criterion for the *DSM-III-R* diagnosis of PTSD. Yet it is all too easy to attempt to establish some external criteria of *traumatic*, especially in cases of low-magnitude trauma. For example, the victim of a hostage taking whose life is directly threatened and the witness to a motor vehicle accident may both appraise their respective situations as traumatic, even though the objective degree of life threat differs greatly. As a result, it is essential to assess in detail the victim's idiographic appraisal at the time of, and following, the event (see Parrott & Howes, 1991).

The second cognitive factor is a *generalized belief of vulnerability*. Following trauma, there is dissolution of the victim's beliefs of personal invulnerability and an adoption of a belief of personal vulnerability (Janoff-Bulman, 1985; Parrott & Howes, 1991). Due to its personal relevance, belief of vulnerability often becomes a central or core (Safran et al., 1986) belief of the PTSD victim (e.g., the victim expects something horrible to happen and is constantly vigilant). Consistent with the influence of core beliefs, beliefs of personal vulnerability generalize and lead to functional incapacitation.

A brief case example illustrates this clearly. Ms. K. is a 30-year-old woman who was sexually assaulted while walking in her neighborhood one evening. During the attack, her life was repeatedly threatened. Following the assault, she became increasingly fearful of further harm and of another assault. Her feelings of personal vulnerability were aggravated when the police did not inform her for several months that the assailant had been apprehended. During this time, she stopped working and was unable to leave her house alone, due to the overwhelming fear of, and generalized belief that she was vulnerable to, further harm. Her sense of vulnerability generalized to her family, and she became increasingly vigilant and protective of their well-being. Clearly, Ms. K.'s strong sense of vulnerability to further harm was associated with significant functional impairment.

The third cognitive factor is *self-questioning*, which involves the victim's attempts to attribute meaning to the traumatic experience and why it occurred. Maladaptive and/or adaptive attributions may develop and influence whether the traumatic experience and its sequelae are resolved in an adaptive or maladaptive manner (Peterson et al., 1991). Because the development of maladaptive attributions may help to maintain PTSD symptoms, assessment of and intervention targeting the victim's explanatory model are often necessary (Parrott & Howes, 1991). Maladaptive attributions are not uncommonly associated with Lerner's (1980) "just world hypothesis," in which victims perceive themselves, and are perceived by others, as responsible for their own misfortune. For example, a gay male victim of a brutal physical assault may be perceived by family or friends as having "provoked" the assailant by virtue of his lifestyle (i.e., homosexuality) and in this way being responsible for it. Adoption of such an explanatory model by the victim, and its reinforcement by others, may lead to maladaptive coping styles. The functional consequences of such beliefs need to be assessed carefully, however, because not all beliefs of personal responsibility are dysfunctional. For example, if the assault of the above victim is seen by him as due to a failure to take adequate safety precautions (e.g., traveling in an unsafe neighborhood late at night), this may lead to beliefs of potential control. Commitment to take steps to reduce the likelihood of similar events in the future may therefore be adaptive (see Davis & Friedman, 1985). Janoff-Bulman (1985) differentiated behavioral and characterological self-blame. Behavioral self-blame involves attributing causality to specific acts (e.g., a victim did not take appropriate precautions) and may be adaptive in that future control is possible. Characterological self-blame, on the other hand, involves attributing causality to stable personal characteristics (e.g., a victim who attributes being assaulted to getting what he or she deserves) and is often maladaptive.

The fourth cognitive factor is *self-appraisal*, which refers to the effect of the trauma and its sequelae on the individual's view of him- or herself (Janoff-Bulman, 1985; Parrott & Howes, 1991). The frightening symptoms a survivor experiences after a traumatic event (i.e., reexperiencing the trauma, increased arousal, sense of personal vulnerability to future harm) may lead to negative self-appraisals, such as a view of self as weak and helpless, with little personal control (e.g., it is common for victims to report a fear of "going crazy"). Negative self-appraisal following trauma has been reported in a wide range of victims, including injured workers, crime victims, incest survivors, and holocaust survivors (Blume, 1990; Howes, 1991; Janoff-Bulman, 1985; Nadler & Ben-Shushan, 1989; Parrott & Howes, 1991).

Analogue research by Pennebaker and Beall (1986) suggested that trauma survivors' difficulty in disclosing to others about the trauma and its sequelae may lead to increased stress-related problems. Clinically, victims are often reticent to disclose their post-trauma emotional difficulties due to fear of negative appraisal by others and possible judgmental reactions. This may increase the likelihood of their developing chronic PTSD prior to being referred for treatment. As Schwarz and Prout (1991) indicated, the prognosis for "acute Post-Traumatic Stress Disorder is considered to be good," whereas the prognosis for "chronic Post-Traumatic Stress Disorder tends to be more guarded and complicated" (p. 364). This is illustrated by the following tragic case, in which a young refugee displayed a PTSD for several years before seeking treatment. The PTSD developed following political incarceration and torture in his homeland. His chronic PTSD symptoms were complicated by issues of alcohol abuse, suicidal ideation, and depression. Despite short-term improvement following intensive treatment, he committed suicide at a time of increased stress unrelated to the traumatic event and its sequelae. Data from Vietnam veterans with PTSD indicating considerable risk for suicide also support this point and the destructive effect of negative self-appraisal (Hendin & Haas, 1991).

Cognitive Therapy Techniques

The above cognitive factors are important guides for conceptualizing PTSD cases. They can also guide treatment. That is, specific intervention strategies and techniques can be identified to address each of the four PTSD-specific cognitive factors. Prior to beginning CT for PTSD, assessing suitability for CT can be useful—for example, by using the Suitability for Short-Term Cognitive Therapy Scale (Safran, Segal, Vallis, Shaw, & Samstag, 1993). As well, it is important to emphasize that timing and flexibility in the use of these intervention strategies are important.

Clinically, when addressing *appraisal of trauma* (i.e., perception of life threat/harm), acknowledgment and support are central interventions. The therapist must demonstrate acknowledgment and understanding of the victim's phenomenological view of the trauma. This is essential in building a strong therapeutic alliance, as well as in normalizing the victim's emotional reactions. With a strong alliance as a base, the victim can be educated about the nature and effects of traumatic experiences. Understanding and support are also helpful in having the victim decrease avoidance of the trauma and its sequelae, and this lays the groundwork for later reappraisal of the trauma. Further, confronting the trauma in a direct but supportive manner conveys the implicit message that the trauma and its sequelae are not too horrible or frightening to discuss.

Existing CT techniques are well developed to help the victim and clinician address *core beliefs of personal vulnerability*. However, it is important to understand that with PTSD these beliefs often are not irrational but, by definition, are based on actual experience. For example, a motor vehicle accident victim may have assumed, before the trauma, that driving was quite safe. After the trauma, however, the victim may think, "If it happened once, it, or something else just as bad or worse, could happen again." Further, if closure has not been achieved in crime or court-related cases, an ongoing threat to the victim remains (e.g., the assailant is not apprehended or has been charged but is out on bail pending trial; Howes, 1991). In cases in which victims' beliefs in personal vulnerability are not irrational, change may be difficult. Compounding this is the notion that core beliefs, because they are directly related to the experience of the self, are difficult to change (Safran et al., 1986). At the same time it should be noted that changing core beliefs is hypothesized to lead to longer-lasting change. Nonetheless, the more entrenched the beliefs of personal vulnerability (and the more chronic the PTSD), the more guarded the prognosis (Parrott & Howes, 1991; Schwarz & Prout, 1991).

In addition to education about the effects of trauma and associated symptoms, it is important to provide the victim with adaptive coping strategies to help him or her gain control of frightening symptoms (e.g., reexperiencing phenomena), decrease helplessness, and increase adaptive functioning. Strategies that are helpful include relaxation, distraction, coping thoughts/images, and mobilization of supports. Coping thoughts may focus on peripheral and/or core beliefs, depending on the victim's progress, and the therapist's conceptual framework (see earlier). Cognitive reframing and restructuring strategies are also recommended. Strategies to redress probability overestimation (Barlow & Cerny, 1988) are particularly useful in helping the victim reframe his or her belief of personal vulnerability. Timing is important in the use of these restructuring techniques. Restructuring the trauma and its sequelae can involve long-term therapy, and therapists as well as victims need to be realistic in their expectations concerning outcome. Because traumas most often have long-lasting, if not permanent, effects on the victim (Schwarz & Prout, 1991), it is unlikely that the victim will return to his or her pretrauma state. The virtually unlimited number of stimuli that can elicit symptoms and exacerbate the PTSD requires the therapist to prepare the victim for the inevitability of periodic setbacks. Active coping strategies are extremely useful in helping victims maintain a sense of control and reduce feelings of vulnerability during these episodes.

The above interventions illustrate the value of content-based and tripartite cognitive conceptualizations when treating PTSD. At the same time, developmental issues are often important when focusing on the core beliefs of personal vulnerability, especially in cases in which past traumas have occurred (e.g., the case of an injured worker whose sister committed suicide when he was a teenager; the case of a rape victim who suffered childhood sexual abuse). Imaginal rehearsal and flooding may be helpful in some cases by directly reducing anxiety and by indirectly providing the victim the message that he or she can survive reexperiencing the trauma in a controlled manner. However, some victims cannot tolerate the sustained and high levels of anxiety associated with imaginal rehearsal (Parrott & Howes, 1991; Schwarz & Prout, 1991).

When addressing the victim's *self-questioning* about why the traumatic event occurred, it is important to explore developmental issues and affect by probing for deeper meaning (i.e., attributions about the event vis-à-vis the sense of self; see Schwarz & Prout, 1991). A focus on adaptive coping strategies is helpful. It is also useful to use cognitive reframing and reattribution techniques (Beck et al., 1979). The therapist plays a central role in helping the victim to reframe the experience (e.g., from victim to survivor) and to explore, as well as reframe, negative or maladaptive attributions. Chronicity and developmental issues can affect the victim's ability to do this. In such cases, exploration of developmental issues must be integrated with a strong focus on coping in the here and now (Schwarz & Prout, 1991).

The victim's *negative self-appraisal* requires exploration and focus on developmental and interpersonal issues, as well as affect. Pre- and post-trauma stressors, which can be mediating factors, are important to consider, especially with respect to how the victim has integrated these stressors into his or her view of self. Reattribution strategies (e.g., viewing life as changed, not ruined), decentering techniques, self-integration, and reappraising the trauma in an affectively real manner are helpful. Additional strategies used to deal with the above cognitive factors also affect the victim's negative self-appraisal. For example, normalizing the victim's emotional reaction can reduce his or her concern that he or she is going crazy. Similarly, coping strategies to gain control over generalized anxiety symptoms and to increase functioning also positively affect the victim's self-appraisal.

It must be emphasized that examination of these cognitive factors in assessment and treatment should occur in a flexible manner. Clearly, establishing rapport and therapeutic alliance is, as with other populations, a necessary first step in therapy. This is especially important with PTSD, as the victim must feel safe in order to deal with the emotional sequelae of the trauma. CT with PTSD may be short-term or long-term, depending on the nature of the trauma, the chronicity of symptoms, and the victim's self-appraisals and attributions. Flexibility in timing, process, and procedure is necessary in the treatment of PTSD. Treatment is facilitated by use of the metamodel presented in the first section of this chapter to guide the therapist in selecting the type of intervention and the rationale behind its implementation.

COGNITIVE THERAPY
FOR PERSONALITY DISORDERS

Until recently, cognitive therapists have focused exclusively on the assessment and treatment of symptom disorders, which correspond to Axis I of the *DSM-III-R* (American Psychiatric Association, 1987). This has been productive work, as evidenced by the convincing data that continue to amass on the importance of cognitive factors in a variety of symptom disorders (e.g., major depressive episode, Beck et al., 1979; panic disorder, Barlow, 1988; generalized anxiety disorder, Butler et al., 1987; anorexia nervosa, Garner & Bemis, 1985), as well as on the demonstrated efficacy of cognitive-behavioral interventions in reducing symptoms (e.g., Borkovec et al., 1987; Clark et al., 1985; Murphy et al., 1984). However, as CT continues to be developed and is integrated into the mainstream of psychological treatment, non-symptom-based issues (e.g., personality traits, relationship patterns) are becoming a focus for cognitive therapists.

There are numerous reasons supporting the application of CT to personality disorder (PD), despite the current lack of empirical validating data.

First, symptom-based disorders and personality disorders are not completely independent, even though they have been placed on different axes in the *DSM-III-R* diagnostic system (see Mavissakalian & Hamann, 1988; Millon, 1981; Shea, Glass, Pilkonis, Watkins, & Docherty, 1987). Second, the more severe the personality disturbance, the more likely it is that the individual will display distressing clinical symptoms (Millon, 1981). This follows given that more severe personality disturbance generally results in greater difficulty with life tasks (e.g., maintaining self-esteem, developing and maintaining relationships, functioning productively in a variety of roles), thereby producing distress. The high degree of overlap between symptom distress and personality disorder justifies applying CT to PD because CT is perhaps the psychological treatment of choice for symptom distress.

In this final section of our chapter, the focus is on how CT can be adapted to treating individuals with PD. At the outset, it must be emphasized that to date there are virtually no empirical outcome studies on the efficacy of CT with PD. It is therefore essential not to assume that CT will be effective because it is effective with selected symptom disorders. Efficacy must be demonstrated, not assumed. After all, a major strength of the CT approach has been its empirical base. At present, the field is at a conceptual, not empirical, level with respect to CT and PD. Two primary questions need to be addressed to guide the necessary future research adequately. First, to what extent must CT be modified from its traditional protocol with symptom disorders to be maximally applicable to PD? Second, what current approaches are being attempted, and do these approaches incorporate the necessary adaptations to conceptualization, procedure, and intervention techniques?

Personality Disorders:
Methodological and Validity Concerns

A central premise is that working with PD requires specific adaptations to traditional CT. The PD population poses a number of challenges, particularly from an empirical perspective. Perhaps the most difficult, and basic, problem relates to poor reliability. It is generally agreed that *personality* refers to enduring patterns of perceiving, relating to, and thinking about the environment, others, and oneself (Millon, 1986b). Further, the concept of personality disorder as resulting from inflexible, inadequate, and unstable personality traits that produce distress is relatively noncontentious. However, the *DSM-III-R* categorization of PD into 11 separate categories, organized around three clusters (odd/eccentric, dramatic/emotional/erratic, and anxious/fearful) is marked by poor reliability of diagnosis (Francis & Widiger, 1986; Garfield, 1986). Without agreement on the presence of specific PD diagnoses in individual patients, any model that proposes specific cognitive profiles for the different PD categories rests on shaky ground. The reliability of the categorization scheme is necessary for the validity of the cognitive profiles. As will be discussed below, this is a major drawback of CT models proposing cognitive specificity of *DSM-III-R* PD categories. It suggests that a process-based, as opposed to a content-based, approach to PD might be more productive at this stage.

Recent methodological work on PD is useful to guide cognitive therapists interested in adapting CT to fit PD populations. Frances and Widiger (1986) examined specific classification models of PD and differentiated dimensional from categorical models. It is interesting that personality theory has been primarily driven by a dimensional model (e.g., the continuous traits of neuroticism-psychoticism; Eysenck, 1970), whereas psychiatric diagnosis has been driven by a categorical model, specifically, the classical model of categorization (Francis & Widiger, 1986). In this model, categories are considered as discrete entities, in which the defining features are singly necessary and jointly sufficient, the boundaries between categories are distinct, and the members of each category are homogeneous (Cantor, Smith, French, & Mezzick, 1980). There are convincing arguments, however, that PD categories do not demonstrate any of these features but are fuzzy categories (Cantor & Genero, 1986). As an alternative, prototypical categories have been advocated to describe PD more accurately and to increase compatibility with a dimensional model (Cantor & Genero, 1986; Frances & Widiger, 1986; Millon, 1986a; Widiger, Trull, Hurt, Clarkin, & Frances, 1987). Prototypes describe a theoretical ideal or standard against which real people can be compared and consist of the most common features of members of a category (Millon, 1986a). Within a prototypical model, categories are not homogeneous, they do not have distinct boundaries, and defining characteristics vary in their validity (Frances & Widiger, 1986). Using this model, one can expect greater variability in presentation between individuals with the same PD diagnosis and greater overlap between diagnoses (i.e., a larger proportion of mixed PD diagnoses). These conditions certainly appear to apply in clinical work with PD cases. The increased variability that follows from a prototypical model of PD implies that a highly idiographic approach is needed when working with this population.

If one adopts a dimensional, prototypical approach to PD, which appears to be the most valid approach, this has implications for cognitive models of PD vis-à-vis cognitive specificity. At best, a cognitive profile for any PD category is prototypical; exceptions to the rule and fuzzy cases are likely to be the norm.

Cognitive Therapy for Personality Disorders: What Adaptations Are Required?

We have presented conceptual reasons that justify examining the application of CT to PD. Some of the specific features of CT that offer potential for the treatment of PD are (a) the phenomenological focus, which may be helpful in developing a strong working therapeutic alliance; (b) the active development of self-control (a major deficit in most individuals with PD); (c) therapeutic flexibility that allows blending of problem-solving strategies with a focus on underlying dysfunctional processes; and (d) recent theoretical developments that lend themselves particularly well to PD.

The above factors notwithstanding, the successful implementation of standard cognitive interventions requires the following patient characteristics: (a) an ability to view problems in a way that is (or becomes) compatible with the cognitive therapy rationale; (b) a willingness to learn coping strategies and to accept the therapist as an educator; (c) an ability to implement CT techniques (e.g., monitor and record dysfunctional thoughts, collect evidence, role-play, challenge negative thoughts); and (d) an ability to follow a structured approach. Several recent studies have confirmed that these characteristics are indeed central to the efficacy of CT (Fennell & Teasdale, 1987; Persons, Burns, & Perloff, 1988). Interestingly, Persons et al. also reported that the presence of PD was a significant predictor of premature termination in their study of depressed outpatients in a private practice setting. In related work, Safran and colleagues (Safran et al., 1993; Safran, Segal, Shaw, & Vallis, 1990) developed an interview-based scale to assess suitability for cognitive therapy. The items of this scale assess accessibility of automatic thoughts, awareness and differentiation of emotions, acceptance of personal responsibility for change, compatibility with the CT rationale, alliance potential (both in- and out-of-session alliance), chronicity of problems, security operations, focality, and patient optimism/pessimism. Safran et al. (1993) found that this scale was predictive of outcome for

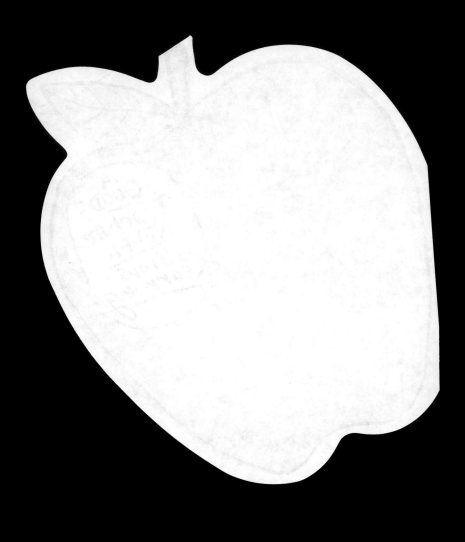

short-term cognitive therapy for a mixed anxious-depressed group. However, examination of these criteria in light of what is known about PD suggests that many, if not most, individuals with PD would score low on these items, suggesting poor suitability for CT.

On the basis of the above, we suggest that there is a conflict between what we know about the general characteristics of individuals with PD and what we know about CT and how it works. Individuals with PD have, by definition, long-standing problems that impair adaptive functioning at a number of levels, including self issues, interpersonal functioning, and role adaptation. The presence of these characteristics is likely to interfere with many of the structure- and technique-oriented features of CT. Two strategies could be adopted to deal with this problem. One strategy would be to select patients who are likely to benefit from CT (e.g., those scoring high on the suitability scale) and to refuse to treat those who do not meet these selection criteria. A second strategy would be to modify CT to address the particular problems presented by those with PD. Clearly, one important criterion on which to judge the value of current cognitive models for CT with PD is the extent to which these issues are addressed.

Current Approaches to Cognitive Therapy for Personality Disorders

Existing approaches to CT with PD can be divided into content-based models and process-based models. Further, some models examine a specific PD category—namely, borderline personality disorder—whereas others deal with the full range of PD categories.

Content-Based Approaches

Three groups of investigators have proposed content-based models of CT for PD (Beck and his colleagues—e.g., Beck, Freeman, & Associates, 1990; Young—e.g., Young, 1990; and Turner—e.g., Turner, 1989). Two of these groups, Beck and his colleagues and Young, have developed specific cognitive profiles of the various PD categories.

Beck's Cognitive Therapy Model. Beck and his colleagues (Beck et al., 1990; Freeman & Leaf, 1989; Freeman, Pretzer, Fleming, & Simon, 1990; Weishaar, 1989) have proposed a comprehensive CT model for the conceptualization and treatment of PD. Central to this approach are dysfunctional schemas (cognitive structures). In fact, Beck et al. (1990) stated that "the personality disorder is probably one of the most striking representations of Beck's concept of 'schema' " (p. 8). The concept of schemas is elaborated in this model, with differentiations being made between types of schemas (e.g., personal, familial, cultural, religious, gender, occupation), their structural qualities (e.g., breadth, flexibility, density, valence), and their degree of prepotency (see Beck et al., 1990). An example might be a 23-year-old man who has a schema of himself as inadequate (personal). Such a schema might influence all aspects of this man's life (broad), be unresponsive to any contrary feedback provided (inflexible), and be activated extremely (prepotent).

With this framework as a base, Beck and colleagues proposed cognitive "profiles" for the *DSM-III-R* PD categories. For each PD category they identified view of self, view of others, main belief, and main behavioral/interpersonal strategy. The criteria become central guideposts, influencing the nature of assessment and determining the focus of intervention. In terms of therapeutic principles, Beck and his colleagues (e.g., Beck et al., 1990) explicitly recognized that therapy with PD patients would be more time consuming and effortful than therapy with symptom disorder patients. As well, greater attention to the therapeutic relationship, as a model to the patient, was highlighted. With these modifications, many of the same techniques as used with symptom-disorder patients were applied (see Beck et al., 1990).

Although validating data are needed, several comments on Beck's model can be made. First, a great deal of attention and effort has been devoted to constructing cognitive "profiles" for each of the 11 PD categories. As mentioned above, the reliability/validity of the *DSM-III-R* categories themselves is somewhat questionable. Without such validity, proposing cognitive specificity of the 11 categories may be premature. Second, Beck and his colleagues (Beck et al., 1990; Freeman et al., 1990) did not make reference to the recent theoretical work on constructivist-developmental and interpersonal models of CT. As a result, although many important issues in treating PD patients are addressed (e.g., the therapeutic relationship, the need to address the developmental issues), Beck's approach remains more rationalist based than constructivist based. That is, the interventions suggested by Beck and his colleagues are primarily based on content, tripartite, and, to some degree, core models of CT. In that constructivist-developmental and interpersonal models of CT are not included, the range of interventions suggested by Beck and colleagues is limited.

Young's Schema-Focused Cognitive Therapy. Young (1987, 1990) also developed a cognitive model of PD, called *schema-focused cognitive therapy.* Briefly, Young proposed that individuals with PD could be characterized by the formation of early maladaptive schemas, a new construct that was differentiated from automatic thoughts, cognitive distortions, and underlying assumptions/schemas (i.e., the tripartite distinction). Early maladaptive schemas were proposed to be stable and enduring thought patterns that developed early in an individual's life (i.e., "during the first few years of an individual's life"; Young, 1990, p. 11) and influenced later functioning in a dysfunctional and self-perpetuating manner. Central to Young's model were the constructs of schema maintenance, schema avoidance, and schema compensation.

Young (1990) defined 15 early maladaptive schemas that reflected four major areas of vulnerability: autonomy, connectedness, worthiness, and limits and standards. In an earlier description of schema-focused CT, Young (1987) categorized the *DSM-III-R* PD categories according to these four areas of vulnerability and 15 early maladaptive schemas. This matching of early maladaptive schemas to PD categories is not included in his most recent version of the model.

Young (1987, 1990) described interventions focused directly on the early maladaptive schemas. Once specific schemas are identified, a number of strategies are employed, including educating patients about the schemas, triggering the schemas (through a variety of specific techniques), confronting schema avoidance, and identifying schema-driven behavior. Strategies for changing schemas include emotive, interpersonal, and cognitive techniques.

Like the model of Beck and his colleagues, Young's approach to working with PD patients incorporates a number of dramatic changes from traditional CT. Both models share a strong focus on cognitive structure, explicitly recognize the importance of the therapeutic relationship, and attempt to integrate cognitive with noncognitive interventions. Despite these positive developments, considerable effort has gone into proposing very elaborate cognitive profiles with virtually no supporting data. This makes these content-based models vulnerable when compared with more process-based approaches. Specifically, it is possible that the detailed conceptual frameworks will not be validated by subsequent research, and this may lead some to conclude that the approaches should be abandoned. Yet it may well be the case that such approaches are important, not so much on the basis of the content of their approach as on the basis of their process.

Turner's Biosocial Learning Approach for Borderline Personality Disorder. Turner has developed an intensive treatment program, labeled the *biosocial learning approach,* based on the *DSM-III-R* definition of borderline personality disorder. In this model, the importance of dealing with micropsychotic episodes is stressed. The biosocial learning approach is a treatment package that systematically combines pharmacotherapy (primarily anxiolytics), anxiety management techniques, standard cognitive therapy techniques, and interpersonal skills training. Interventions are implemented in an intensive manner. Turner (1989) reported on the efficacy of this program for four BPD individuals and concluded that treatment was associated with reductions in depression, anxiety, and general psychopathology. Although the limited sample involved in this study makes reliability questionable, these data are encouraging, and the fact that Turner empirically evaluated his package is noteworthy. Although this approach has not received a great deal of attention, it offers potential that should be further evaluated.

Process-Based Approaches

In contrast to CT approaches that stress cognitive content specific to the PD categories, two models focus on process issues in treating PD patients. One model (Rothstein & Vallis, 1991) is proposed to apply to all PD categories, and the other (Linehan, 1989) focuses specifically on the treatment of borderline personality disorder.

Rothstein and Vallis's Process-Based Model. It has been argued that individuals with PD often have difficulty following through on many of the specific tasks of CT. As a result, Rothstein and Vallis (1991) proposed that CT is best implemented within the context of a conceptual model that integrates technique with process variables (such as the development of dysfunctional self-beliefs, interpersonal schemas, and the meaning of the therapeutic relationship). This requires conceptual, procedural, and process adaptations of many common practices within CT.

Conceptually, CT is seen as an integrated, systemic form of psychotherapy, in which the central focus of therapy is on dysfunctional beliefs concerning the self and one's world (i.e., core beliefs; Safran et al., 1986) and in which the therapist's conceptualization includes cognitive processes, both conscious (automatic thoughts) and nonconscious (dysfunctional schemas; Turk & Salovey, 1985). The constructivist-developmental and interpersonal models of CT, described in the first section of this chapter, are emphasized by Rothstein and Vallis (1991) and are proposed to fit most closely with issues presented by PD patients.

Integrating the constructivist-developmental model into CT when treating PD patients has a number of advantages. First, there is increased flexibility that allows the therapist to track the patient more closely. Second, there is greater attention placed on developmental issues. Third, more focus is placed on the process of therapy, including the meaning of the therapeutic relationship itself. This allows a range of problem issues such as trust, intimacy, and resistance to be addressed.

Procedurally, modification of the structure of CT is required because of the difficulty PD patients often have with issues such as compatibility with the CT rationale and the ability to implement homework exercises. The following structural adaptations are recommended. First, CT should not be guided by a strict limit on the number of sessions. Second, the structure of an individual session should be guided by relevant process issues as opposed to a standard protocol.

Attention to the process of CT is important because the development and maintenance of a working therapeutic alliance with PD patients are often tenuous. The therapist needs to be highly sensitive to the state of the alliance, and much work should go into establishing and maintaining a functional alliance (see Jacobson, 1989). For this reason, the therapist should be prepared to deviate from ongoing or planned interventions so as to maintain the alliance. In fact, the relationship between the patient and therapist becomes a powerful therapeutic tool (Jacobson, 1989; Rothstein & Robinson, 1991; Safran & Segal, 1990; Young, 1990). As part of the relationship, exploration of resistance as a form of self-protection is often a therapeutic focus.

Rothstein and Vallis (1991) outlined general strategies for implementing process-focused CT with PD. The process has two major phases. Phase 1 involves the development of a comprehensive cognitive *conceptualization* of the problem, and Phase 2 involves active *intervention* strategies based on this conceptualization. In developing the case conceptualization, it is essential to consider a number of issues and their meaning. These issues include understanding the symptoms presented by the patient in the context of their current situation and developmental history (e.g., current dysfunction might reflect persistent patterns that were functional at a past point in the patient's development), considering of the therapeutic process and how it can be used in developing a comprehensive conceptualization (e.g., detailed exploration of the patient's reactions to the process of assessment/treatment and how these relate to important intra- and interpersonal processes), exploring the cognitive-developmental process (e.g., tracing the development and maintenance of beliefs about the self), and, finally, conceptualizing core schemas.

In implementing this process-based approach to CT, guided by constructivist/developmental/interpersonal cognitive models, standard cognitive and behavioral strategies are important but are not the sole defining characteristics. Instead, the bulk of the initial therapeutic effort is committed to helping the individual identify, appreciate, and reevaluate core dysfunctional processes. Strategies to accomplish this consist of an exploration of the patient's thoughts, beliefs, and assumptions, the patient's core and peripheral cognitions, affect-cognition relationships, and the capacity of the patient to decenter (see Rothstein & Vallis, 1991; Safran & Segal, 1990). Interventions per se include standard cognitive-behavioral change strategies, as well as the use of the therapeutic relationship to facilitate reappraisal of self- and interpersonal schemas and a focus on the patient's developmental context to facilitate reappraisal of self-schemas.

Linehan's Dialectical Behavior Therapy for Borderline Personality Disorder.   According to Linehan (1989), the primary dysfunction with borderline personality disorder is inadequate affect regulation. Linehan proposed that behavioral patterns in borderline individuals develop along three dialectical poles: emotional vulnerability versus invalidation, active-passive versus competency, and unremitting crises versus inhibited grief (Linehan, 1989). The concept of dialectics is central to Linehan's model, and it is this concept that makes her model a process model. Dialectics is based on the concept of the contradiction of opposites (thesis and antithesis) and their continual resolution (synthesis). Thus, when working with borderline patients, the therapist must be constantly vigilant to the pull between any given state and its opposite. Definitive positions are likely to produce confusion and resistance from borderline patients. Because of poor affect regulation, borderline patients are in almost constant flux, and effective therapy must balance acceptance-oriented strategies with change strategies (e.g., balance messages such as "It's OK to be the way you are" with "Here's a way you can change"). According to Linehan (1989), imbalance on this dimension (acceptance vs. change) will detract from the effectiveness of treatment. The general treatment approach proposed by Linehan focuses on dialectical interventions around the three poles identified above.

Linehan's specific treatment approach combines individual and group therapy and typically extends over 1 year. Treatment focuses on interpersonal skills training, anxiety management, emotion regulation, and distress tolerance. Linehan (1989) categorized her treatment strategies into eight groups, four of which are common to all forms of behavior therapy (problem solving, contingency management, irreverent communication, capability enhancement), and four of which are specific to a dialectical approach (dialectical strategies, consultant strategies, validation strategies, and relationship strategies). Linehan reported data from a randomized study comparing dialectical behavior therapy to treatment as usual. Although the sample was small (11 BPD patients received dialectical behavior therapy), data indicated that dialectical behavior therapy was superior to treatment as usual on variables such as frequency/severity of parasuicidal behavior, employment rate, and, most important, dropout rate.

To conclude, cognitive therapists are beginning to turn their attention toward treating patients with PD. Although there is very little empirical information to provide confidence in the efficacy of these treatment models (Linehan's model being the major exception), preliminary conceptual models, either content or process oriented, have been proposed. Yet all proponents of these models share the assumptions that standard, traditional short-term CT must be modified for use with PD patients. We have most likely reached a point at which there has been sufficient conceptual development with respect to the treatment of PD with CT, and empirical work must now follow.

SUMMARY

Cognitive therapy has been shown to be one of the most effective short-term treatments for a variety of symptom disorders. As we have discussed above, it is now being adapted to the treatment of nontraditional patient groups, such as patients with PTSD, marital problems, and PD. We have presented a review of the recent advances in cognitive therapy, guidelines to idiographic conceptualization of patient problems, and specific models for adapting CT in the treatment of PTSD and PD. At this stage of development of CT, these models are primarily conceptual and based on clinical experience. It is our hope that future empirical studies will advance the use of CT with nontraditional patient groups.

REFERENCES

American Psychiatric Association. (1980). *Diagnostic and statistical manual of mental disorders* (3rd ed.). Washington, DC: Author.

American Psychiatric Association. (1987). *Diagnostic and statistical manual of mental disorders* (3rd ed., Rev.). Washington, DC: Author.

Barlow, D. H. (1988). *Anxiety and its disorders: The nature and treatment of anxiety and panic.* New York: Guilford.

Barlow, D. H., & Cerny, J. A. (1988). *The psychological treatment of panic.* New York: Guilford.

Beck, A. T. (1988). Cognitive approaches to panic disorder: Theory and therapy. In S. Rachman & J. D. Maser (Eds.), *Panic: Psychological perspectives.* Hillsdale, NJ: Lawrence Erlbaum.

Beck, A. T., & Emery, G. (1985). *Anxiety disorders and phobias: A cognitive perspective.* New York: Basic Books.

Beck, A. T., Freeman, A., & Associates. (1990). *Cognitive therapy of personality disorders.* New York: Guilford.

Beck, A. T., Hollon, S. D., Young, J. P., Bedrosian, R. C., & Budenz, D. (1985). Treatment of depression with cognitive therapy and amitriptyline. *Archives of General Psychiatry, 42,* 142-148.

Beck, A. T., Rush, A. J., Shaw, B., & Emery, G. (1979). *Cognitive therapy of depression.* New York: Guilford.

Blackburn, I. M., Bishop, S., Glen, A. I. M., Whalley, L. T., & Christie, J. E. (1981). The efficacy of cognitive therapy in depression: A treatment trial using cognitive therapy and pharmacotherapy, each alone, and in combination. *British Journal of Psychiatry, 139,* 181-189.

Blume, E. S. (1990). *Secret survivors: Uncovering incest and its aftereffects in women.* New York: John Wiley.

Borkovec, T. D., Mathews, A. M., Chambers, A., Ebrahimi, S., Lytle, R., & Nelson, R. (1987). The effects of relaxation training with cognitive therapy or nondirective therapy and the role of relaxation-induced anxiety in the treatment of generalized anxiety. *Journal of Consulting and Clinical Psychology, 55,* 883-888.

Bowlby, J. (1985). The role of childhood experience in cognitive disturbance. In M. Mahoney & A. Freeman (Eds.), *Cognition and psychotherapy* (pp. 181-200). New York: Plenum.

Bownes, I. T., O'Gorman, E. C., & Sayers, A. (1991). Adult characteristics and posttraumatic stress disorder in rape victims. *Acta Psychiatrica Scandinavica, 83,* 27-30.

Brickman, J., & Briere, J. (1984). Incidence of rape and sexual assault in an urban Canadian population. *International Journal of Women's Studies, 7*, 195-206.

Brom, D., Kleber, R., & Defares, P. (1989). Brief psychotherapy for posttraumatic stress disorder. *Journal of Consulting and Clinical Psychology, 57*, 607-612.

Butler, G., Cullington, A., Hibbert, G., Klimes, I., & Gelder, M. (1987). Anxiety management for persistent generalized anxiety. *British Journal of Psychiatry, 151*, 535-542.

Cantor, N., & Genero, N. (1986). Psychiatric diagnosis and natural categorization: A close analogy. In T. Millon & G. L. Klerman (Eds.), *Contemporary directions in psychopathology: Towards the DSM-IV* (pp. 233-256). New York: Guilford.

Cantor, N., Smith, E., French, R. D., & Mezzick, J. (1980). Psychiatric diagnosis as a prototype categorization. *Journal of Abnormal Psychology, 89*, 81-89.

Clark, D. M., Salkovskis, P. M., & Chalkley, A. J. (1985). Respiratory control as a treatment for panic attacks. *Journal of Behavior Therapy and Experimental Psychiatry, 16*, 23-30.

Craik, F. I. M., & Tulving, E. (1975). Depth of processing and retention of words in episodic memory. *Journal of Experimental Psychology: General, 104*, 268-294.

Davidson, J. R. T., & Foa, E. B. (1991). Diagnostic issues in posttraumatic disorder: Considerations for the *DSM-IV. Journal of Abnormal Psychology, 100*, 346-355.

Davidson, L. M., & Baum, A. (1986). Chronic stress and posttraumatic stress disorders. *Journal of Consulting and Clinical Psychology, 54*, 303-308.

Davis, R. C., & Friedman, L. N. (1985). The emotional aftermath of crime and violence. In C. R. Figley (Ed.), *Trauma and its wake: The study and treatment of posttraumatic stress disorder* (pp. 90-112). New York: Brunner/Mazel.

Dye, E., & Roth, S. (1991). Psychotherapy with Vietnam veterans and rape and incest survivors. *Psychotherapy, 28*, 103-120.

Eichelman, B. (1985). Hypnotic change in combat dreams in two veterans with posttraumatic stress disorder. *American Journal of Psychiatry, 142*, 112-114.

Elkin, I., Parloff, M., Hadley, S., & Autry, J. (1985). NIMH treatment of depression collaborative research program: Background and research plan. *Archives of General Psychiatry, 42*, 305-316.

Elkin, I., Shea, M. T., Watkins, J. T., Imber, S. D., Sotsky, S. M., Colins, J. F., Glass, D. R., Pilkonis, P. A., Leber, W. R., Docherty, J. P., Fiester, S. J., & Parloff, M. B. (1989). NIMH Treatment of Depression Collaborative Research Program: I. General effectiveness of treatments. *Archives of General Psychiatry, 46*, 971-982.

Eysenck, H. (1970). A dimensional system of psychodiagnostics. In A. Maher (Ed.), *New approaches to personality classifications* (pp. 169-207). New York: Columbia University Press.

Fairburn, C., & Cooper, P. (1989). Eating disorders. In K. Hawton, P. M. Salkovskis, J. Kirk, & D. M. Clark (Eds.), *Cognitive behavior therapy for psychiatric problems: A practical guide* (pp. 277-314). New York: Oxford University Press.

Fennell, M., & Teasdale, J. (1987). Cognitive therapy for depression: Individual differences and the process of change. *Cognitive Therapy and Research, 11*, 253-272.

Foa, E. B., Rothbaum, B. O., Riggs, D. S., & Murdoch, T. B. (1991). Treatment of posttraumatic stress disorder in rape victims: A comparison between cognitive behavioral procedures and counselling. *Journal of Consulting and Clinical Psychology, 59*, 715-723.

Frances, A., & Widiger, T. (1986). Methodological issues in personality disorder diagnosis. In T. Millon & G. Klerman (Eds.), *Contemporary directions in psychopathology: Towards the DSM-IV* (pp. 381-400). New York: Guilford.

Freeman, A., & Leaf, R. C. (1989). Cognitive therapy applied to personality disorders. In A. Freeman, K. Simon, L. Beutler, & H. Arkowitz (Eds.), *Comprehensive handbook of cognitive therapy* (pp. 403-434). New York: Plenum.

Freeman, A., Pretzer, J., Fleming, B., & Simon, K. (1990). *Clinical applications of cognitive therapy*. New York: Plenum.

Garfield, S. L. (1986). Problems in diagnostic classification. In T. Millon & G. Klerman (Eds.), *Contemporary directions in psychopathology: Towards the DSM-IV* (pp. 99-114). New York: Guilford.

Garner, D. M., & Bemis, K. M. (1985). Cognitive therapy for anorexia nervosa. In D. M. Garner & P. E. Garfinkel (Eds.), *Handbook of psychotherapy for anorexia and bulimia* (pp. 107-146). New York: Guilford.

Goldfried, M. (1982). *Converging themes in psychotherapy: Trends in psychodynamic, humanistic and behavioral practice*. New York: Springer.

Goldfried, M., Padawer, N., & Robins, C. (1984). Social anxiety and semantic structure of heterosocial interaction. *Journal of Abnormal Psychology, 93*, 87-97.

Greenberg, L., & Safran, J. (1987). *Emotions in psychotherapy*. New York: Guilford.

Grigsby, J. P. (1987). The use of imagery in the treatment of post-traumatic stress disorder. *Journal of Nervous and Mental Disease, 175*, 55-59.

Guidano, V. F., & Liotti, G. (1983). *Cognitive processes and emotional disorders: A structural approach to psychotherapy*. New York: Guilford.

Hawton, K., Salkovskis, P. M., Kirk, J., & Clark, D. M. (1989). *Cognitive behavior therapy for psychiatric problems: A practical guide*. New York: Oxford University Press.

Helzer, J. E., Robins, L. N., & McEvoy, M. A. (1987). Post-traumatic stress disorder in the general population: Findings of the epidemiologic catchment area survey. *New England Journal of Medicine, 317*, 1630-1634.

Hendin, H., & Haas, A. P. (1991). Suicide and guilt as manifestations of posttraumatic stress disorder in Vietnam combat veterans. *American Journal of Psychiatry, 148*, 586-591.

Hickling, E. J., Sison, G., & Vanderploeg, R. D. (1986). Treatment of post-traumatic stress disorder with relaxation and biofeedback training. *Biofeedback and Self-Regulation, 11*, 125-134.

Hollon, S., & Kriss, M. (1984). Cognitive factors in clinical research and practice. *Clinical Psychology Review, 4*, 35-76.

Hollon, S. D., & Najavits, L. (1989). Review of empirical studies on cognitive therapy. *Review of Psychiatry, 7*, 643-666.

Horowitz, M. J. (1976). *Stress response syndromes*. New York: Jason Aronson.

Horowitz, M. (1986). *Stress response syndromes* (2nd ed.). New York: Jason Aronson.

Howes, J. L. (1991, June). *Assessment and treatment issues in crime-related posttraumatic stress disorder*. Paper presented at the annual meeting of the Canadian Psychological Association, Calgary, Alberta.

Howes, J. L., & Parrott, C. (1991). Conceptualization and flexibility in cognitive therapy. In T. M. Vallis, J. L. Howes, & P.C. Miller (Eds.), *The challenge of cognitive therapy: Applications to nontraditional populations* (pp. 25-41). New York: Plenum.

Jacobson, N. S. (1989). The therapist-client relationship in cognitive behavior therapy: Implications for treating depression. *Journal of Cognitive Psychotherapy, 3*, 85-96.

Janoff-Bulman, R. (1985). The aftermath of victimization: Rebuilding shattered assumptions. In C. R. Figley (Ed.), *Trauma and its wake: The study and treatment of post-traumatic stress disorder* (pp. 15-35). New York: Brunner/Mazel.

Jones, J. C., & Barlow, D. H. (1990). The etiology of posttraumatic stress disorder. *Clinical Psychology Review, 10*, 299-328.

Keane, T. M., Fairbank, J. A., Caddell, J. M., & Zimering, R. T. (1989). Implosive (flooding) therapy reduces symptoms of PTSD in Vietnam combat veterans. *Behavior Therapy, 20*, 245-260.

Keane, T. M., Fairbank, J. A., Caddell, J. M., Zimering, R. T., & Bender, M. E. (1985). A behavioural approach to assessing and treating post-traumatic stress disorder in Vietnam veterans. In C. R. Figley (Ed.), *Trauma and its wake: The study and treatment of post traumatic stress disorder* (pp. 257-294). New York: Brunner/Mazel.

Keane, T. M., & Kaloupek, D. G. (1982). Imaginal flooding in the treatment of a post-traumatic stress disorder. *Journal of Consulting and Clinical Psychology, 50*, 138 140.

Kelly, G. (1955). *The psychology of personal constructs*. New York: Norton.

Kilpatrick, D. G., Saunders, B. E., Amick-McMullan, A., Best, C. L., Veronen, L. J., & Resnick, H. S. (1989). Victim and crime factors associated with development of crime related posttraumatic stress disorder. *Behavior Therapy, 20*, 199-214.

Kolb, L. C. (1987). A neuropsychological hypothesis explaining posttraumatic stress disorder. *American Journal of Psychiatry, 144*, 989-995.

Lerner, M. J. (1980). *The belief in a just world*. New York: Plenum.

Linehan, M. M. (1989). Cognitive and behavior therapy for borderline personality disorder. *Annual Review of Psychiatry, 8*, 84-102.

Litz, B. T., & Keane, T. M. (1989). Information processing in anxiety disorders: Application to the understanding of post-traumatic stress disorder. *Clinical Psychology Review, 9*, 243-257.

Louisy, H. (1989). *Automatic activation of core and peripheral self-knowledge: An idiographic approach*. Unpublished master's thesis, University of Saskatchewan, Saskatoon, Canada.

Mahoney, M. (1988). The cognitive sciences and psychotherapy: Patterns in a developing relationship. In K. Dobson (Ed.), *Handbook of cognitive-behavior therapies* (pp. 357-386). New York: Guilford.

Mahoney, M., & Freeman, A. (Eds.). (1985). *Cognition and psychotherapy*. New York: Plenum.

Mavissakalian, M., & Hamann, M. S. (1988). Correlates of *DSM-III* personality disorder in panic disorder and agoraphobia. *Comprehensive Psychiatry, 29*, 535-544.

McCaffrey, R. J., & Fairbank, J. A. (1985). Behavioral assessment and treatment of accident-related PTSD: Two case studies. *Behavior Therapy, 16*, 404-416.

Meichenbaum, D., & Gilmore, B. (1984). The nature of unconscious processes: A cognitive behavioral perspective. In K. S. Bowers & D. Meichenbaum (Eds.), *The unconscious reconsidered*. New York: John Wiley.

Millon, T. (1981). *Disorders of personality: DSM-III, Axis II*. New York: John Wiley.

Millon, T. (1986a). Personality prototypes and their diagnostic criteria. In T. Millon & G. Klerman (Eds.), *Contemporary directions in psychopathology: Towards the DSM-IV* (pp. 671-712). New York: Guilford.

Millon, T. (1986b). A theoretical derivation of pathological personalities. In T. Millon & G. Klerman (Eds.), *Contemporary directions in psychopathology: Towards the DSM-IV* (pp. 639-669). New York: Guilford.

Murphy, G. E., Simons, A. D., Wetzel, R. D., & Lustman, P. J. (1984). Cognitive therapy and pharmacotherapy, singly and together in the treatment of depression. *Archives of General Psychiatry, 41*, 33-41.

Nadler, A., & Ben-Shushan, D. (1989). Forty years later: Long-term consequences of massive traumatization as manifested by Holocaust survivors from the city and the kibbutz. *Journal of Consulting and Clinical Psychology, 57*, 287-293.

Parrott, C., & Howes, J. L. (1991). The application of cognitive therapy to posttraumatic stress disorder. In T. M. Vallis, J. L. Howes, & P. C. Miller (Eds.), *The challenge of cognitive therapy: Applications to nontraditional populations* (pp. 85-109). New York: Plenum.

Pennebaker, J., & Beall, S. (1986). Confronting a traumatic event: Toward an understanding of inhibition and disease. *Journal of Abnormal Psychology, 95,* 274-281.

Persons, J., Burns, D., & Perloff, J. M. (1988). Predictors of dropout and outcome in cognitive therapy for depression in a private practice setting. *Cognitive Therapy and Research, 12,* 557-576.

Peterson, C., Prout, M., & Schwarz, R. (1991). *Post-traumatic stress disorder: A clinician's guide.* New York: Plenum.

Rapee, R. M., & Barlow, D. H. (1991). *Chronic anxiety: Generalized anxiety disorder and mixed anxiety-depression.* New York: Guilford.

Rogers, T. B., Kuiper, N. A., & Kirker, W. S. (1977). Self-reference and the encoding of personal information. *Journal of Personality and Social Psychology, 35,* 677-688.

Roth, S., Dye, E., & Lebowitz, L. (1988). Group therapy for rape victims. *Psychotherapy, 25,* 82-93.

Rothstein, M. M., & Robinson, P. J. (1991). The therapeutic relationship and resistance to change in cognitive therapy. In T. M. Vallis, J. L. Howes, & P. C. Miller (Eds.), *The challenge of cognitive therapy: Application to nontraditional populations* (pp. 43-55). New York: Plenum.

Rothstein, M. M., & Vallis, T. M. (1991). The application of cognitive therapy to patients with personality disorders. In T. M. Vallis, J. L. Howes, & P. C. Miller (Eds.), *The challenge of cognitive therapy: Application to nontraditional populations* (pp. 59-84). New York: Plenum.

Rush, A. J., Beck, A. T., Kovacs, M., & Hollon, S. D. (1977). Comparative efficacy of cognitive therapy and pharmacotherapy in the treatment of depressed out-patients. *Cognitive Therapy and Research, 1,* 17-37.

Rush, A. J., & Shaw, B. F. (1983). Failure in treating depression by cognitive behavior therapy. In E. B. Foa & P. M. G. Emmelkamp (Eds.), *Failure in behavior therapy* (pp. 217-228). New York: John Wiley.

Rychtarik, R. G., Silverman, W. K., VanLandingham, W. P., & Prue, D. M. (1984). Treatment of an incest victim with implosive therapy. *Behavior Therapy, 15,* 410-420.

Safran, J. D. (1984). Assessing the cognitive-interpersonal cycle. *Cognitive Therapy and Research, 8,* 333-348.

Safran, J. D. (1988). *A refinement of cognitive behavioral theory and practice in light of interpersonal theory.* Toronto: Clarke Institute of Psychiatry.

Safran, J. D., & Greenberg, L. S. (1982). Eliciting "hot cognitions" in cognitive behavior therapy: Rationale and procedural guidelines. *Canadian Psychologist, 23,* 83-87.

Safran, J. D., & Greenberg, L. S. (1986). Hot cognition and psychotherapy process: An information processing/ecological approach. *Advances in Cognitive-Behavioral Research and Therapy, 5,* 143-177.

Safran, J., & Segal, Z. V. (1990). *Cognitive therapy: An interpersonal process perspective.* New York: Basic Books.

Safran, J. D., Segal, Z. V., Shaw, B. T., & Vallis, T. M. (1990). Suitability for short-term cognitive interpersonal therapy: Interview and rating scales. In J. D. Safran & Z. V. Segal (Eds.), *Interpersonal processes in cognitive therapy* (pp. 229-238). New York: Basic Books.

Safran, J. D., Segal, Z. V., Vallis, T. M., Shaw, B. F., & Samstag, L. W. (1993). Assessing patient suitability for short-term cognitive therapy with an interpersonal focus. *Cognitive Therapy and Research, 17,* 23-38.

Safran, J., Vallis, T. M., Segal, Z. V., & Shaw, B. F. (1986). Assessment of core cognitive processes in cognitive therapy. *Cognitive Therapy and Research, 10,* 509-526.

Schwarz, E., & Prout, M. (1991). Integrative approaches in the treatment of posttraumatic stress disorder. *Psychotherapy, 28,* 364-373.

Shea, M. T., Glass, D. R., Pilkonis, P. A., Watkins, J., & Docherty, J. P. (1987). Frequency and implications of personality disorders in a sample of depressed outpatients. *Journal of Personality Disorders, 1,* 27-42.

Stretch, R. H. (1991). Psychosocial readjustment of Canadian Vietnam veterans. *Journal of Consulting and Clinical Psychology, 59,* 188-189.

Stretch, R. H., Vail, J. D., & Maloney, J. D. (1985). Post-traumatic stress disorder among army nurse corps Vietnam veterans. *Journal of Consulting and Clinical Psychology, 53,* 704-708.

Sullivan, H. S. (1953). *The interpersonal theory of psychiatry.* New York: Norton.

Trimble, M. R. (1985). Post-traumatic stress disorder: History of a concept. In C. R. Figley (Ed.), *Trauma and its wake: The study and treatment of post-traumatic stress disorder* (pp. 5-14). New York: Brunner/Mazel.

Turk, D., & Salovey, P. (1985). Cognitive structures, cognitive processes and cognitive behavior modification: I. Client issues. *Cognitive Therapy and Research, 9,* 1-18.

Turner, S. M. (1989). Case study evaluations of a bio-cognitive-behavioral approach for the treatment of borderline personality disorder. *Behavior Therapy, 20,* 477-489.

Vallis, T. M. (1991). Theoretical and conceptual basis of cognitive therapy. In T. M. Vallis, J. L. Howes, & P. C. Miller (Eds.), *The challenge of cognitive therapy: Application to nontraditional populations* (pp. 3-24). New York: Plenum.

Weishaar, M. E. (1989, June). *Cognitive therapy of histrionic and passive-aggressive personality disorders.* Paper presented at the World Congress of Cognitive Therapy, Oxford, UK.

Widiger, T., Trull, T., Hurt, S., Clarkin, J., & Frances, A. (1987). A multi-dimensional scaling of the *DSM-III* personality disorders. *Archives of General Psychiatry, 44,* 557-563.

Young, J. E. (1987). *Schema-focused cognitive therapy for personality disorders.* Unpublished manuscript, Columbia University.

Young, J. E. (1990). *Cognitive therapy for personality disorders: Schema-focused approach.* Sarasota, FL: Professional Resource Exchange, Inc.

Author Index

Aberger, E. W., 104, 114
Abramson, L. Y., 67, 70, 80, 225, 232
Achmon, J., 50, 60
Ackerman, P. L., 3, 27
Adams, A., 97, 114
Adams, N. E., 138, 140
Addis, M. E., 81, 180, 191
Affleck, G., 100, 110
Agras, W. S., 131, 140, 154, 167, 169
Ahern, D. K., 104, 111
Ahern, D. L., 97, 101, 114
Ajzen, I., 14, 25
Alexander, J. F., x, xiv, 174-175, 177-178,
    185-186, 190-192, 195, 200, 204-205,
    206-208, 275
Alloy, L. B., 63, 67, 80, 82
Alnaes, R., 149, 169
American Psychiatric Association, x, xii,
    xiv, 31, 60, 63, 65, 75, 80, 86, 110,
    117-118, 140, 145, 169, 187, 190, 193,
    207, 246-247, 255, 266
Amick-McMullan, A., 247, 269
Amies, P., 131, 141
Anastasiades, P., 141, 170
Anderson, D., 214, 235
Andrasik, F., 98, 112
Andrews, G., 150-151, 162, 171
Anthony, J., 171
Antonakes, J. A., 84, 110
Antony, M., 151, 169
Appley, M. H., 2, 26
Arconad, M., 67-68, 81

Arias, I., 232
Arkowitz, H., xv, 80
Arnkoff, D. B., 138, 140, 142
Arnow, B. A., 154, 169
Arntz, A., 96, 113
Atkinson, J. H., 94, 114
Autry, J., 243, 267
Azjen, I., 26

Babich, K., xiv
Baer, R. A., 175, 190
Bagnall, J., 18, 28
Baldwin, D. V., 196, 207
Bandura, A., ix, xiv, 8, 25, 93, 99-100, 103,
    106, 108, 110, 138, 140, 179, 190,
    202, 207, 210, 222, 232
Bank, L., 177, 191
Bank, S., 234
Baptiste, S., 98, 111
Barbaree, H. E., 98, 102, 113
Barber, T., 107, 110
Barchas, J. D., 106, 110
Bargh, J. A., 6, 25, 28
Barkley, R. A., xiv
Barlow, D. H., ix, xiv, 125, 128-129, 136,
    139, 140-141, 143, 146, 148-151,
    153-155, 157, 166-173, 238, 248-249,
    253, 255, 266, 268, 270
Barnett, P. A., 80
Baron, R. M., 138, 140
Barry, W. A., 211, 235

Subject Index

Affect regulation
    and borderline personality disorder, 264
Aggression
    definition of, 33
Agoraphobia
    and anxiety disorders, 116-117, 123-131,
        136-137, 139
    and cognitive-behavioral therapy, 145-173
    definition of, 148
    development of, 148
    and differential diagnosis, 154-155
    and treatment, 157-167
    and treatment efficacy, 167-168
Agoraphobic Cognitions Questionnaire, 124,
    156
Anger
    and anxiety management training, 47
    and appraisal processes, 37-39, 49-51
    and cognitive-behavioral therapy, 31-62
    and cognitive restructuring, 38, 46, 48,
        51, 54-55
    and desensitization, 46-47
    and ego identity, 37
    and humor, 54-55
    and imagery, 44-45, 48, 51
    and insight, 35-36
    and problem-solving, 50-51, 56
    and related behavior, 39
    and relaxation, 45-50, 58-59
    and stimulus control, 42-45
    and stress inoculation, 46, 50
    and the preanger state, 36-37, 42

cognitive responses to, 38
definition of, 33
emotional responses to, 38
intervention strategies for, 39-59
model of, 34
physiological responses to, 38
precipitants of, 34-35
Anger Expression Inventory, 41
Anger Inventory, 41
Anxiety disorders
    and Beck-Emery cognitive behavioral
        therapy, 118, 124-126, 128-130,
        139
    and behavior therapy, 122-123
    and cognitive-behavioral therapy, 116-
        144
    and comorbidity, 129, 131, 134, 137
    and depression, 122-123, 129, 134-136
    and disorder specificity in anxious
        cognitions, 116-117
    and dysthymia, 122, 129, 134
    and effect sizes, 117-121, 125-128, 132-
        134
    and exposure, 122, 124-125, 128-131,
        134, 136
    and generalized anxiety disorder (GAD),
        117-122, 136-137
    and maintenance of treatment gains, 131,
        136, 138
    and nondirective therapy, 119-123,
    and nonspecific treatment effects, 119,
        122

About the Editors

Keith S. Dobson, Ph.D., is Professor of Psychology of the University of Calgary, where he is also the Director of the Programme in Clinical Psychology. He is a Professional/Scientific Member of the Department of Psychiatry at Foothills Hospital and a Consulting Psychologist at the Calgary Group District Hospital, Calgary. His research interests center on the issues of cognition and psychopathology (particularly anxiety and depression), gender issues in psychopathology, cognition and interpersonal relationships, cognitive-behavioral therapies, and professional issues in psychology. He is the editor or coeditor of several volumes, including the *Handbook of Cognitive-Behavioral Therapies, Psychopathology and Cognition,* and *Professional Psychology in Canada.* In addition to his research interests, he has been active in professional psychology and has served on many committees of several organizations. He is the current Chair of the National Professional Psychology Consortium and the immediate Past-President of the Canadian Psychological Association.

Kenneth D. Craig, Ph.D., is Professor of Psychology in the Department of Psychology at the University of British Columbia. His postsecondary education was at Sir George Williams University (B.A.), the University of British Columbia (M.A.), and Purdue University (Ph.D. in Clinical Psychology, 1964). At the University of British Columbia, he has served as Director of the Graduate Programme in Clinical Psychology on two occasions. His teaching currently focuses on abnormal psychology and health psychology at the undergraduate level and psychological assessment and supervision in the Psychological Clinic at the graduate level. He has authored numerous research papers and chapters on the psychology of pain and on the anxiety disorders. His research has won a number of awards, including the Canada Council Killam Research Fellowship. He has been the editor of the *Canadian Journal of Behavioural Science* and currently is an associate editor of the journal *Pain*. He has coedited the following books: *Anxiety and Depression in Adults and Children; Health Enhancement, Disease Prevention and Early Intervention: Bio-Behavioral Perspectives;* and *Advances in Clinical Behavior Therapy.* He is a Fellow of the Canadian Psychological Association, the American Psychological Association, and the Society for Behavioral Medicine; a founding member of the International Association for the Study of Pain; and a member of the Academy of Behavioral Medicine Research. Service for scientific and professional organizations has included terms as President of the Canadian Psychological Association, President of the British Columbia Psychological Association, and Treasurer of the Social Science Federation of Canada. He currently is President of the Banff International Conferences on Behavioural Science and President of the Canadian Pain Society.

About the Contributors

James F. Alexander, Ph.D., is Professor of Psychology and past Director of Clinical Training at the University of Utah. He is Past-President of Division 43, Family Psychology, and Fellow of the American Psychological Association. He has presented as a "Master Therapist" at the Annual Convention of American Association for Marriage and Family Therapy, and he is currently on the Board of Directors of the American Family Therapy Academy as well as the past recipient of that organization's Award for Contributions to Family Therapy Research. He has presented over 100 training workshops and has published extensively in the clinical and research literature on family therapy. He currently has a grant from the National Institute of Drug Abuse as part of the multisite Center for Research on Adolescent Drug Abuse (CRADA: Howard Liddle, Temple University, P.I.) to study culturally sensitive and empirically based family therapy process and outcome with substance-abusing adolescents.

Donald H. Baucom, Ph.D., is Pardue Professor of Psychology and Director of the Clinical Psychology Program at the University of North Carolina at Chapel Hill. For the past 20 years, he has been conducting research on marriage from a cognitive-behavioral perspective. He has conducted a number of treatment outcome investigations, evaluating the relative effectiveness of different treatment interventions in working with maritally distressed couples. In addition, he has focused a great deal of attention on the role of cognitive factors in marriage. In the early 1980s, he began a collaborative relationship with Norman Epstein, Ph.D., and the two of them have continued to pursue research on cognitive variables in marriage.

They have attempted to delineate the important types of cognitions in marriage, along with developing appropriate assessment strategies for each of these cognitive variables. In 1990, they published *Cognitive Behavioral Marital Therapy.* In addition to his research efforts in the marital domain, Dr. Baucom also trains graduate students in marital therapy and is an active clinician. He has won several undergraduate awards for excellence in undergraduate teaching as well. He has served as associate editor for *Behavior Therapy* and has served on the editorial boards of numerous journals in psychology.

Charles K. Burnett is currently a Postdoctoral Fellow in the Division of Digestive Diseases and Nutrition at the University of North Carolina School of Medicine. He is a graduate of the Clinical Psychology Program at the University of North Carolina at Chapel Hill, where he received the 1993 Wallach Award for outstanding graduate of the clinical program. He completed his internship in health psychology at Duke University Medical Center. Prior to returning to graduate school in clinical psychology, he received his doctorate in maternal and child health from the University of North Carolina School of Public Health. He also holds a master's degree in pediatric psychology from the University of Colorado at Denver and a bachelor's degree in psychology from Hastings College. His current research interests include strategies for the prevention of marital distress, the content of couple cognitions, and cognitive/behavioral factors in somatization.

Dianne L. Chambless received her Ph.D. in clinical psychology from Temple University in 1979 and is currently Professor of Psychology at the American University. For the past 20 years, she has specialized in research and treatment of anxiety disorders, especially panic disorder with agoraphobia. In 1979 she received the New Researcher Award from the Association for Advancement of Behavior Therapy for her research on phobias. She has served on the editorial boards of journals such as *Behavior Therapy, Journal of Anxiety Disorders, Clinical Psychology Review, Anxiety,* and *Cognitive Therapy and Research.* Her current research projects on the effects of family relationships on treatment outcome for obsessive-compulsive disorder and agoraphobia and on assessment of social phobia and avoidant personality disorder are funded by the National Institute of Mental Health.

Michelle G. Craske received her Ph.D. from the University of British Columbia in 1985, She was a Senior Research Scientist and Associate Director at the Center for Stress and Anxiety Disorders of the State University of New York at Albany from 1986 through 1989. She joined the University of California, Los Angeles, in 1990, where she is now an Associate Professor in the Department of Psychology, and Director of the Anxiety Disorders Behavioral Program. She has published many articles on the topic of fear and anxiety. In particular, her work focuses on developing cognitive-behavioral assessments and treatments for the anxiety disorders and furthering our understanding of the etiology and maintaining factors in fear and anxiety. She was a member of the DSM-IV Anxiety Disorders Taskforce subcommittees for panic disorder and specific phobia. Most recently, she received funding from the National Institute of Mental Health to examine the phenomenology and treatment of nocturnal panic attacks.

Jerry L. Deffenbacher, Ph.D., is a Professor of Psychology in the Department of Psychology at Colorado State University, where for a number of years he has been a member of and former Director of Training of the doctoral program in counseling psychology. He is a Fellow of the American Psychological Association and of the American Association for Applied and Preventive Psychology and a diplomate in counseling psychology from the American Board of Professional Psychology. His primary clinical and research interests involve the nature and expression, correlates, diagnosis, and treatment of various general and specific anger problems.

Norman Epstein, Ph.D., is Professor of Family Studies at the University of Maryland, College Park. He is a Fellow in the divisions of Family Psychology and Psychotherapy of the American Psychological Association, a licensed psychologist, and a clinical member of the American Association for Marriage and Family Therapy. In addition to his teaching, research, and clinical supervision within the marital and family therapy training program at the University of Maryland, he has a part-time private practice, specializing in cognitive-behavioral work with couples and individuals. For over 20 years, the primary focus of his research has been on the development of assessment and treatment approaches for distressed couples from a cognitive-behavioral perspective. His Relationship Belief Inventory, developed with Roy Eidelson, was the first standardized measure of marital cognition and has been used widely in the field. He also conducts research on intra- and interpersonal factors in depression and anxiety disorders. He and Donald Baucom have a long-term collaborative program of research involving the development of instruments for assessing cognitive variables influencing couples' relationships. They also have collaborated on the refinement of therapeutic approaches for couples, and their book *Cognitive-Behavioral Marital Therapy* was published by Brunner/Mazel in 1990. Many of Dr. Epstein's other publications, including the edited book *Cognitive-Behavioral Therapy With Families* (with Stephen Schlesinger and Windy Dryden), have dealt with a variety of relationship issues, including stepfamily relationships, family crisis intervention, family factors in adolescent depression, and coping among adult children of alcoholic parents.

Martha M. Gillis received her B.A. from Sophia University in Tokyo, Japan, in 1975 and an M.A. in counseling psychology from George Mason University in 1978. She is currently a fifth-year doctoral student in clinical psychology at the American University.

Donna Gunderson is a third-year doctoral student in the clinical program of the Psychology Department of the University of Utah. Her primary interests include multicultural issues that affect mental health, particularly in situations where underserved ethnic minority populations are involved, and adolescent psychopathology, specifically conduct disorder and related factors. Currently, she is working on a thesis project that involves an analog study of gender effects and religiosity on the effectiveness of culturally sensitive interventions. She has also been involved in compiling an information synthesis on assessing adolescent substance abuse and comorbid conditions in a Native American population as part of a prospective consultation with a residential treatment center for American Indian adolescent substance abusers.

Janice L. Howes completed her undergraduate training at Dalhousie University and obtained her M.A. and Ph.D. (1984) in clinical psychology from the University of Western Ontario. After completing her doctoral studies, she worked as a Staff Psychologist at the Downsview Rehabilitation Centre, Toronto, Ontario (1984-1988). She is currently a psychologist at the Queen Elizabeth II Health Sciences Centre, Halifax, Nova Scotia, and is an Assistant Professor in the Department of psychiatry, Dalhousie University, Halifax, Nova Scotia. She also holds an Honorary Adjunct Professor status in the Psychology Department, Dalhousie University. She is Past-Chair of the Section on Clinical Psychology of the Canadian Psychological Association. She is active in clinical work, research, teaching, and psychotherapy supervision of predoctoral psychology interns and residents in psychiatry. She is interested in the application of cognitive therapy, especially to health and post-traumatic stress disorder populations. She is coinvestigator of a research study focusing on the psychological sequelae of individuals affected by the recent Westray Mine Disaster. She regularly presents talks to professional groups focusing on the short- and long-term effects of trauma and the treatment of such difficulties. She is active in the development and provision of brief intervention services following critical incidents at Queen Elizabeth II Health Sciences Centre. She is coeditor of the text entitled *The Challenge of Cognitive Therapy: Applications to Nontraditional Populations* and has published several articles.

Susan Jackman-Cram is a doctoral student in the Clinical Psychology Programme at the University of Calgary. Her theoretical and empirical interests are in three areas: depression, marriage, and professional issues in psychology. Her interest in depression has focused on the roles of cognitive and interpersonal factors, psychotherapies for depression, and gender differences in depression; her interest in marriage has focused on the examination of affect, cognition, and communication; and her work on professional issues has included a survey of Canadian psychologists' attitudes and management of confidentiality. She is currently completing her predoctoral internship in clinical psychology at the Holy Cross Hospital, Calgary District Hospital Group.

Penny Brooke Jameson received her doctorate in developmental psychology from the University of Wisconsin. She was a member of the Psychology Department of Saint Mary's College, Notre Dame, Indiana, from 1970 to 1990. She retrained as a clinical psychologist at the University of Utah and the University of Colorado Health Sciences Center and is currently in private practice in Salt Lake City, Utah.

Charlotte Johnston received her B.A. with honors in psychology from the University of Calgary and her M.Sc. in experimental psychopathology from this same institute. She completed her doctoral work in clinical child psychology at Florida State University, received her internship training at Chedoke-McMaster Hospitals, McMaster University, and graduated in 1987. She is currently an Associate Professor in the Psychology Department at the University of British Columbia. Her research program focuses on families of children with disruptive behavior disorders, particularly attention deficit hyperactivity disorder (ADHD). She has published studies describing the social interactions of ADHD children, the family characteristics associated with this disorder, parent attributions for the behavior of ADHD children, and the influence of comorbidity of ADHD and oppositional defiant disorder on family interactions and responsiveness to behavioral parent training. She is a registered clinical psychologist and is actively involved in the clinical training program at the University of British Columbia, supervising students in both research and clinical experiences. She is a professional advisor to several parent support associations, including the Canadian Children and Adults with Attention Deficit Disorder (ChADD) Association, and has given numerous workshops for parents, teachers, and health professionals on the topics of ADHD and behavior management.

Frederick H. Kanfer obtained his Ph.D. from Indiana University. He has served on the faculties of Washington University, Purdue University, the University of Oregon Medical School's Department of Medical Psychology and Psychiatry, and the University of Cincinnati. He is currently Professor at the University of Illinois at Champaign-Urbana. His major interests have been the development of self-regulation theory and the application of resultant research to a self-management approach to psychotherapy. More recently, he has also spelled out the implicit basis for his work—that is, the scientist-professional model. He has published 148 articles and book chapters and has authored or coauthored nine books. Among numerous honors are a Fulbright Professorship in 1968, the Alexander Von Humboldt Prize in 1987, the University Scholar Prize from the University of Illinois from 1990 to 1993, and Visiting Professorships at numerous universities both in the United States and in Europe. From 1955 to 1981 he was principal investigator of National Institute for Mental Health research grants. He has been on advisory boards of various institutes, both in the United States and abroad. He has been a member of numerous editorial boards of American and international journals and is a diplomate in clinical psychology of the American Board of Professional Psychology. He has served as a program and research consultant to various treatment facilities, both in the United States and in Europe.

Robert M. Newell is currently a Ph.D. student in clinical psychology at the University of Utah. He obtained his B.S. from the University of Washington in 1991. His research and clinical interests include family-based approaches to treatment with adolescent substance abusers and victims of child sexual abuse. He has over 13 years of applied experience working with troubled youth in a variety of treatment modalities.

Lynn A. Rankin, Ph.D., attended Bucknell University as an undergraduate, where she completed a double major in Biology and English. She attended the University of North Carolina at Chapel Hill for her doctoral work in clinical psychology, where she was the 1994 recipient of the Wallach Award for outstanding graduate of the clinical psychology program. During her time at the University of North Carolina, she was selected as one of the top 10 teaching assistants in the university by the undergraduates and served as student representative to the North Carolina Psychological Association. During the 1994-1995 year she completed her internship at the Palo Alto VA in Palo Alto, California, followed by a 2-year postdoctoral position at Stanford University Medical Center. She has focused her research in the marital field, with a particular emphasis on cognitive variables and effects on marital interaction, distress, and communication patterns. Her current work further explores cognitions in marriage by examining potential gender differences in cognitive processes in marital interaction. In addition, she has developed a focus on individual factors in marriage. This individual focus continues with her work at Stanford, investigating the marital interactions of persons with either anxiety or mood disorders.

Dennis C. Turk is Professor of Psychiatry, Anesthesiology, and Behavioral Science and Director of the Pain Evaluation and Treatment Institute at the University of Pittsburgh School of Medicine. He is a founding member of both the International Association for the Study of Pain and the American Pain Society. He is a Fellow of the American Psychological

Association, the Academy of Behavioral Medicine Research, and the Society of Behavioral Medicine. In 1993, he was the recipient of the American Psychological Association, Division of Health Psychology, Outstanding Scientific Contribution Award. His research has been funded by the National Institute of Dental Research, the National Institute of Arthritis, Musculoskeletal and Skin Diseases, the National Center for Health Statistics, and the Arthritis Foundation, as well as a number of private foundations and companies. He has published over 190 journal articles and chapters in edited books and has written or edited eight books: *Pain and Behavioral Medicine: A Cognitive-Behavioral Perspective; Pain Management: A Handbook of Psychological Treatment Approaches; Facilitating Treatment Adherence: A Practitioner's Guidebook; Health, Illness, and Families: A Life-Span Perspective; Psychosocial Assessment in Terminal Care; Reasoning, Inference, and Judgment in Clinical Psychology; Handbook of Pain Assessment; Non-Invasive Approaches to Pain Control in the Terminally Ill*; and *Psychological Approaches to Pain Management: A Practitioners Handbook*. He is currently editor of the *Annals of Behavioral Medicine*.

T. Michael Vallis, Ph.D., is a registered psychologist currently employed at Queen Elizabeth II Heath Sciences Centre, Halifax, where he functions as Coordinator of Clinical Training and provides service within health psychology. A native of Dartmouth, he obtained his undergraduate training from Dalhousie University (1977). He went on to obtain his M.A. (1979) and Ph.D. (1983) in clinical psychology from the University of Western Ontario. After holding clinical positions at the Clarke Institute of Psychiatry, Toronto (1982-1985) and the Credit Valley Hospital, Mississauga (1985-1988), he returned to Nova Scotia, to his present position, in 1988. He has held academic appointments at the University of Toronto (Lecturer, Department of Psychiatry, 1984-1988) and currently is Assistant Professor, Department of Psychiatry, and Adjunct Professor, Department of Psychology, Dalhousie University. His main area of expertise is in adult clinical psychology, with an emphasis on cognitive-interpersonal psychotherapy and health psychology. He was Codirector of the Anxiety Disorders Clinic while it was operating in the Psychiatry Outpatient Services. Currently, he functions as part of the Nova Scotia Diabetes Centre and the Gastroenterology programs at Queen Elizabeth II Health Sciences Centre. He has strong interest in psychotherapy, clinical research, and training. He has also maintained academic interests and is currently involved in several funded clinical research trials. He has published journal articles and book chapters and has edited three textbooks. Professionally, he has been active in the Canadian Psychological Association (former Chair of the Section on Clinical Psychology, currently a member of the Continuing Education Committee), the Canadian Council of Professional Psychology Programs (former secretary-treasurer), and the Association of Psychologists of Nova Scotia.